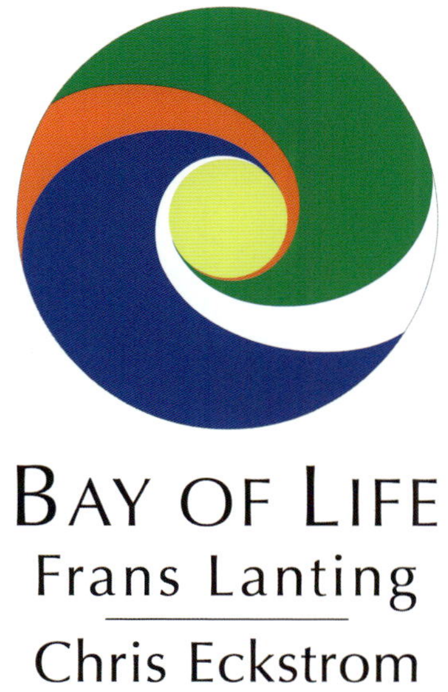

BAY OF LIFE
Frans Lanting
Chris Eckstrom

THE BAY OF LIFE IS A UNIQUE CONFLUENCE

OF LAND AND SEA,

ENERGIZED BY THE SUN,

SHAPED BY THE FORCES OF FOG AND FIRE,

AND INFLUENCED BY THE ACTIONS OF PEOPLE.

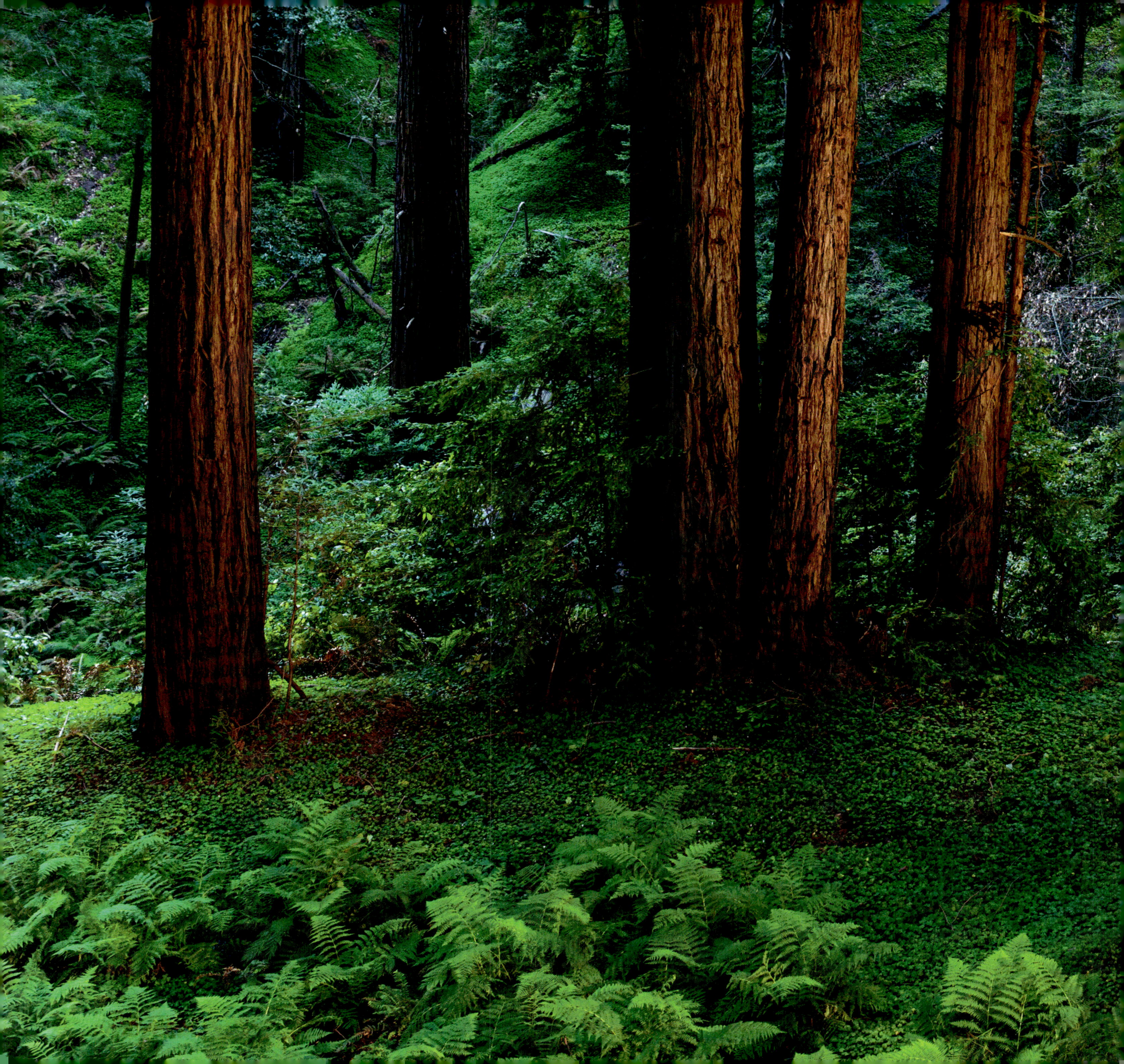

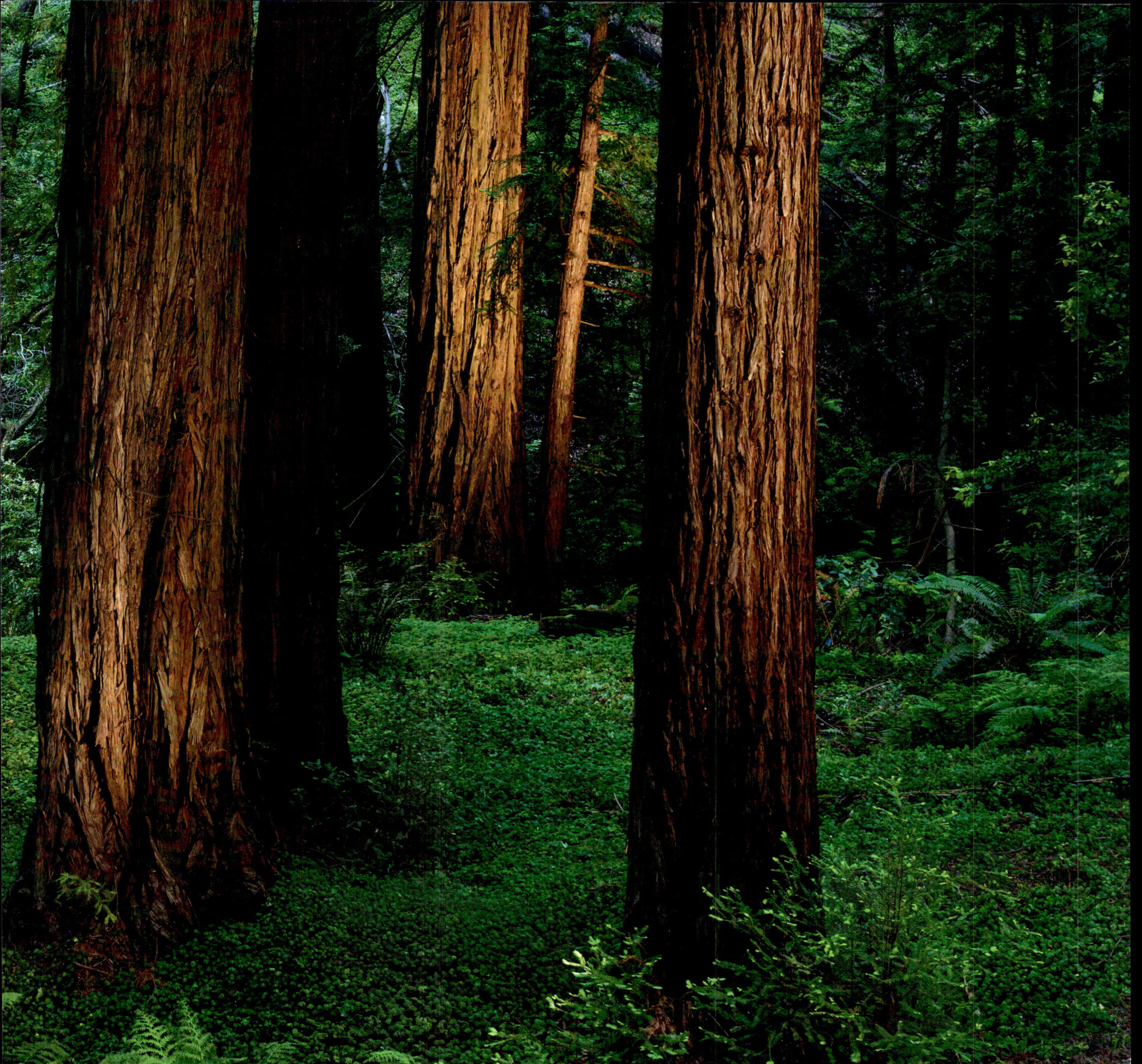

From redwoods come silence and awe.
They are ambassadors from another time.

—JOHN STEINBECK

PREVIOUS PAGES: REDWOODS, MOLINO CREEK FARM

Here from this mountain shore, headland beyond stormy headland
plunging like dolphins through the grey sea-smoke
Into pale sea—look west at the hill of water: it is half the planet.

—ROBINSON JEFFERS

BIG SUR AT DAWN

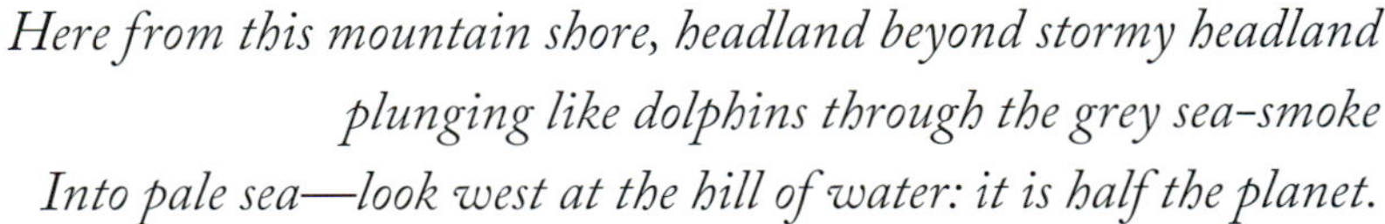

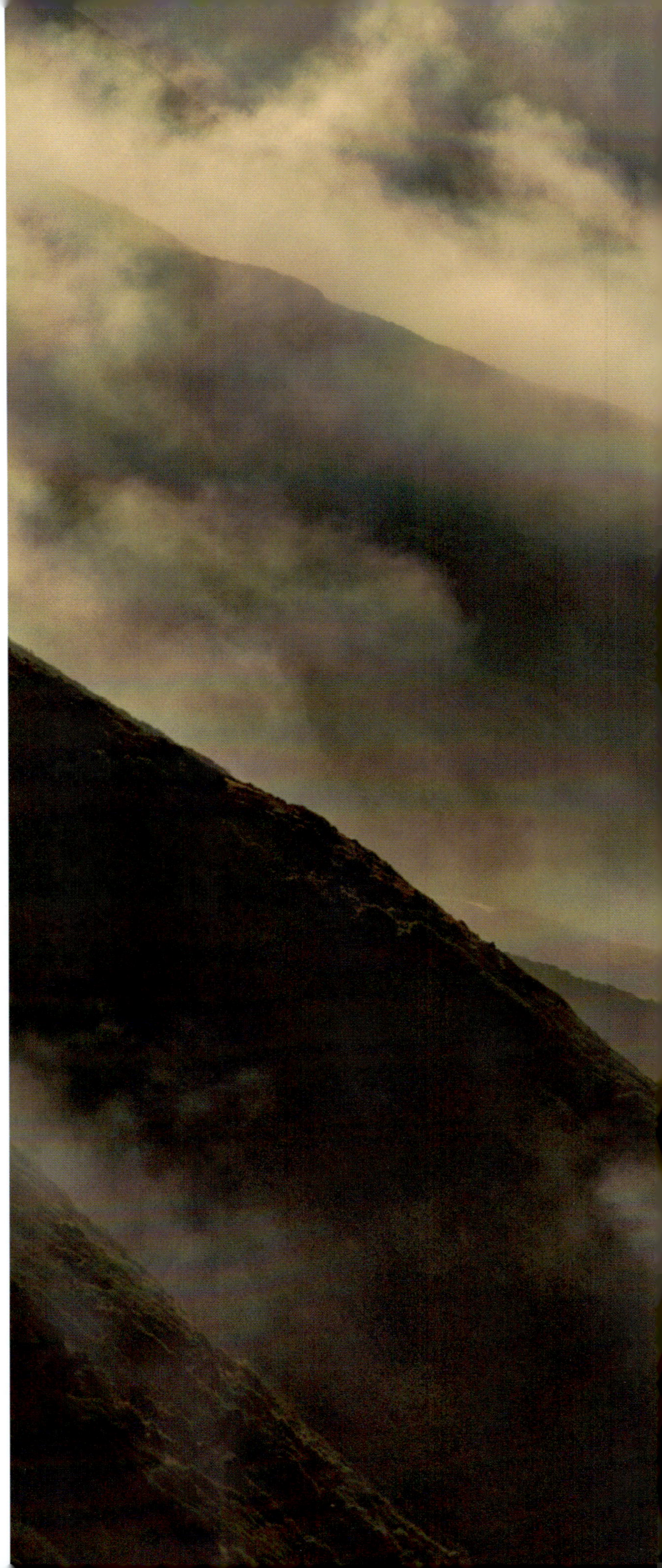

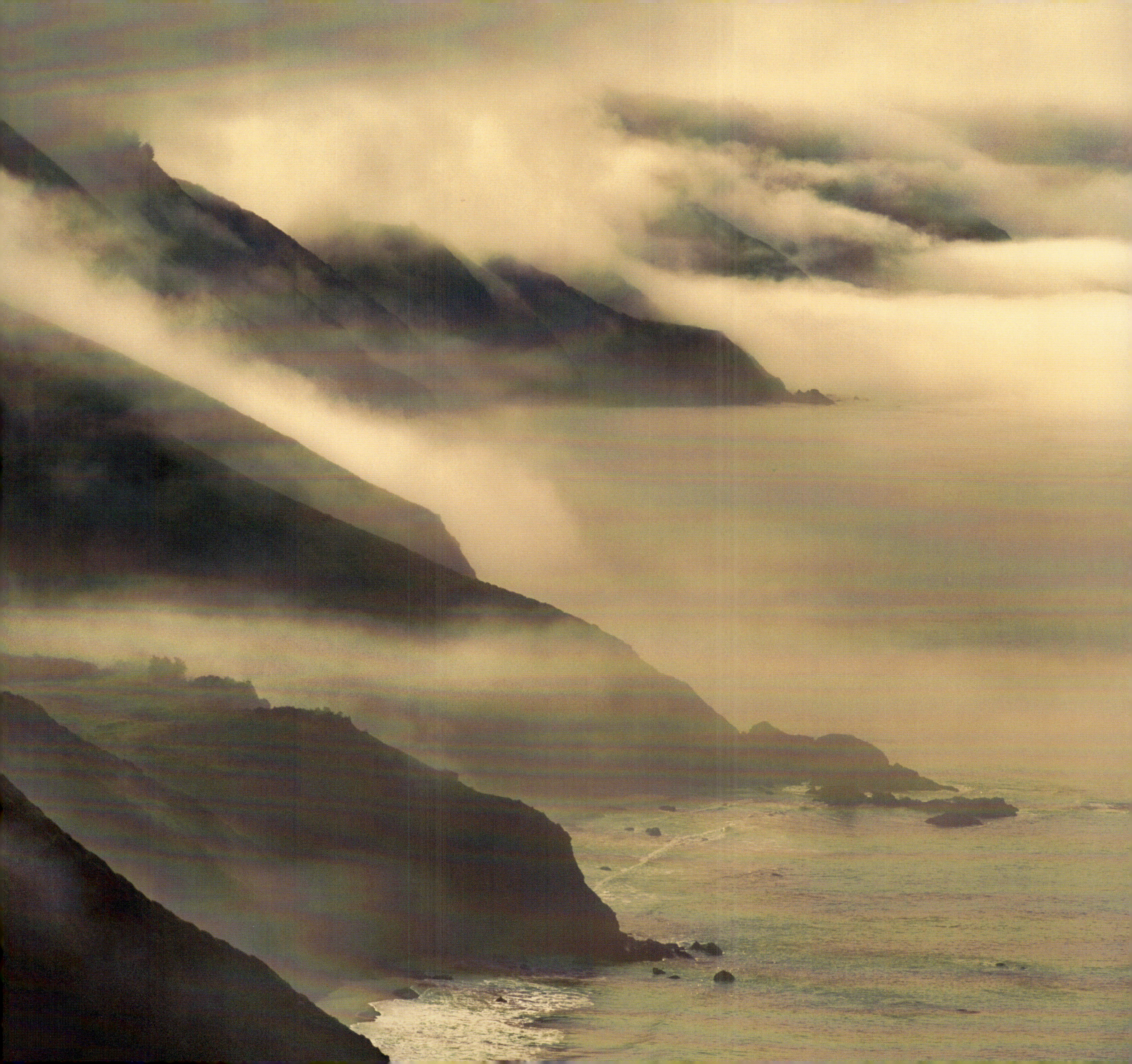

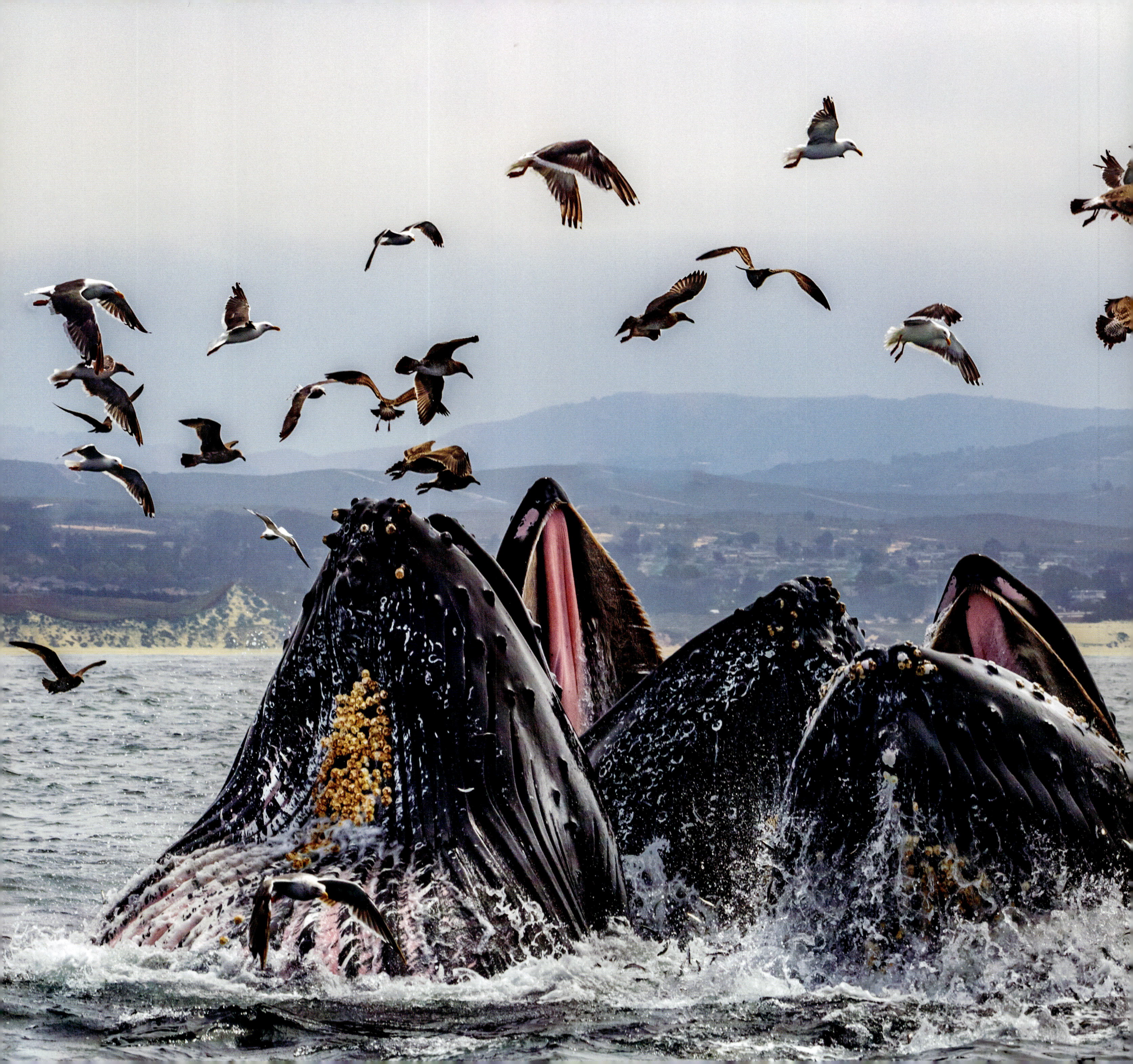

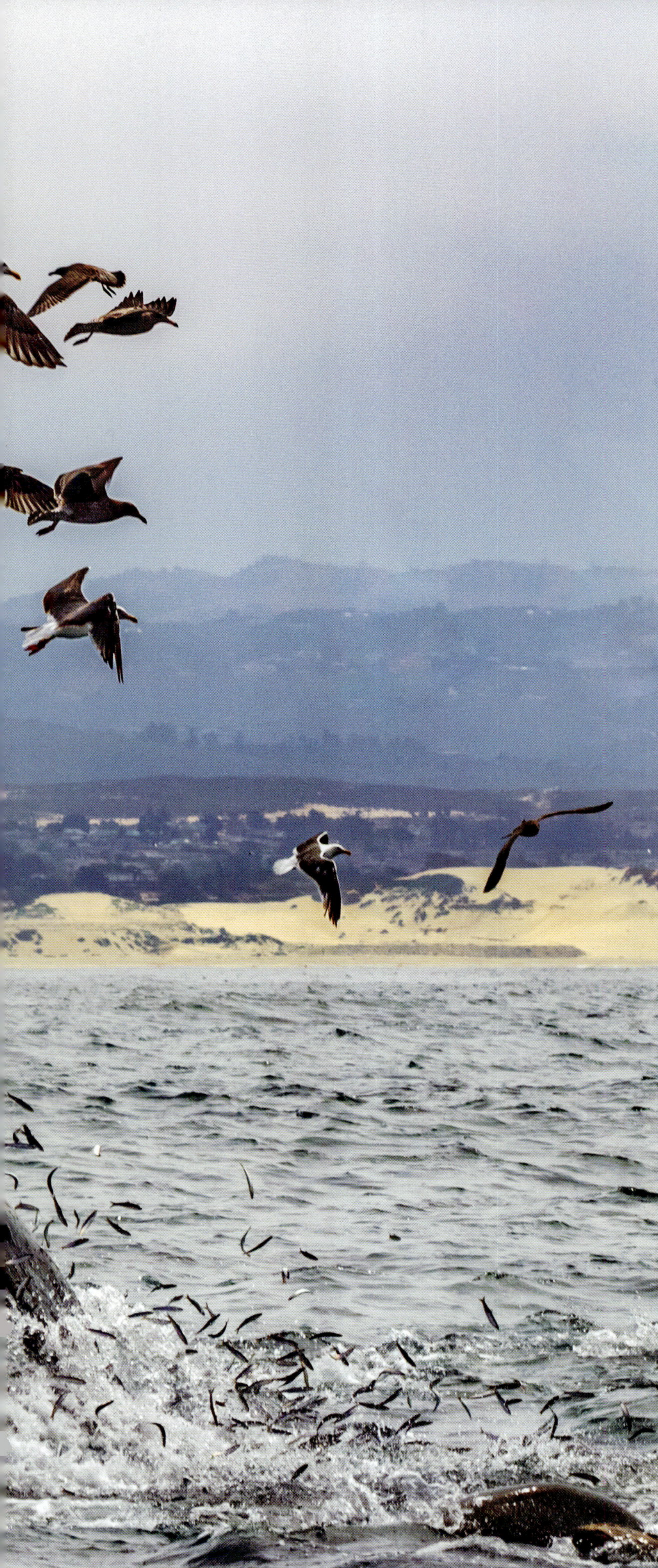

It is the winds of spring that bring the whales of summer to the Bay of Life. When the wind begins to blow, cold, nutrient-rich water wells up from the deep and is exposed to sunlight. That leads to massive blooms of phytoplankton that nourish everything up the food chain.

Humpback Whales, Monterey Bay National Marine Sanctuary

FOLLOWING PAGE: Mountain lions are fiercely private, yet they manage to survive in the Santa Cruz Mountains, surrounded by urban development. Their future depends on our ability to coexist with this apex predator in our midst. Creating habitat corridors and safeguarding denning sanctuaries are crucial parts of the solution.

Mountain Lion, Sierra Azul Open Space Preserve

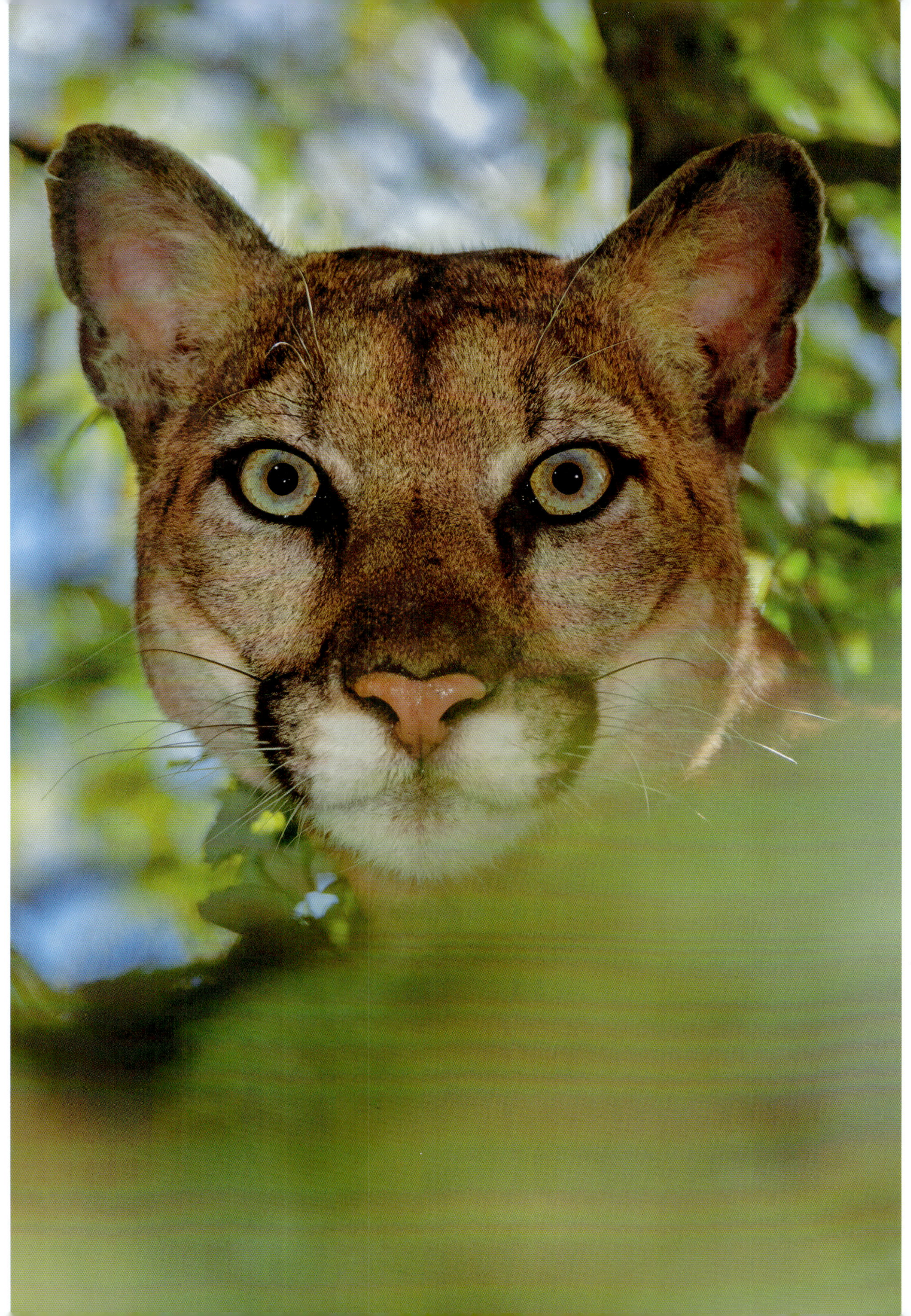

BAY OF LIFE

FROM WIND TO WHALES

FRANS LANTING

CHRIS ECKSTROM

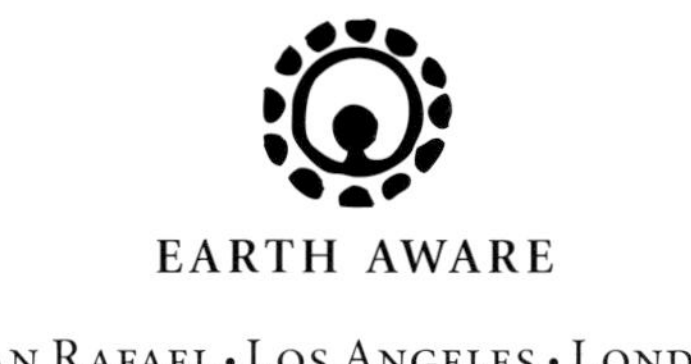

EARTH AWARE

San Rafael · Los Angeles · London

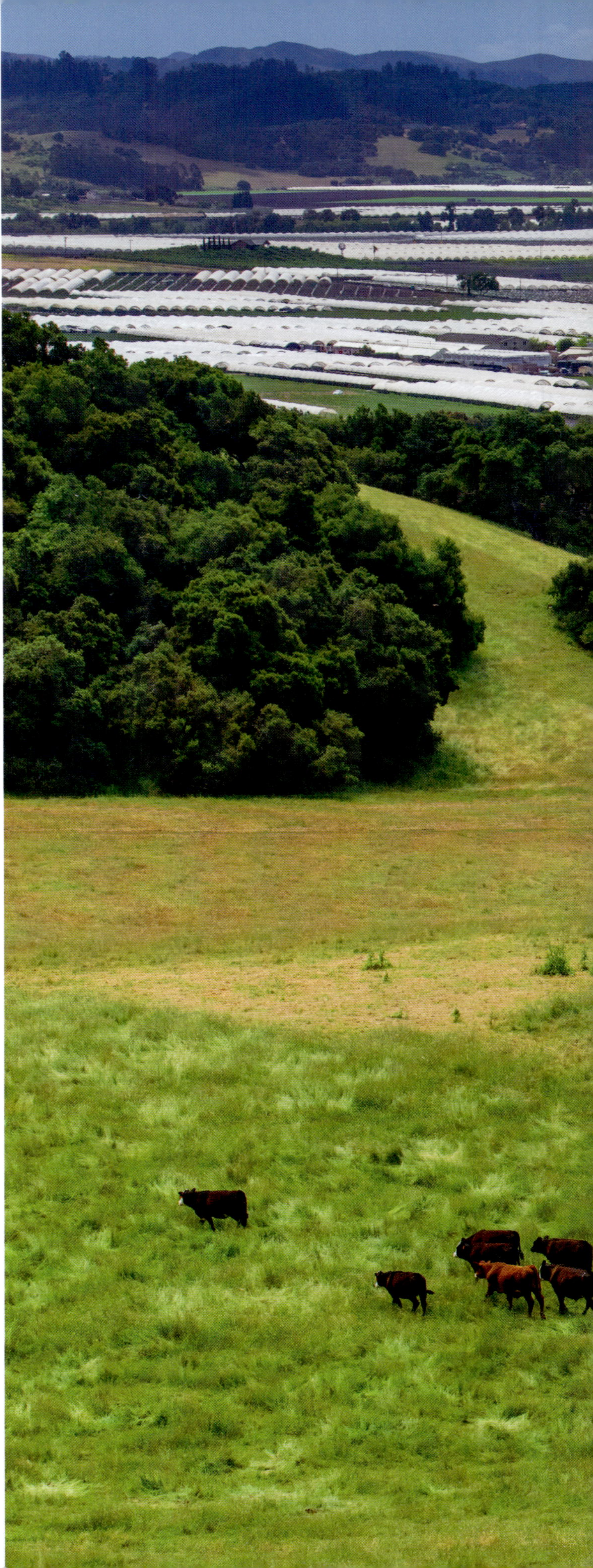

Working lands around Monterey Bay, managed by people who care, are an important
part of its rich mosaic of habitats. Joe Morris rounds up cattle in the foothills of
the Santa Cruz Mountains. In the distance, the fertile agricultural fields of the
Pajaro Valley stretch toward the shores of the bay.

HERDING CATTLE, KELLY-THOMPSON RANCH, WATSONVILLE

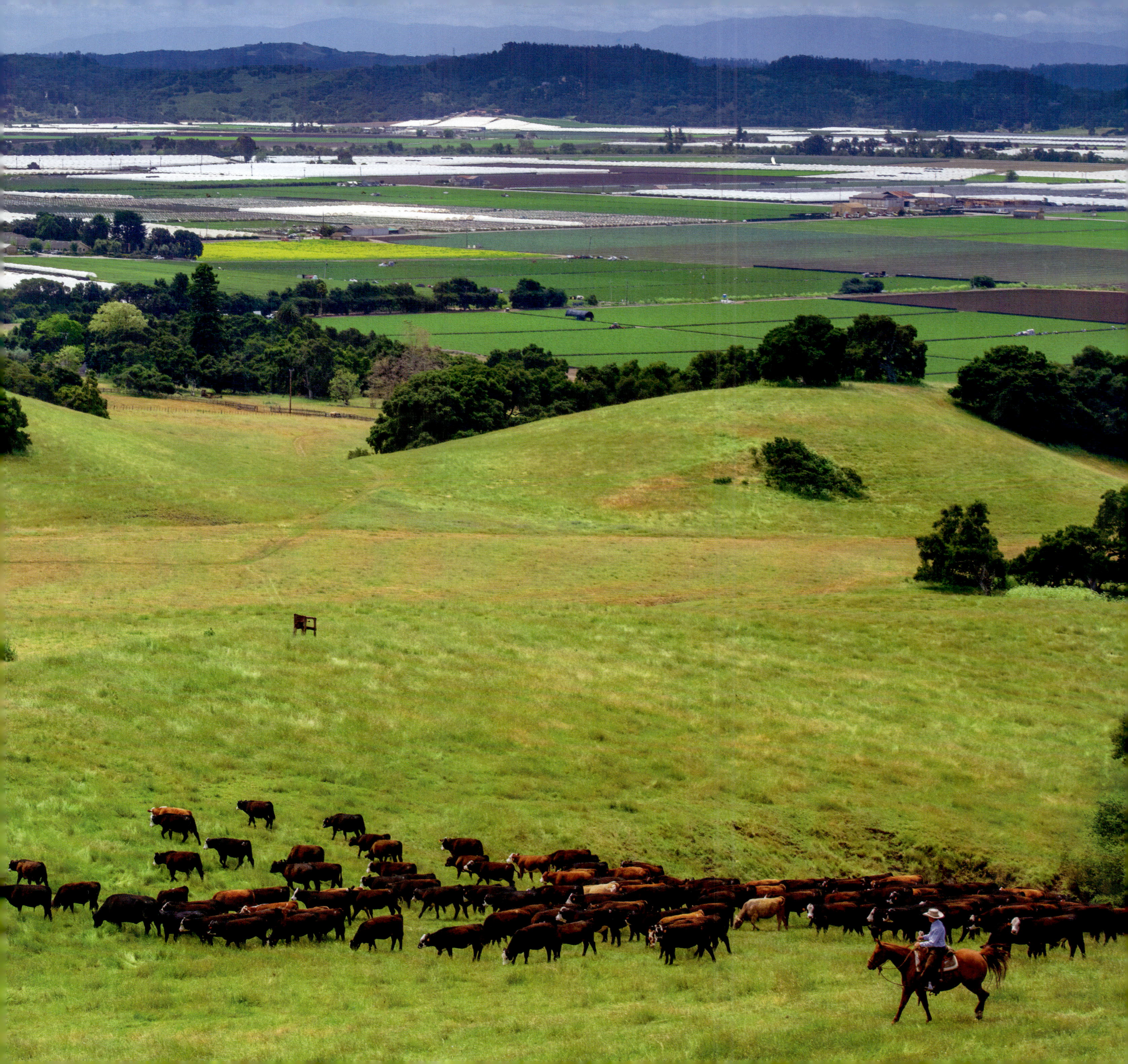

The Monterey Bay region includes the traditional and unceded lands
and waters of the Ohlone and Esselen people. We recognize them
as the original inhabitants and pay respect to the enduring relationship
they have with the natural world through their ancestral wisdom.
We acknowledge their special role in the
stewardship of this precious land.

CONTENTS

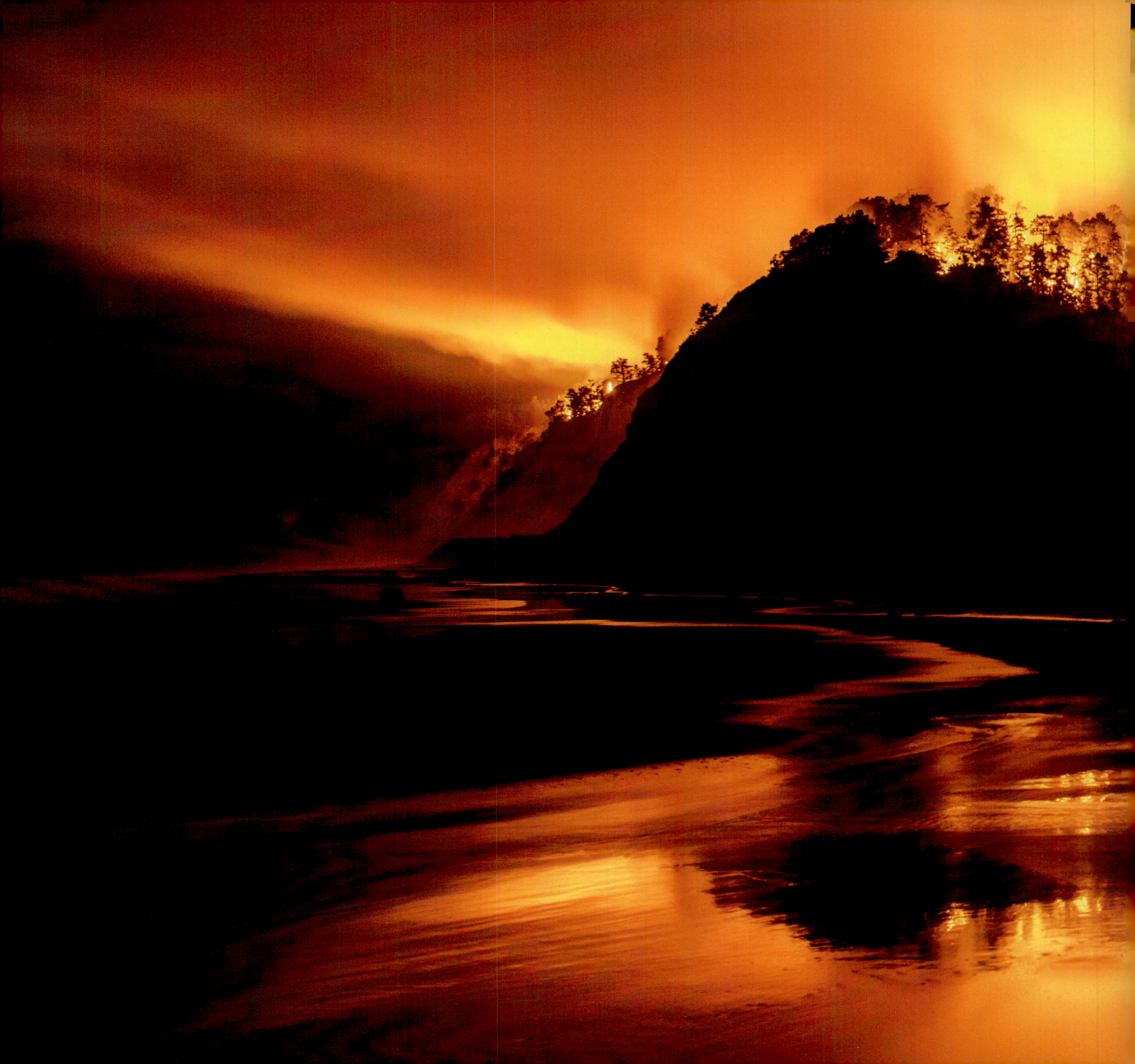

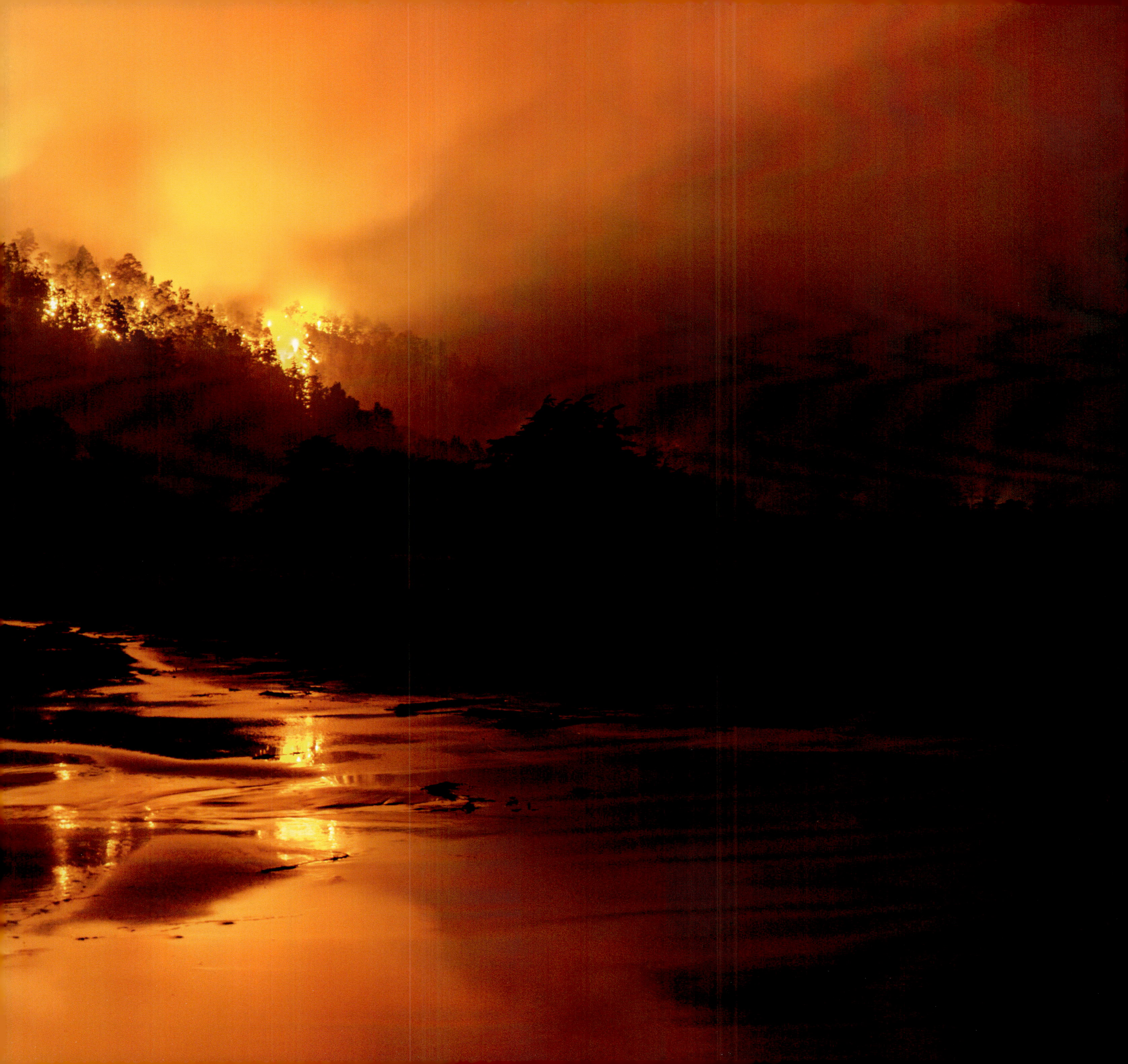

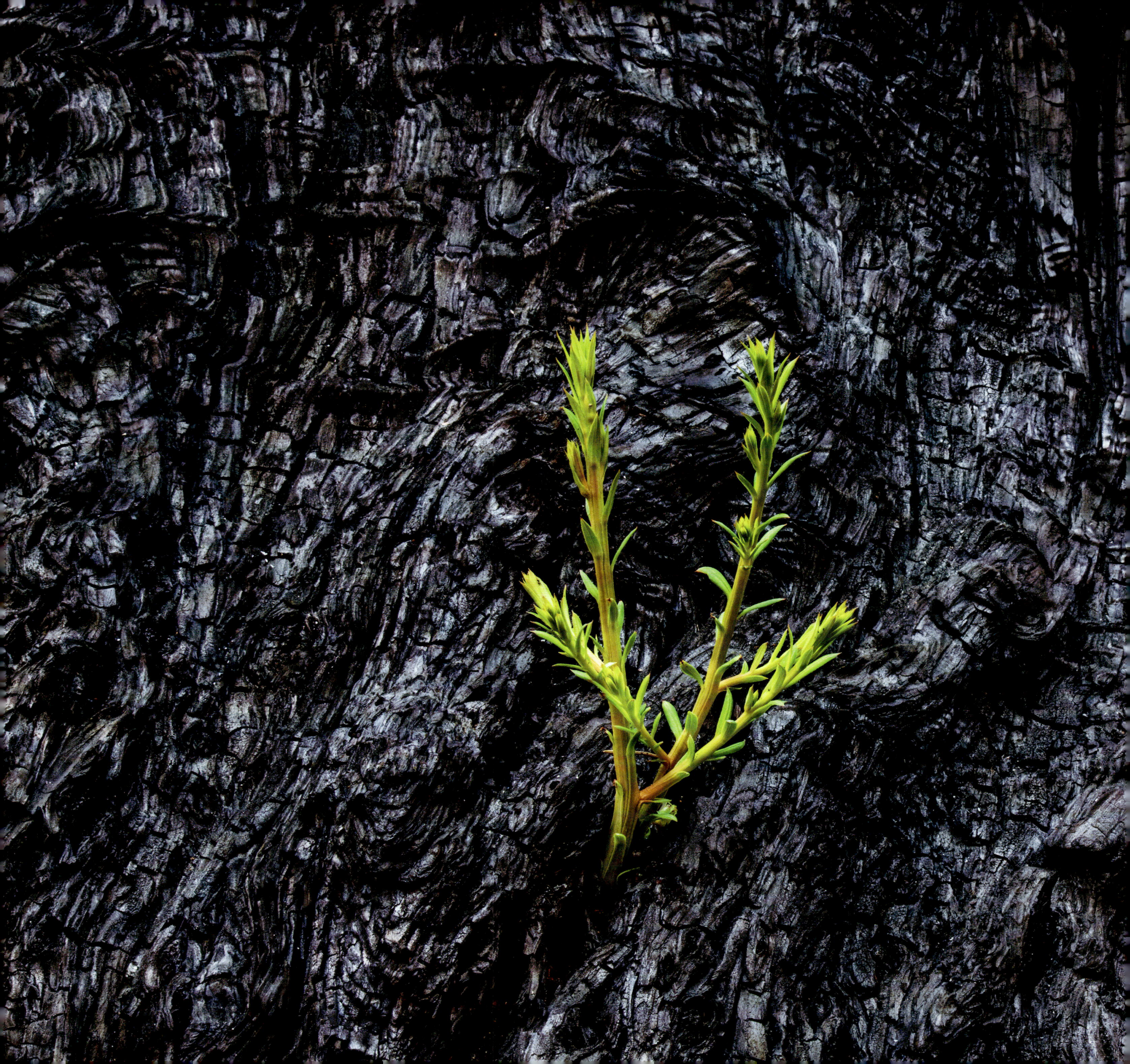

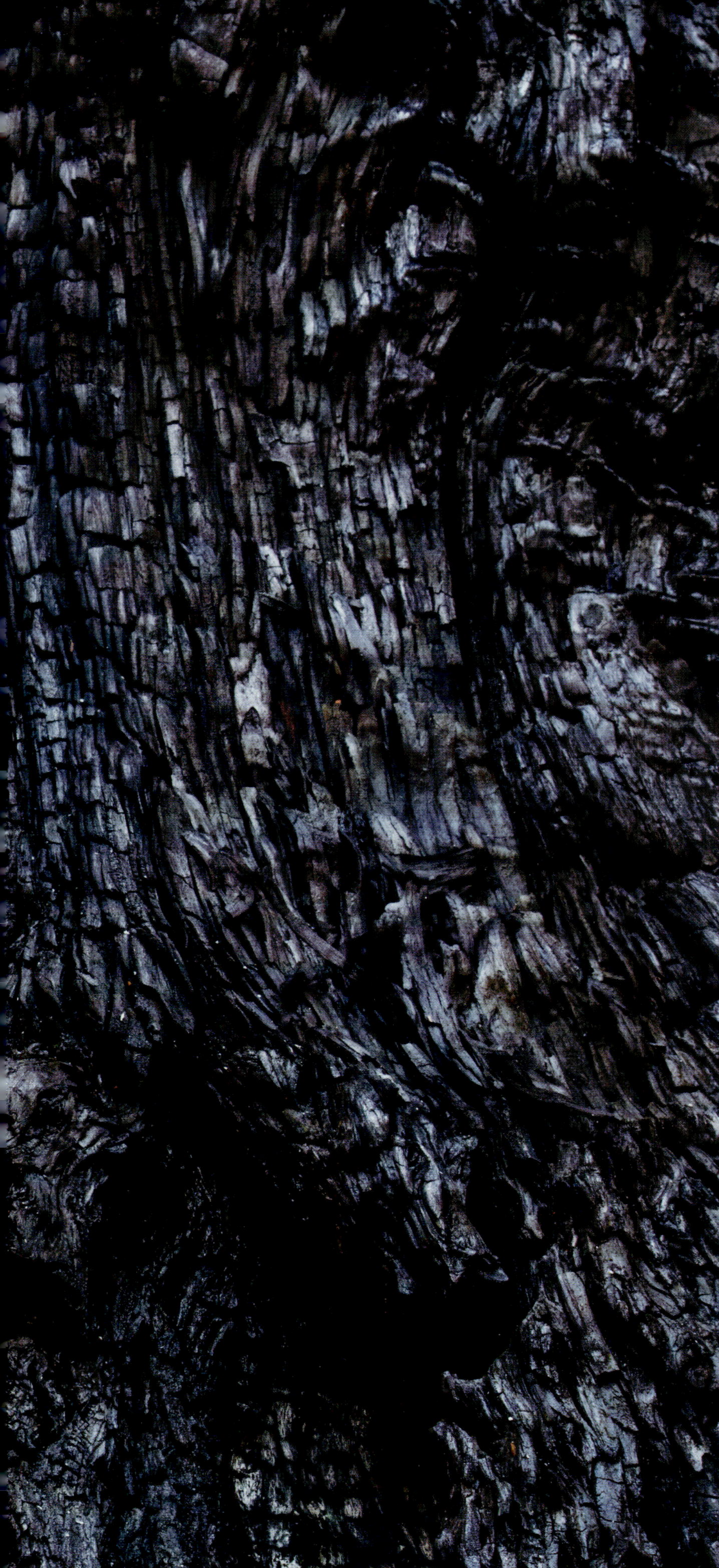

Fire is a natural part of the Monterey Bay's Mediterranean life cycle,
but in an era of climate change it is taking on a new dimension.
The wildfires that swept through the Santa Cruz Mountains in 2020
burned to the sea at the Waddell Bluffs in Big Basin Redwoods State Park
(previous pages). Most of the park went up in flames, but redwoods have
evolved to live with fire. Within months, new sprouts began to
emerge from blackened tree trunks.

WILDFIRE AND REDWOOD SPROUT, BIG BASIN REDWOODS STATE PARK

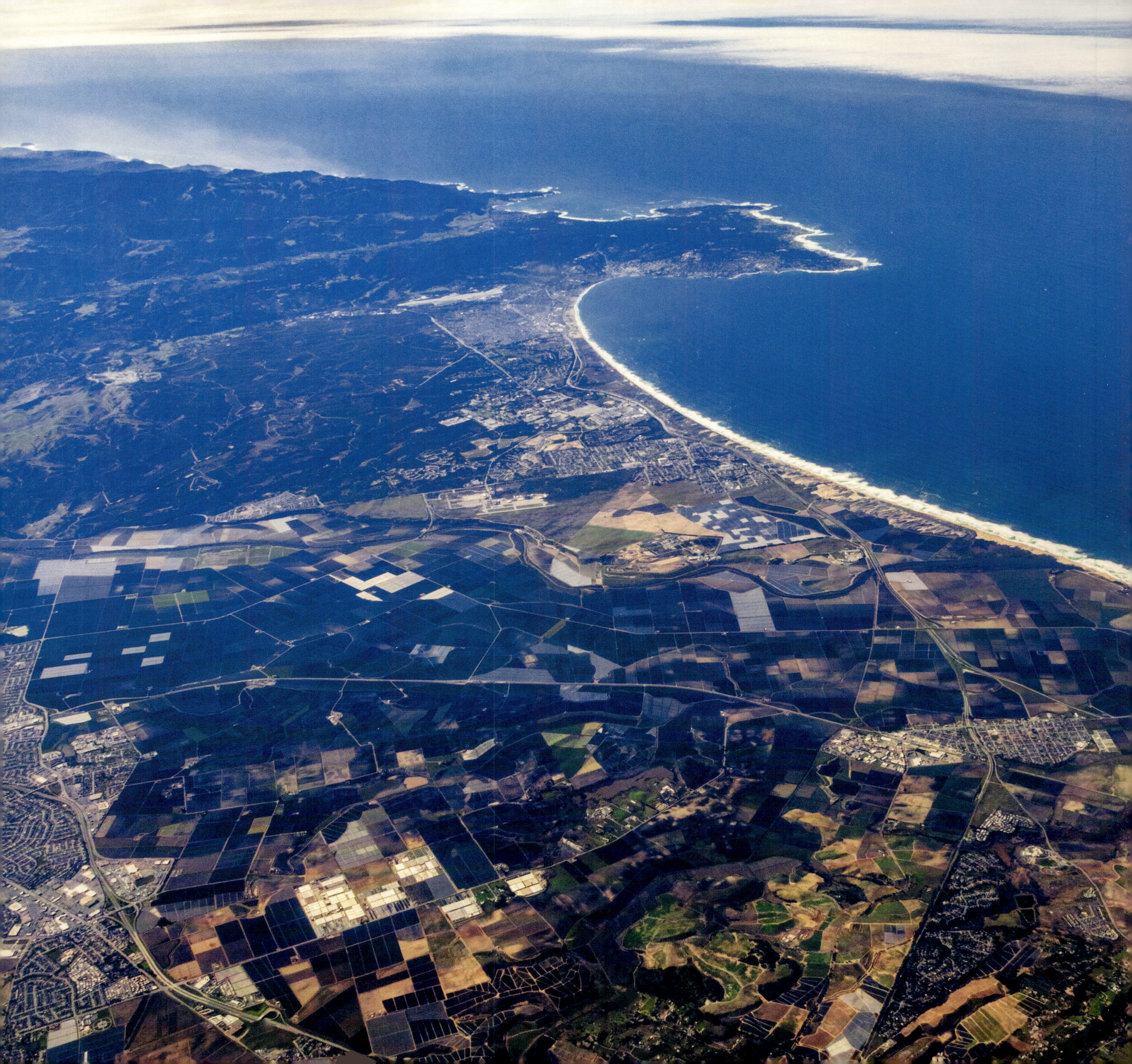

FOREWORD

BY LEON E. PANETTA

CO-CHAIR, MONTEREY BAY NATIONAL MARINE SANCTUARY FOUNDATION

*All of us have in our veins the exact same percentage of salt in our blood that exists in the ocean,
and therefore, we have salt in our blood, in our sweat, in our tears. We are tied to the ocean.*

—John F. Kennedy

This book celebrates the Monterey Bay as the world-class environment it is and pays tribute to the people who are taking care of it. When we are good stewards of our natural environment, we are fulfilling our responsibility to future generations to ensure that they too can reap the benefits of the Monterey Bay's magnificence.

When I asked my Italian immigrant parents why they came all that distance to a strange land, I never forgot my father's response: "Because your mother and I believed that we could give our children a better life in this country." That is the American Dream that we all want for our children and their children—to give them a better life. And what greater legacy can we leave them than the natural beauty of the Monterey Bay.

We have learned not to take that beauty for granted. In the 1980s the federal government wanted to sell leases to vast areas of our coastline for offshore oil drilling. The people of the Central Coast rose up in opposition. As their congressman, I authored a moratorium on offshore drilling that passed each year for 20 years. But that fight made clear that permanent protection was needed. With the support of leaders from business, conservation, research, fishing, agriculture, recreation, education, and politics, we were able to pass legislation in the U.S. Congress to create the Monterey Bay National Marine Sanctuary—the largest marine sanctuary in the continental United States.

The ocean is critical to our lives and our economies. The Marine Sanctuary is critical to our mental health and to our spirit. It exists because people cared and came together. But the battle to protect Monterey Bay is not over. There are continuing impacts from coastal development, pollution, and threats to wildlife, along with new impacts from climate change—warming and rising seas, changing ocean currents, and toxicity damaging to both sea life and fisheries.

This book showcases the Monterey Bay's natural richness, but it also chronicles the ecological collapse that has been reversed by committed conservationists, visionary scientists, dedicated philanthropists, enlightened politicians, and an engaged citizenry. By celebrating our region's natural wonders and demonstrating that damaged ecosystems can be restored, it provides an inspiration to all of us that we have the power to celebrate and protect our national treasure—Monterey Bay—for future generations. This book makes clear that our stewardship is critical to the legacy we need to leave our children.

A sweeping aerial view of the southern part of Monterey Bay shows coastal features from Big Sur and the Monterey Peninsula at the top to inland farmlands along the Salinas River.

FOLLOWING PAGES: Sea lions and elephant seals pack the beaches of Año Nuevo Island Reserve at the northern end of the bay.

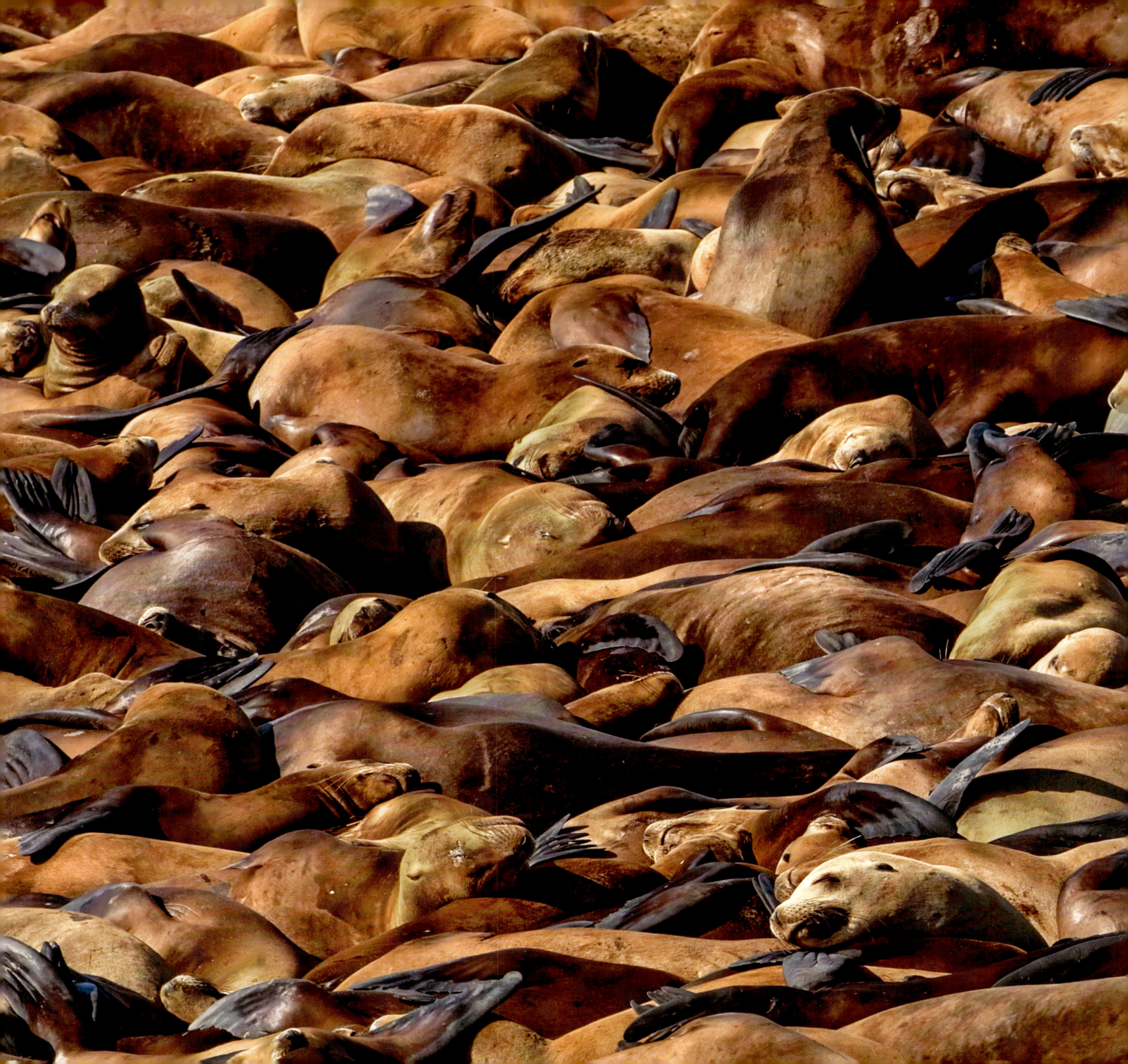

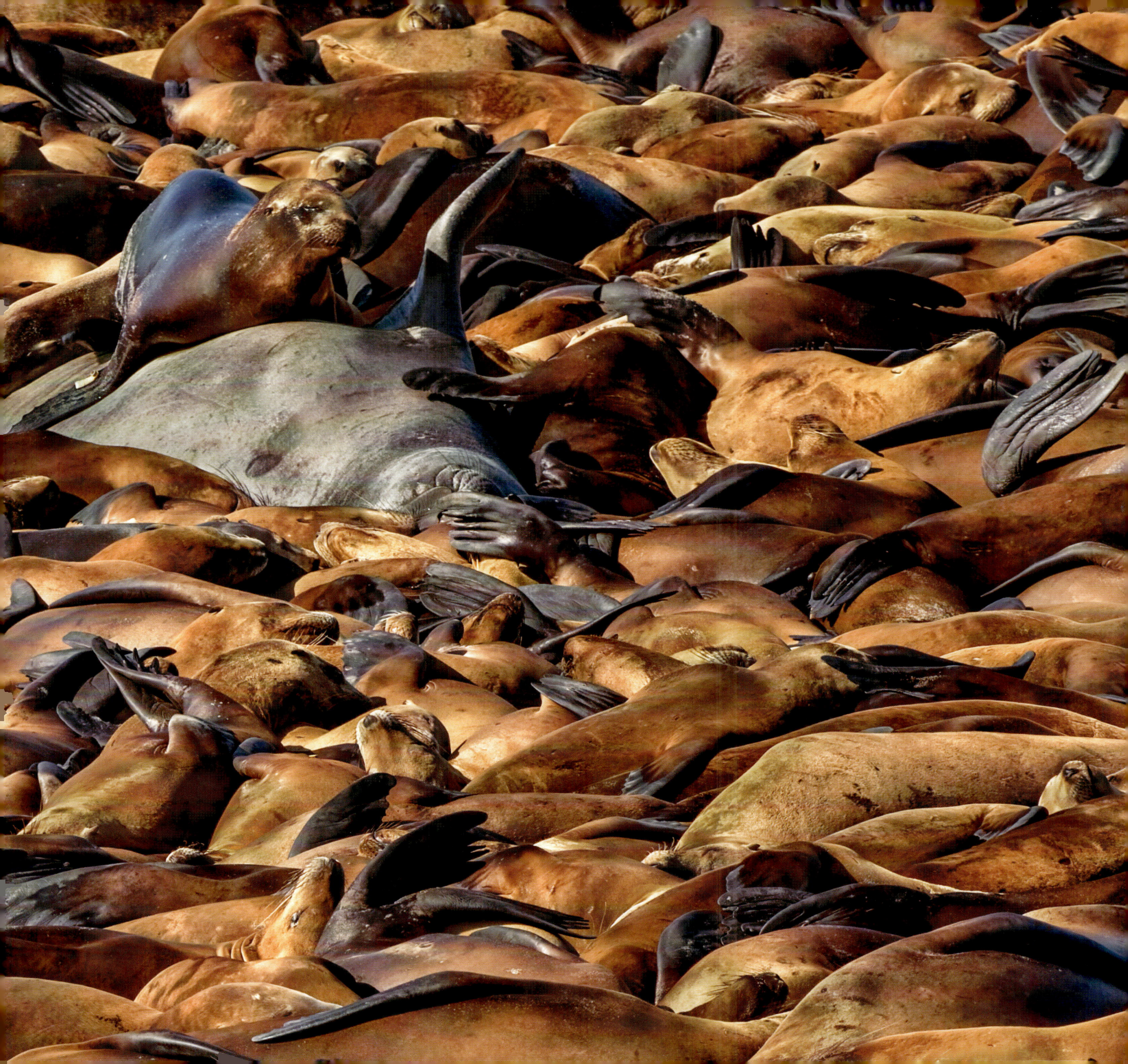

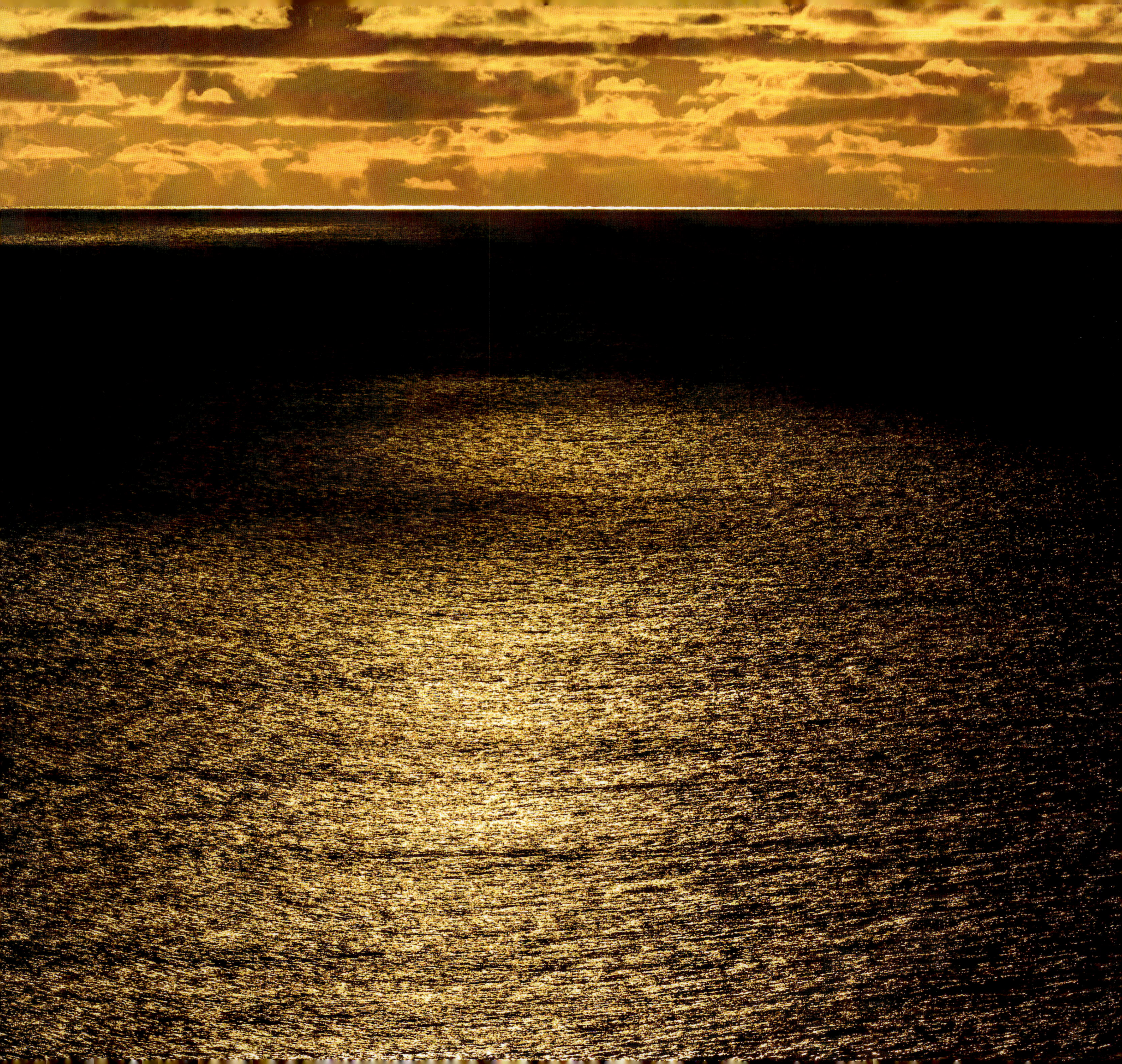

PREFACE

BY JULIE PACKARD

EXECUTIVE DIRECTOR, MONTEREY BAY AQUARIUM

The choice, after all, is ours to make.

—Rachel Carson

The story of Monterey Bay begins far from the shoreline. It starts on the highest peaks in the Coast Ranges, whose waters feed into the bay. It's also a story about people—our imprint on the land and seascapes over time, and where this place has taken us in our own paths.

My path began inland, in the Santa Clara Valley, where my parents made their home in an apricot orchard alongside the meadows and oak woodlands of the bay's watershed. I know now how privileged I was to be surrounded by so much pastoral beauty and open space, but at the time, we all took it for granted. Later, I migrated to the coast, where at UC Santa Cruz my interest in nature shifted from terrestrial plants to marine algae. I learned then what a truly remarkable place the Monterey Bay region is, teeming with life—both known and unknown—and awaiting research and protection. At the time we called it pristine, but we soon came to understand that the ocean—like the land—was in peril from human activities. The 1969 Santa Barbara oil spill was perhaps the biggest wake-up call in the imperative to take action. It was time to embrace the ocean in our definition of doing conservation work.

I've had the immense privilege of leading the Monterey Bay Aquarium since our founding nearly 40 years ago. We initially aimed to showcase the amazing diversity of life in the bay. Over time, our vision expanded. We began to tell the larger story of how the bay is connected to the global ocean. And, most importantly, we wanted to acknowledge the human impact on the bay and the coast. Today, the Aquarium's mission is to inspire conservation of the ocean. Together with a remarkable array of research, education, government, and private organizations we are working toward a common goal—a healthy coast and ocean. We have much to be proud of: miles and miles of protected coastline, world-renowned academic and research organizations, strong coastal development policies, the nation's first statewide integrated network of marine protected areas, and more.

The challenges ahead are daunting, from stemming global climate change and ocean plastic pollution, to achieving just and equitable conservation solutions that ensure food and socioeconomic security for those most in need. I know that our region has the talent and resources to contribute to a positive future not only for our treasured place but also for people and places far from our shores.

Like the Monterey Bay Aquarium, what Frans Lanting and Chris Eckstrom have created here is another portal that connects us with the remarkable life in Monterey Bay. Their images, and those of other contributors to *Bay of Life*, are stunning and inspiring. Their stories weave together the living fabric of the entire Monterey Bay ecosystem and its human connections.

And they make the compelling case for the continuing role each of us must play to safeguard its future.

Evening light illuminates the surface of Monterey Bay where it blends into the Pacific Ocean beyond. Hidden from view is an extraordinary diversity of marine life.

The rugged topography of Monterey Bay's coastal mountains is matched by
the depth of its marine canyons; that contributes to a unique array of microclimates and habitats
onshore and offshore that supports the greatest hotspot of biodiversity in North America.

Monterey Bay National Marine Sanctuary

Map by the National Oceanic and Atmospheric Administration

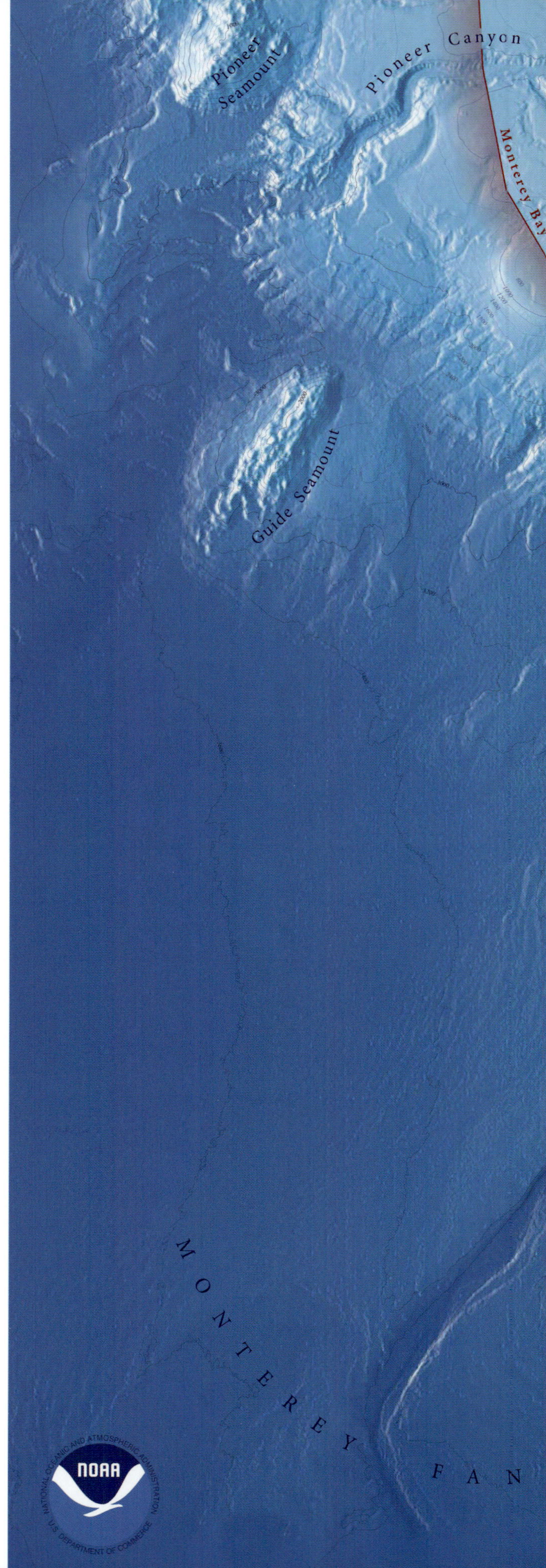

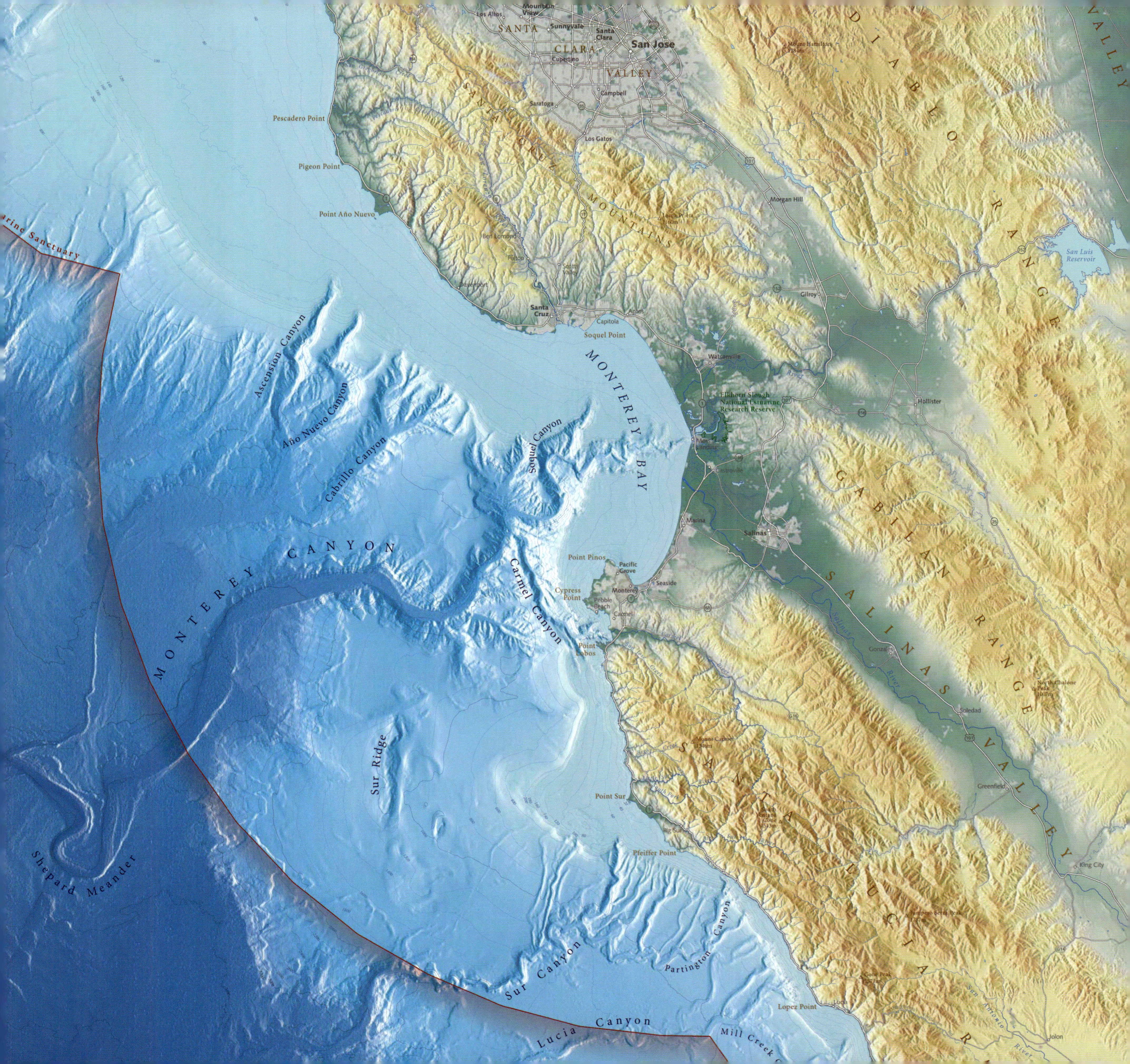

VALLEY
DIABLO
SANTA
CLARA
Sunnyvale
Santa Clara
Mountain View
Los Altos
Cupertino
San Jose
VALLEY
Campbell
Saratoga
Mount Hamilton
Lick Obs.
Los Gatos
Pescadero Point
Morgan Hill
DIABLO RANGE
Pigeon Point
San Luis
Reservoir
Point Año Nuevo
Ben Lomond
Gilroy
Felton
Scotts Valley
Santa Cruz
Capitola
Soquel Point
Watsonville
MONTEREY BAY
Hollister
Ascension Canyon
Elkhorn Slough
National Estuarine
Research Reserve
Moss Landing
Año Nuevo Canyon
Soquel Canyon
Castroville
Cabrillo Canyon
GABILAN RANGE
Marina
Salinas
MONTEREY CANYON
Point Pinos
Pacific Grove
Seaside
Monterey
Cypress Point
Carmel Canyon
Gonzales
Point Lobos
Carmel
Sur Ridge
SALINAS RANGE
North Chalone
Peak
SANTA LUCIA RANGE
SALINAS VALLEY
Mount Carmel
Soledad
Point Sur
Greenfield
Shepard Meander
Pfeiffer Point
Sur Canyon
Partington Canyon
King City
Cone Peak
Lopez Point
Lucia Canyon
Mill Creek
Jolon
marine Sanctuary

INTRODUCTION

BY FRANS LANTING AND CHRIS ECKSTROM

What is such a resource worth? Anything it costs.

—WALLACE STEGNER

We have been privileged to document our planet's natural heritage on assignment for National Geographic for more than 30 years—from the icy edges of Antarctica to the savannas of Africa and the jungles of Borneo. But the place we know best and love most is California's Monterey Bay. We have lived here for many years, and we come home from our travels to a secluded coastal meadow north of Santa Cruz. To us, Monterey Bay is one of Earth's natural crown jewels.

The richness of the bay's marine wildlife reminds us of islands near Antarctica, like South Georgia, whose shores are packed with seals and seabirds, much like the beaches of Año Nuevo. Cold water supports an abundance of life here as it does in the subantarctic. The botanical richness of the Monterey Bay region reminds us of parts of South Africa, which is an epicenter of floral diversity just like the Central Coast of California.

Monterey Bay is the hottest hotspot for biodiversity in all of North America, according to a study by The Nature Conservancy. But that assessment did not include its marine life, which is astonishing in its own right. Land and sea are often looked at separately by researchers and planners. In this book we bring the two together for a unified view of the bay and its natural abundance, which is due to a unique mix of physical features and microclimates, shaped by the powerful influence of the ocean. We know of no other place in the world where land and sea connect in such an extraordinary way.

This is a place of giants, from redwood forests standing tall on land to forests of kelp swaying in the currents offshore. It supports iconic wildlife from secretive mountain lions to majestic blue whales in a region where far-flung migrants mix with local endemics. Monterey Bay is both a crossroads and an epicenter for many forms of life. It is the southern boundary for species like coast redwoods and coho salmon, and it is the northern boundary for roadrunners

and Monterey pines. It is an epicenter for sea otters rafting by the dozens in sheltered waters and for spectacular summertime congregations of sooty shearwaters. And it is the only place where you can find the Santa Cruz cypress and the Ohlone tiger beetle—two of many species that live nowhere else in the world.

On maps, Monterey Bay appears as a crescent-shaped bight in the California coast, but what are its boundaries? On the ocean side we recognize the borders of the Monterey Bay National Marine Sanctuary. On the landward side, we regard watersheds as one natural definition. A map on page 230 shows them, from the streams of the Santa Cruz Mountains in the north to the creeks of the Santa Lucia Range in the south, and the Pajaro, Salinas, and Carmel Rivers in between.

Fog is vital to life here. It brings moisture during dry summer months that helps sustain natural habitats and agricultural enterprises alike. Fog is a physical expression of the ocean's influence onshore. We consider the extent of summer fog to be an important way to define the bay as an ecoregion. A map on page 231 shows just how far it spreads inland.

As we view it, most of the Monterey Bay region can be contained within a simple 50-mile circle, with Moss Landing at the center. Along the coast, that circle reaches up to Half Moon Bay in the north and down to Lucia in the south. In the east it includes Henry W. Coe State Park and Pinnacles National Park, and to the west it stretches into the open Pacific Ocean and includes much of the Monterey Canyon. We know of very few places in the world where a 50-mile circle encloses an ecoregion of such variety and complexity.

Monterey Bay is unique because of its seasonal pulse and its diverse habitats but also because of its environmental history. We recognize the region's natural richness in the context of the imprints of people who have made their home here, beginning with Native

Americans, who lived off the land and the sea for at least 10,000 years. A map on page 232 shows the diversity of tribal groups and languages in the Monterey Bay area. Spanish colonizers arrived in the late 1700s, and in the century after the Gold Rush began in 1848, American settlers were joined by immigrants from Europe, Asia, and many other places. They all left their marks. But the Gold Rush accelerated an over-exploitation of nature, which stripped the land of trees and depleted the sea of marine mammals and fish.

As redwoods were being cut down at an alarming rate in the early 20th century, concerned citizens banded together to protect the last of the big trees in the Santa Cruz Mountains. Today redwood forests have grown back in many areas that were once denuded. Offshore, the multitudes of marine mammals are living proof of the success of the Marine Mammal Protection Act and other policies that have enabled wildlife to repopulate the bay. To us, this shows that species can be rewilded and ecosystems can be restored when people take action together, and we believe it may offer a model for other places at a time when we need such stories of hope.

There has been a significant expansion of protected areas around Monterey Bay in the last 50 years. They have become magnets for many millions of people living within two hours of its shoreline. Every year more than ten million visitors come to its National Parks, Monuments, Forests, Wildlife Refuges, and BLM lands, the Marine Sanctuary, State and County Parks and Beaches, regional Open Space Preserves, and local Land Trust properties. A map on page 233 shows them all. During the Covid pandemic, these places provided people relief from the confines of their homes—and an opportunity to connect with nature.

We recognize the need for more urban parks closer to population centers that are easier for people to reach, and we endorse efforts to develop more inclusive experiences for our diverse communities.

With increasing numbers of people coming to our protected places, there is a need for more professionals on the ground to interpret their significance for visitors, who can be allies for environmental initiatives. Caring for our precious resources can involve citizens as well as land managers. We applaud the new partnerships between State Parks, local land trusts, and Native Americans to collaborate on projects that engage them as stewards of the land.

We support efforts to link protected areas together to strengthen them collectively. Connectivity is a crucial response to the habitat fragmentation that jeopardizes the survival of mountain lions that roam our hills. It also creates more opportunities for plants and animals to move as they have to adapt to new conditions in an era of climate change.

We have long known that fire is a fundamental feature of Monterey Bay's Mediterranean life cycle, but it became a frightening reality for us when the CZU megafire engulfed our rural community in 2020. We watched a firestorm develop that billowed above the forest while tall trees turned into rockets of flame. The fire came close to our home in the hills, but we were spared because neighbors banded together to fight its advance. Nearly a thousand families in the Santa Cruz Mountains were not so lucky. They lost their homes, and we hurt for them. Along with others, we learned invaluable lessons about how to adapt to fire and make our communities and wildlands more resilient.

Monterey Bay has a special history of people joining forces to safeguard what they cherish. Witness our extensive network of protected lands. Consider the marine sanctuary that stretches far beyond the bay. The next time you stand in awe before an ancient redwood in the forest or watch a whale breach offshore, remember that they are here today because of people who acted. We hope you will join us and contribute to a future worthy of our magnificent Bay of Life.

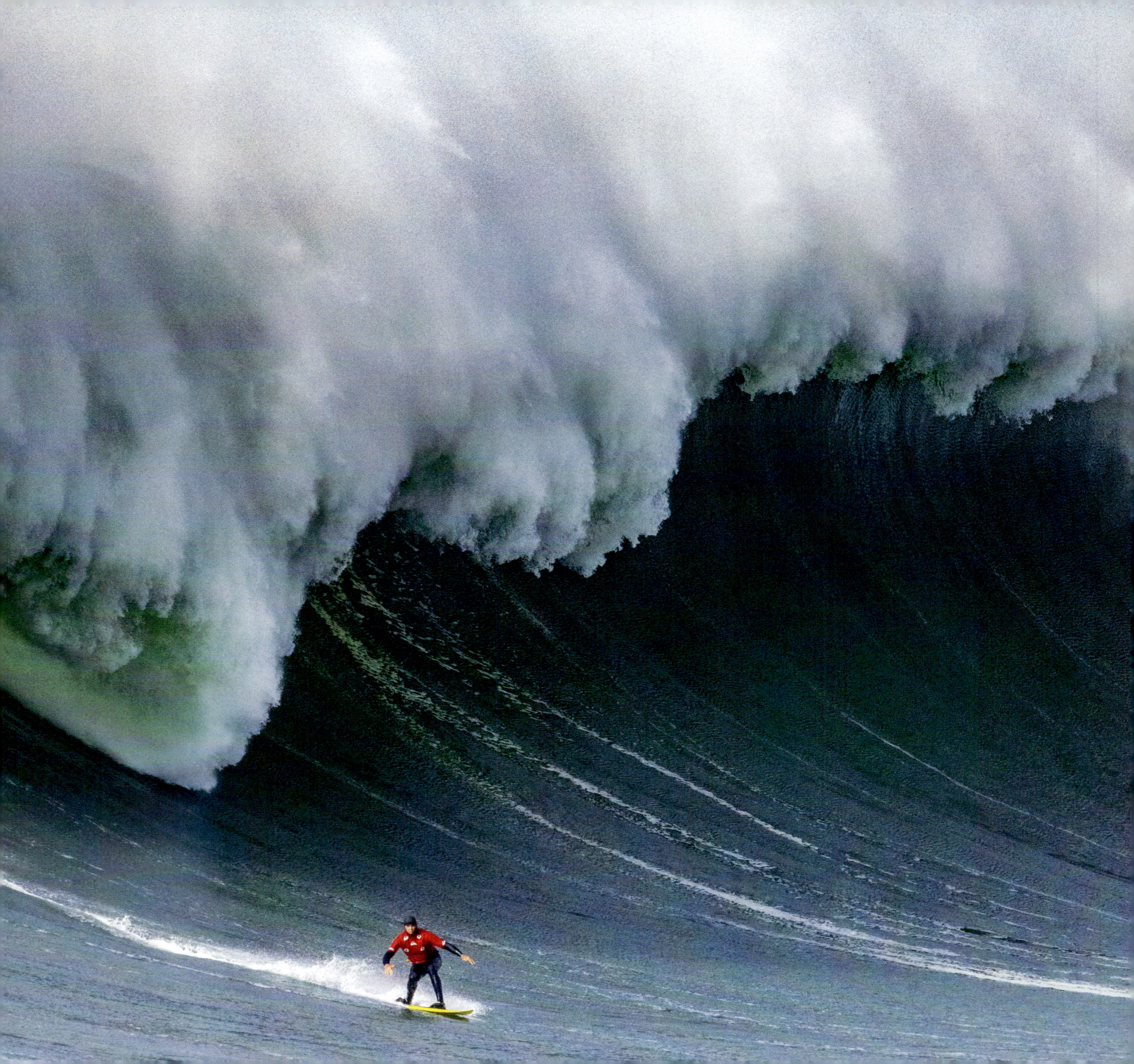

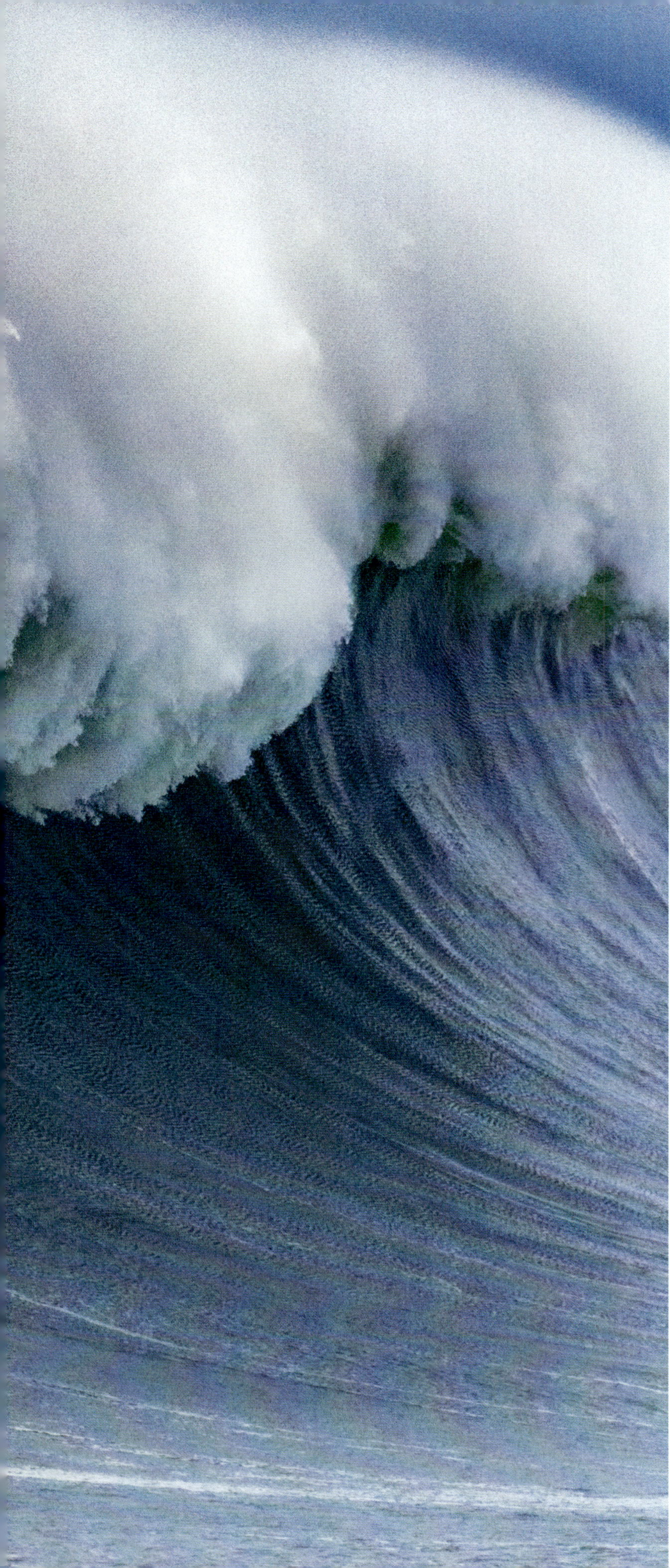

The power of a winter storm from the Pacific Ocean
is expressed in a 50-foot wave at Mavericks,
where Santa Cruz surfer Peter Mel keeps his cool.

BIG WAVE SURFER, PILLAR POINT STATE MARINE CONSERVATION AREA

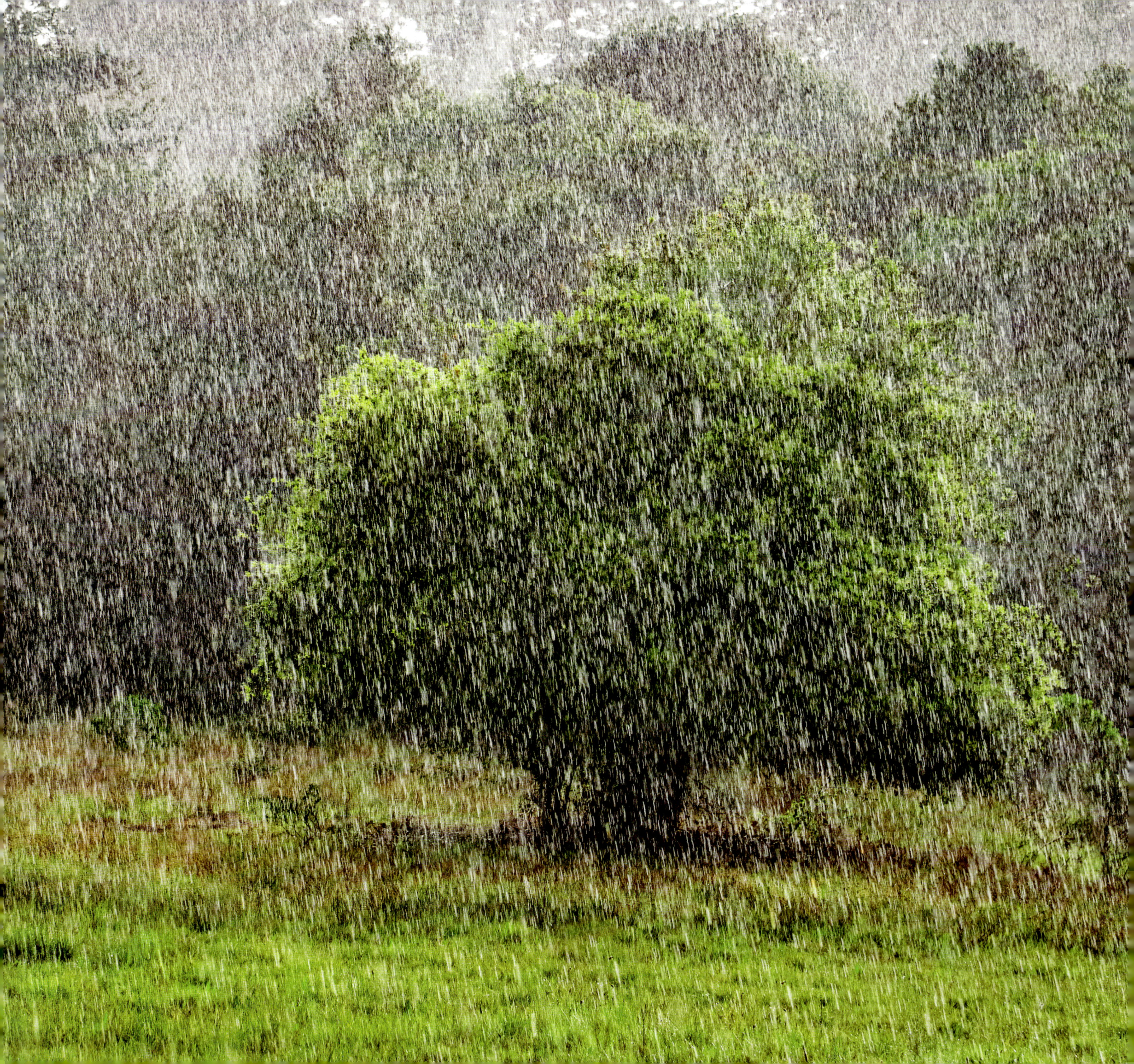

SEASONS

FROM WIND TO WHALES

I've lived in a good climate, and it bores the hell out of me.
I like weather rather than climate.

—John Steinbeck

Most people who visit Monterey Bay, and those lucky to live here, don't think very often about the climate—but everyone likes the weather. While millions of people elsewhere in the United States swelter through the heat of summer, most of the Monterey Bay remains cool. And when much of the country struggles through the cold of winter, the Monterey Bay stays mild. There is a different pulse to the seasons here than in any other part of the United States.

Life in the Monterey Bay is shaped by a temperate Mediterranean climate of rainy winters and dry summers that is found in only five regions in the world: parts of California, Chile, South Africa, Australia, and Europe's Mediterranean Basin. Combined, they cover only 2 percent of the Earth's landmass, yet they nurture 20 percent of all the plant species in the world. While these five places are distinctly different from one another, they are all located along the western edge of continents where cold, offshore ocean currents moderate summer temperatures.

Monterey Bay has a remarkable array of microclimates, from a fog belt in the north around Pigeon Point to a banana belt inside the bay around Santa Cruz and another fog belt around Monterey. The topography of rugged hills and steep valleys contributes to this diversity. Two mountain ranges running parallel to the coast create rain shadows that keep interior valleys dry. Annual rainfall in the Santa Lucia Range of Big Sur can be 60 inches, while the

Salinas Valley to the east receives less than 15 inches. Gaps in the coastal ranges allow fog to penetrate the Salinas and Pajaro Valleys, moderating heat in these agricultural regions. Farmers here depend on fog.

In this complex setting the bay's seasons unfold, each marked by a change in the air. The powerful winds of spring whip whitecaps across the surface of the bay before the moist waves of fog roll inland during summer. The clear skies of autumn can gust with hot winds that feel like the breath of fire. They give way to the puffed cumulus clouds of winter that cast flickering shadows across land and sea in the wake of storms.

Monterey Bay's seasons are shaped by a dome of high pressure that spreads across the northeastern Pacific Ocean for many thousands of square miles. Known as the North Pacific High, it consists of a vast, clockwise circulation of winds that shifts north and south during the year. As it does, it influences the bay's weather. In spring, the Pacific High moves north and grows stronger. It drives winds across the ocean toward the California coast, where they are sucked inland by the heat of the Central Valley. This creates the northwest winds that sweep into the bay. Salt spray flies from ocean breakers, sands swirl across beaches, grasslands ripple in mesmerizing waves—and workers and surfers alike duck into their hoodies.

The winds of spring trigger a transformational event: Blowing along the shore, they push surface water away, allowing cold

Rain renews the land. It turns meadows green, replenishes streams, and nurtures new life in the forest.

Oak in Rain, Rancho Refugio

water to surge from the deep in great upwellings. These pumping plumes of seawater last from spring through summer and are an important reason why marine life is so abundant here. Water from the deep is high in nutrients, and when it wells up to the surface, sunlight stimulates massive blooms of phytoplankton that nourish huge swarms of krill—a vital food source for everything higher up the food chain, from fish to seabirds to dolphins. And it sustains the largest animals on Earth—the great whales that converge on Monterey Bay every year. This miraculous chain of events can be summarized simply: The winds of spring bring the whales of summer.

August is a great time to see humpback whales in the bay. On a foggy morning when the water is calm, they can be heard before they're seen as they surface and exhale explosively. Their main prey, krill and anchovies, respond to strong upwellings by swarming together in huge aggregations—an ideal opportunity for humpbacks, which search for dense patches of food. As a big school of anchovies ruffles the surface and sea lions porpoise in frenzied circles to feed on them, humpbacks corral the fish underwater. Suddenly the whales burst up from the sea in synchrony, forcing out streams of water through baleen plates in their mouths as they swallow masses of anchovies and sink back down, out of sight until their next lunge.

Summer is the season of fog. When cold upwellings chill the ocean's surface, they cool the moist maritime air above it, which condenses and forms great banks of fog that stretch across the bay. Fog is a shapeshifter. It can look like a mountain range far out at sea; it can come ashore in an advancing wave, with a feathery leading edge drawn inland by heat. It can engulf everything in a cottony whiteness, cool and misty and dense with moisture that feels like horizontal rain. Fog is fickle. It can persist for days or dissipate in minutes. In the Monterey Bay, fog cools the streams salmon depend on in summer and during low tides, it reduces the desiccating impact of the sun on intertidal life.

During the long, rainless months of summer, fog provides critical moisture to both natural systems and agricultural operations. Redwoods receive as much as 40 percent of their annual water from fog; without it, they might not survive here. In heavy coastal mists, redwood trees become so laden with moisture that they create their own rain—a fog drip that waters their roots.

In autumn, westerly winds die down, upwellings slow, and the fog wanes away. September and October are the warmest months of the year. Skies turn blue, and warm water flows into the bay. Fall in the Monterey Bay is what many visitors expect summer to be.

But autumn is also a season of fire. When high pressure develops east of the Sierra Nevada while a low-pressure system forms offshore, winds from the interior can rush toward the coast. These devilish winds take their name from the Diablo Range east of the Monterey Bay, but the term "Diablo wind" is now used to refer to dry offshore winds that race through the Coast Ranges, including the Santa Cruz Mountains. When winds from the Sierras cascade down into the Central Valley and over the crests of the Diablo Range, they can reach speeds of hurricane force. As they descend toward the coast, they heat up and lose humidity, funneling through canyons and gaps in powerful gusts. Everyone's nerves are on edge when this wind hits the hills while vegetation is at its driest, primed for fire.

The first rain showers that break the long dry season in late summer and early fall can arrive as monsoon storms that blow in from the south. But these systems become dangerous when they develop into dry lightning storms. That was the cause of the massive fires of 2020 in the Santa Cruz Mountains: Dry lightning strikes on a parched landscape ignited scattered blazes that merged together; fanned by winds from the interior, it became a firestorm.

Fire can be destructive when it rages through a drought-stricken forest, driven by high winds, scorching everything in its path. Yet it can also rejuvenate nature when it creeps along the ground, burning brush and nourishing the soil in grasslands and woodlands. Many plants in Monterey Bay are adapted to fire, and some conifers like knobcone pines actually rely on intense heat to open their cones so their seeds can disperse after a fire.

Real relief doesn't come back to the land until the first winter rains arrive later in the year. By then, the Pacific High has moved south and its counterpart, the Aleutian Low, has expanded to dominate the northeastern Pacific Ocean. Centered on the Aleutian Islands off Alaska, this low-pressure system is the place where cold winter storms are born—and propelled toward California. Other storms, known as atmospheric rivers, extend in long bands of moisture from the tropics to higher latitudes and can slam into the coast with torrential downpours that last for days. When the storms end and skies clear again, the land is soggy and green, with a bright sun steaming moisture from vegetation in vaporous billows.

Winter is a season of renewal. Rain soaks down into thirsty soil and transforms grasses from gray to green. Streams come back to life, with rivulets gurgling in unexpected places. The forest floor turns soft and glistens with mushrooms. An earthy scent of damp soil and new growth rises up to tickle the senses.

At the coast, the beaches at Año Nuevo are packed with elephant seals that converge here every winter to reproduce. From a distance the crowded colony looks like a mass of giant boulders piled together along the shore. Up close, it is a cacophony of sounds. Females bark to defend personal space, pups squeal to maintain contact with their mothers, and massive males trumpet deep, guttural warnings to ward off rivals. To human ears and eyes it may seem like utter chaos, but research has shown that males know the status of other males by their distinctive vocalizations. Long-term studies by researchers from UC Santa Cruz reveal the intricacy of relationships between individual elephant seals and their connections with the seasons at this place near the northern end of Monterey Bay.

By February when other parts of the United States are still blanketed with snow, signs of spring already appear around the bay: Frogs call in pulsing choruses from pools and ponds, golden poppies bloom in meadows, and offshore, kelp forests grow taller under the influence of a strengthening sun.

Mediterranean climates are fickle by nature. Dry years alternate with wet ones, and periodic droughts are a fact of life. Climate change is making some local weather patterns more extreme. Warming temperatures create a "thirstier" atmosphere that increases evaporation, leaving less water for people and habitats alike—in a region already stressed by population growth and greater demands for water. It is sobering to contemplate how much Monterey Bay's precious water systems depend on a handful of serendipitous winter storms each year. Yet they support the lives and livelihoods of a million people, a multi-billion-dollar agriculture sector, and an equally valuable tourism economy.

Fog and fire are crucial components of the unique seasonal pulse that shapes life in the Monterey Bay, and both are influenced by the activities of people. Fog is a natural air conditioner, and an unpaid ecosystem service whose value to the region has yet to be calculated. There is increasing concern that coastal fog may be affected by global warming. One study concludes that fog along the Pacific coast has decreased by a third in the past 60 years. An assessment by the State of California projects that by 2080, Santa Cruz may have a climate like that of Goleta, near Santa Barbara, which is more than two degrees warmer and 30 percent drier. How that may impact fog is uncertain, but we do need to better understand what is at stake and how we can prepare for a future with less fog.

Ever since indigenous practices of burning landscapes on a regular basis came to an end, fire has been treated as an adversary, and fire suppression has been institutionalized. As a result, huge amounts of combustible materials have built up in our wildlands at the same time as more people have built homes there. That has created a volatile situation exacerbated by longer fire seasons and more catastrophic megafires. In the aftermath of the 2020 fires, we need to reinvent our relationship with fire as a fundamental reality of nature in the Bay of Life.

SPRING

Spring is marked by a bloom of poppies but also by
blustery winds that begin to blow in from the bay.

Poppies in Wind, Andrew Molera State Park

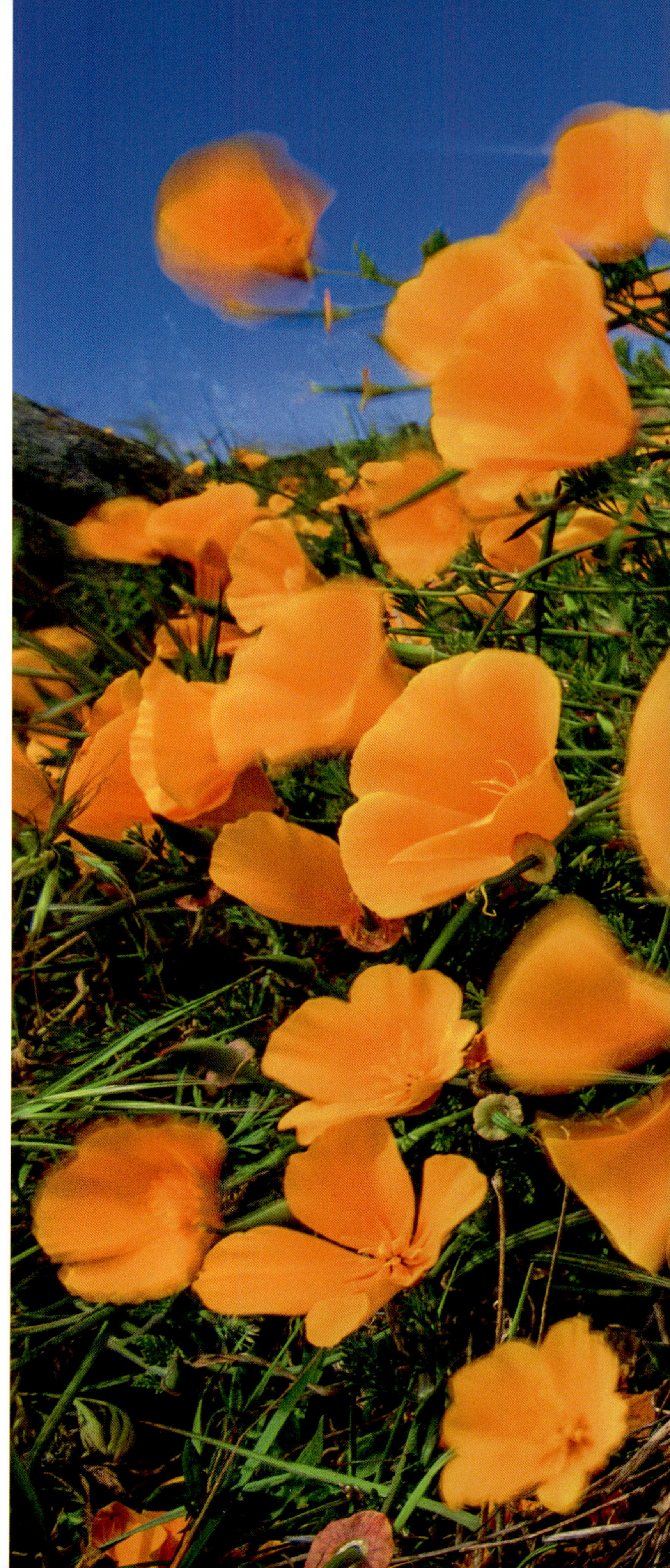

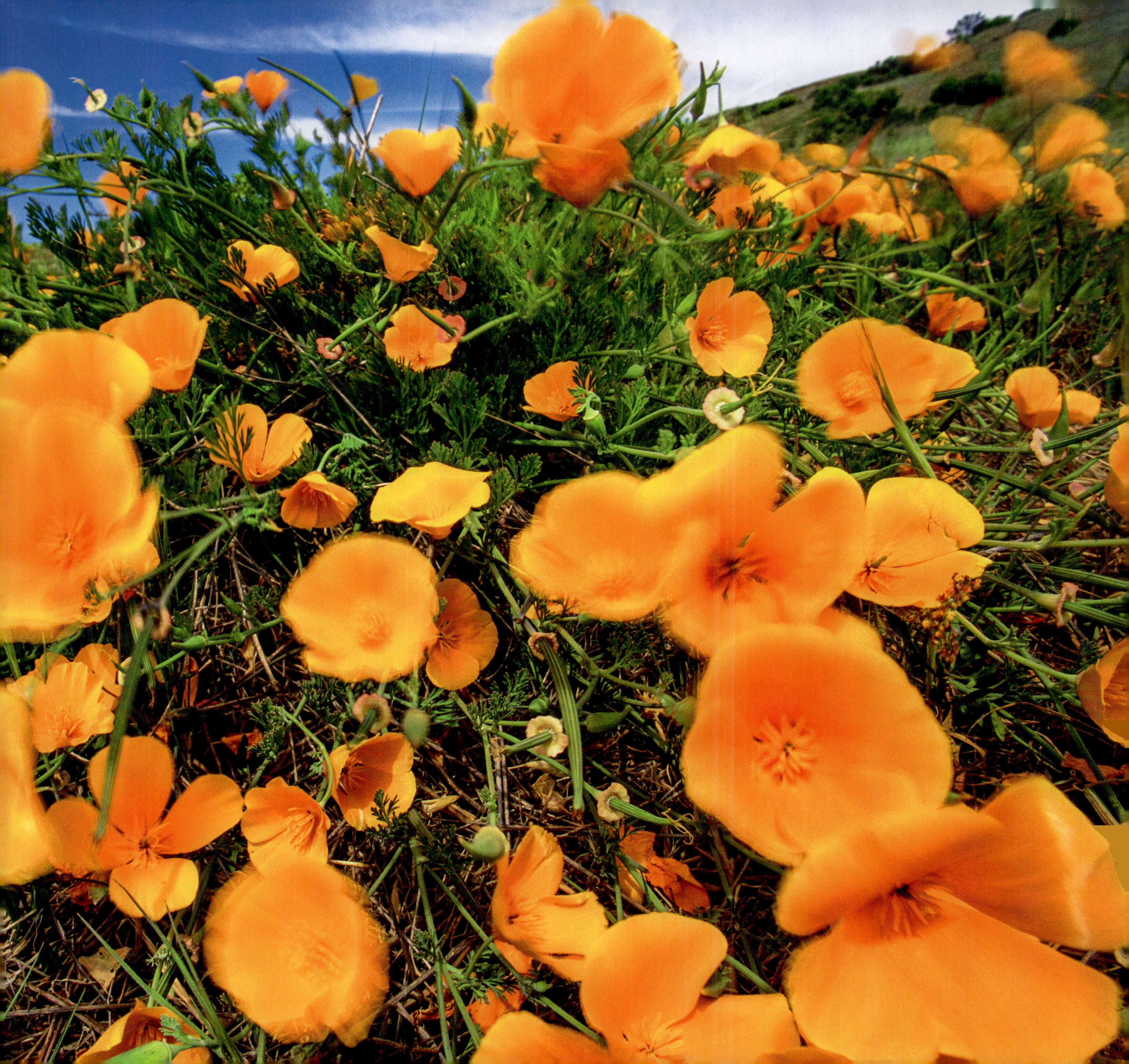

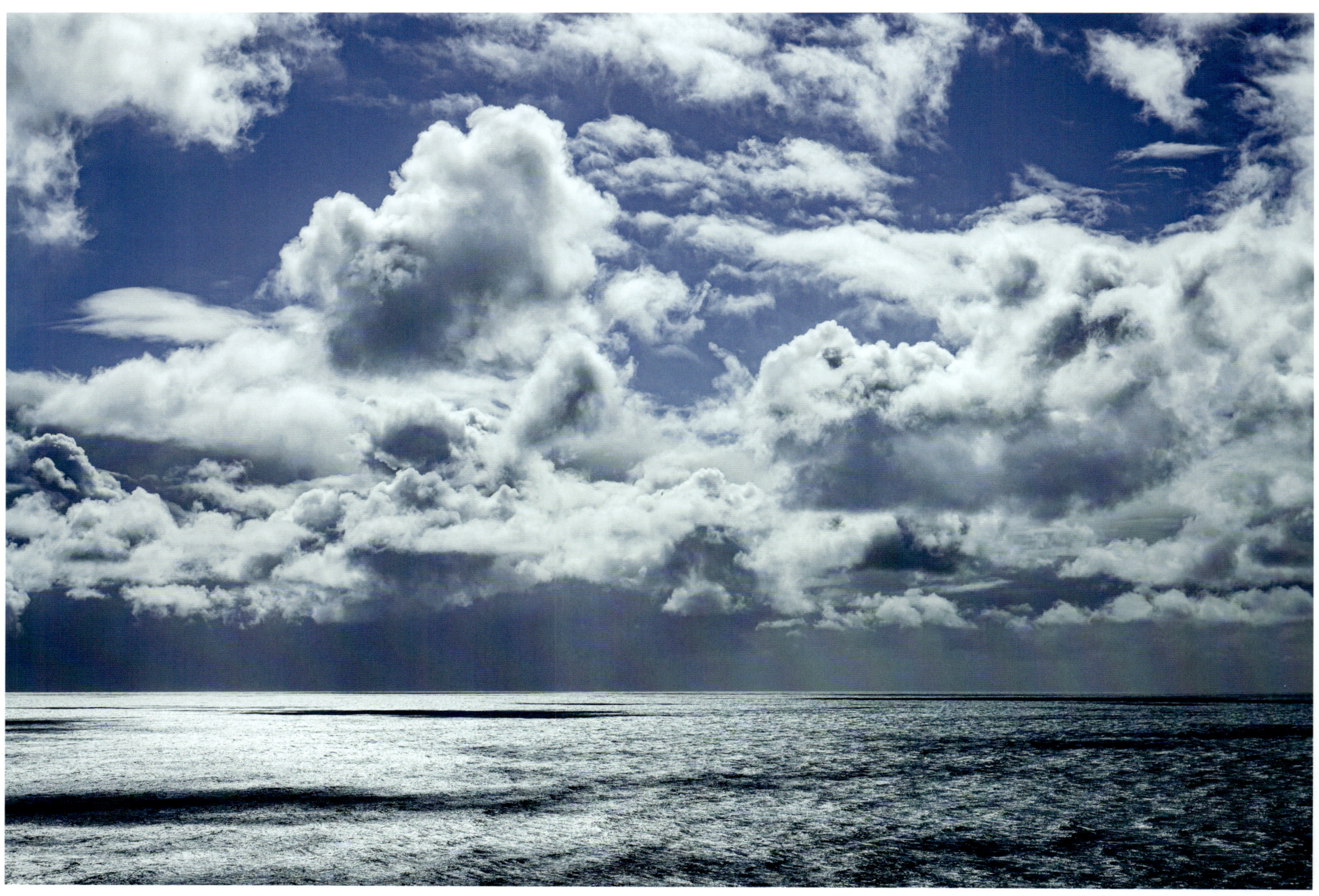

Cloud shadows shimmer as approaching rain squalls darken the horizon. The arrival of spring winds signals a great change in the Monterey Bay, when upwellings of cold, nutrient-rich water stimulate blooms of phytoplankton. These microscopic plants nourish swarms of krill and other tiny animals that then feed everything in the bay from jellyfish to seabirds to whales.

Rain Clouds, Monterey Bay National Marine Sanctuary

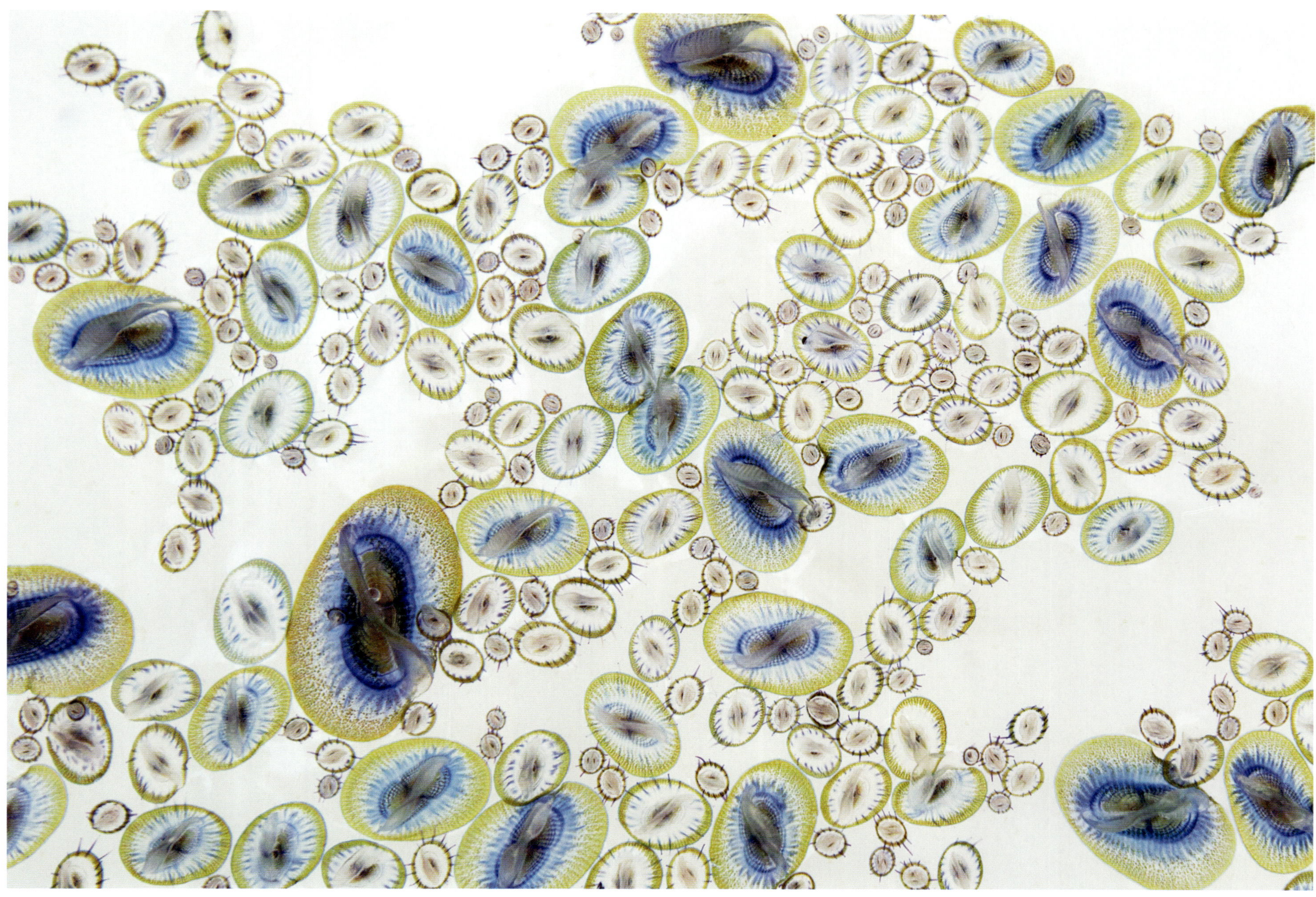

Also known as "by-the-wind sailors," these gelatinous ocean drifters live at the interface of water and air. Their tentacles dangle in the sea to capture prey while a small stiff sail catches the breeze and propels them across the ocean. Spring winds often blow them onto the beaches of Monterey Bay.

Velella velella, Monterey Bay National Marine Sanctuary | *Photo by Jodi Frediani*

following pages: Budding alder trees in a riparian forest are a pointillist expression of rebirth.

Alder Trees, Butano State Park

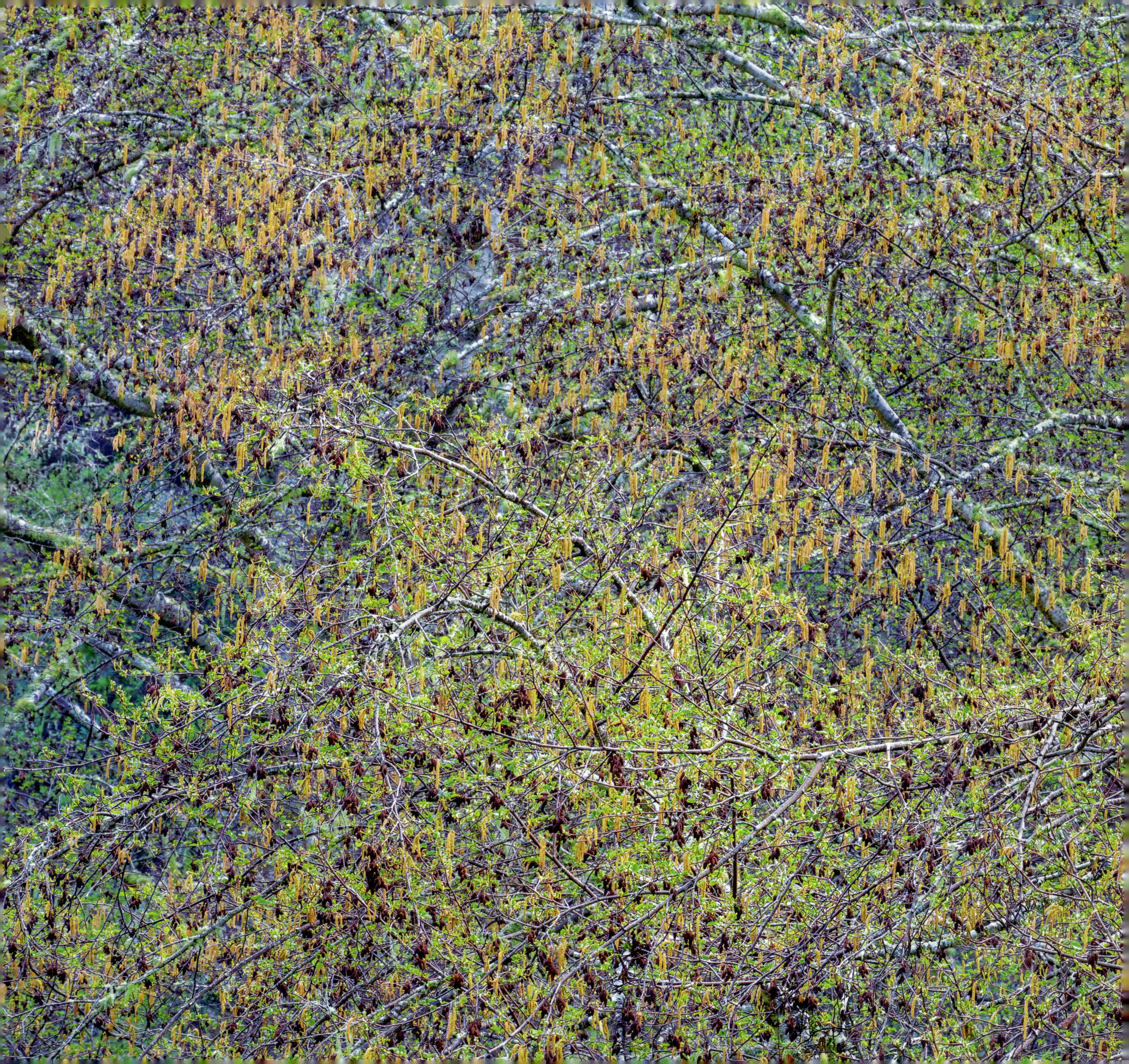

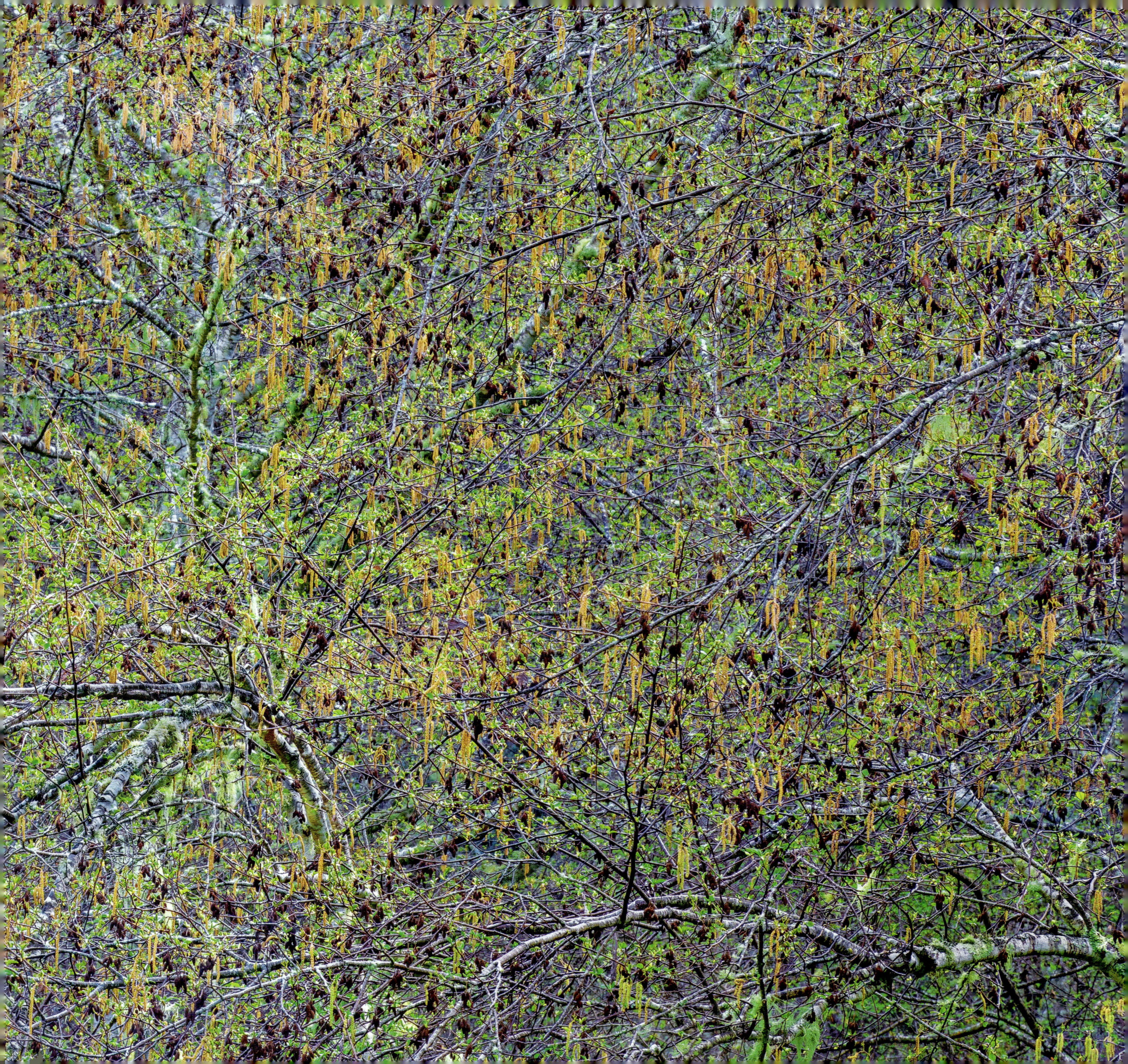

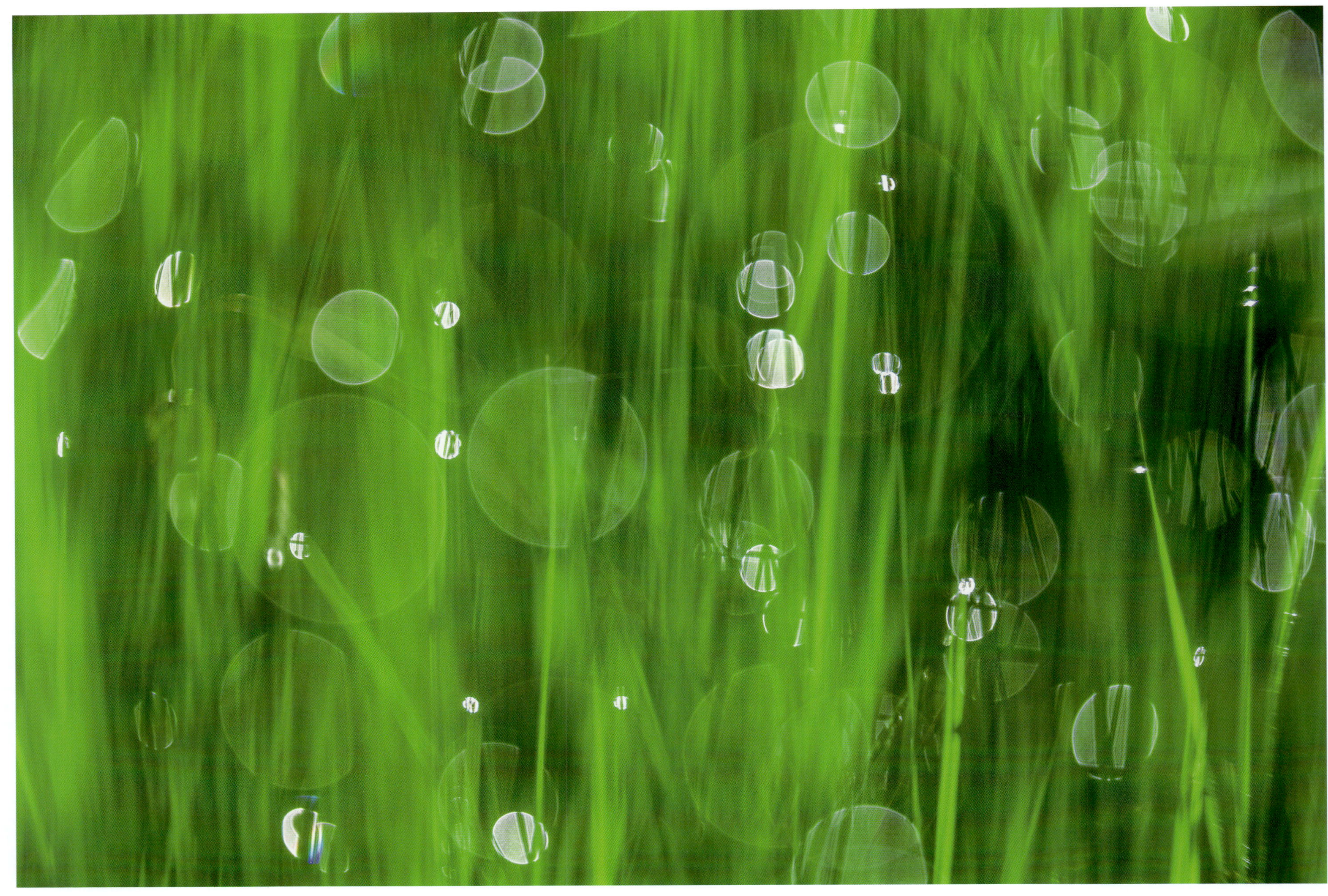

Dewdrops sparkle on meadow grasses that are coming alive in early spring.

MORNING DEW, RANCHO REFUGIO

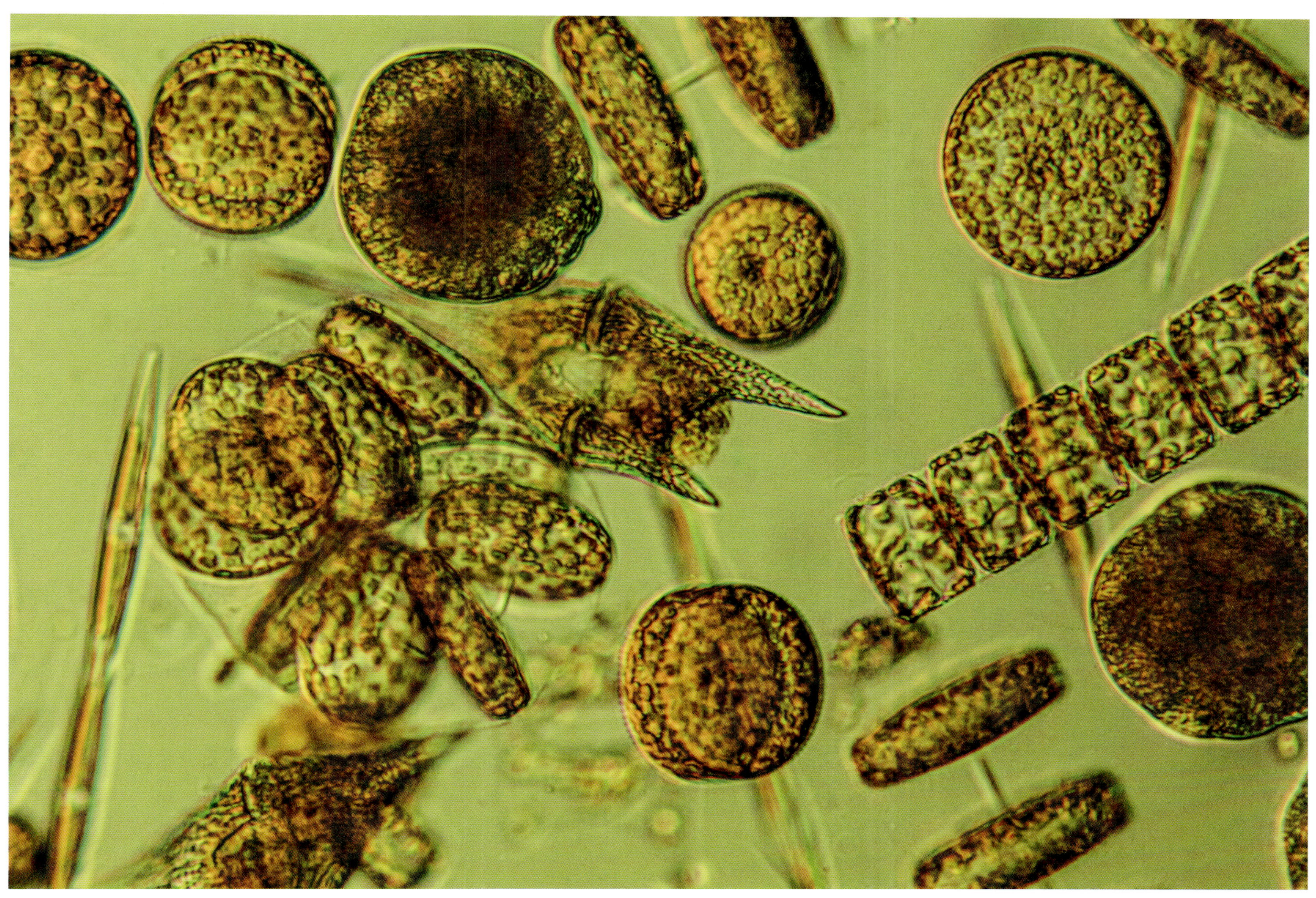

Marine upwellings bring nutrients to the surface that spark the growth of diatoms—microscopic algae that are the basis of the marine food chain.

DIATOMS, SANTA CRUZ WHARF | *Photo by Steve Mandel*

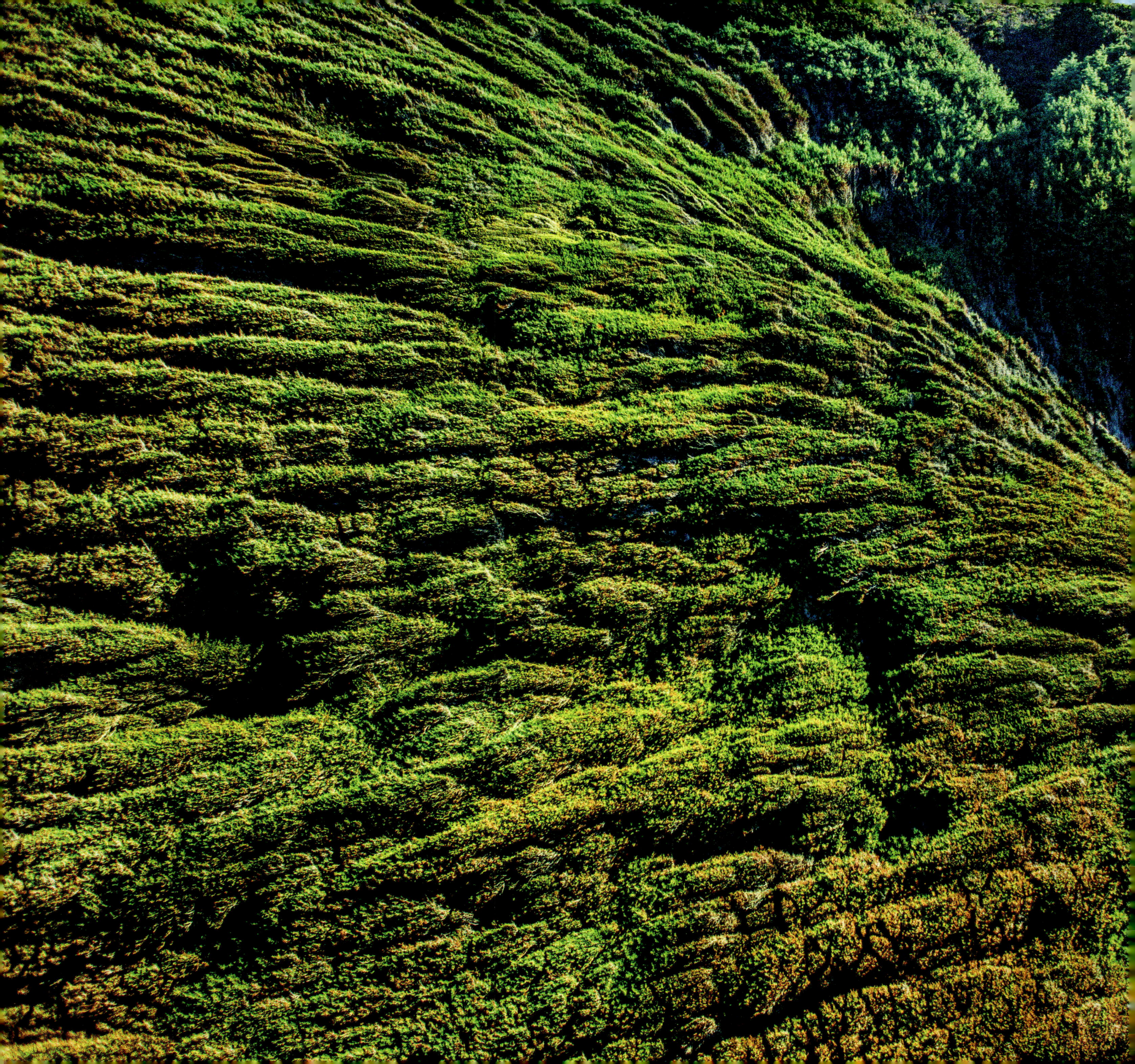

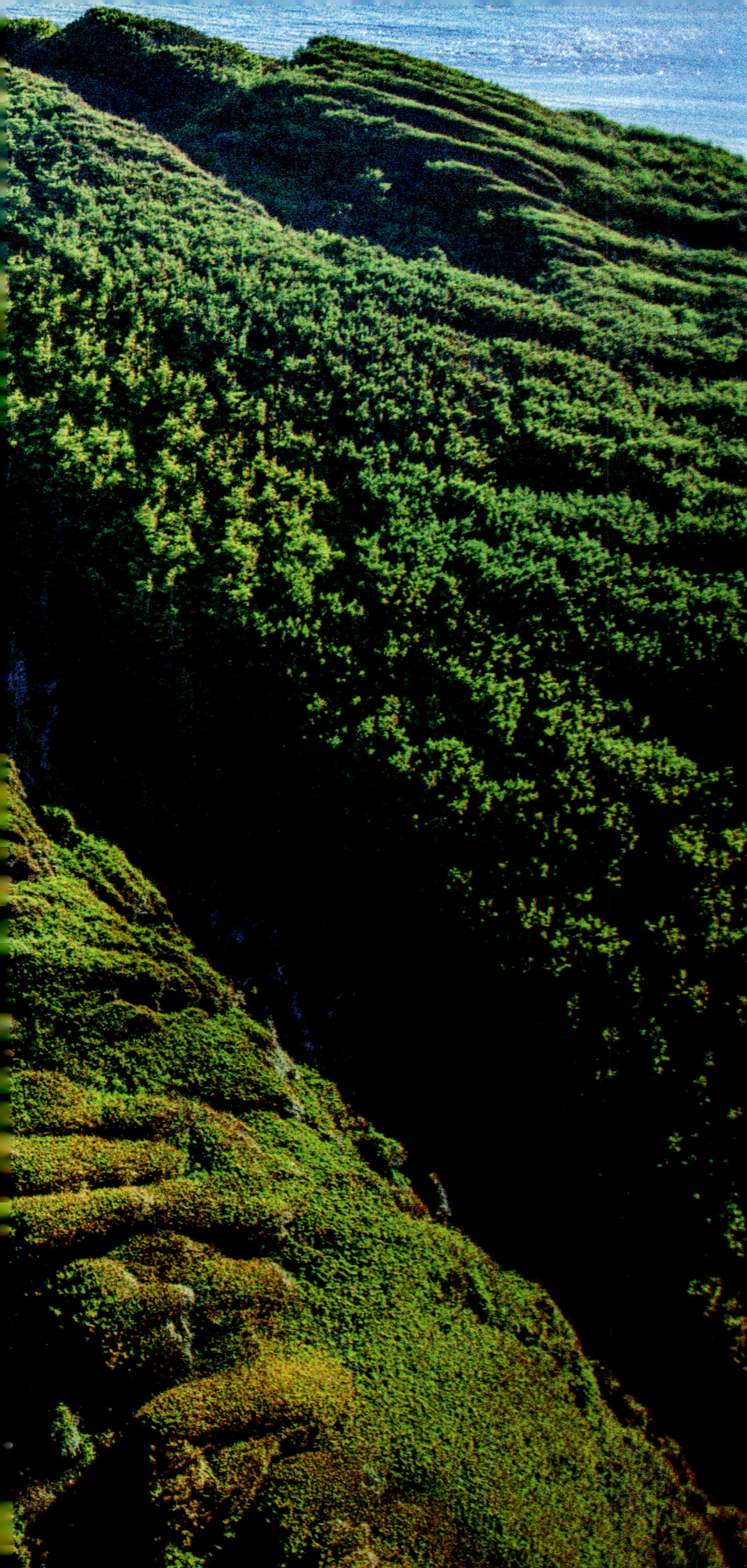

A coastal hillside covered in chaparral shows the power of the wind that blows up steep canyons and sculpts grooved channels into the vegetation.

WINDBLOWN CHAPARRAL, BIG SUR

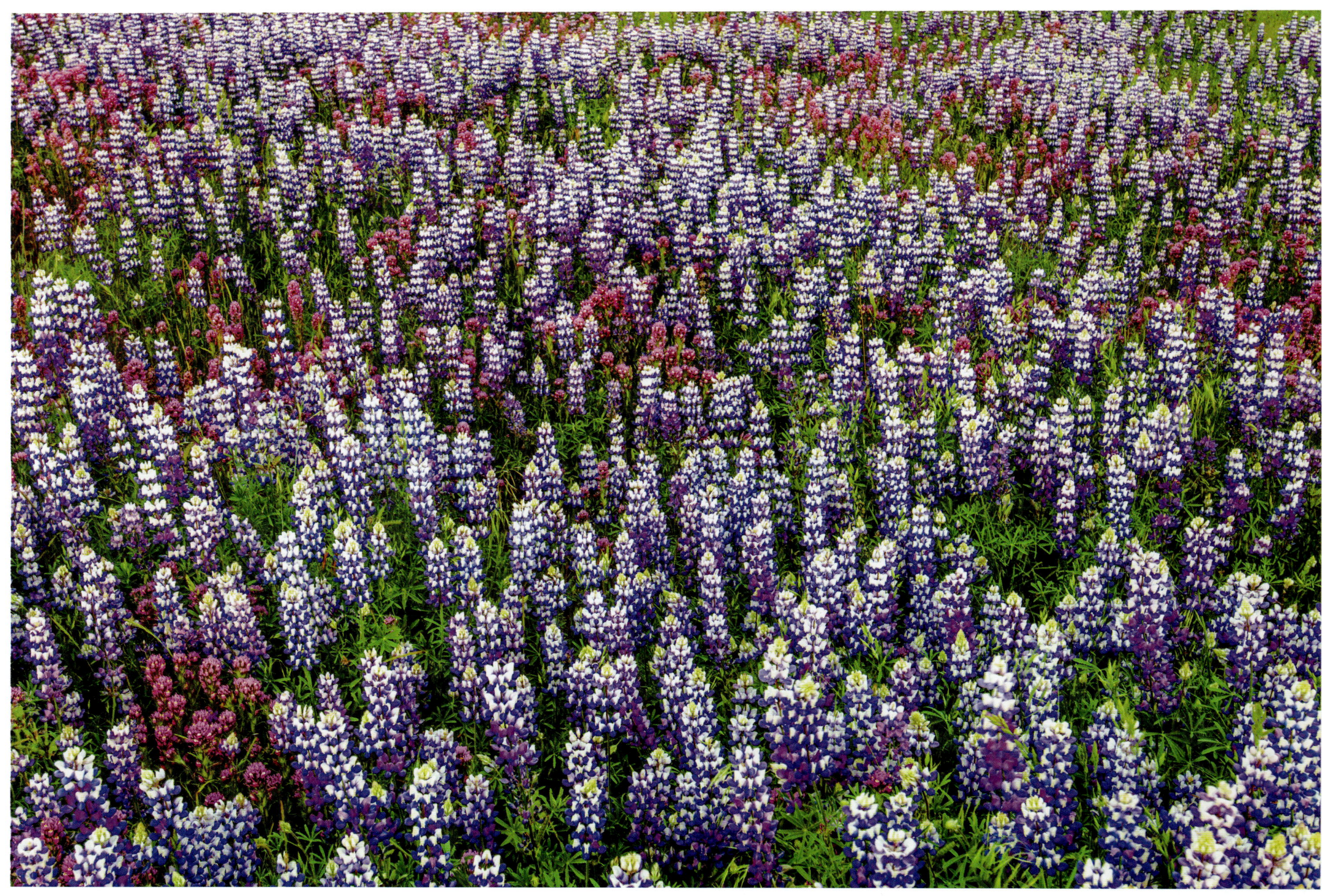

Blue sky lupines mix with purple owl's clover in a dizzying display of color. Tiny
pink tips on some of the lupines indicate native bumblebees have pollinated them.

WILDFLOWERS, LOS PADRES NATIONAL FOREST

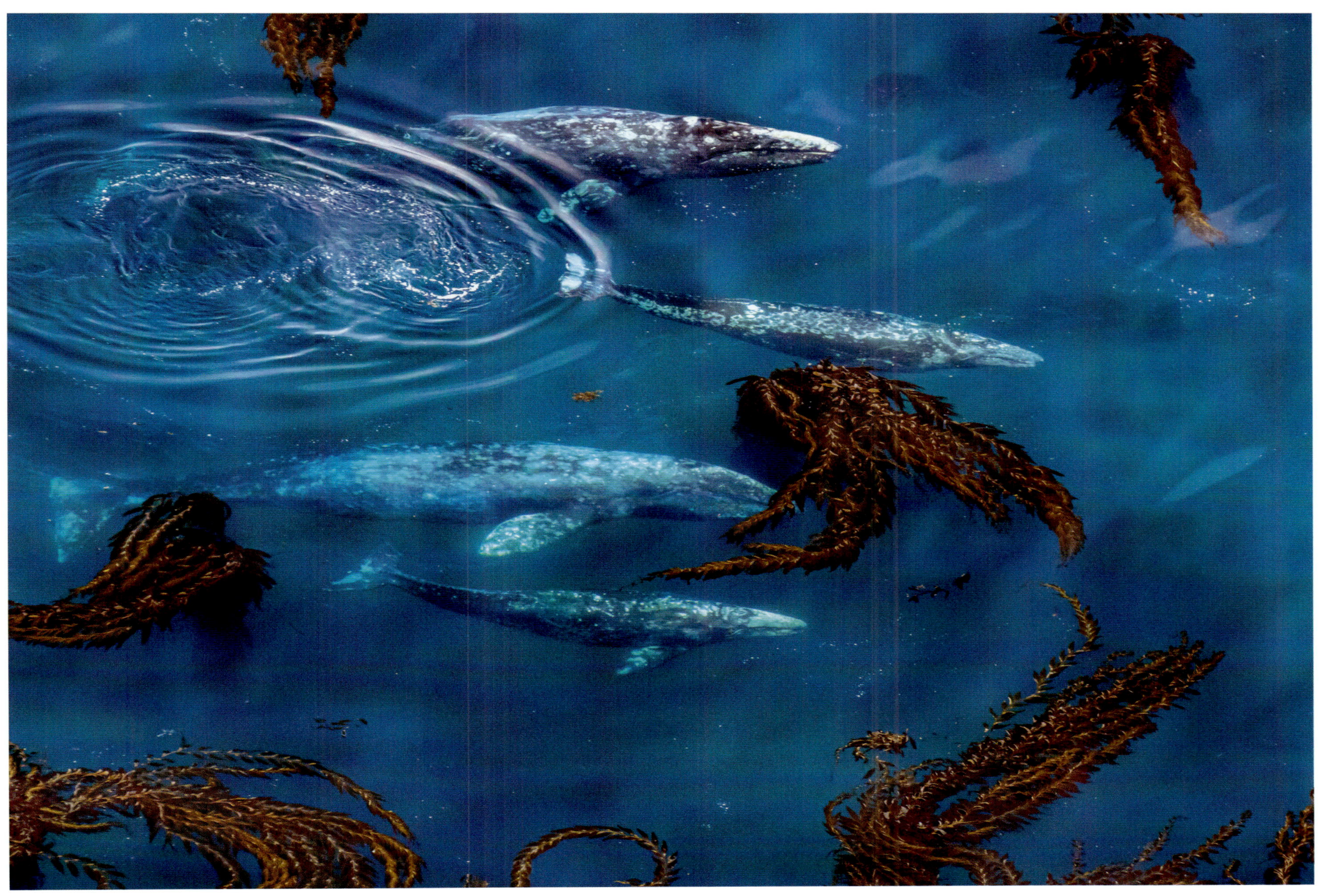

Gray whale mothers and calves make their way north each spring from calving lagoons in Baja California to feeding grounds in the Arctic, a 6,000-mile journey. To avoid attack by orcas they hug the Big Sur coastline, where tangles of kelp and the sound of breaking surf help mask their passage.

GRAY WHALES, BIG SUR | *Photo by Jodi Frediani*

SUMMER

During summer, swells of fog form at sea and roll over the coast in
engulfing waves. The moisture carried ashore sustains life around
Monterey Bay for months, when not a drop of rain falls.

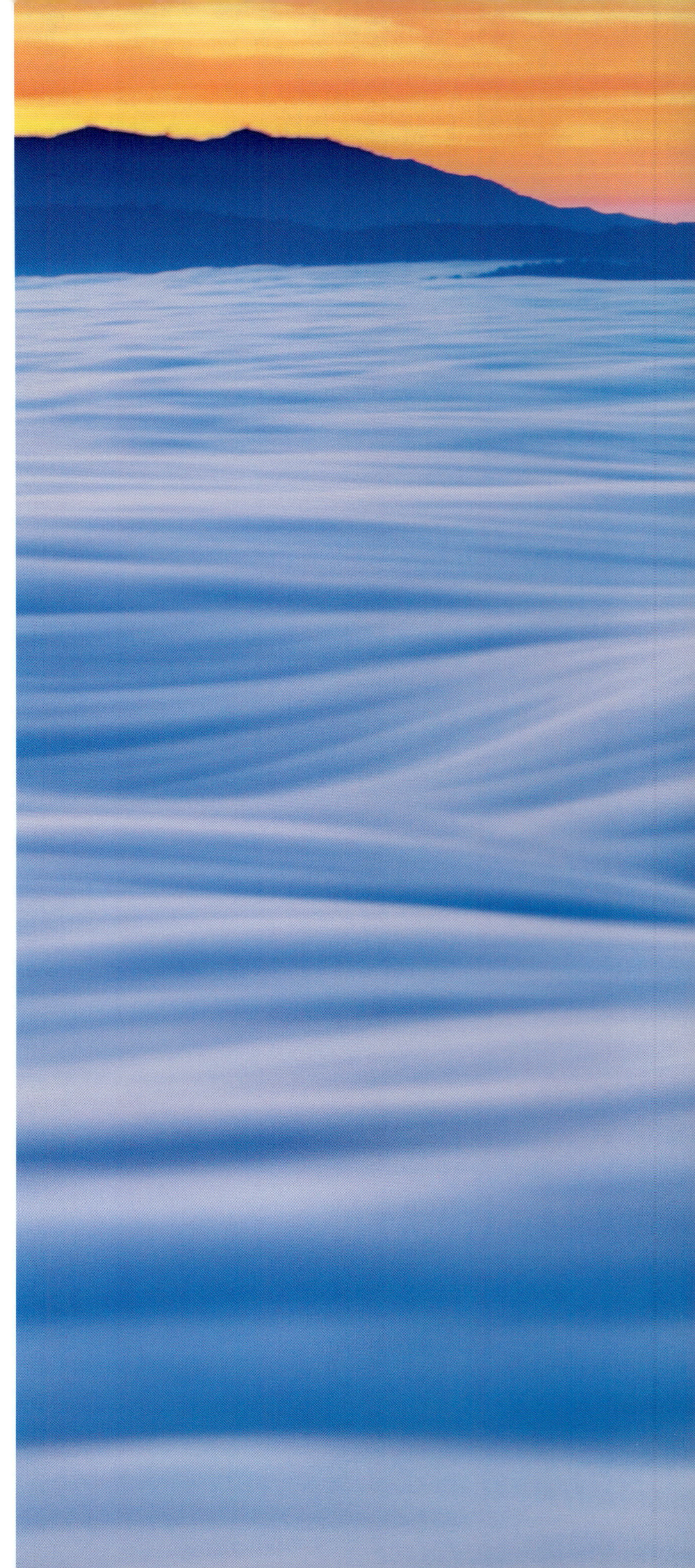

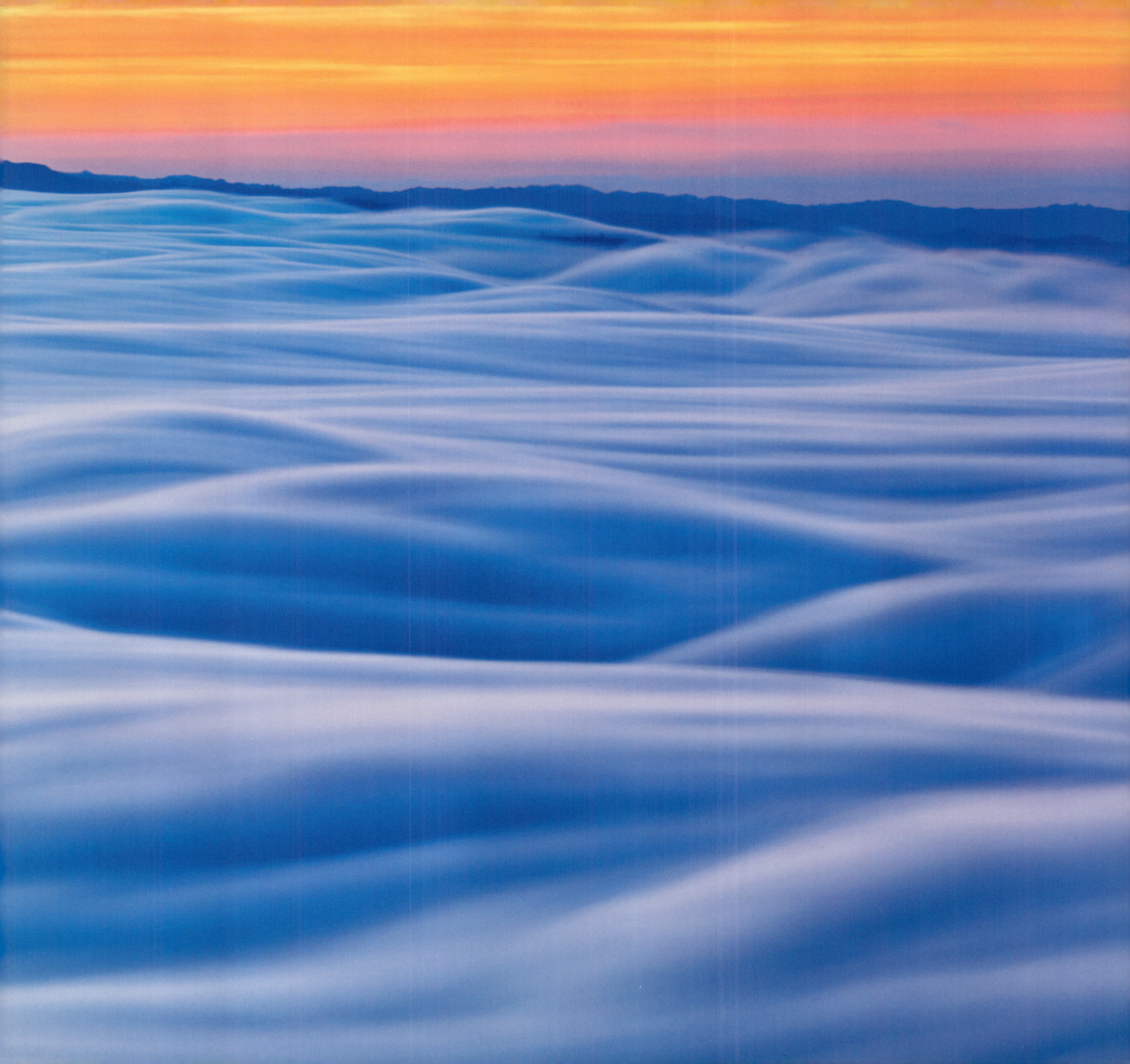

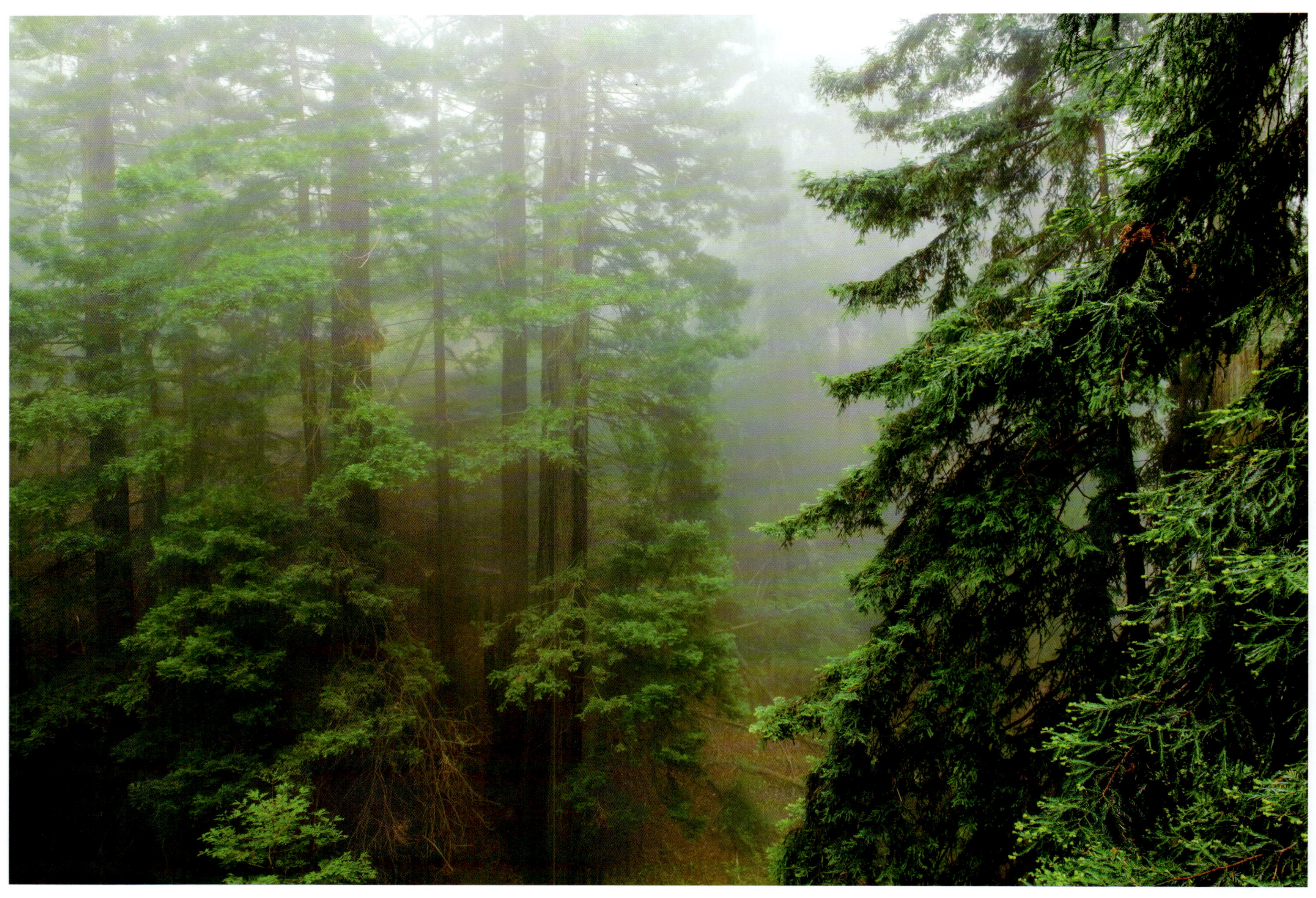

Fog provides redwoods with as much as 40 percent of their annual water.
Moisture combed from the fog by their needles drips down to the roots. Redwoods
live in a narrow strip along the coast and are only found where there is fog.

REDWOOD TREES IN FOG, LOS PADRES NATIONAL FOREST

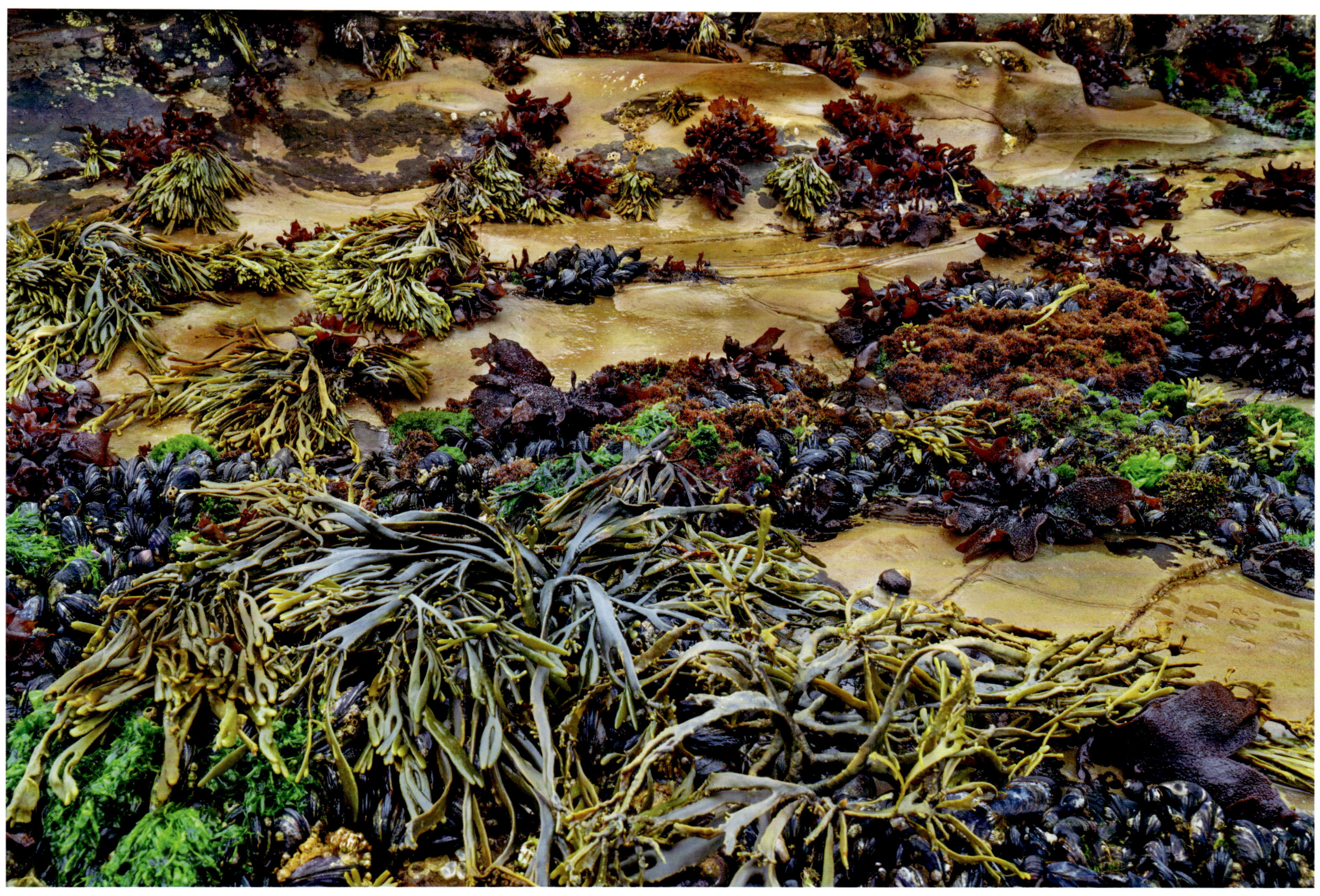

An exquisite array of life is exposed when the tide goes out. Mussels, barnacles, and
kelp and other algae can survive periodic spells in the air, but they belong underwater.
Fog is an umbrella that shields them from the drying impacts of the sun.

Intertidal Life, Wilder Ranch State Park

following pages: The extraordinary shape of a humpback whale tail that propels
an animal weighing thirty tons is briefly exposed as it dives.

Humpback Whale, Monterey Bay National Marine Sanctuary

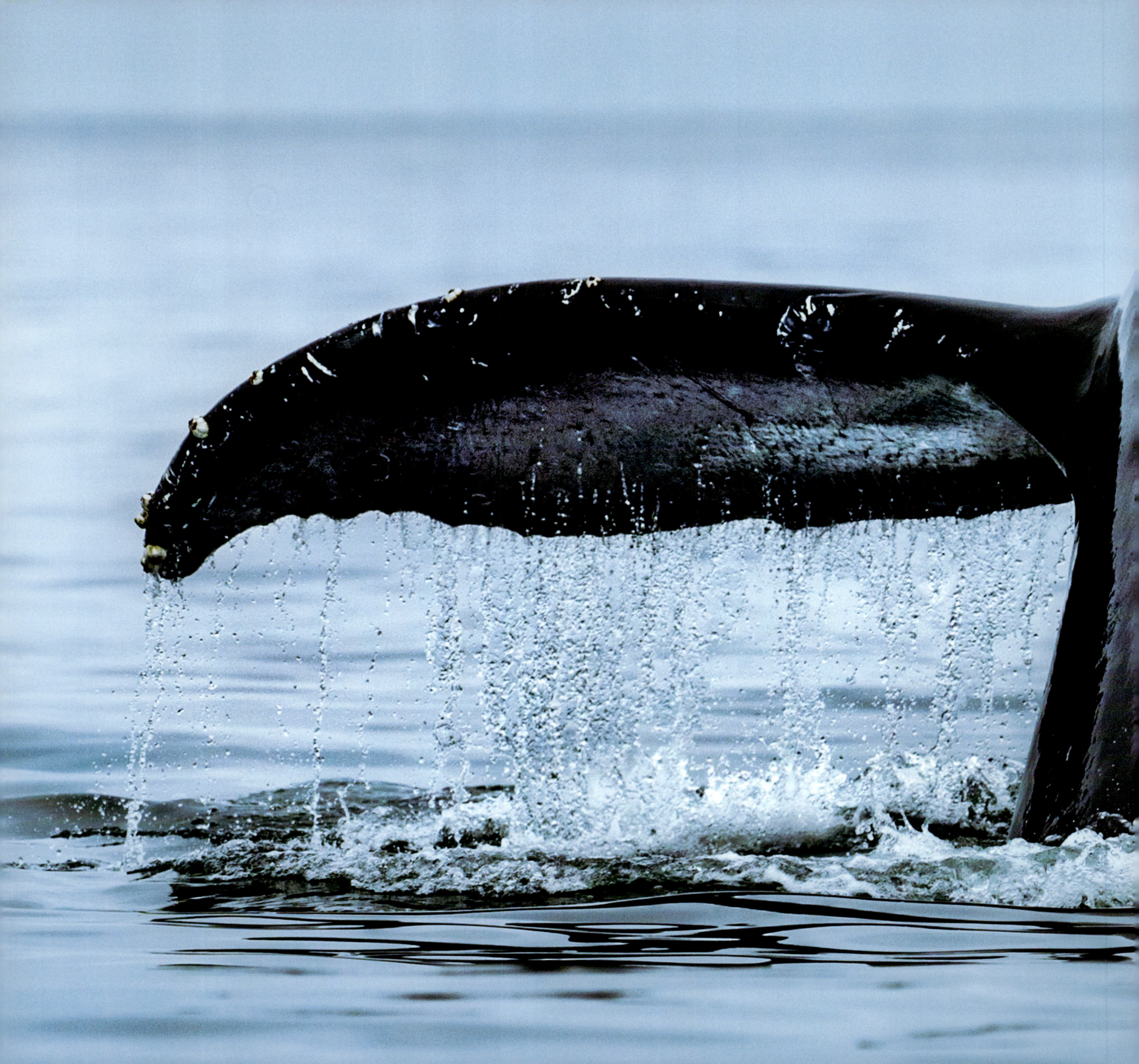

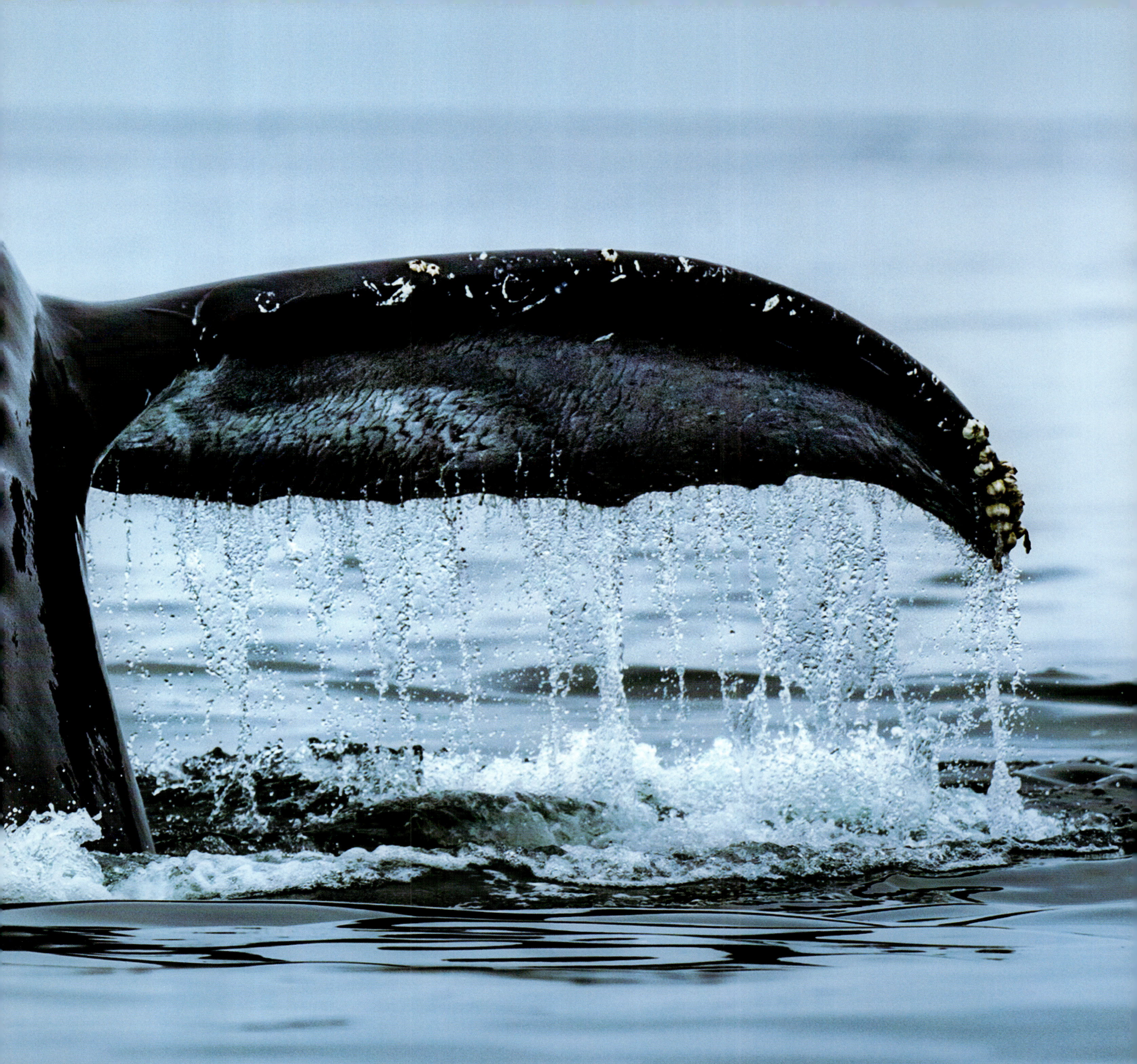

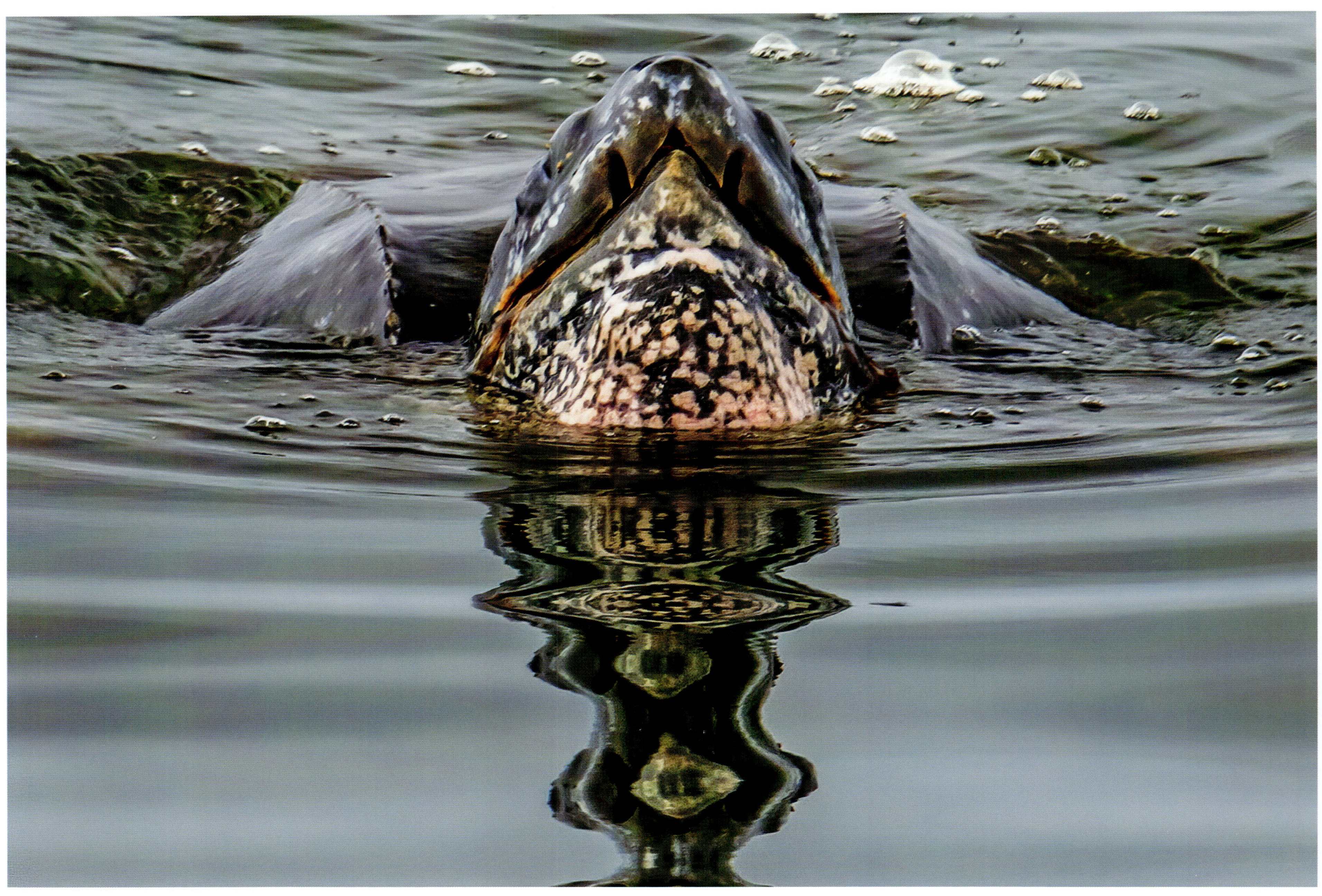

Why would a giant leatherback sea turtle swim 9,000 miles from Indonesia to Monterey Bay?
Because masses of jellyfish thrive here in summer, and jellies are the leatherback's primary food.
The presence of the largest of all sea turtles confirms the significance of the bay to seasonal migrants
from beyond the horizon. But leatherback populations are declining due to entanglements with
fishing gear and the pervasive presence of plastics—which the turtles mistake for jellies and ingest.

Leatherback Sea Turtle, Monterey Bay National Marine Sanctuary | *Photo by Douglas Croft*

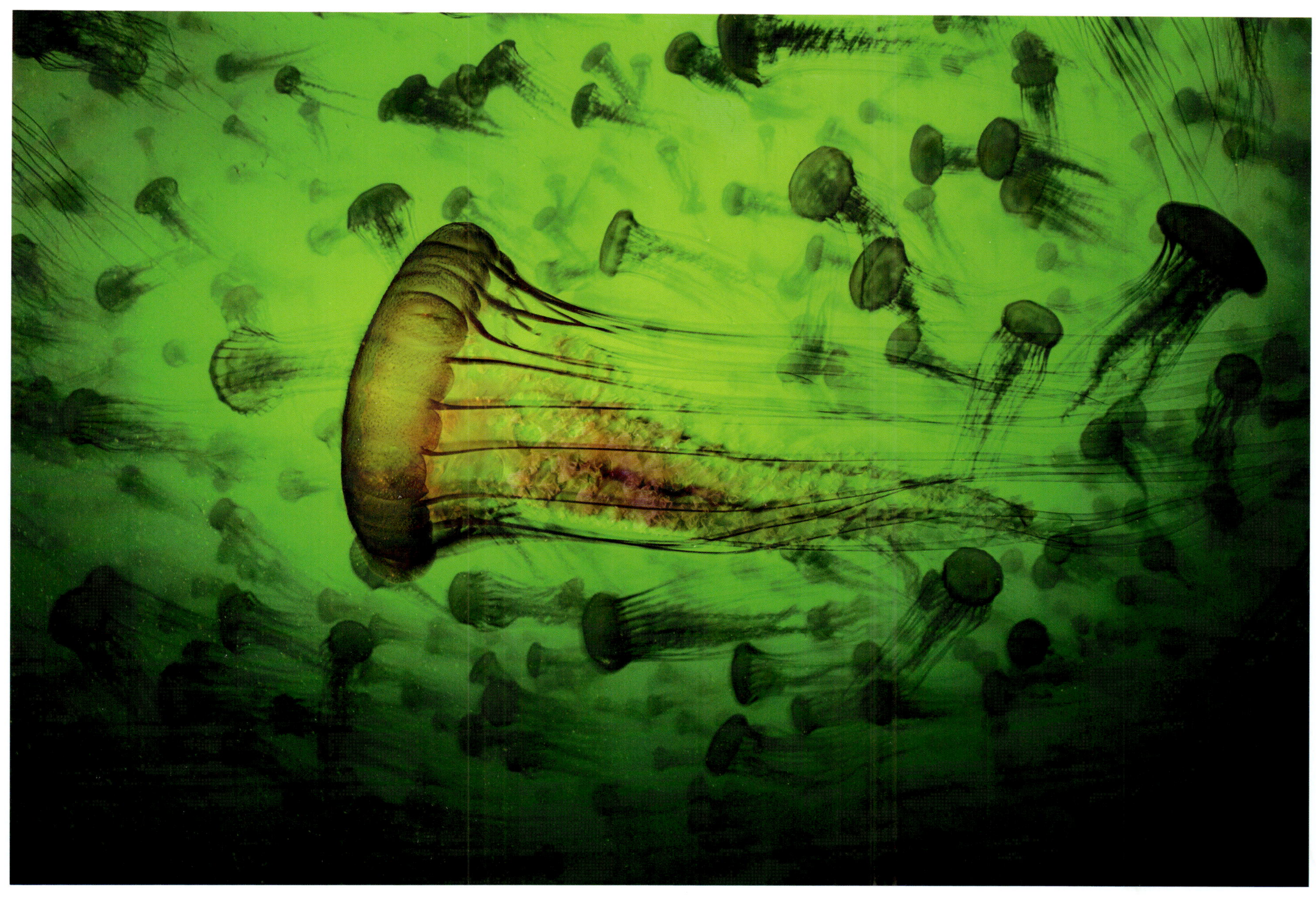

A swirl of sea nettles off San Carlos Beach showcases the fecundity of midsummer life in the bay.
These jellies feed on zooplankton, tiny drifting animals that are abundant during the upwelling season
from March through August. Stinging cells on their trailing tentacles enable the jellies to paralyze prey.

PACIFIC SEA NETTLES, EDWARD F. RICKETTS STATE MARINE CONSERVATION AREA | *Photo by Ralph Pace*

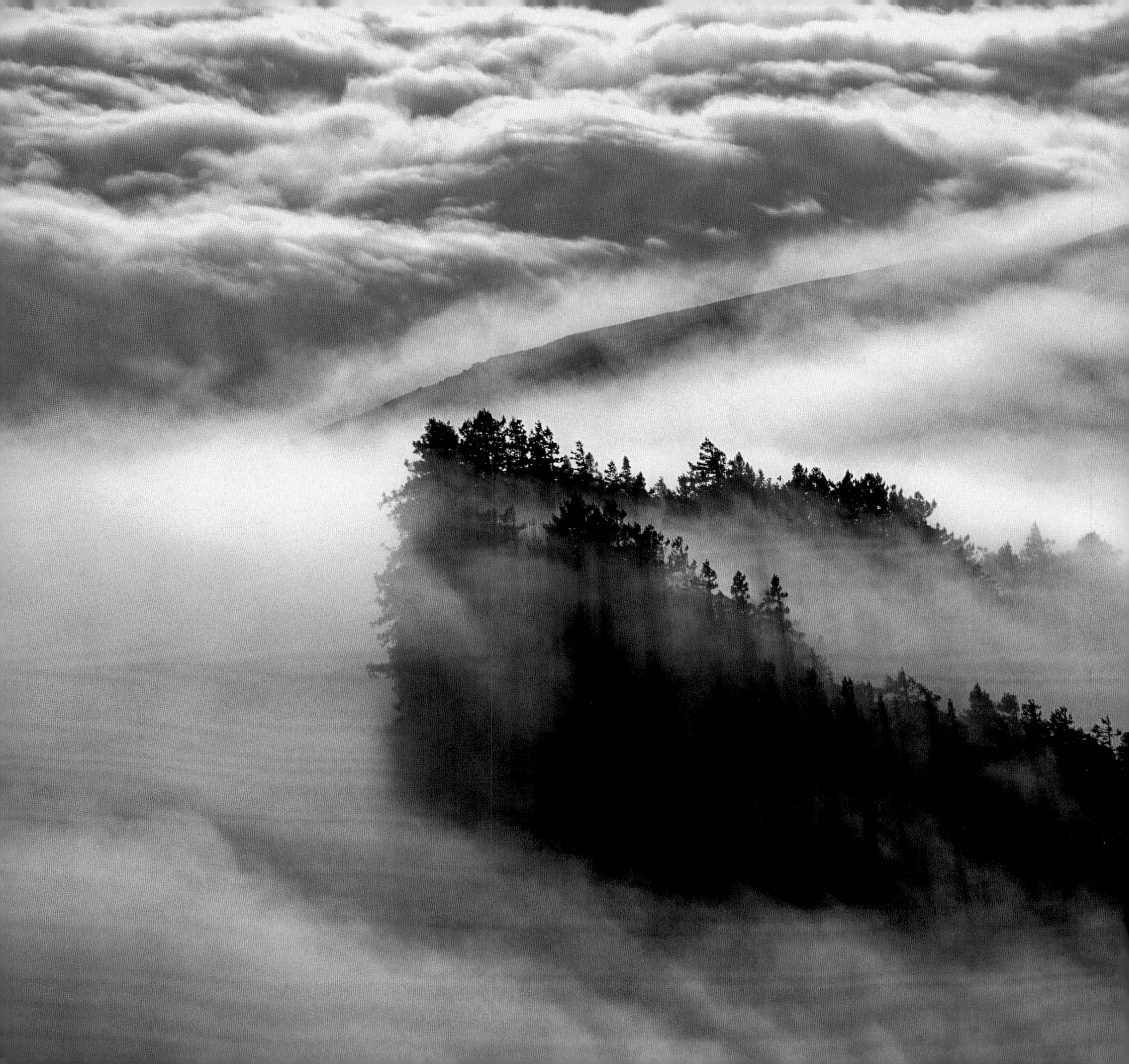

Fog defines where coastal redwoods grow.
Silent, ephemeral, and life-sustaining,
fog renews everything it touches.

REDWOODS IN FOG, BIG SUR

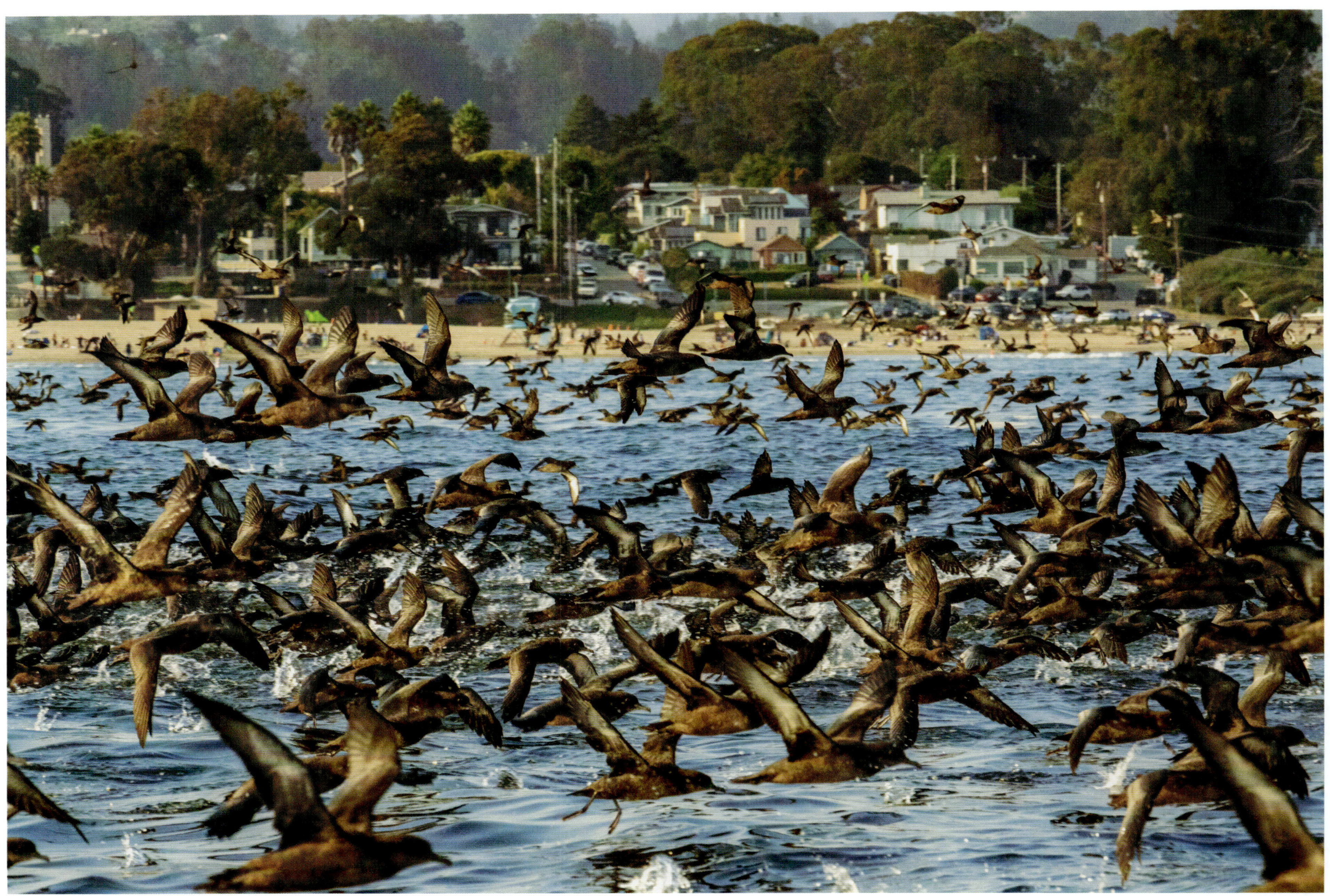

For sooty shearwaters, Monterey Bay is an essential stop on a great migration that takes
them around the Pacific Ocean Basin. From breeding islands near New Zealand, they
fly via Japan to Alaska and California before heading back to the Southern Ocean.
It is a 40,000-mile round trip—the longest known animal migration in the world.

Sooty Shearwaters, Santa Cruz

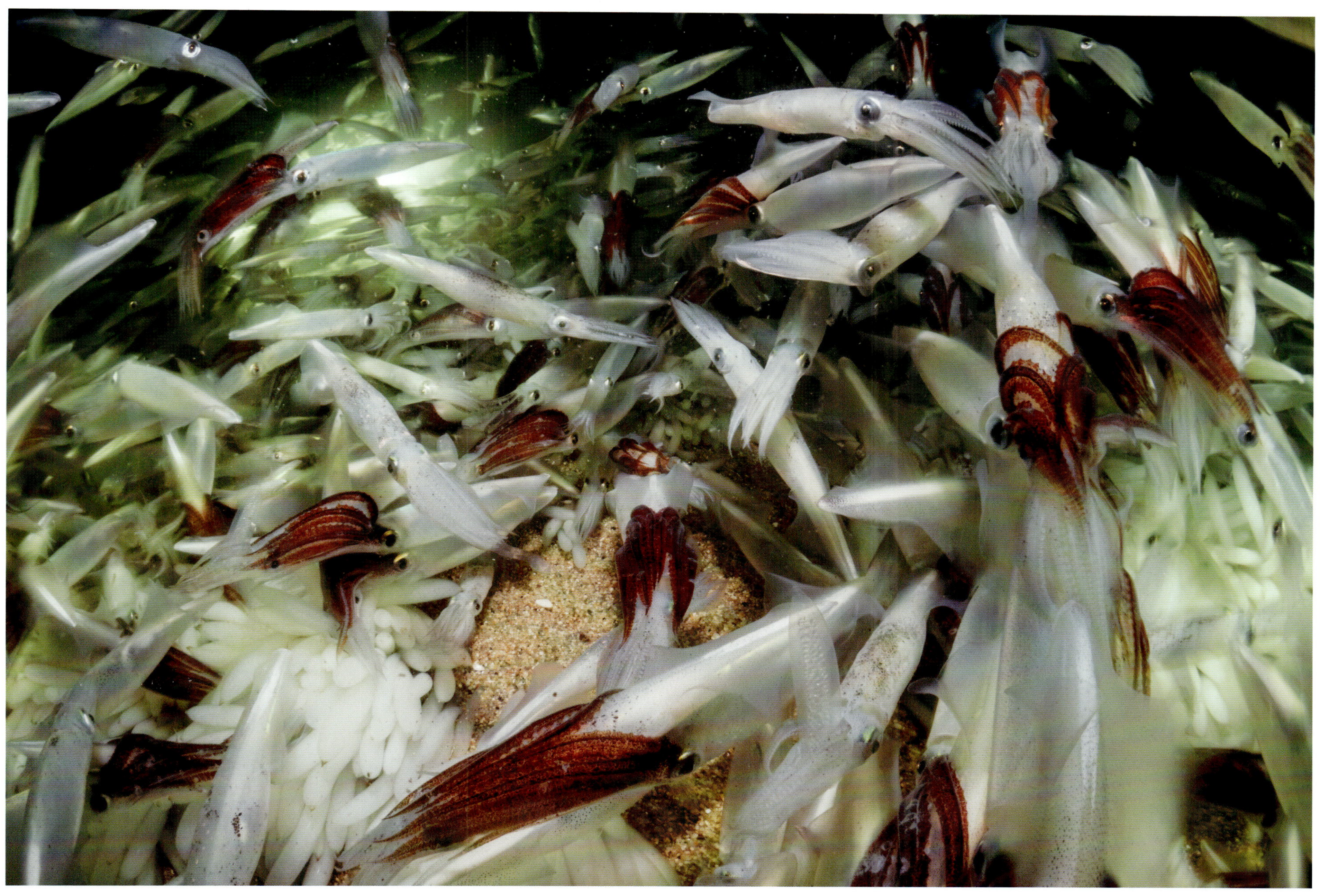

In a breeding frenzy, dense shoals of California market squid mate on the sandy bottom off Monastery Beach. Male arms flush red as females dig into the sand to anchor their egg masses with a sticky substance. Egg cases sway in the surge, which aerates them as the young squid grow. Some egg beds can cover acres of seafloor.

SPAWNING SQUID, POINT LOBOS STATE MARINE RESERVE | *Photo by Patrick Webster*

FALL

Strong winds whipped a fire started by lightning into an
inferno that engulfed Big Basin and burned almost the
entire park and many places beyond.

FIRESTORM, BIG BASIN REDWOODS STATE PARK

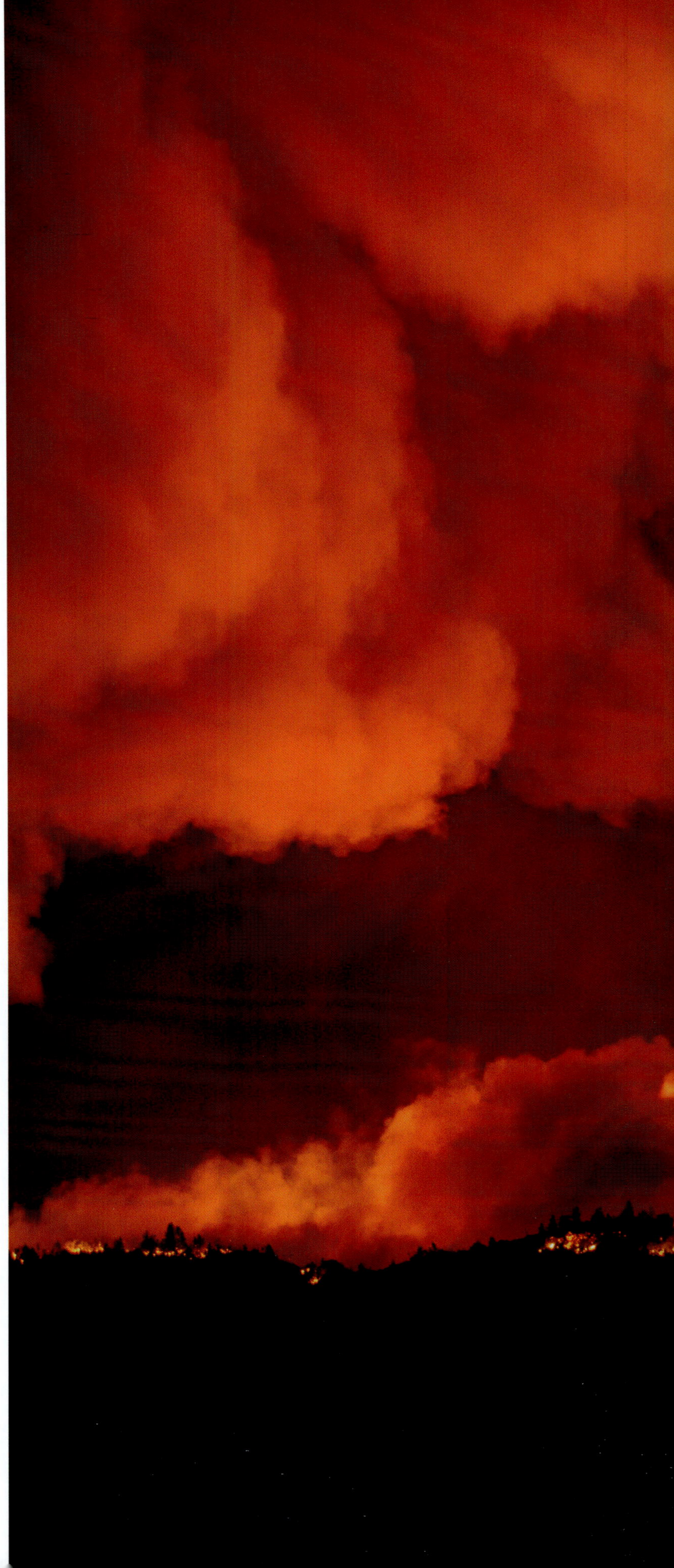

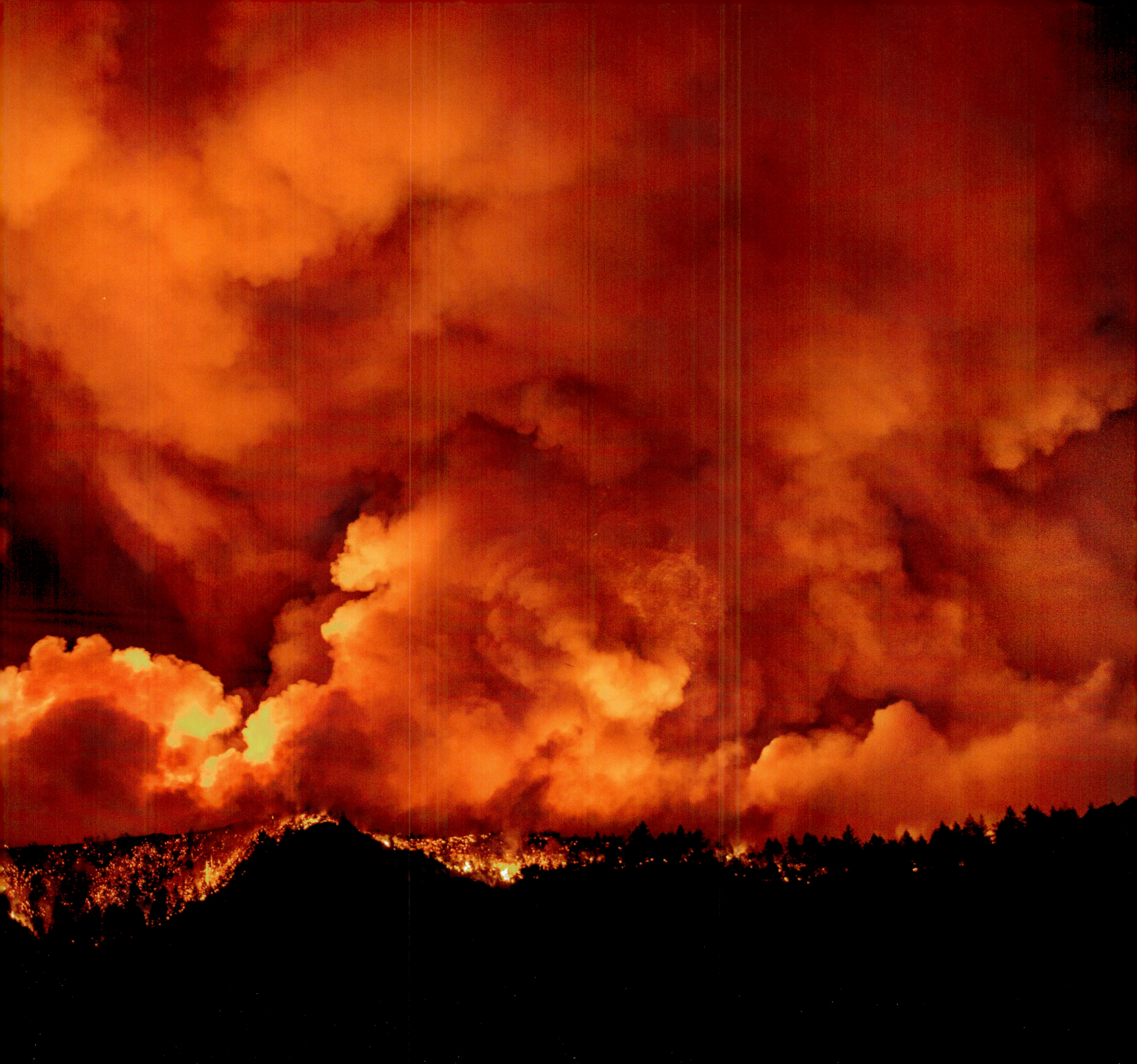

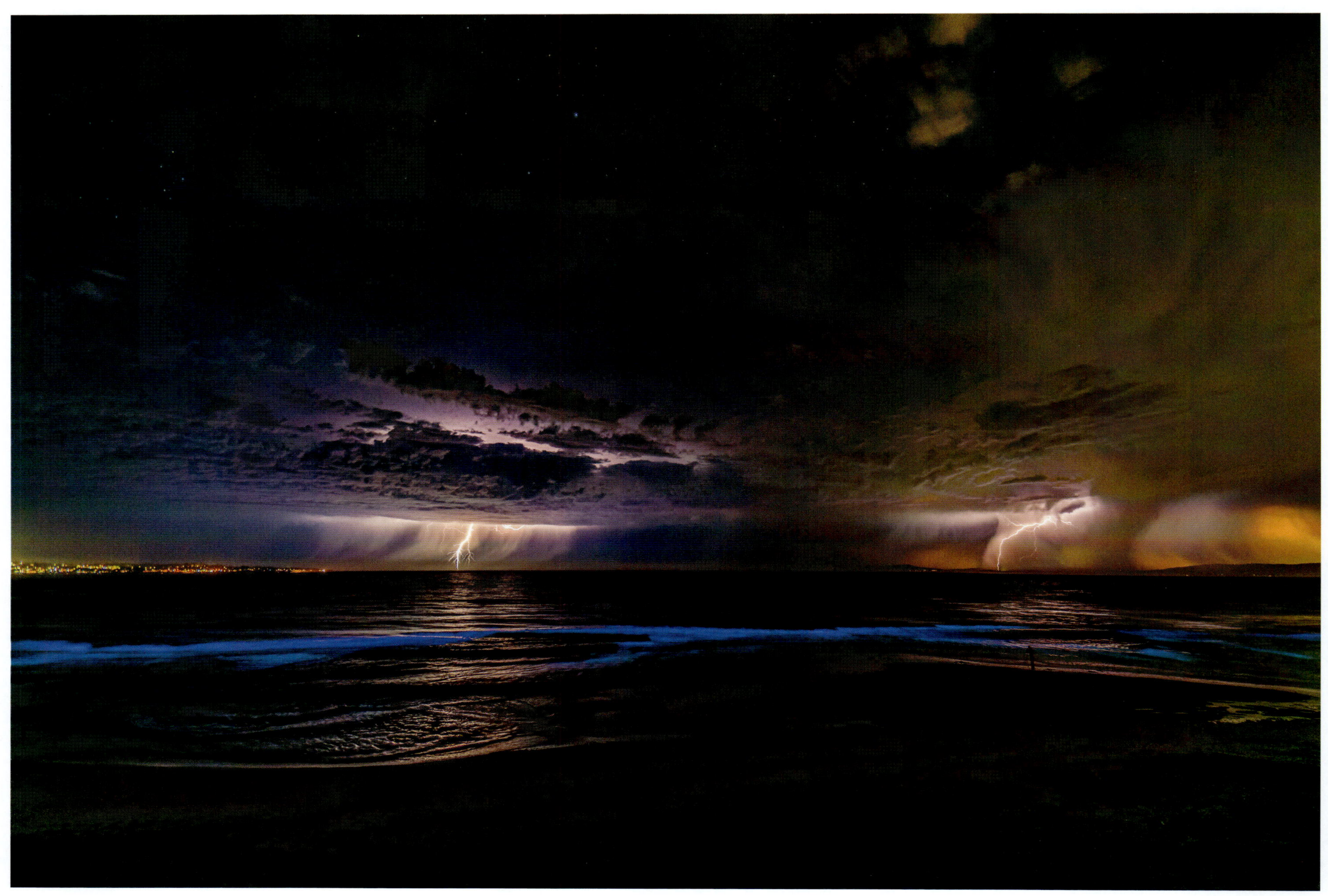

On a sweltering night during a heat wave, a tropical weather system unleashed thousands of lightning strikes that sparked fires across Monterey Bay. This image also captures a turquoise bioluminescent glow in the waves caused by a bloom of light-producing plankton.

LIGHTNING AND BIOLUMINESCENCE, MONTEREY BAY | *Photo by George Krieger*

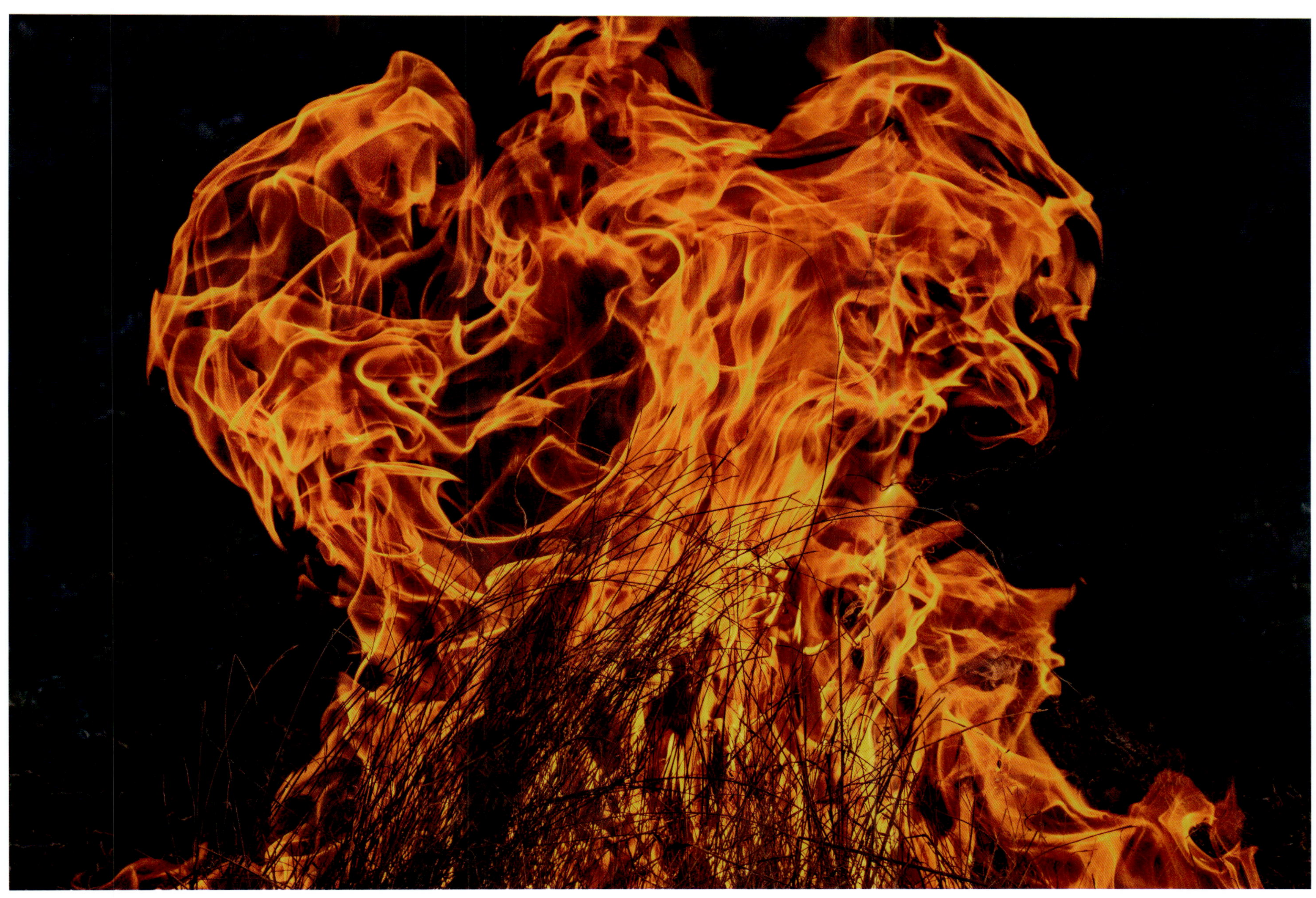

Flames are the visible part of fire. They consist of carbon dioxide, water vapor, oxygen, and nitrogen, which dissipate into the air while elements in the ash, including potassium and phosphorus, are deposited back into the soil.

FIRE, WILDER RANCH STATE PARK

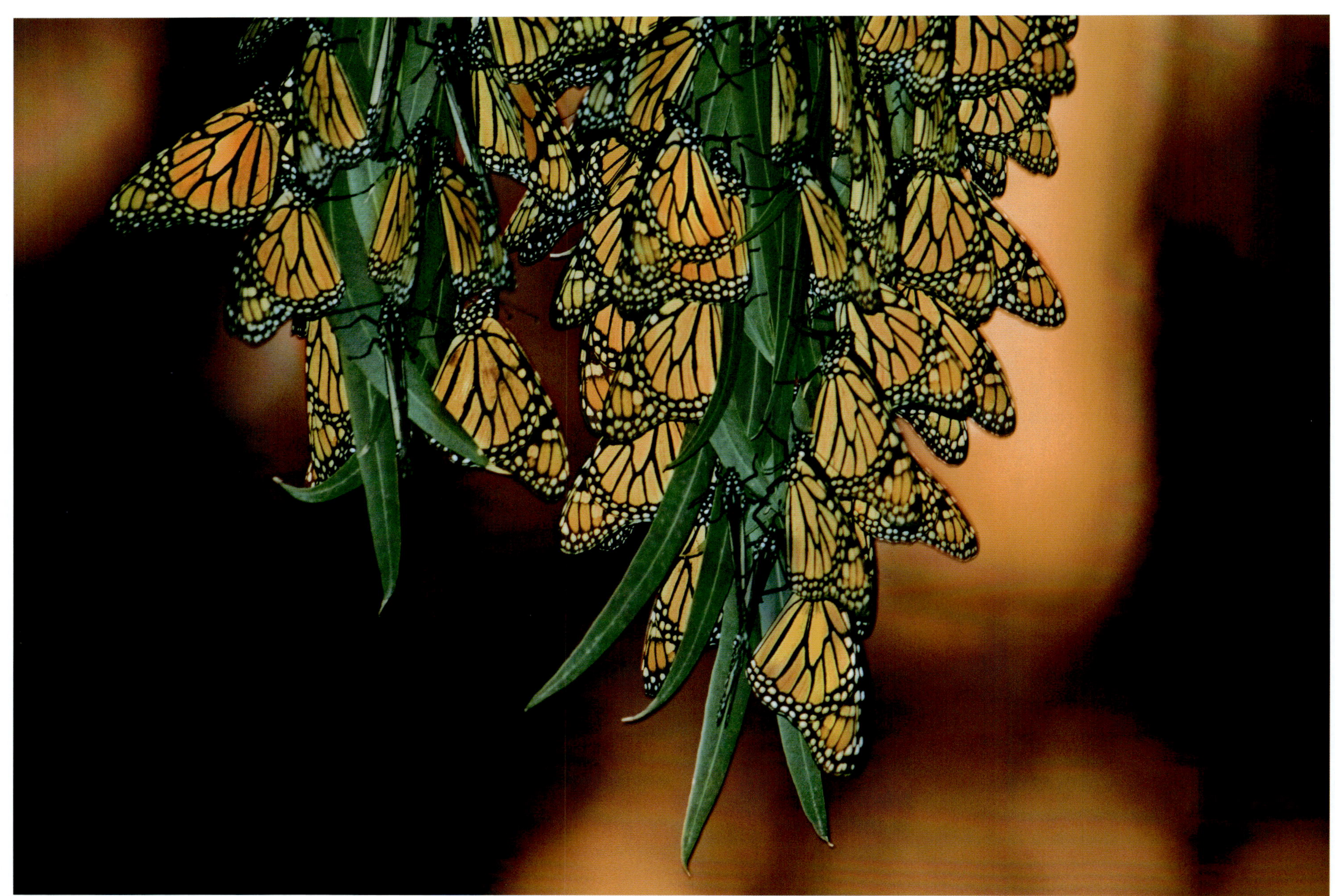

Monarch butterflies flutter in from all over the American West to overwinter in sheltered sites along the California coast. Santa Cruz and Pacific Grove have historically drawn the largest populations. In the 1980s, Natural Bridges State Beach hosted hundreds of thousands, as in the image at right. Since then, the population has plummeted due to habitat loss and pesticide use in places farther inland where monarchs spend their summers. A low point was reached in 2020 when only 550 of the endangered butterflies were counted in Natural Bridges.

Monarch Butterflies, Natural Bridges State Beach

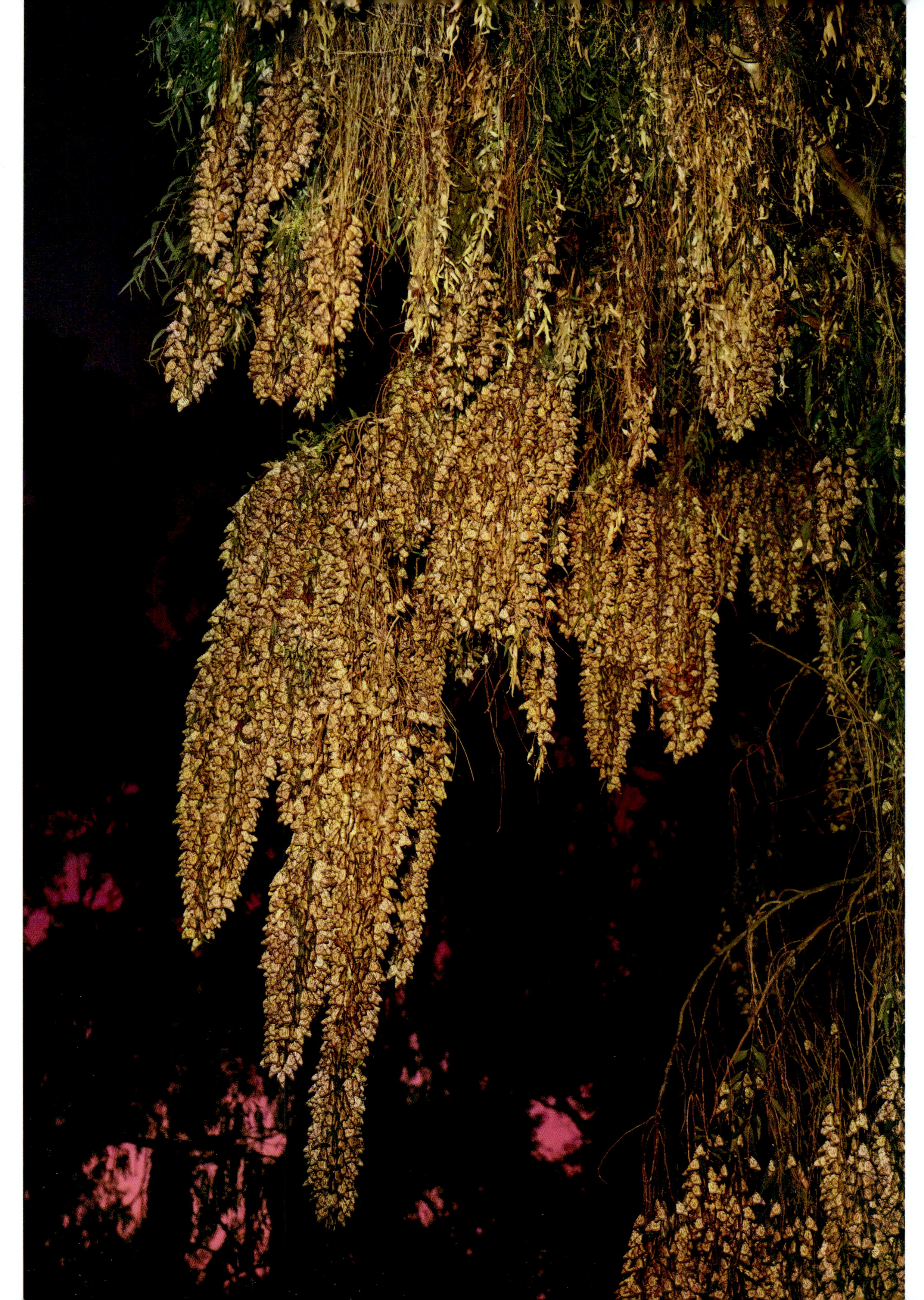

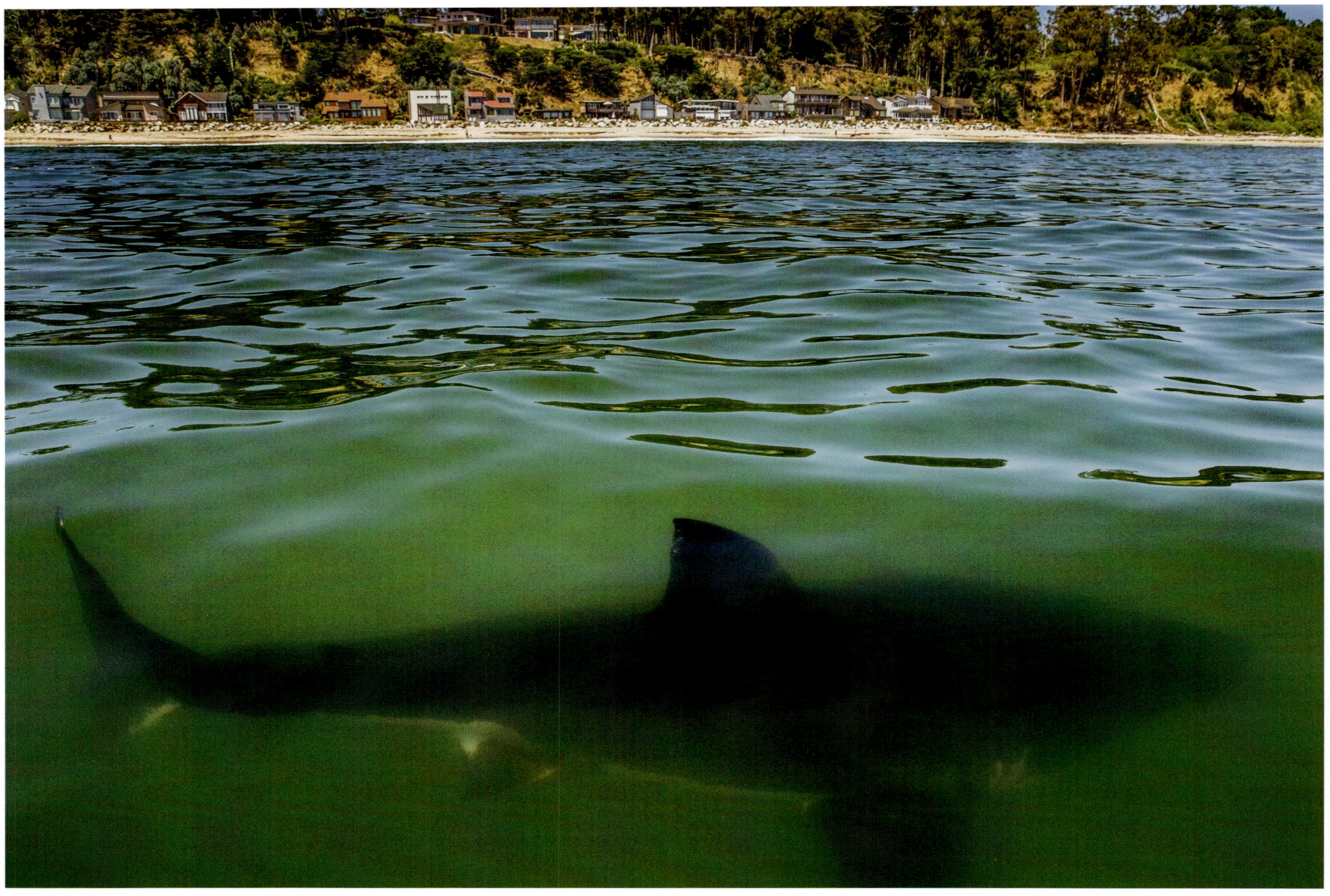

Juvenile great white sharks have been gathering in increasing numbers near Capitola. Warming ocean water has attracted them here from nursery sites in Mexico and southern California. The young sharks stay in warm inshore waters to feed on fish; when they grow more than ten feet long, they head out to colder waters to pursue bigger prey.

GREAT WHITE SHARK, NEW BRIGHTON STATE BEACH | *Photo by Ralph Pace*

OPPOSITE: Blue whales, the largest animals in the world, have a big appetite yet feed almost exclusively on creatures just an inch long. This 90-foot marine mammal can consume nearly 8,000 pounds of krill daily. The whales converge on Monterey Bay in late summer and early fall when krill have matured to adults—the life stage blues prefer.

BLUE WHALE, MONTEREY BAY NATIONAL MARINE SANCTUARY

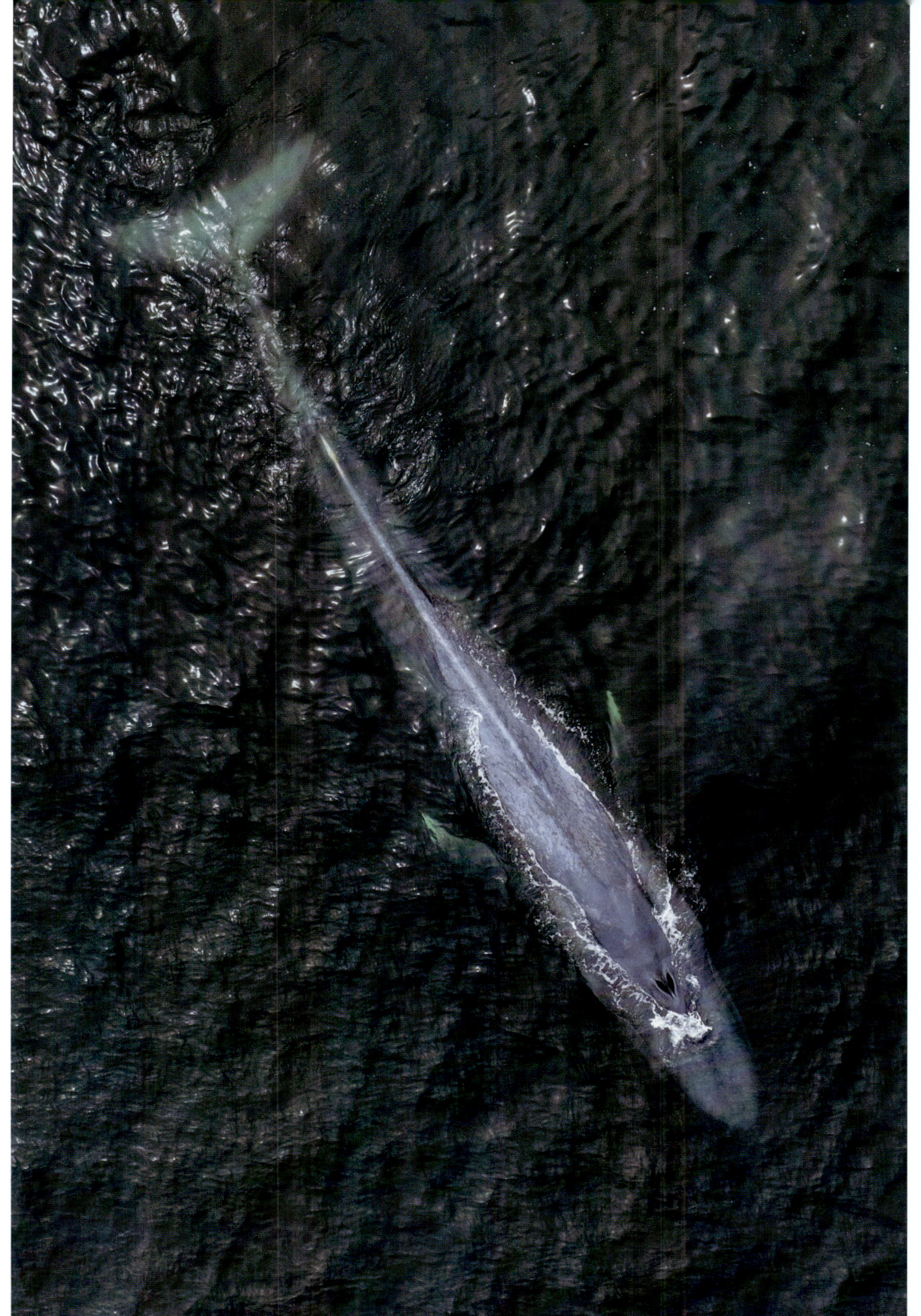

Sanderlings are far-flung shorebirds that pass through Monterey Bay twice a year
as they migrate between nesting grounds in the high Arctic and wintering areas
in Latin America. They feed on tide lines all along the way.

Sanderlings, Año Nuevo State Park

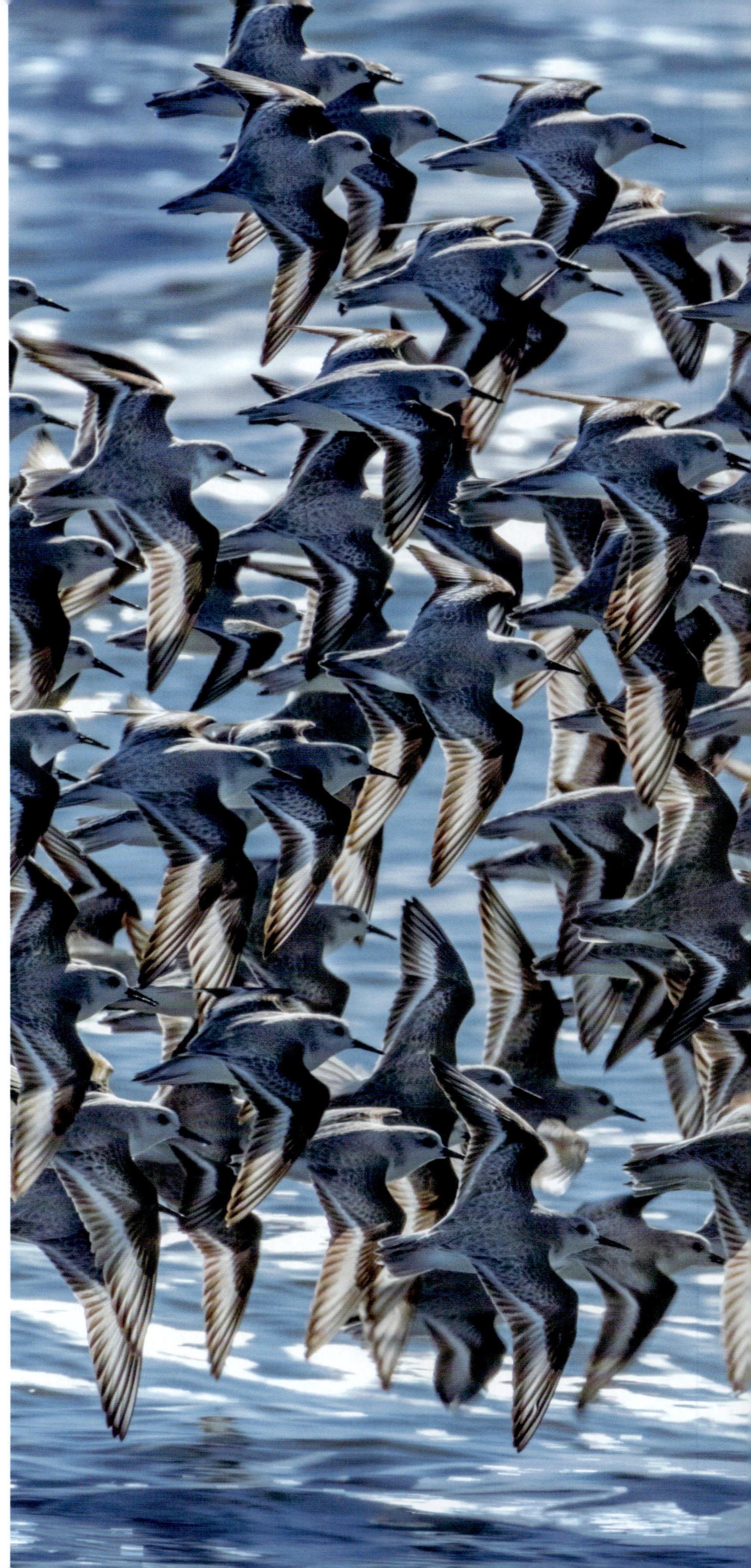

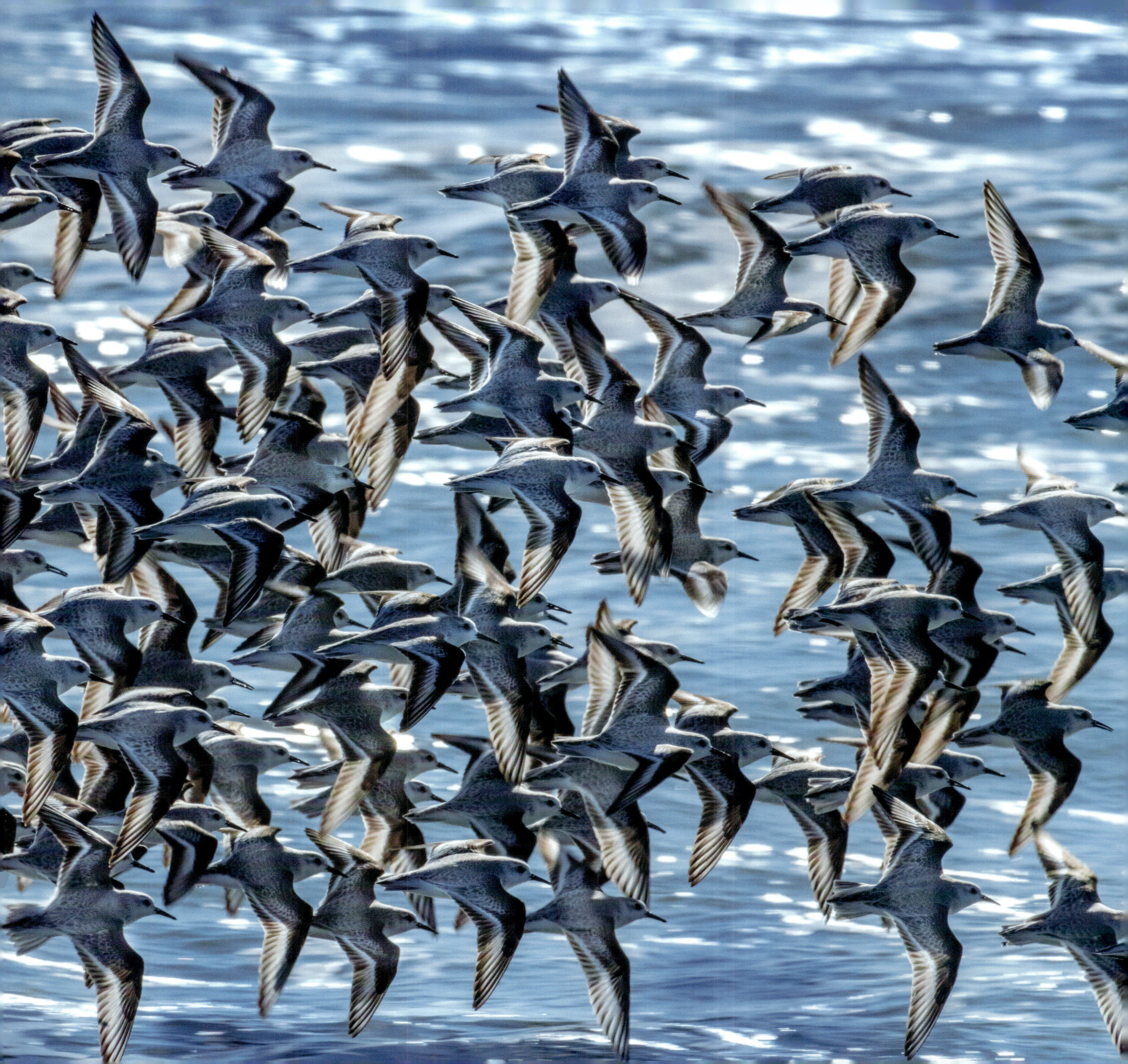

WINTER

Winter storms blowing in from the Pacific Ocean can create swells that
turn into gigantic waves near Half Moon Bay at the Mavericks break,
one of the most famous big waves in the world for daring surfers.

BREAKING WAVE, PILLAR POINT STATE MARINE CONSERVATION AREA

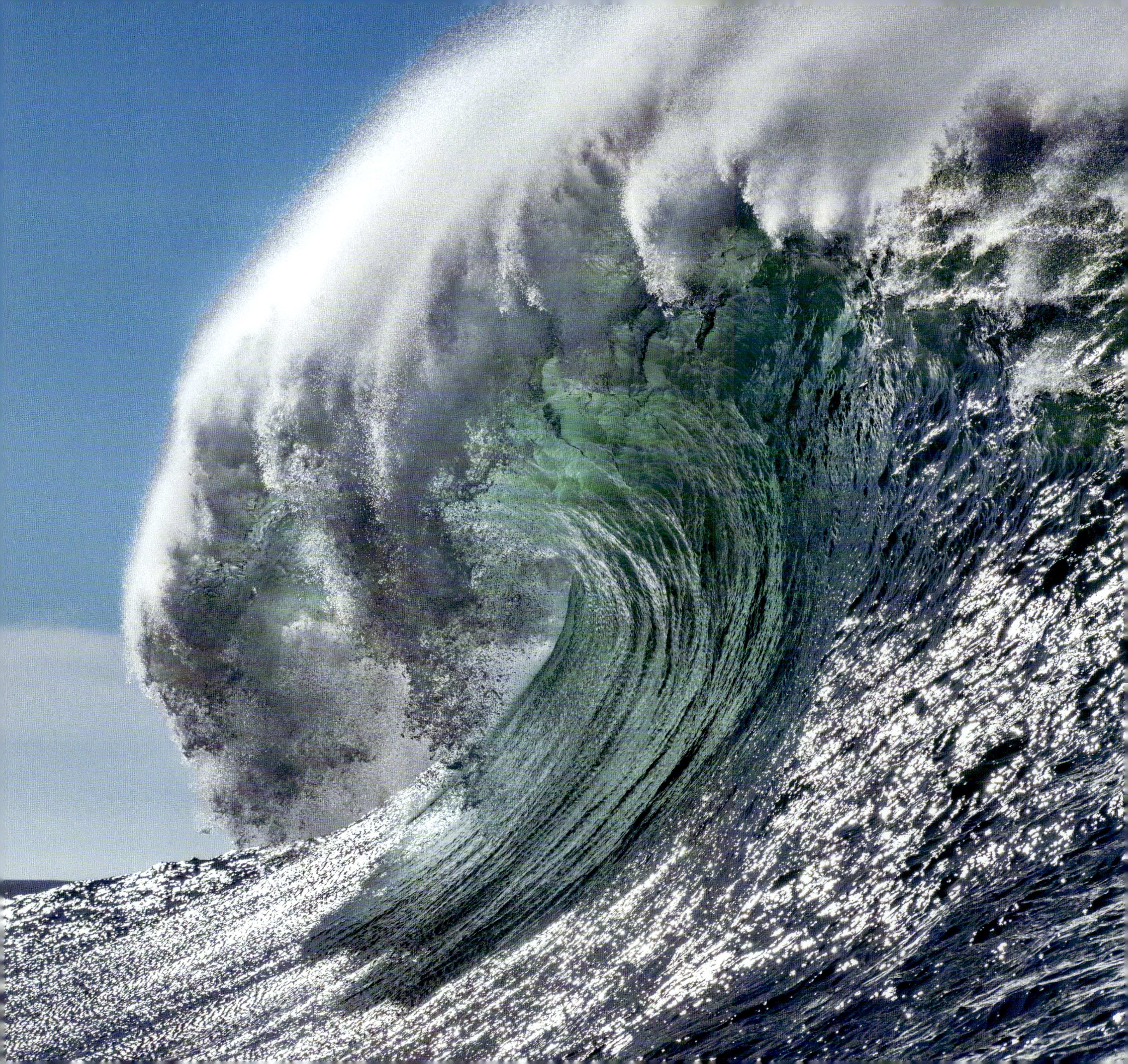

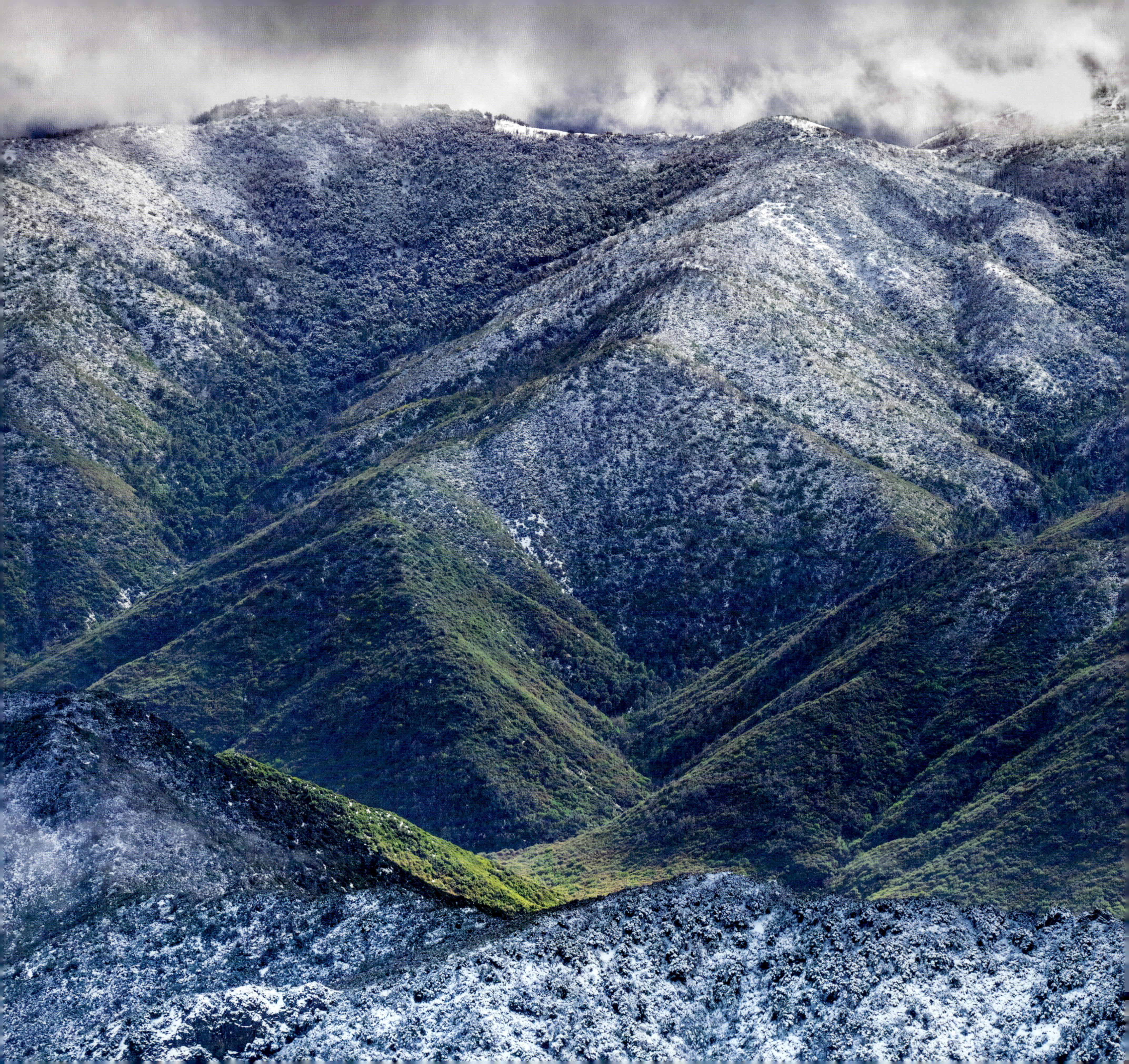

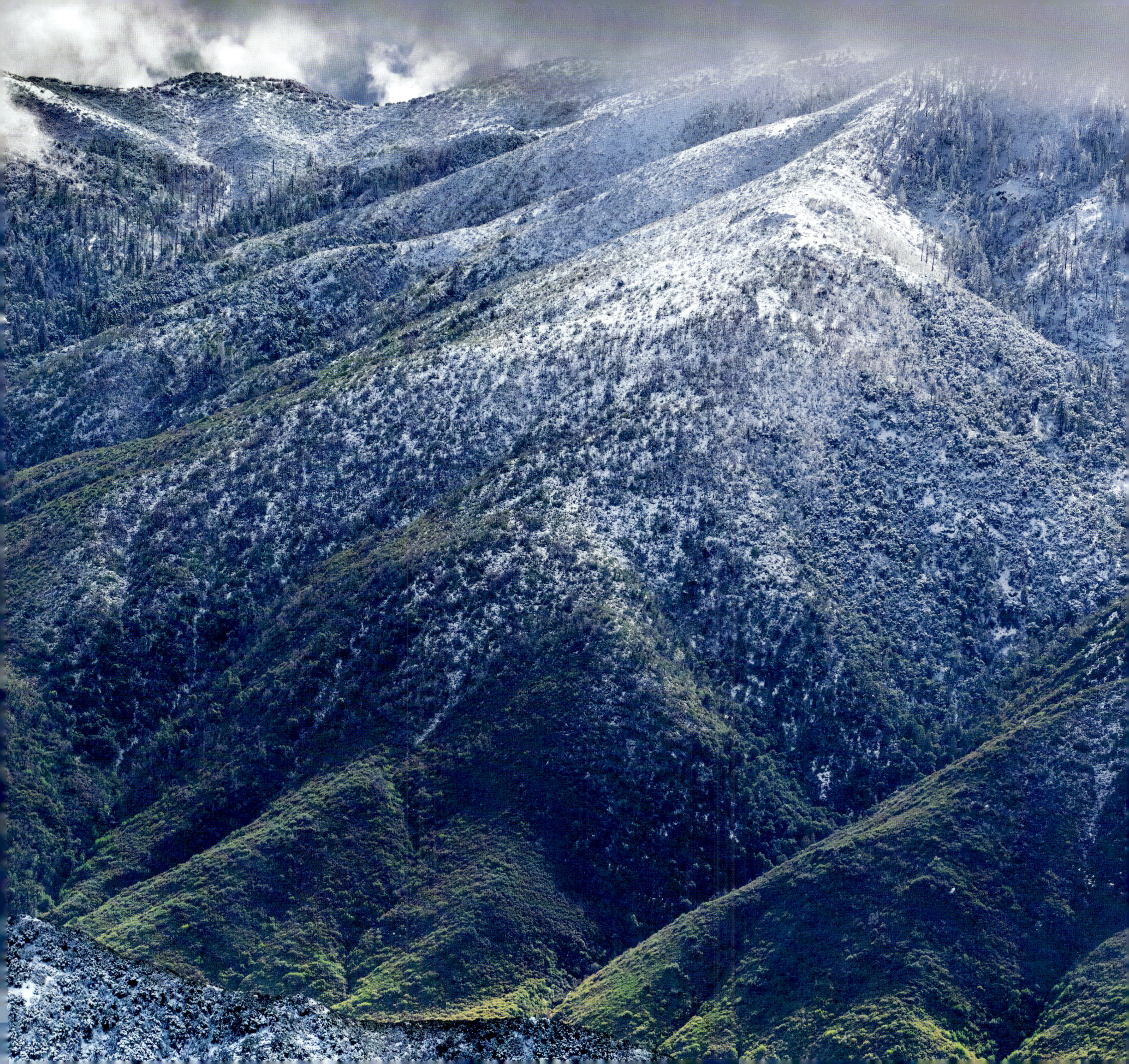

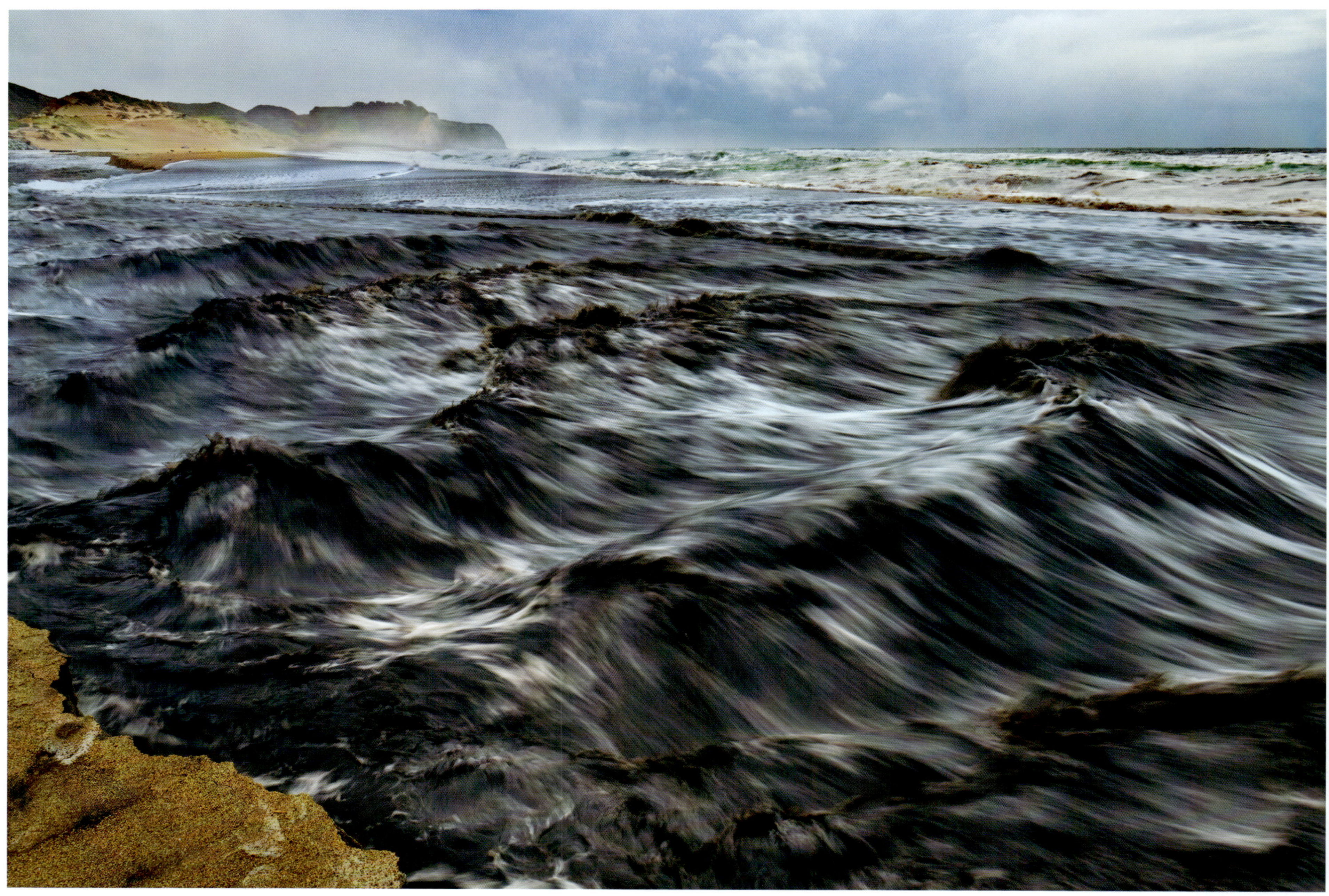

Scott Creek runs black with ash and other fire debris as it flows into the
bay during the first heavy winter storm after the 2020 fire.

Storm Runoff, Scott Creek County Beach

previous pages: Fresh snow blankets mountains in the Ventana Wilderness
of Big Sur—a winter dusting that usually lasts only a few days.

Snow, Santa Lucia Range

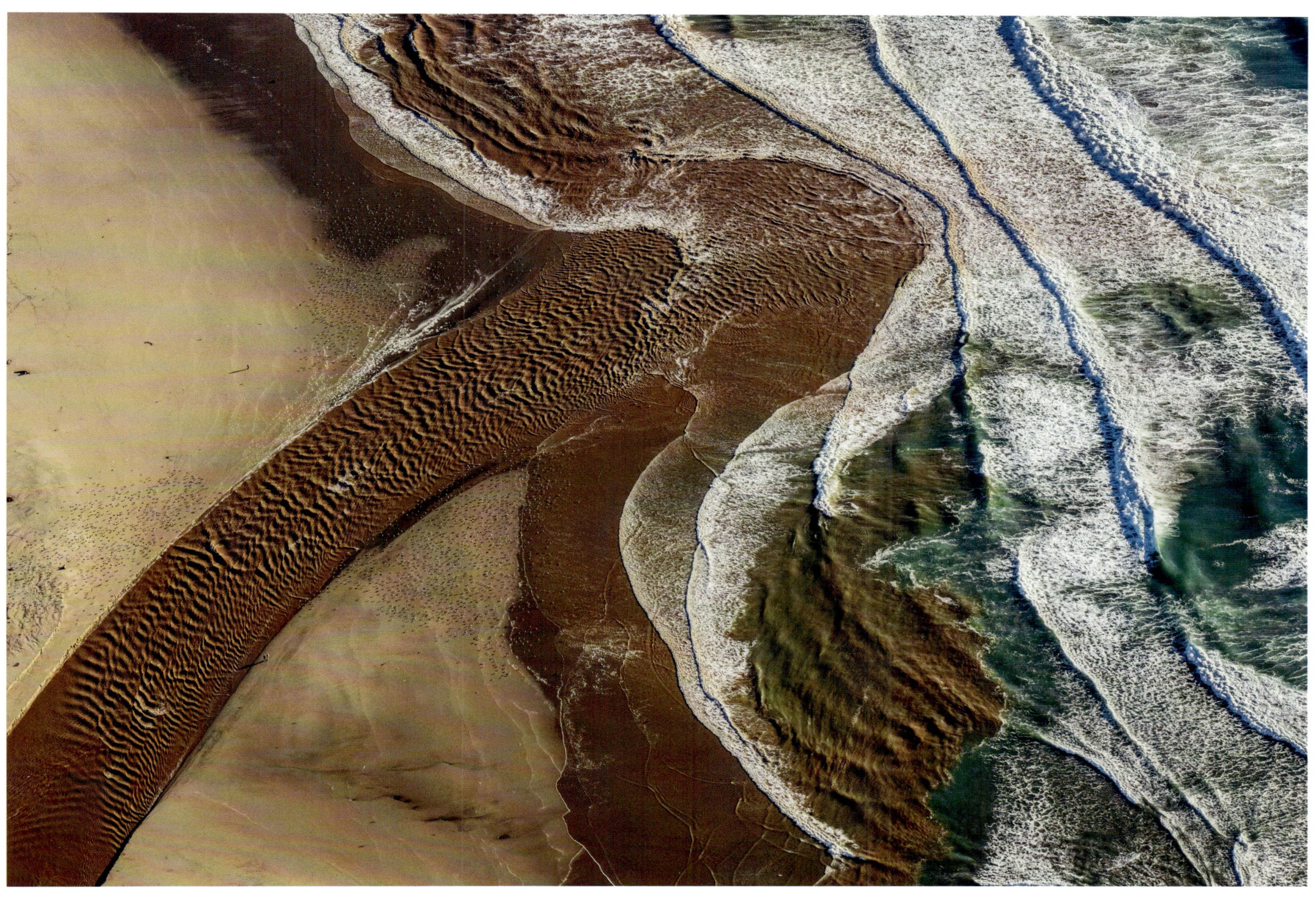

When rains swell coastal creeks and rivers like the Pajaro, they can breach beach barriers to reach the ocean, restoring a vital connection between fresh and salt water that allows steelhead trout to swim upstream to spawn.

Pajaro River Mouth Natural Preserve

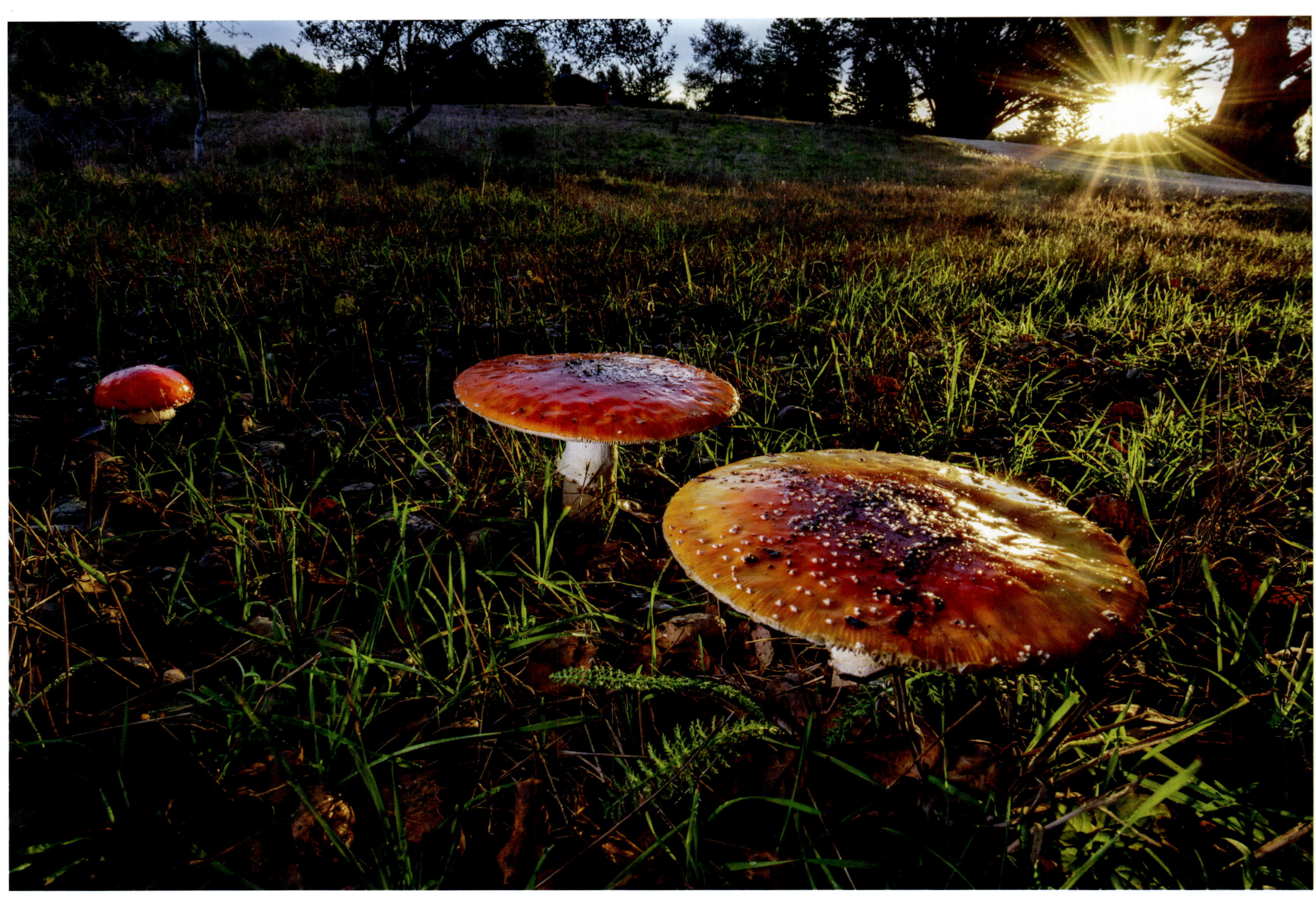

Mushrooms like these fly agarics emerge from the ground soon after the first rains. Thousands of mushroom species thrive in the Monterey Bay region, thanks to its great range of habitats.

MUSHROOMS, RANCHO REFUGIO

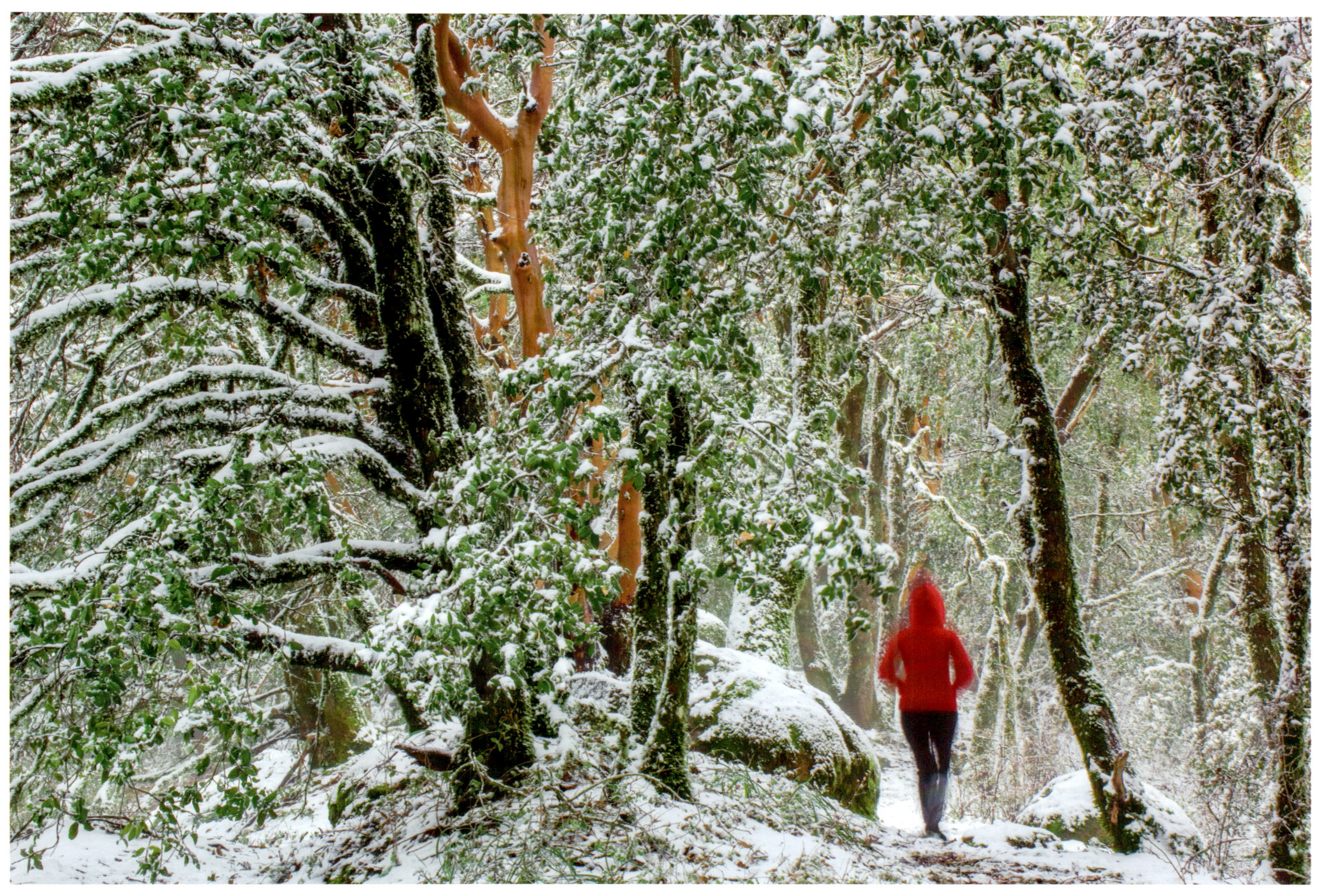

A rare snowfall in the Santa Cruz Mountains coats a grove of sculptural madrones.
Young trees shed their bark, exposing reddish trunks that contrast with the dark older trees.

HIKER, CASTLE ROCK STATE PARK

A waning winter storm leaves clouds on the horizon and
moisture in the air that makes the sky light up at sunset.

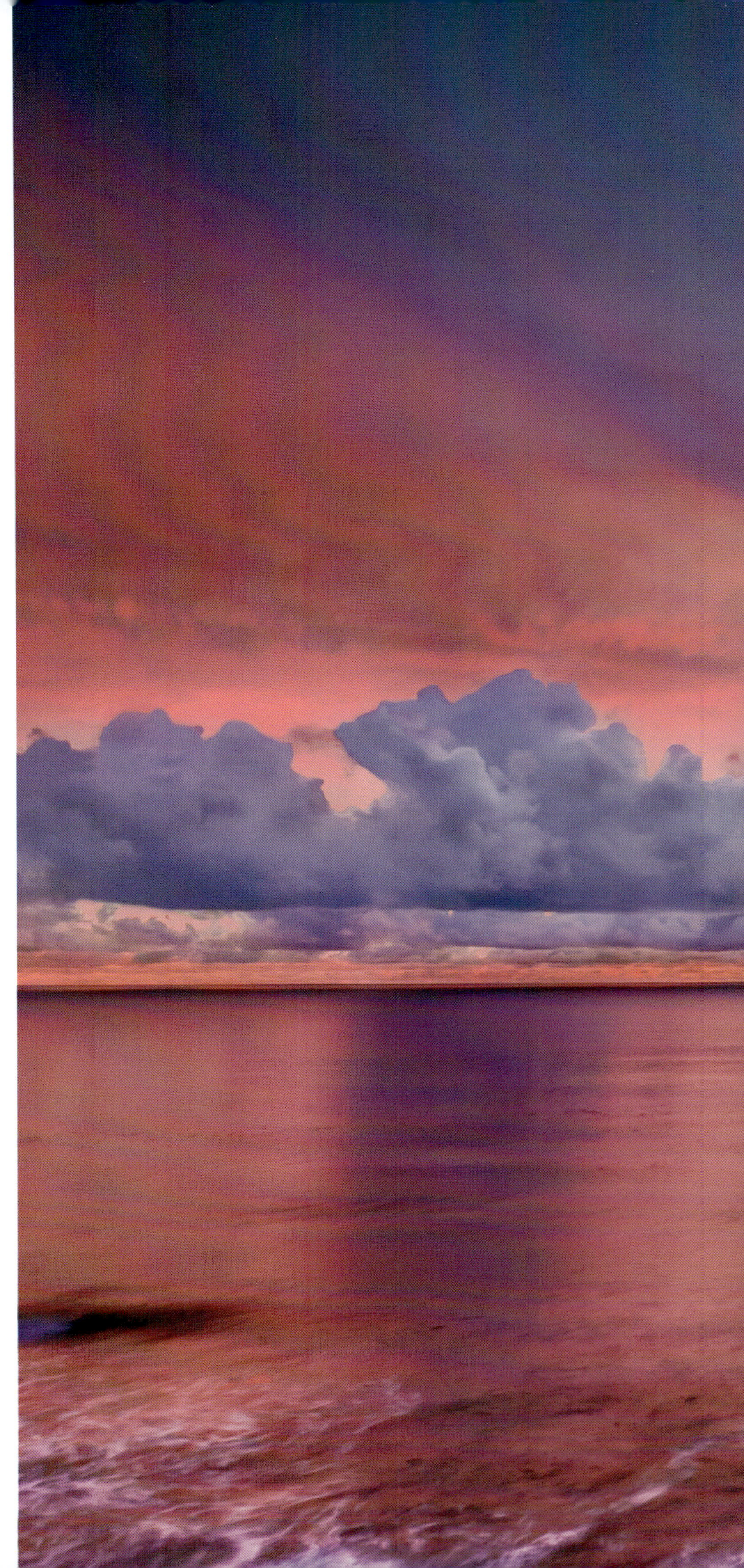

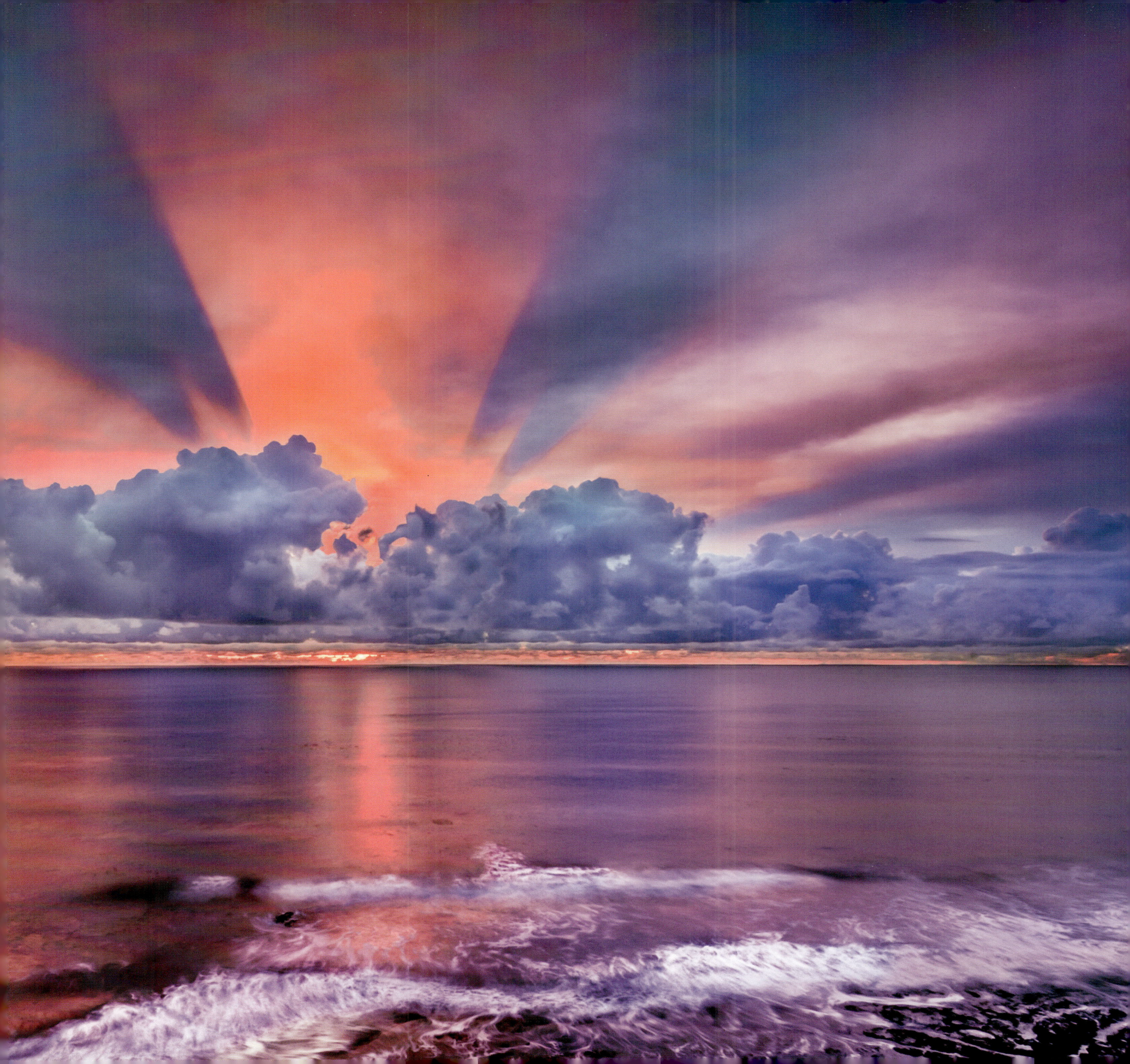

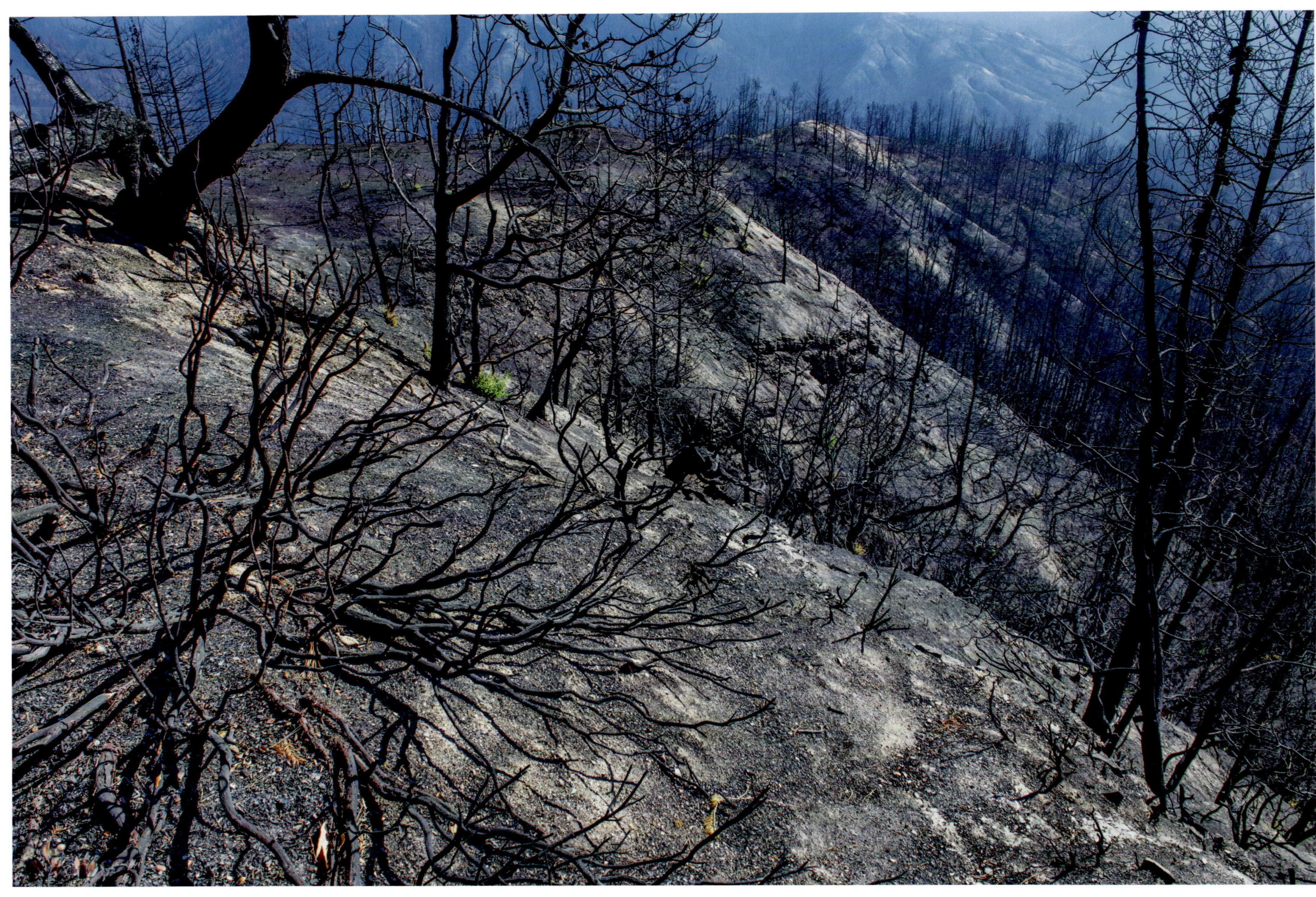

An intense fire fanned by high winds torched steep slopes covered with dense
chaparral and knobcone pines that had not burned in more than a century.
This combustible combination needed only a lightning strike to burst into flames.

After the Fire, Big Basin Redwoods State Park

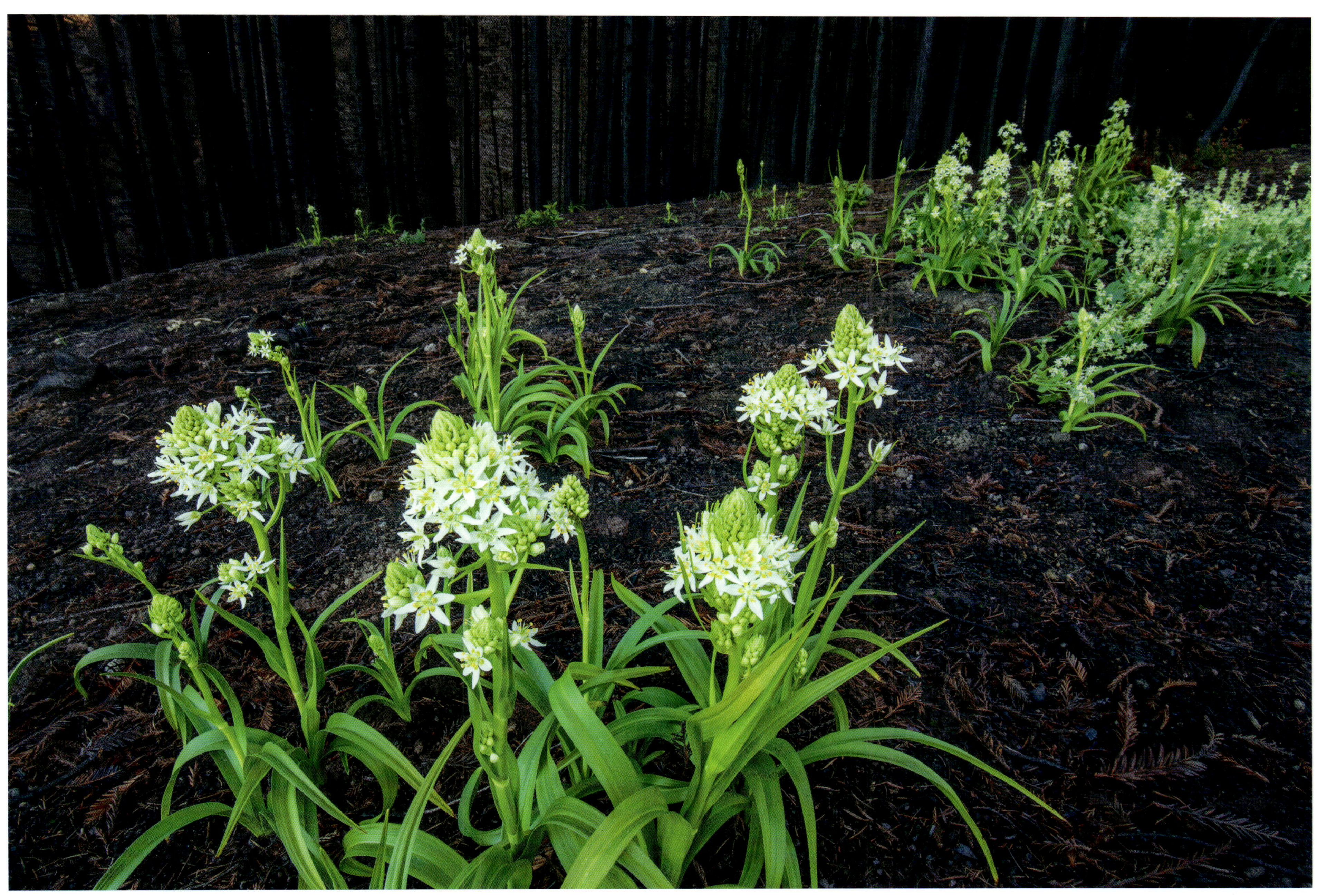

Just months after a fire, Fremont's star lilies emerge with a profusion of cream-colored flowers produced from underground bulbs. Lovely but toxic, these natives don't bloom every year, but they are more prolific after fire. Other plants known as "fire followers" have seeds that can lie dormant for years but germinate when triggered by heat, smoke, or charred soil.

Flowers after Fire, K&S Ranch

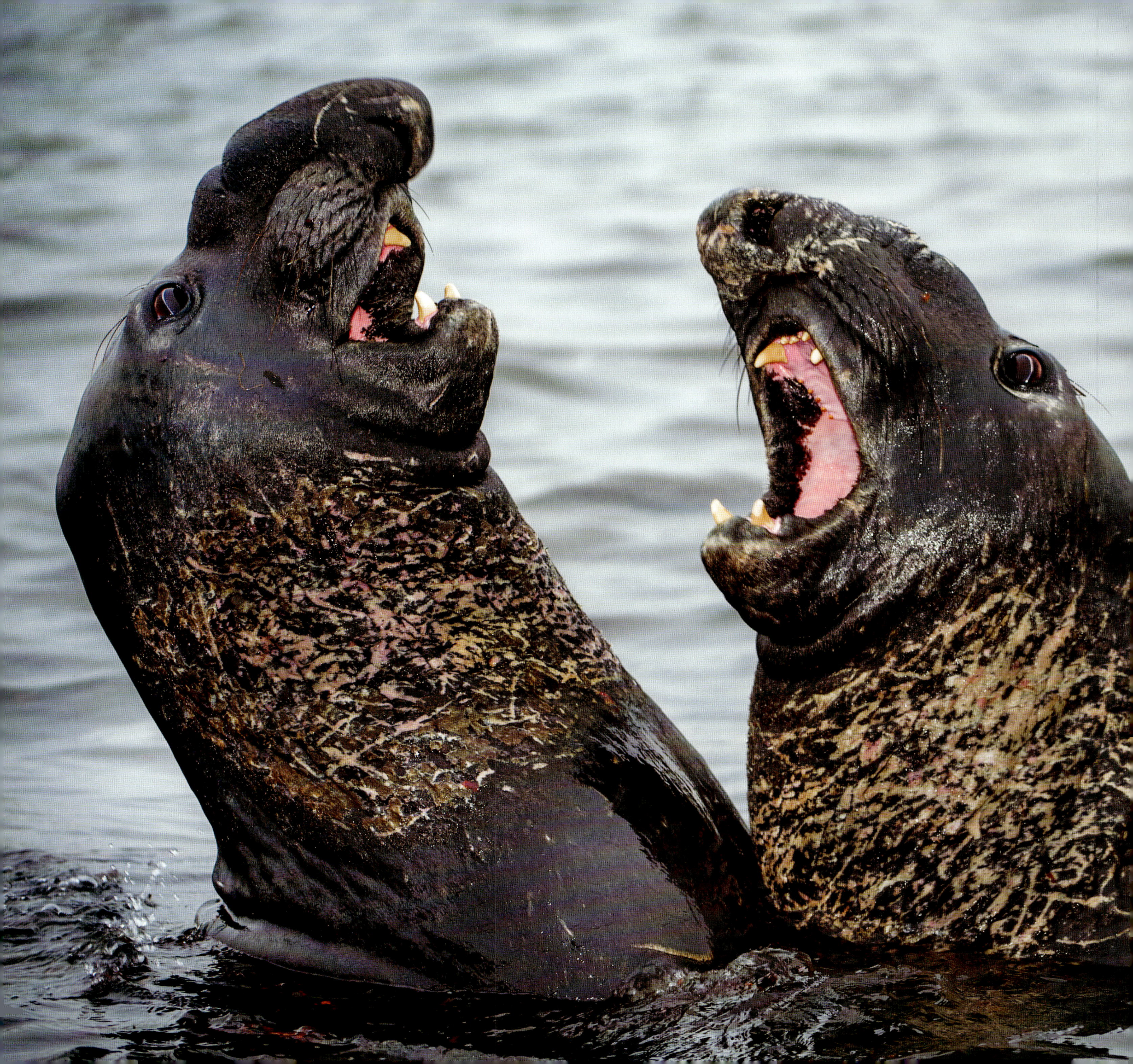

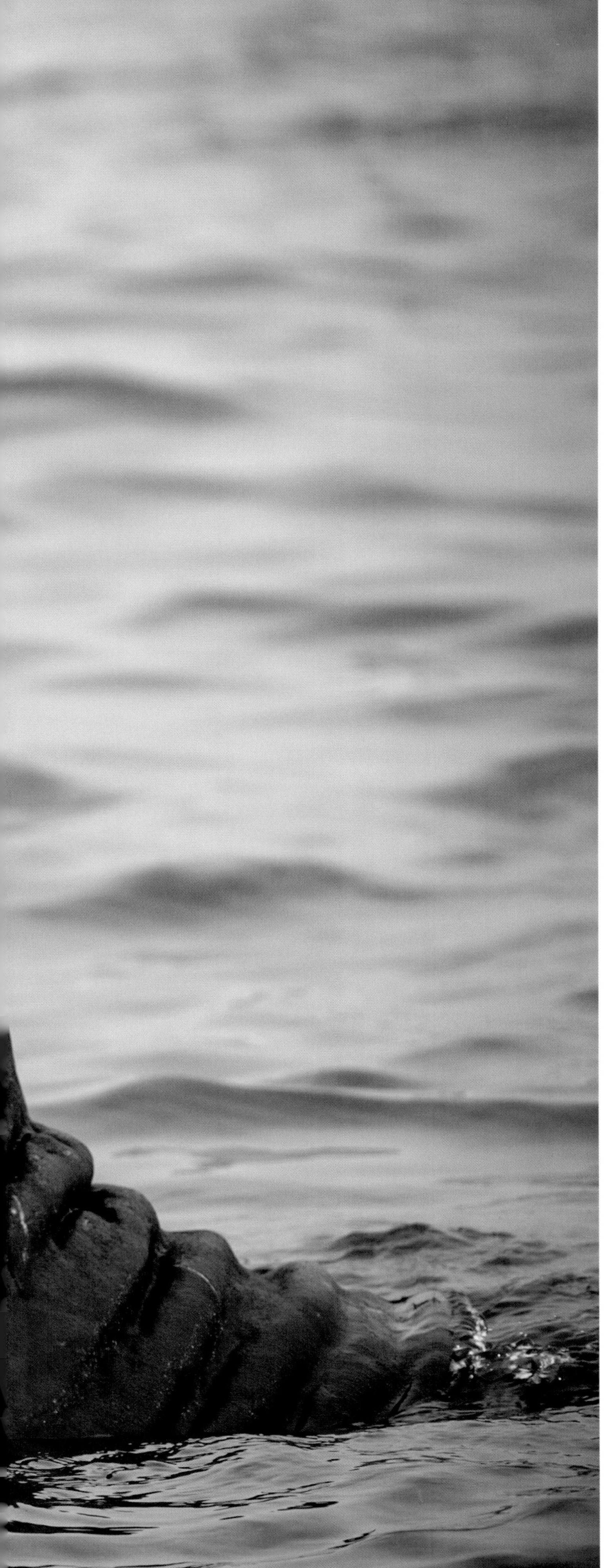

Young male elephant seals practice their fighting skills at the onset of the breeding season in December. Elephant seals are the only mammals known to undertake a double migration each year. Adults come to Año Nuevo in winter to reproduce, then leave to forage in the North Pacific; they return again in spring to molt before leaving once more to feed at sea until the next winter season.

ELEPHANT SEALS SPARRING, AÑO NUEVO ISLAND RESERVE

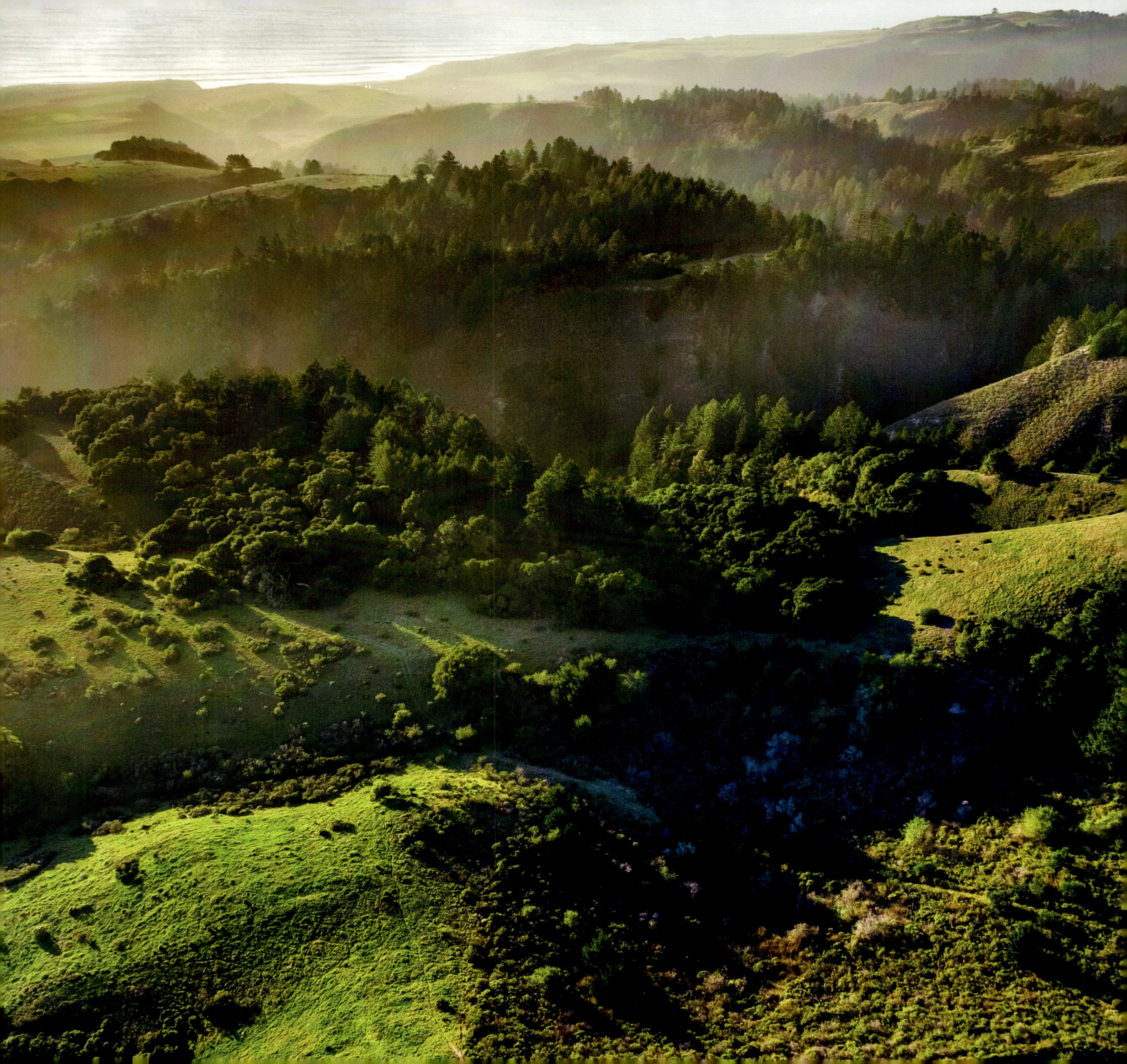

HABITATS

A BAY OF LIFE

As we headed north, there were the thickest, tallest, and straightest trees we had ever seen.

—Fray Francisco Palóu, 1769, Portola Expedition

It would take a lot of time to explore all the habitats of the Monterey Bay, but a simple way to get an overview is to imagine a thrill ride by zip line and submersible from the highest point in the Santa Cruz Mountains to the bottom of the Monterey Bay. What would you see along the way?

At the summit of Loma Prieta, 3,800 feet above sea level, you're surrounded by steep slopes covered with chaparral, an evergreen community of tough shrubs that thrive in central California's Mediterranean climate. Many chaparral plants have seeds that germinate after fire. Shrubs like chamise and manzanita have deep roots as well as burls near the surface that can resprout after fire burns the plants to the ground. Hidden here are creatures just as hardy: rain beetles that survive underground for years and emerge only to mate when it rains, and fire beetles that swarm to burning chaparral to lay eggs on smoldering branches. This is a habitat born and reborn of fire.

As you go downhill, you zip over redwoods with foliage so dense that you can't see the forest floor from above. These are tall trees but their roots are shallow; they extend outward for a hundred feet or more and entwine with the roots of other redwoods, enabling them to withstand wind and grow to dizzying heights. Under the right conditions, they can live seemingly forever, as their scientific name implies: *Sequoia sempervirens*

means "ever-living redwood." Thick bark full of tannins helps them resist insects and fungi—and fire. The needles they shed are high in acids and contribute to a forest floor duff with soils too harsh for many plants, but ideal for these majestic conifers.

Farther downslope, redwoods give way to spacious oak woodlands. Coast live oaks have gnarled trunks and arching limbs that bow toward the ground to form sprawling umbrellas of cool shade. Oak woodlands support more species of plants and animals than any other terrestrial ecosystem in California. As you sweep past the tree crowns, a family of acorn woodpeckers flies off in a noisy dazzle, erupting from a "granary tree"—an oak where generations of the birds have stored their acorns. Thousands of acorns can be packed into a single tree, each wedged in a snug hole in the bark drilled by a woodpecker, to be eaten later, when the time is right.

From the air, the oaks look like green islands in a sea of golden grasses. At the northern end of Monterey Bay, grasslands on marine terraces and hilly slopes are recognized as a unique habitat called California coastal prairie: This is the most species-rich grassland in all of North America. After winter rains, coastal prairies grow lush with perennial grasses like wild rye and purple needlegrass. Native wildflowers add color—from lavender blooms of Douglas iris to pink *Clarkia* and carpets of golden

Marine terraces north of Santa Cruz support habitats from coastal prairie to chaparral and oak woodland, with redwood groves in the canyons.

poppies mingled with blue sky lupines. Yet the coastal prairies first described by Spanish explorers were not a pristine habitat. For thousands of years they were actively managed by Native Americans, who burned them regularly to nurture plants they harvested and to attract animals they hunted. Deer and other wildlife are lured to the fresh growth that appears after a fire. Coastal prairies today are a result of cultural practices as much as they are an expression of nature.

Ahead the surface of Elkhorn Slough shimmers. This is one of the most important estuaries along the entire coast of California—and it is the largest tidal salt marsh outside San Francisco Bay. Its sinuous arms meander for seven miles from its headwater creeks to the edge of Monterey Bay. There it forms a saltwater lagoon with tidal currents that enable a rich exchange of nutrients and organisms between the bay and marshes farther inland. Elkhorn Slough is an essential stop on the Pacific Flyway for many thousands of migrating birds. Looking down, you can see flocks of shorebirds feeding on the mudflats and silvery harbor seals lounging on the banks. In the distance you can hear the barking of sea lions gathered near the mouth of the slough. No other place along the California coast features such a unique combination of fresh, brackish, and saltwater habitats with such a diverse array of life, including the largest concentration anywhere of southern sea otters. They swim into the quiet waters of the slough to rest and shelter from predators at sea.

When you zip past Elkhorn Slough, the mouth of the Salinas River comes into view as it flows through cream-colored sand dunes to reach the sea. The Salinas carries water both above and below ground for 175 miles from its headwaters east of San Luis Obispo. Because of its huge subsurface water flow, it is considered the longest underground river in North America. The Salinas provides water for more than a million acres of agricultural fields in the valley, but the river itself is unknown to most people in the Monterey Bay because there are few points of public access along its course. Yet if you do manage to get onto the river in a kayak, you ease past riverbanks lined with willows flush with bird life—and midstream, shy beavers dunk and disappear.

Where the Salinas River meets the sea, it crosses sand dunes treasured by botanists as one of the most intact and diverse dune communities on the entire west coast of North America. It is a habitat where plants from northern and southern California meet and mix with local endemics like the tiny sand *Gilia*, the lavender Monterey spineflower, and the buttercup-blooms of Yadon's wallflower. Below the dunes, secretive snowy plovers huddle on their nests in the sand. These tiny shorebirds are endangered, and their nearly invisible eggs are easily lost to human disturbance.

As you glide past the Salinas dunes, sandy beaches stretch away toward the Monterey Peninsula, whose rocky shores create an intricate intertidal zone and an underwater substrate where kelp forests form one of the bay's richest habitats. But you are following the sand—from the dunes to the beach and down under the waves to the seafloor beyond. As you plunge underwater, holding your zip line handles and your breath, you slide into an imaginary submersible that will let you experience the marine wonders of the bay.

Beyond the breakers, most of the seafloor in the Monterey Bay is covered with sand or mud, with no place for kelp to attach. It is an abrasive domain with an ever-shifting substrate. Yet worms manage to build tubes to shelter inside. Clams burrow down and poke up snorkel-like siphons to feed, and flatfish press into the sandy bottom to lie in wait for prey.

As you move away from shore, you descend into the astonishing chasm that makes this bay unique. The Monterey Canyon is the largest submarine canyon on the continent's Pacific coast. In sheer size, it is an undersea equivalent of the Grand Canyon, with walls more than a mile deep. This mighty canyon begins just offshore from Moss Landing's shallow harbor. From there it deepens, widens, and plunges farther: Extending more than a hundred miles out into the Pacific Ocean, it finally reaches a depth of more than two and a half miles as it levels off into the abyssal plain of the deep seafloor.

The open ocean is a fluid world with ever-changing boundaries defined by currents, temperature, and light. The upper water layers teem with phytoplankton—free-floating, microscopic plants that support virtually all life in the ocean.

They are grazed by zooplankton—animal drifters ranging from single-celled life-forms to krill, sea snails, jellies, and the myriad larvae of crabs and fish. Many migrate vertically: They rise up to the surface to feed on phytoplankton at night and descend into deeper waters by day for safety. You might not see many of these creatures during your submersible ride, but you may get a glimpse of their predators: glittering schools of sardines, anchovies, mackerel—and whales. From huge humpbacks to gargantuan blues, all of them rely on zooplankton, and the Monterey Bay is a generous provider.

As you sink deeper into the canyon, the water darkens to a shadowy blue. Below 200 feet, there isn't enough light for phytoplankton to grow, and the deep sea begins. When you switch on a floodlight at 700 feet, a curling chain of silver light appears against the velvety blackness. It is a siphonophore, a gelatinous string of clones made up of distinct individuals with dedicated functions. Some segments catch prey with stinging tentacles while others digest, reproduce, or propel the entire organism. Siphonophores can grow to lengths exceeding 120 feet. Like almost all of the animals living at this depth, they are bioluminescent, creating their own light through chemical reactions within their bodies.

At 900 feet another marvel comes into view: a larvacean. The animal may be only the size of a finger, but it spins intricate webs of mucus around itself—a "house" that can be more than three feet wide. The larvacean lives inside, flapping its tail to circulate water and eating organic matter filtered through the mucus walls. When the house gets clogged with debris, the larvacean sheds it and builds a new one. The discarded mucus carries stored carbon—and even microplastics—to the bottom of the bay.

Larvaceans are islands of life in the dark depths of midwater—the habitat between the upper layers of the ocean and the deep seafloor. Worldwide, this midwater habitat is home to the largest animal communities on the planet, yet they are also the least known, due to the difficulty of studying them. For decades scientists used to drag nets from ships to collect midwater organisms, which offered little insight into the lives of these creatures in their own habitat. In 1964 the submersible *Alvin*, a Human Occupied Vehicle (HOV), began to revolutionize our understanding of undersea life with live observations from the depths around the world—including a first dive in the Monterey Canyon in 1988. That knowledge proliferated when smaller and nimbler Remotely Operated Vehicles (ROVs)—with no humans aboard—became more widely available in the 1990s. They have enabled researchers at the Monterey Bay Aquarium Research Institute (MBARI) in Moss Landing to study many animals and behaviors that are new to science.

One mile down, your floodlight reveals steep walls covered with colorful sea lilies, anemones, sponges, and sea stars. To see what exists even deeper down, you have to shift from your submersible to watch the live images transmitted from an ROV descending to the muddy bottom of the canyon.

That is where an astounding scene comes into view: a whale fall. The carcass of a gray whale that died at the surface has sunk to the seafloor, where it is providing a feast for deep-sea organisms that can last for years. Octopuses are crawling over it, along with crabs and grenadier fish. Eelpouts are stripping off blubber, and bone-eating worms are consuming fats from the skeleton. Whale falls have only been observed since the late 1970s, when robotic vehicles first began to explore the marine depths—and their significance to life at the bottom of the sea is still a frontier of science.

The bottom of Monterey Bay is as alien an environment as another planet. No human being has ever been down there in person. Yet just as the surface of Mars is becoming known from the exploits of robotic rovers piloted from afar by people on Earth, the deep-sea world of Monterey Bay is being explored through remote technology applied by scientists and engineers working out of laboratories in Moss Landing. Hundreds of new species have already been identified and many more will come to light in the years ahead. These discoveries reveal a mysterious world that is an extreme extension of life in the Monterey Bay— and of the wondrous diversity of life on Planet Earth.

FOREST

Most of the original forests in the Santa Cruz Mountains were clear-cut
during an intensive logging period that came to an end in the early 20th century.
Remnants of mill sites, flumes, and railroad trestles lie hidden under the
canopy of second-growth redwood trees in a forested landscape
that is a testament to regeneration.

MORNING CLOUDS, SANTA CRUZ MOUNTAINS

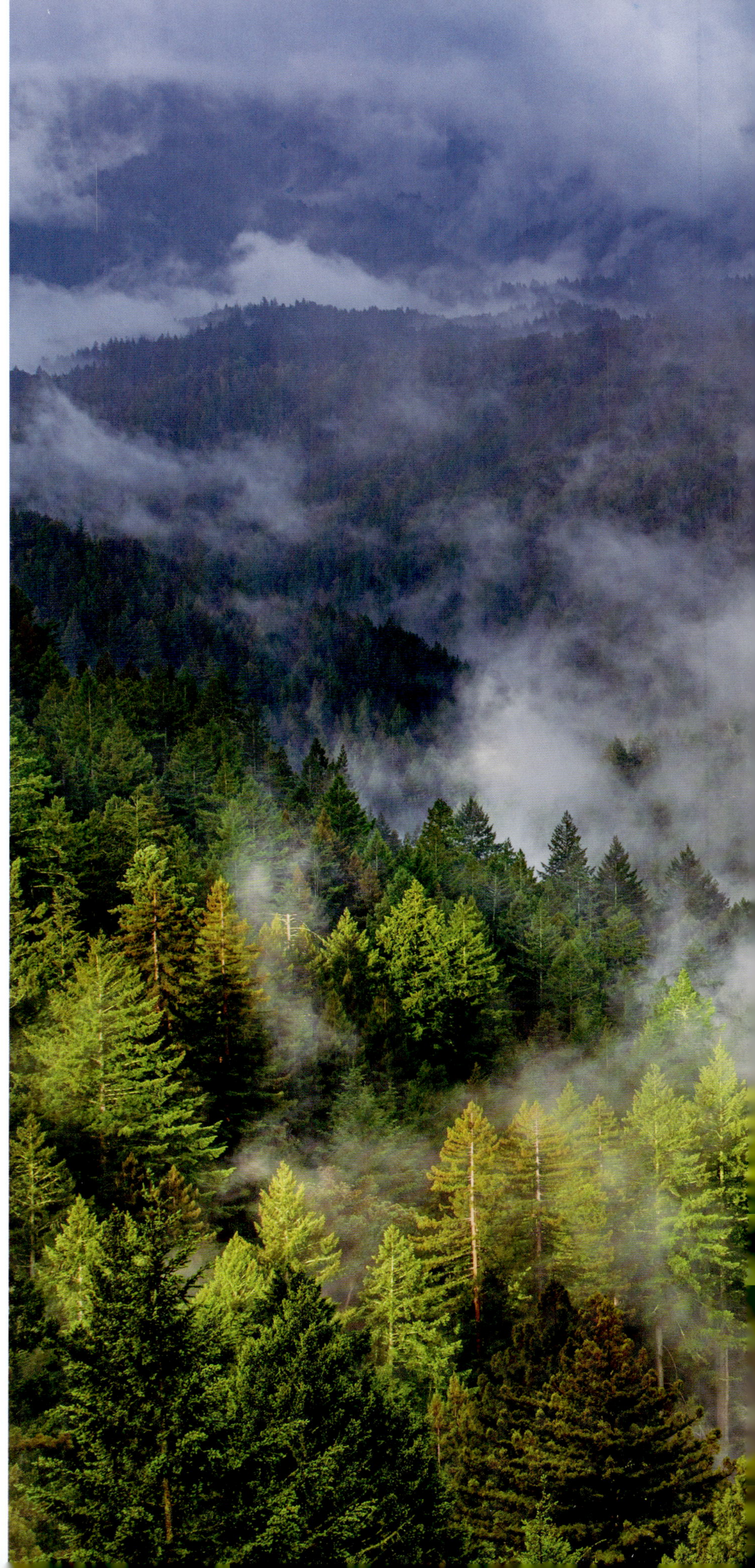

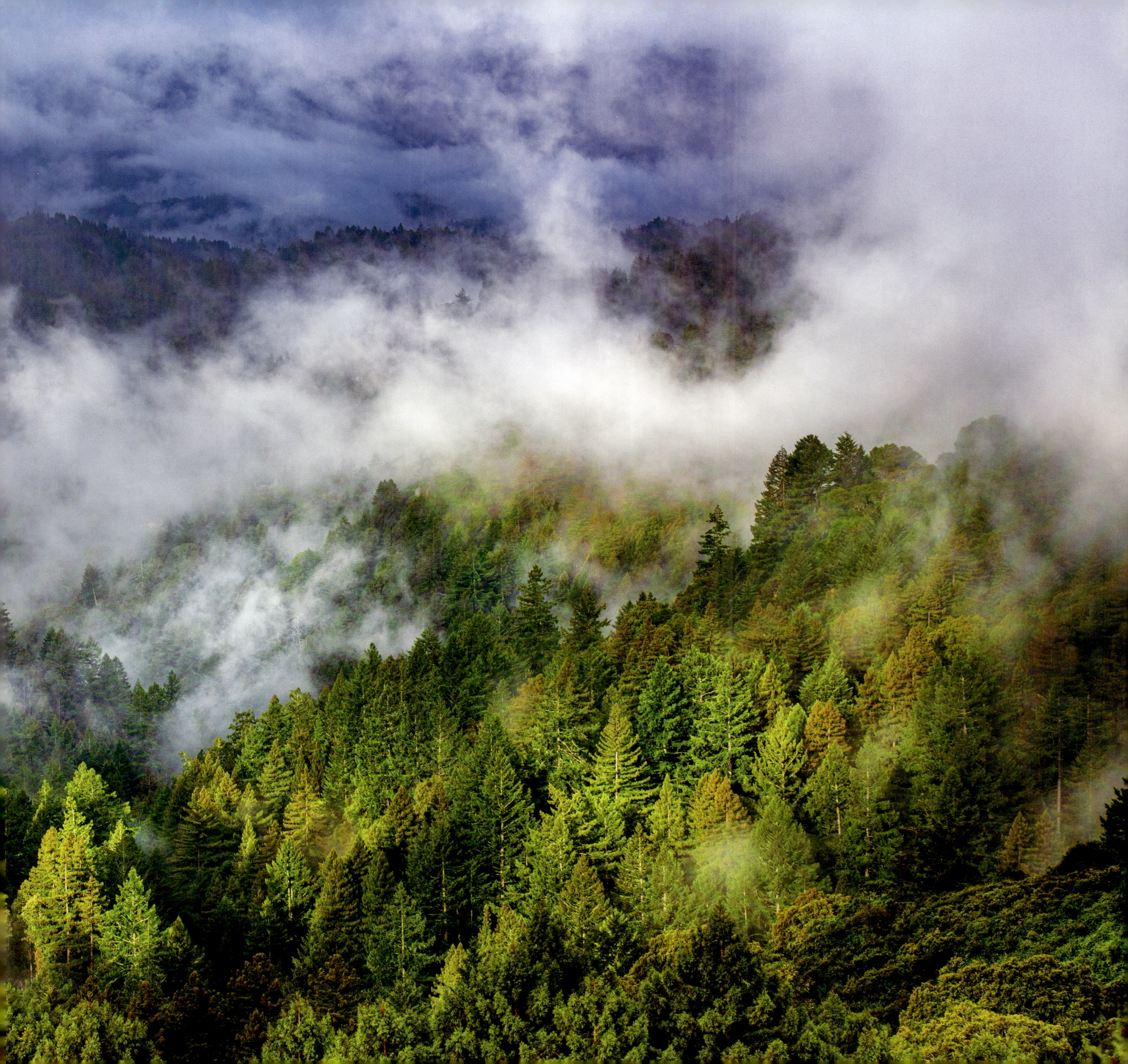

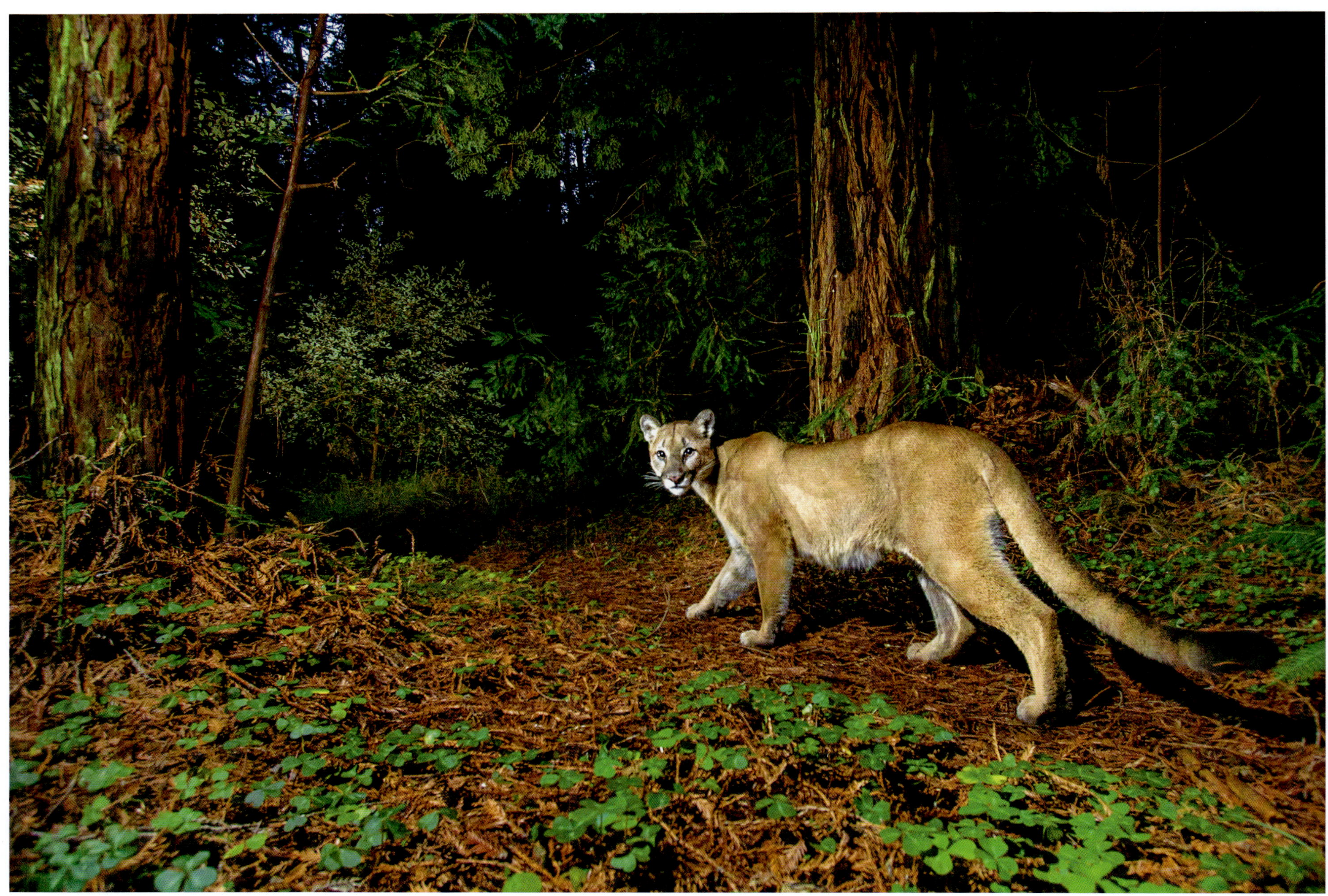

Mountain lions are elusive, so Frans Lanting turned to camera traps to document their presence. One day when a sensor triggered the system, a young lion froze, revealing its long, sinuous body. During a second exposure, it turned to cast a wary look back at the camera—a portrait of stealth foiled.

MOUNTAIN LION, SWANTON

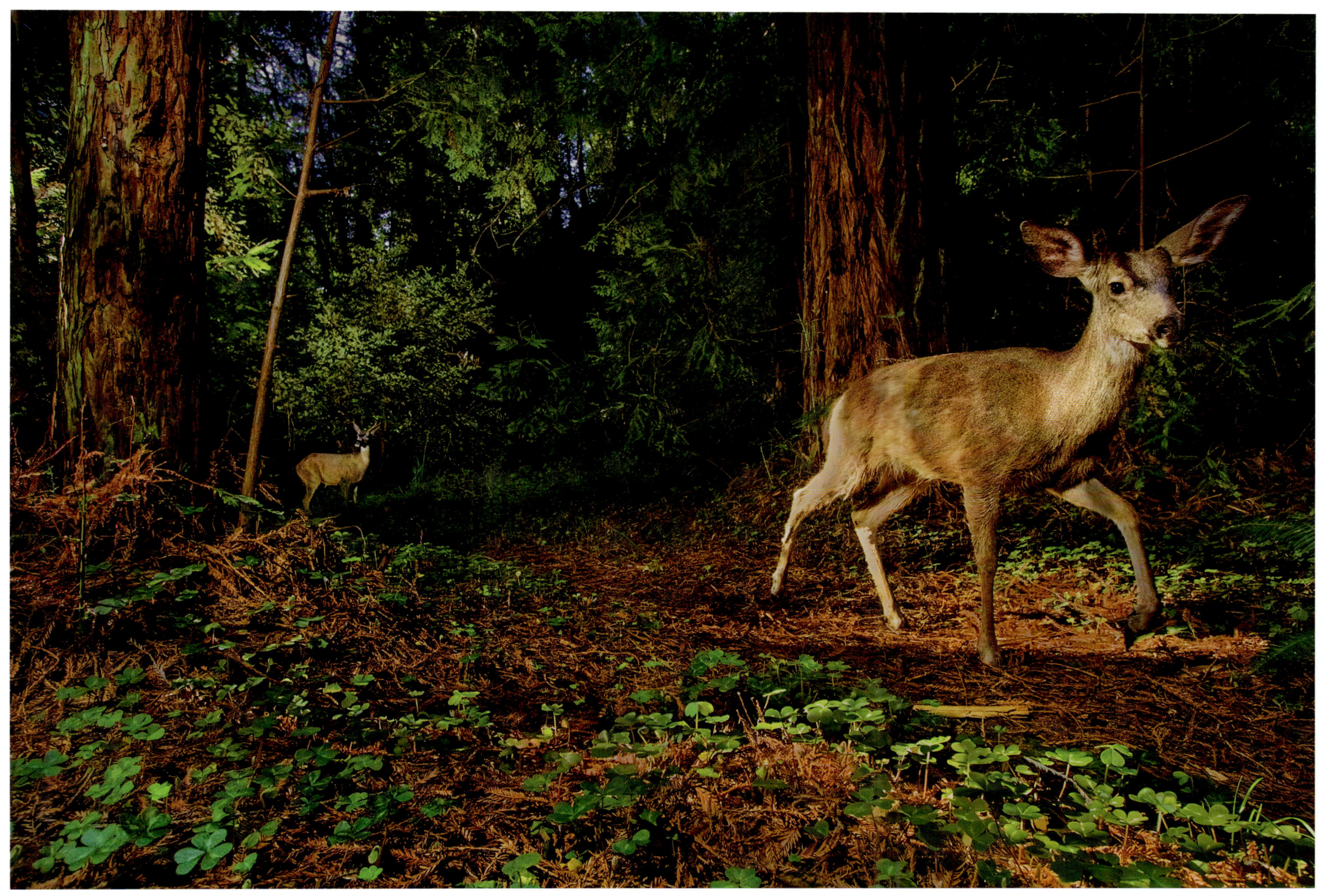

A blacktail deer is caught in the same spot as the mountain lion on the opposite page, confirming that predator and prey may use the same trails through the forest. Research by UCSC's Santa Cruz Puma Project has revealed patterns of lion movements in the region that enable planners to create habitat corridors and protect denning sanctuaries.

Blacktail Deer, Swanton

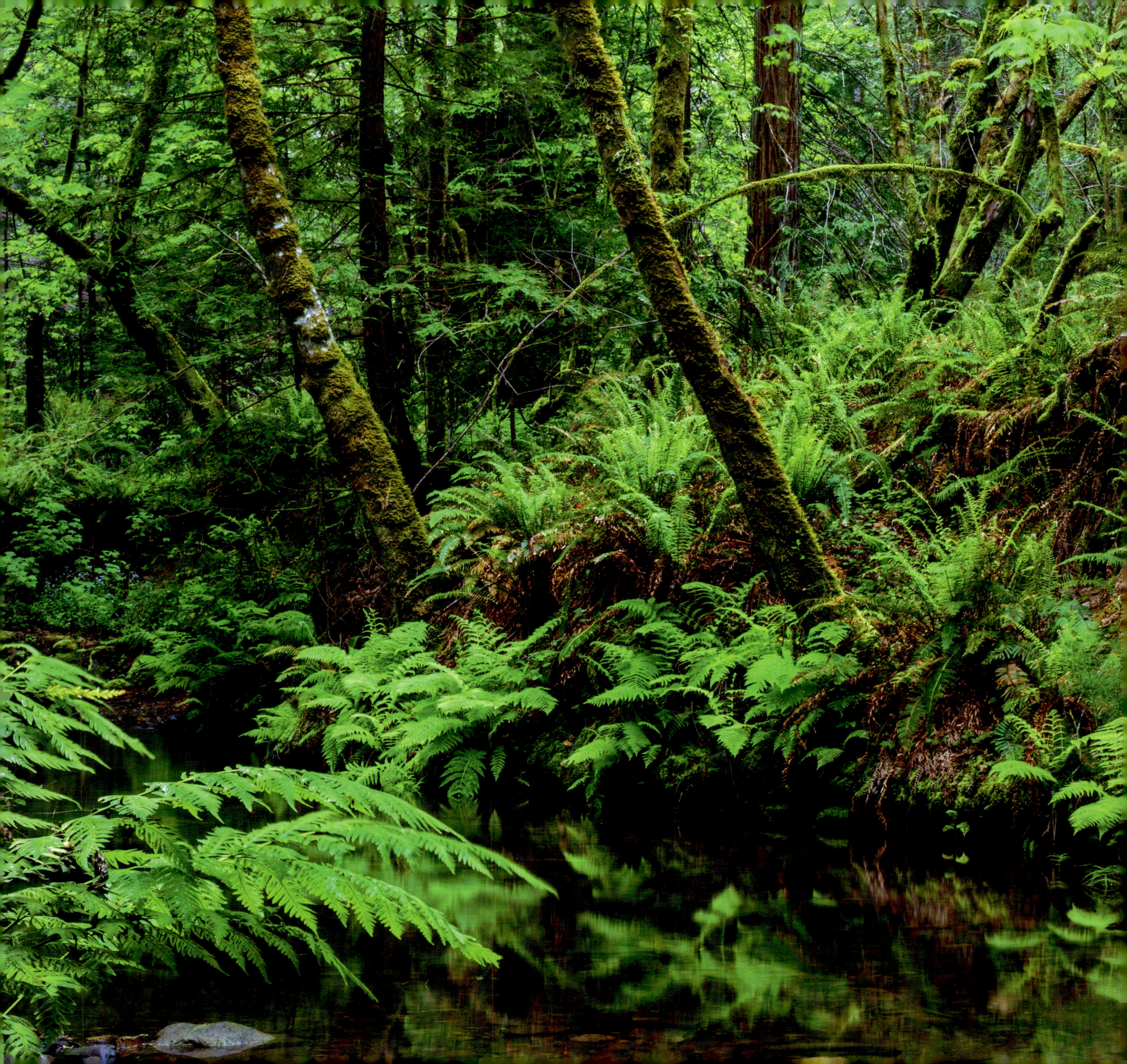

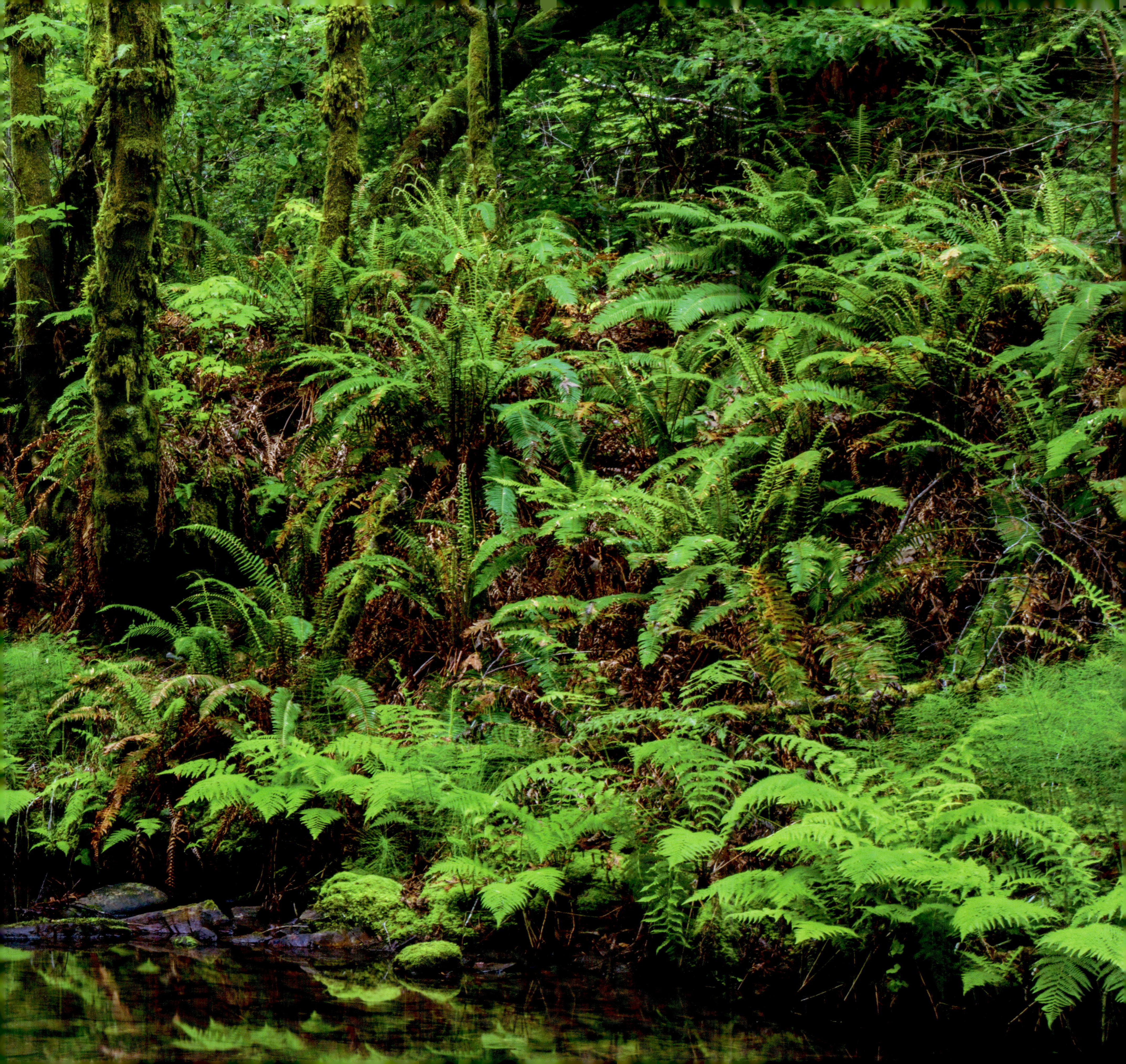

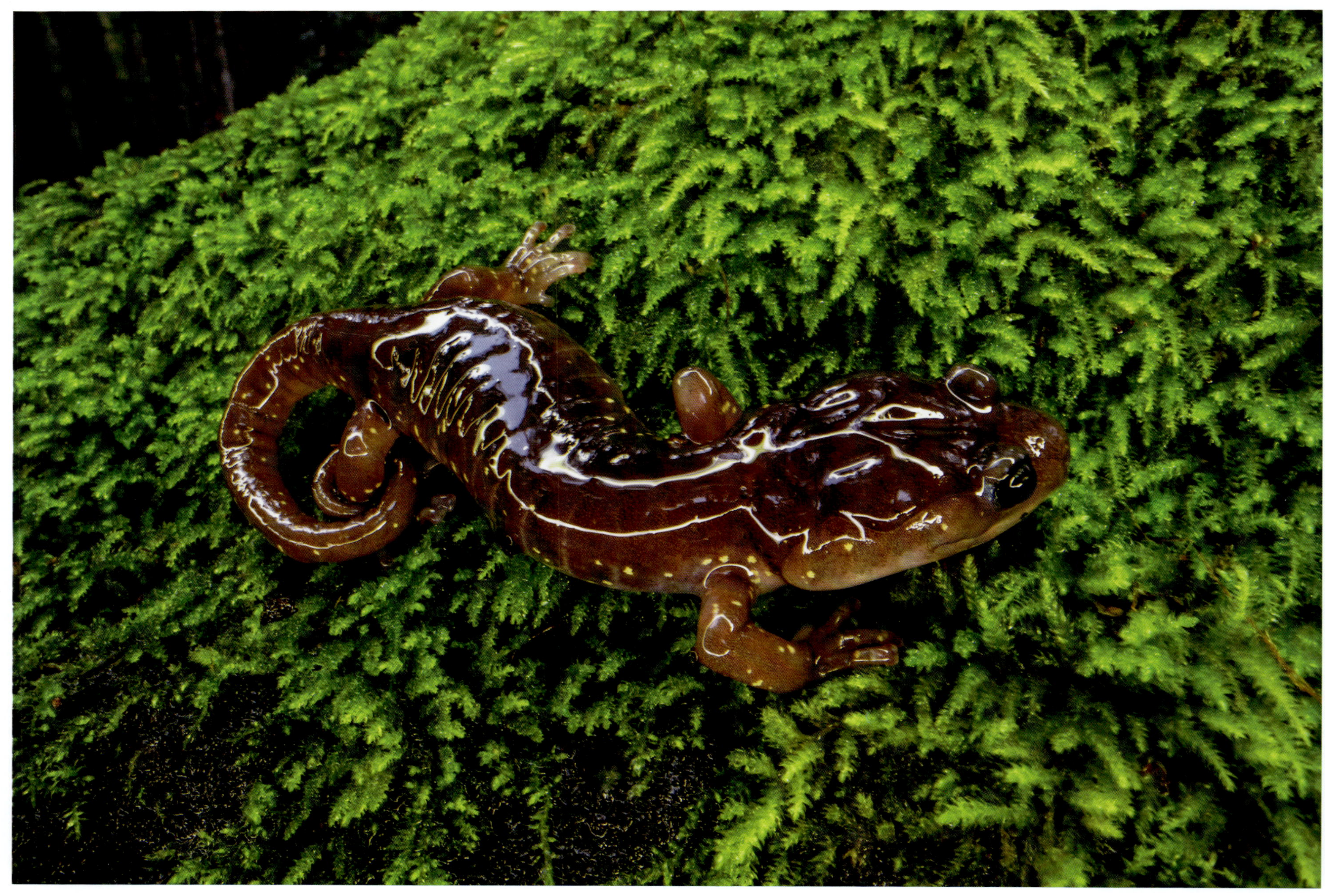

With square toe tips for gripping and semi-prehensile tails for hanging from branches, arboreal salamanders are adapted for life in the trees—though they are also found on the ground. They roam at night to grab spiders, insects, and slugs with their formidable, toothy jaws.

ARBOREAL SALAMANDER, BONNY DOON

PREVIOUS PAGES: Lush forest along a coastal creek features ferns, alders, and redwoods in a moist habitat that is a haven for amphibians.

RIPARIAN FOREST, BUTANO STATE PARK

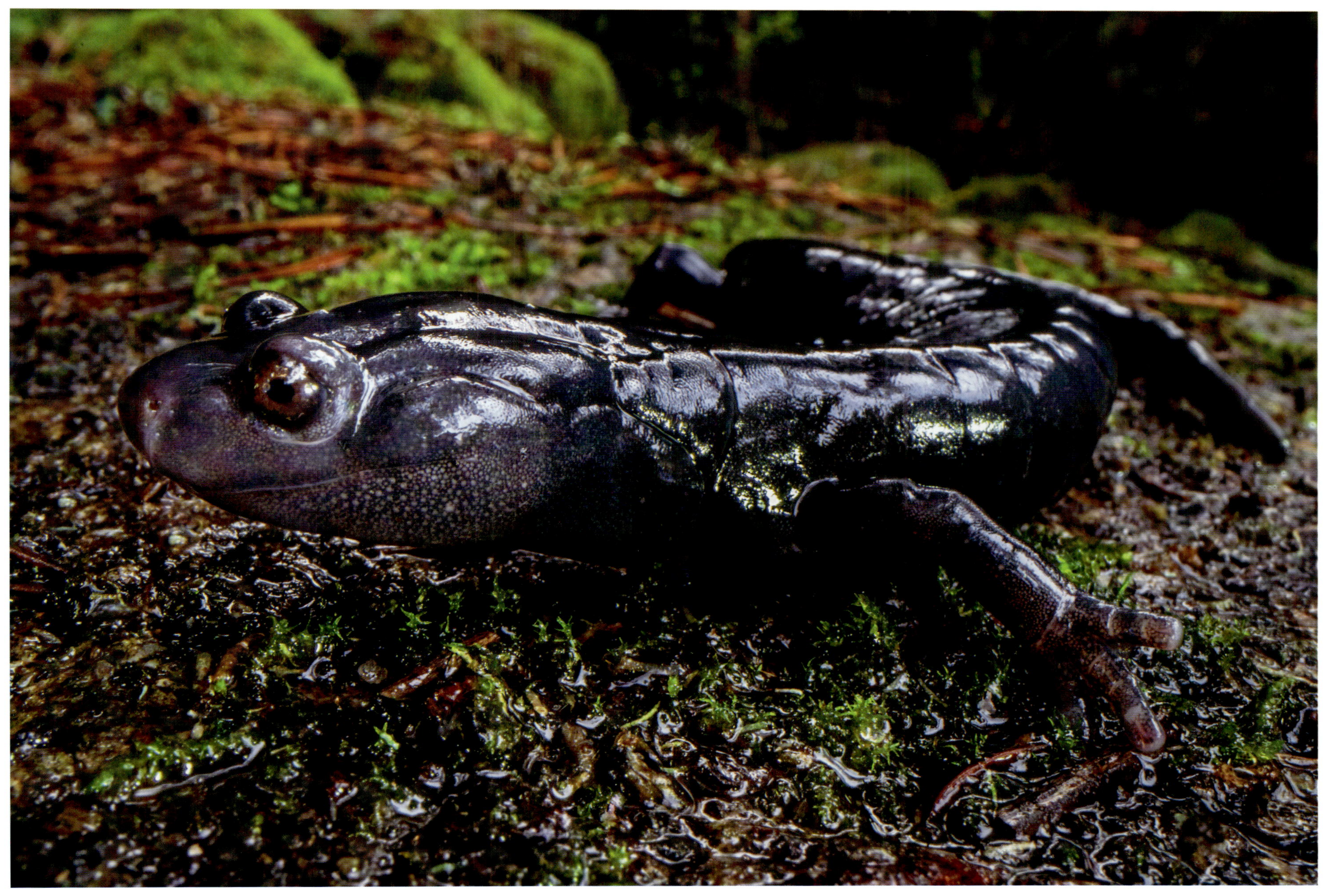

Found only in the Santa Cruz Mountains, the rare black salamander likes to hide under rocks and logs near well-shaded streams. Lacking lungs, it breathes through its skin and only moves when humidity is high, foraging at night for millipedes, ants, and termites.

Santa Cruz Black Salamander, UC Santa Cruz Campus Natural Reserve

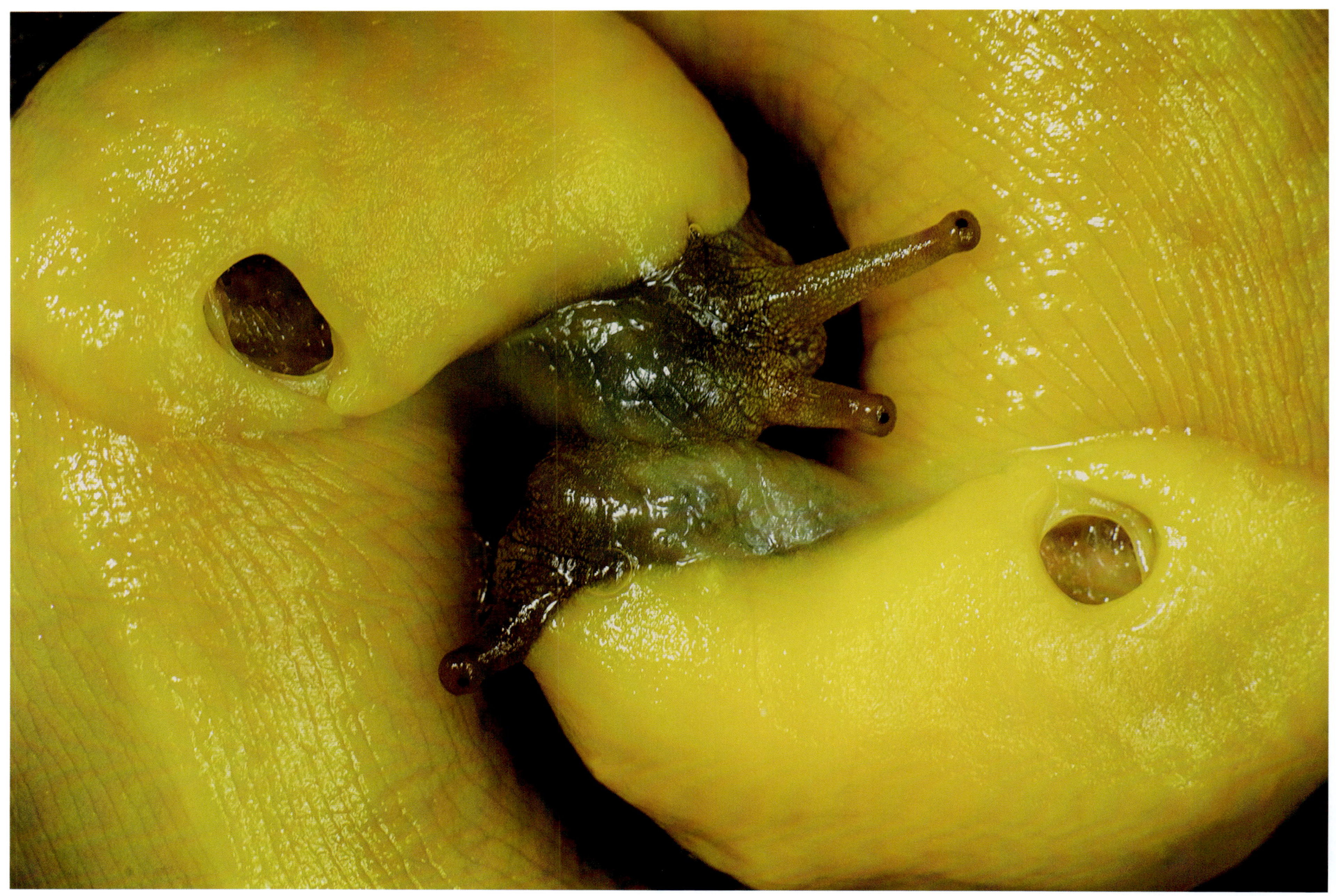

Two banana slugs curl up for an amorous embrace as a prelude to mating. The largest land mollusk in North America can grow to a length of eight inches and live seven years. They are at home in the cool, damp environment of redwood forests. Monterey Bay is the southern end of their range.

BANANA SLUGS, BIG SUR | *Photo by Kevin Osborn*

OPPOSITE: Mock oyster mushrooms grow in overlapping clusters on a decaying log.

MUSHROOMS, QUAIL HOLLOW RANCH COUNTY PARK

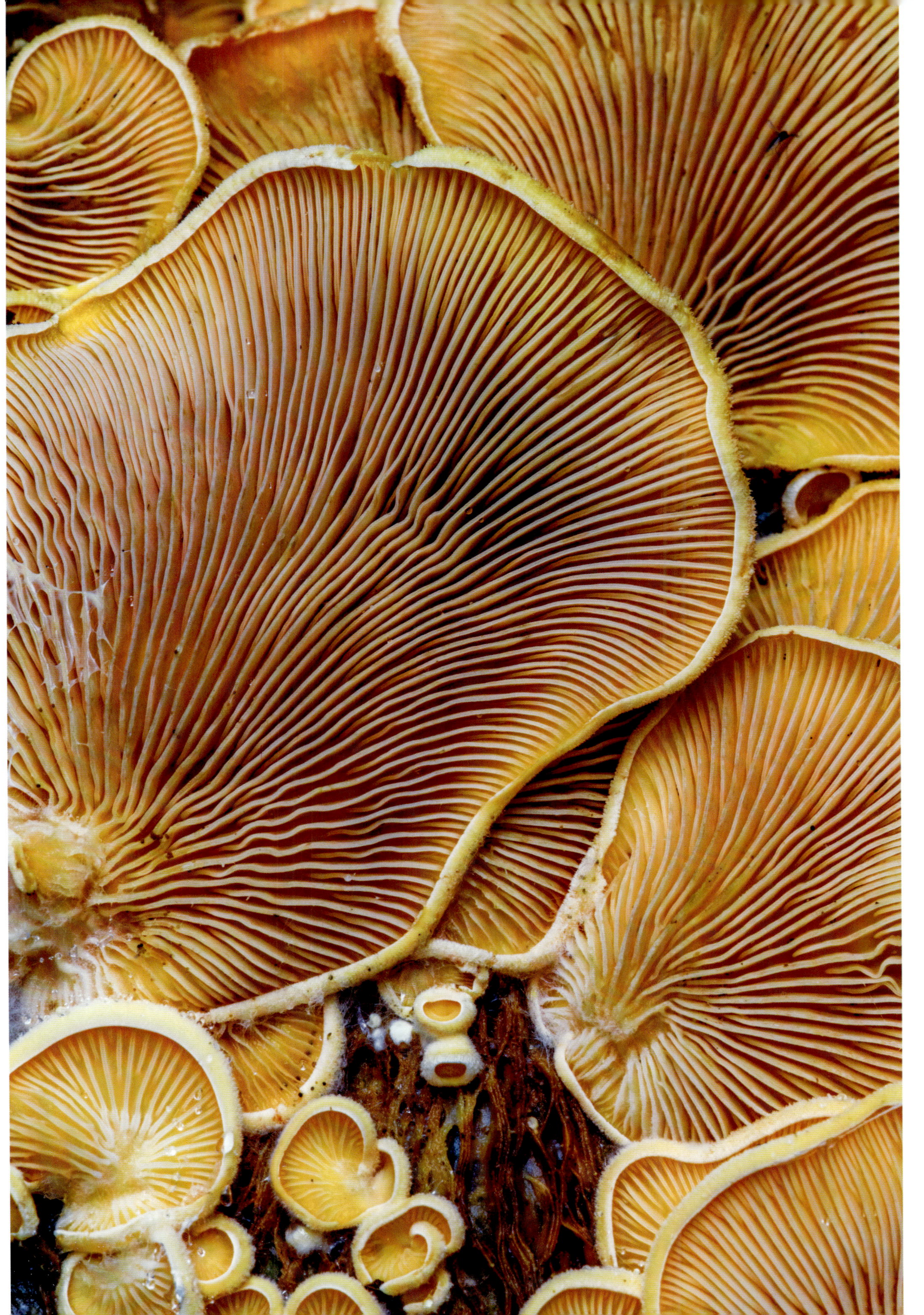

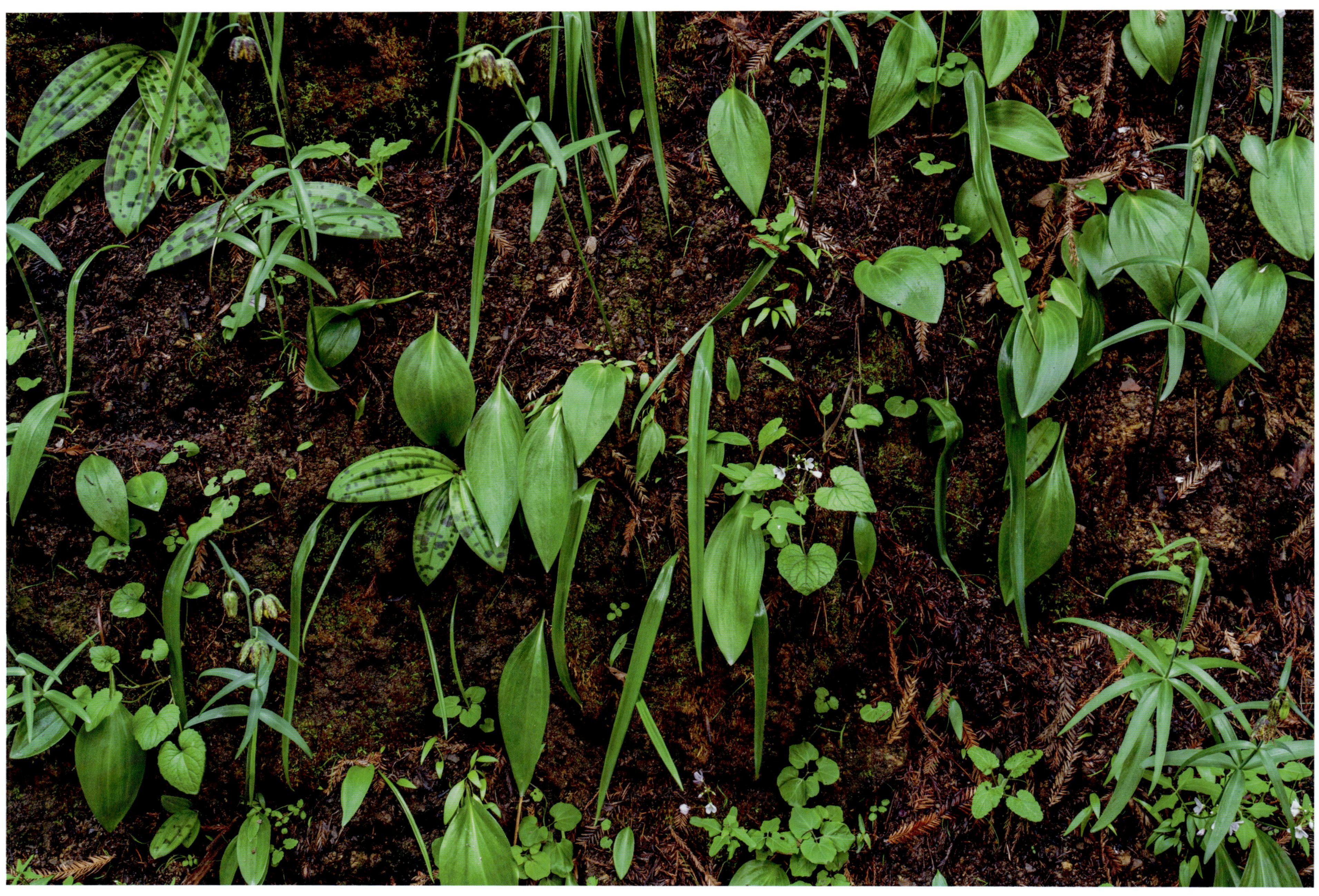

A still life of fragile plants that thrive on the dim-lit forest floor includes checker lilies with mottled petals, heart-shaped stream violet leaves, tiny fairy lantern blossoms, and the spotted leaves of leopard lilies.

FOREST FLORA, BUTANO STATE PARK

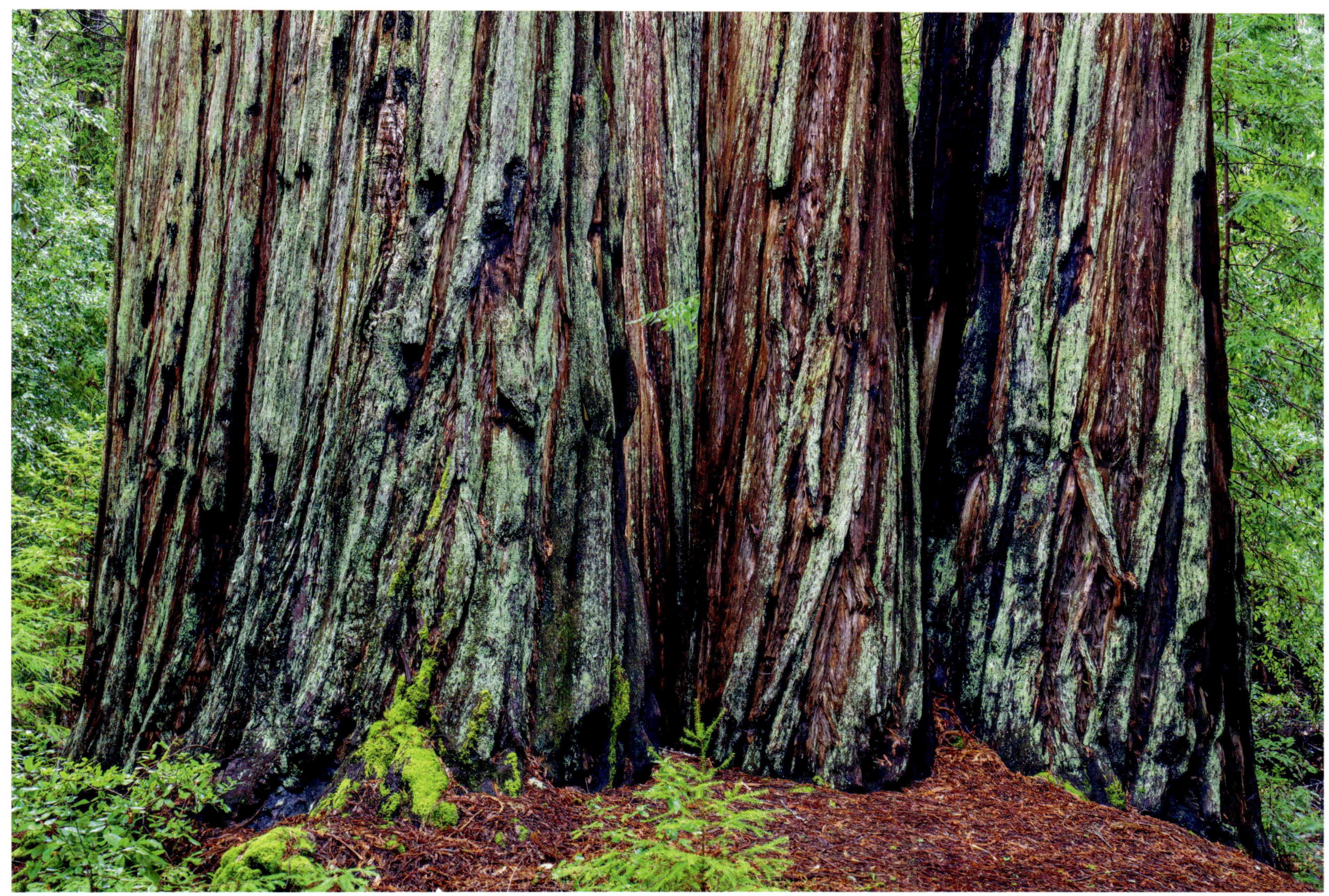

A landmark campaign for the protection of ancient redwoods culminated with the creation of California's first state park in 1902. It was established in Big Basin to save the last of the big trees, thanks to the efforts of the Sempervirens Fund, one of the region's earliest conservation groups.

Ancient Redwood Trees, Big Basin Redwoods State Park

WOODLAND

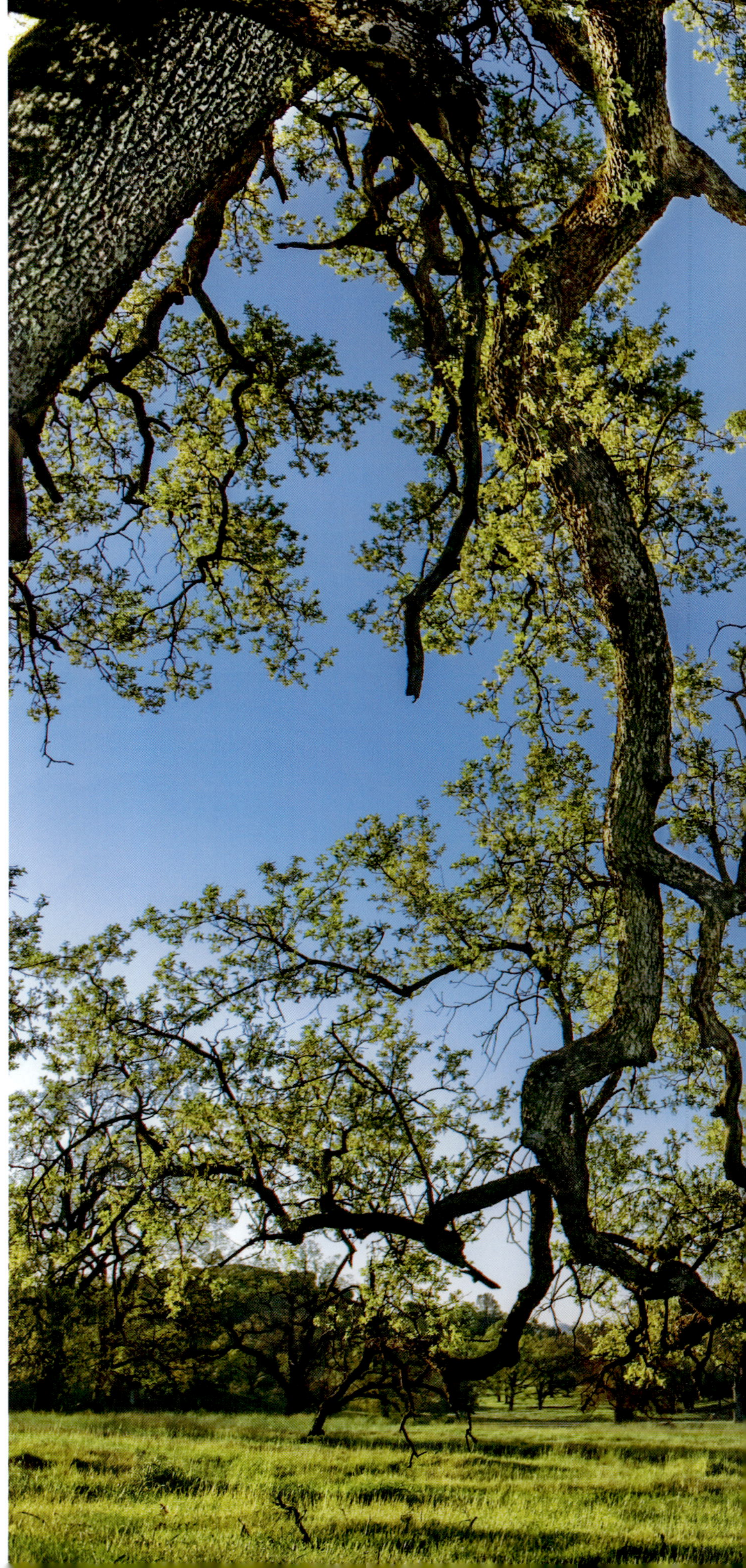

Oak woodlands support more forms of life than any other terrestrial ecosystem in California, including 300 species of mammals, birds, reptiles, and amphibians, and more than 5,000 different kinds of insects.

Valley Oaks, Fort Hunter Liggett

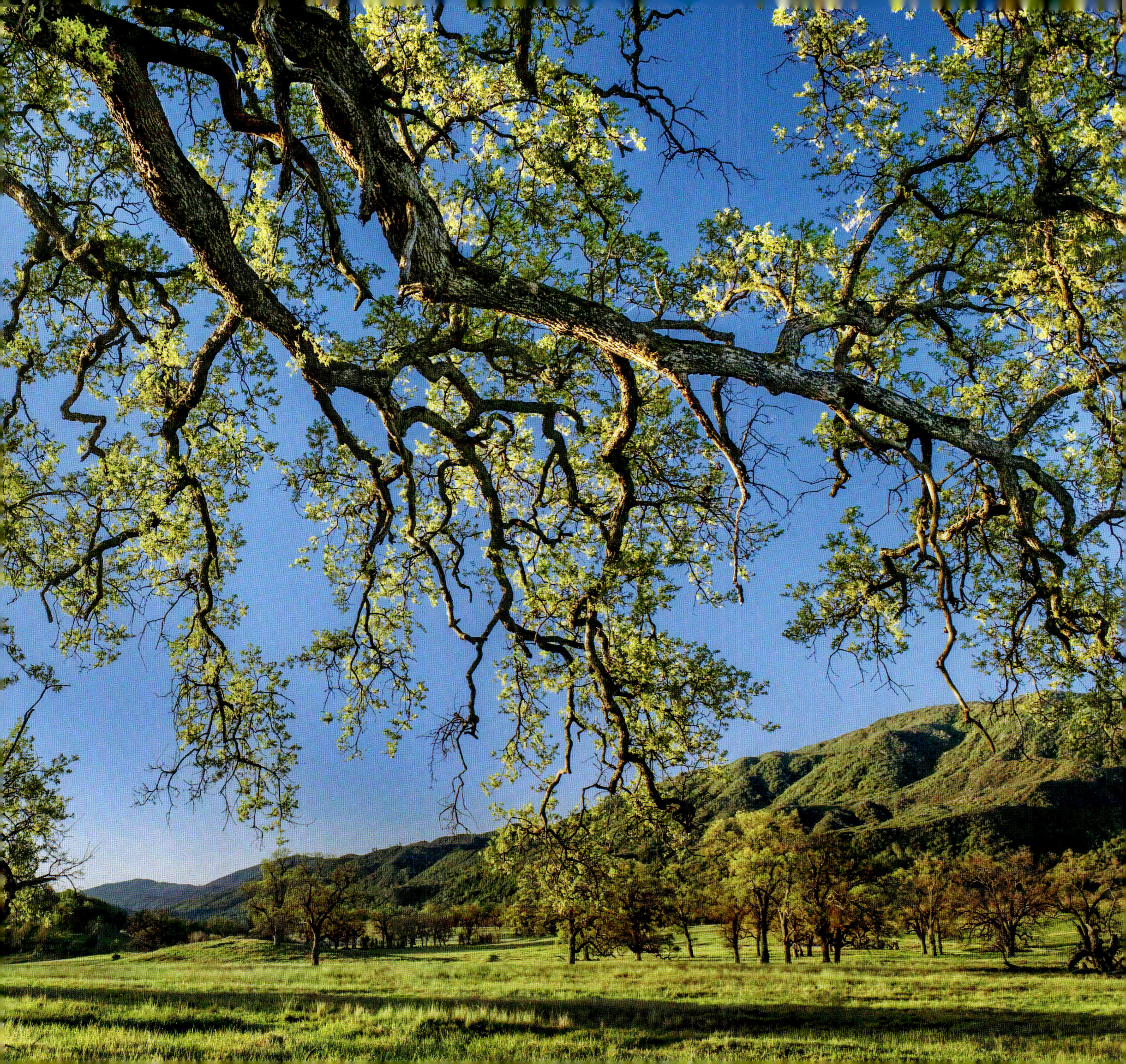

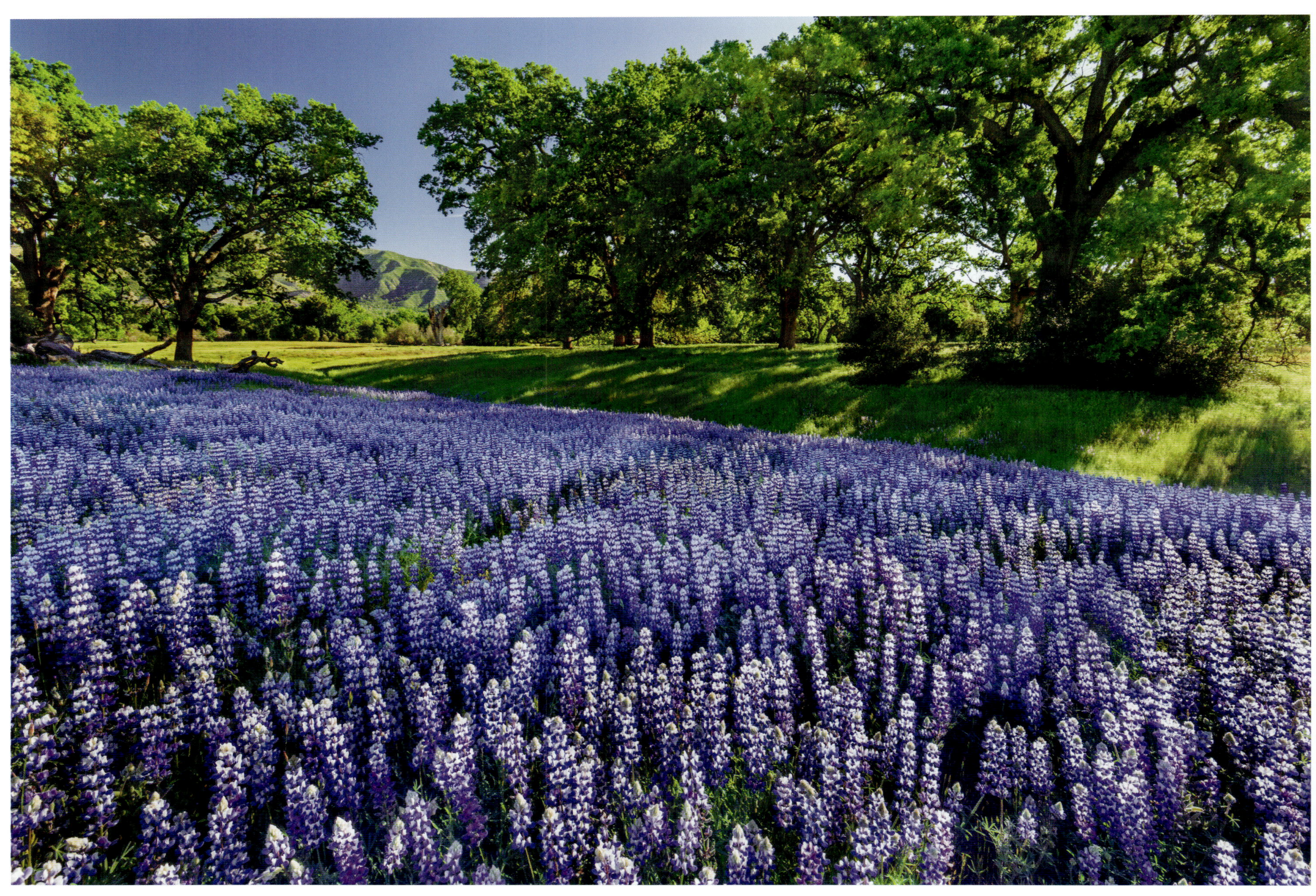

The vibrant color and heady scent of sky lupines in full bloom fill
a scenic valley of oak woodlands near Fort Hunter Liggett.

Sky Lupines, Los Padres National Forest

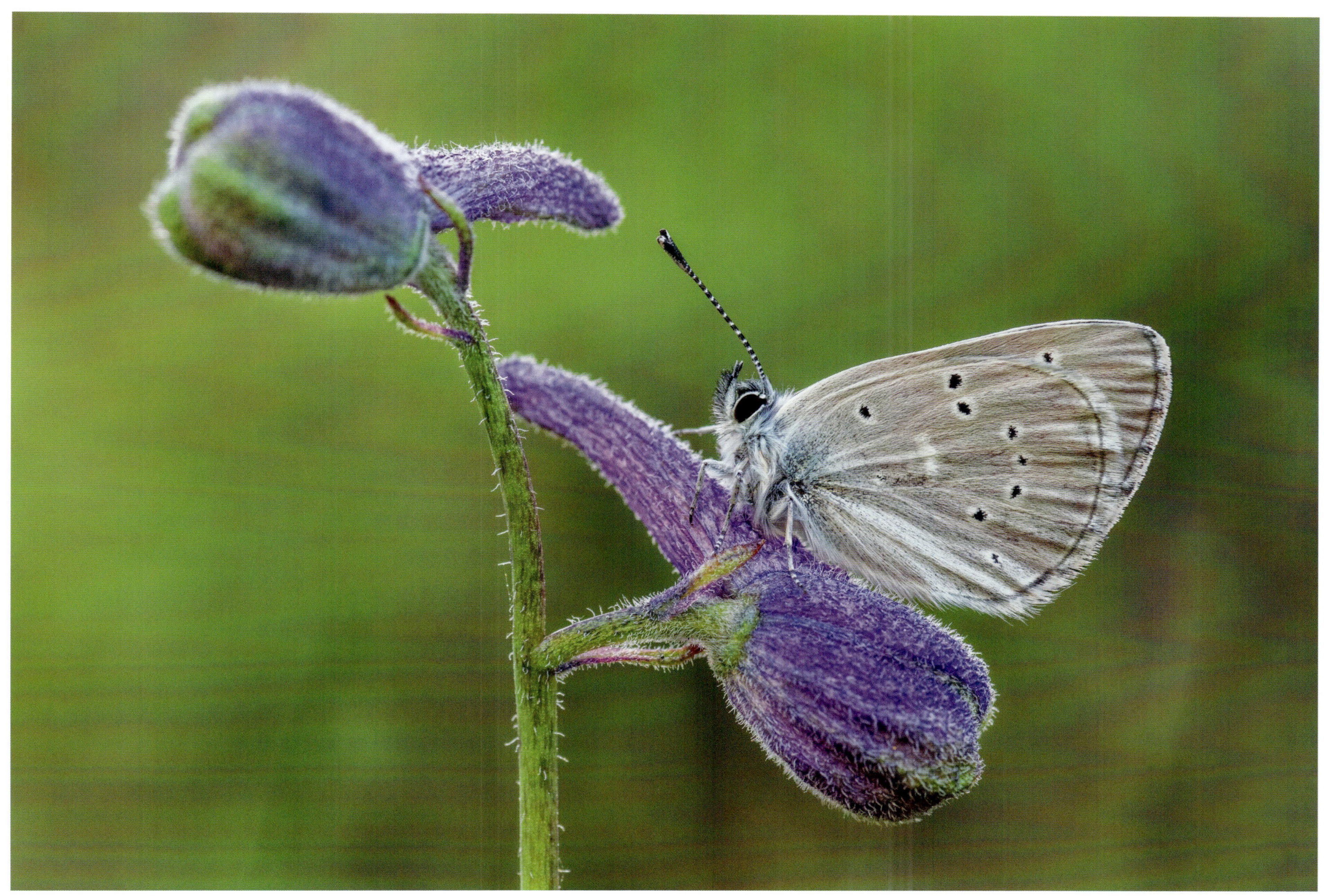

An echo azure butterfly perches on the flower bud of a Monterey larkspur,
a rare plant found only in Monterey County.

Butterfly on Larkspur, Landels-Hill Big Creek Natural Reserve

following pages: The rolling hills of a working ranch in the rugged Sierra de Salinas
contrast with the cultivated farmlands of the Salinas Valley that stretch in the distance.

Aerial View of Ranchland, Sierra de Salinas

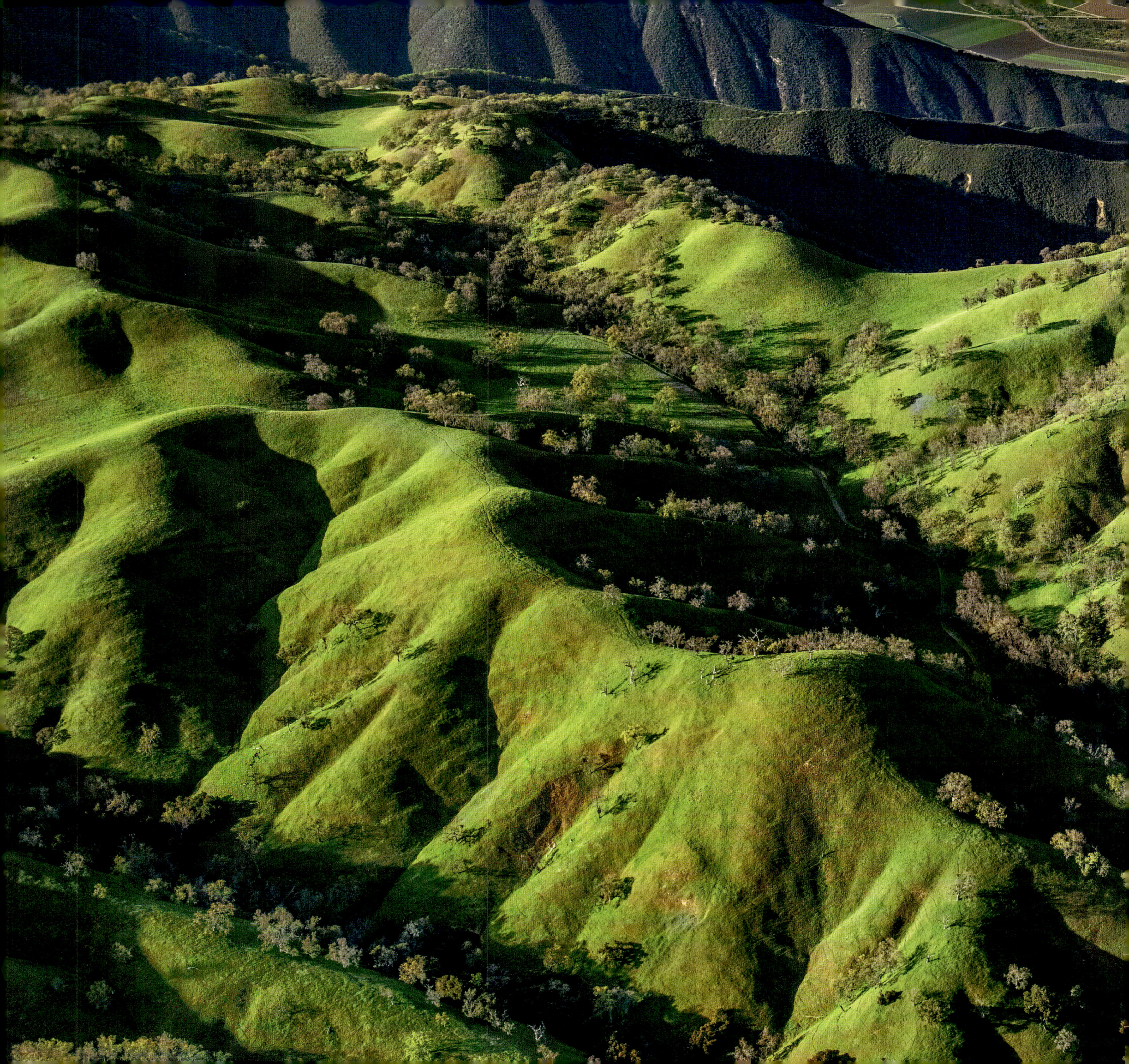

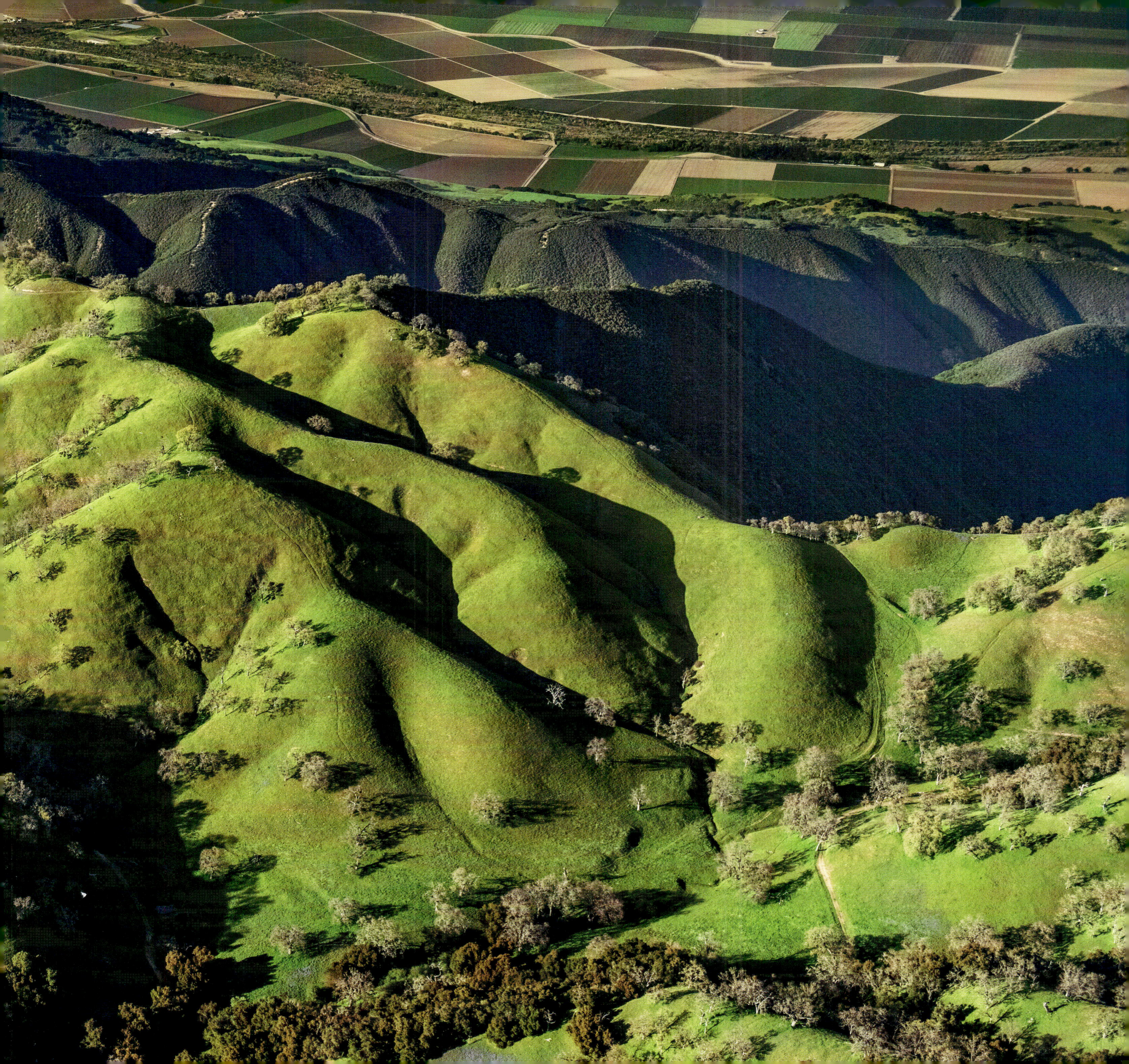

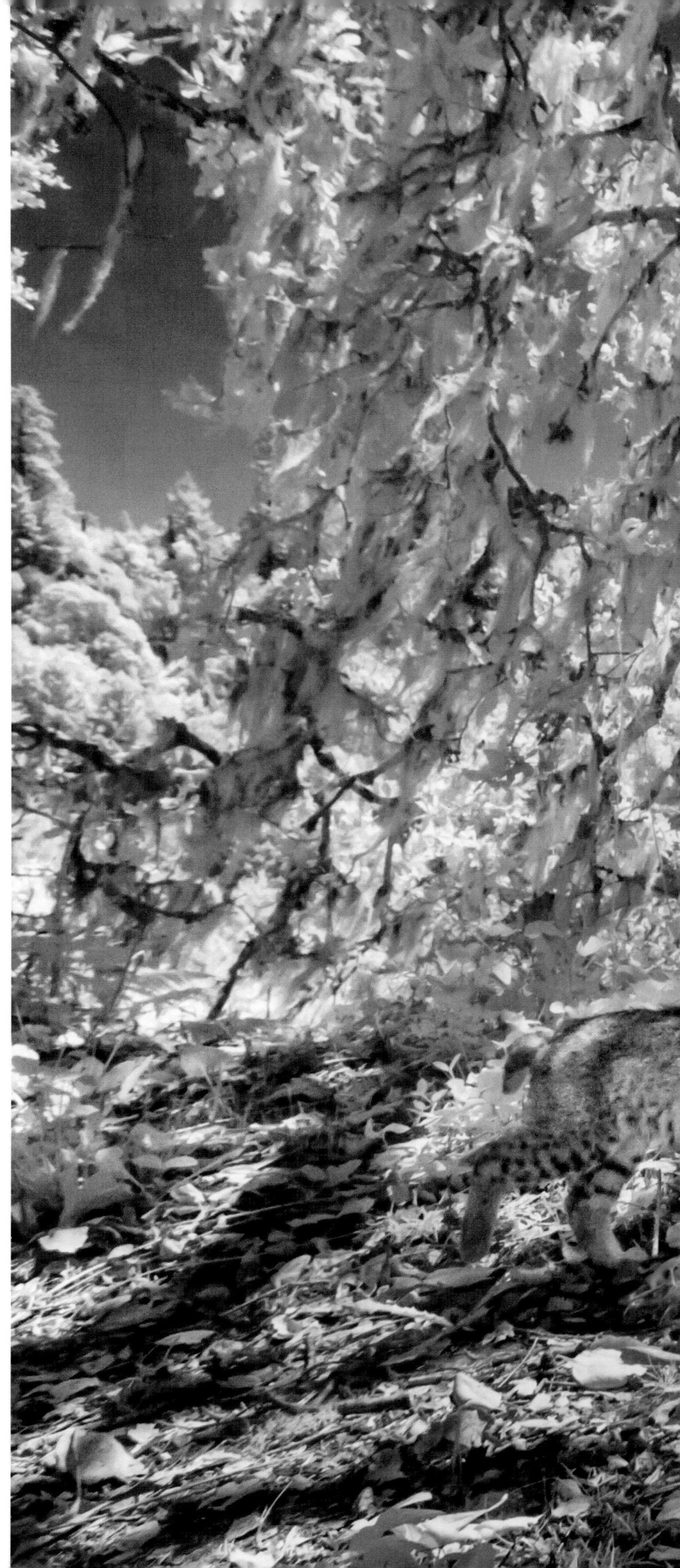

Set up at an oak tree festooned with lichen, a remote camera adapted for infrared photography captured a precious scene of a bobcat mother and her kitten strolling by, a private passage unaffected by the presence of a photographer.

Bobcat and Kitten, Wilder Ranch State Park

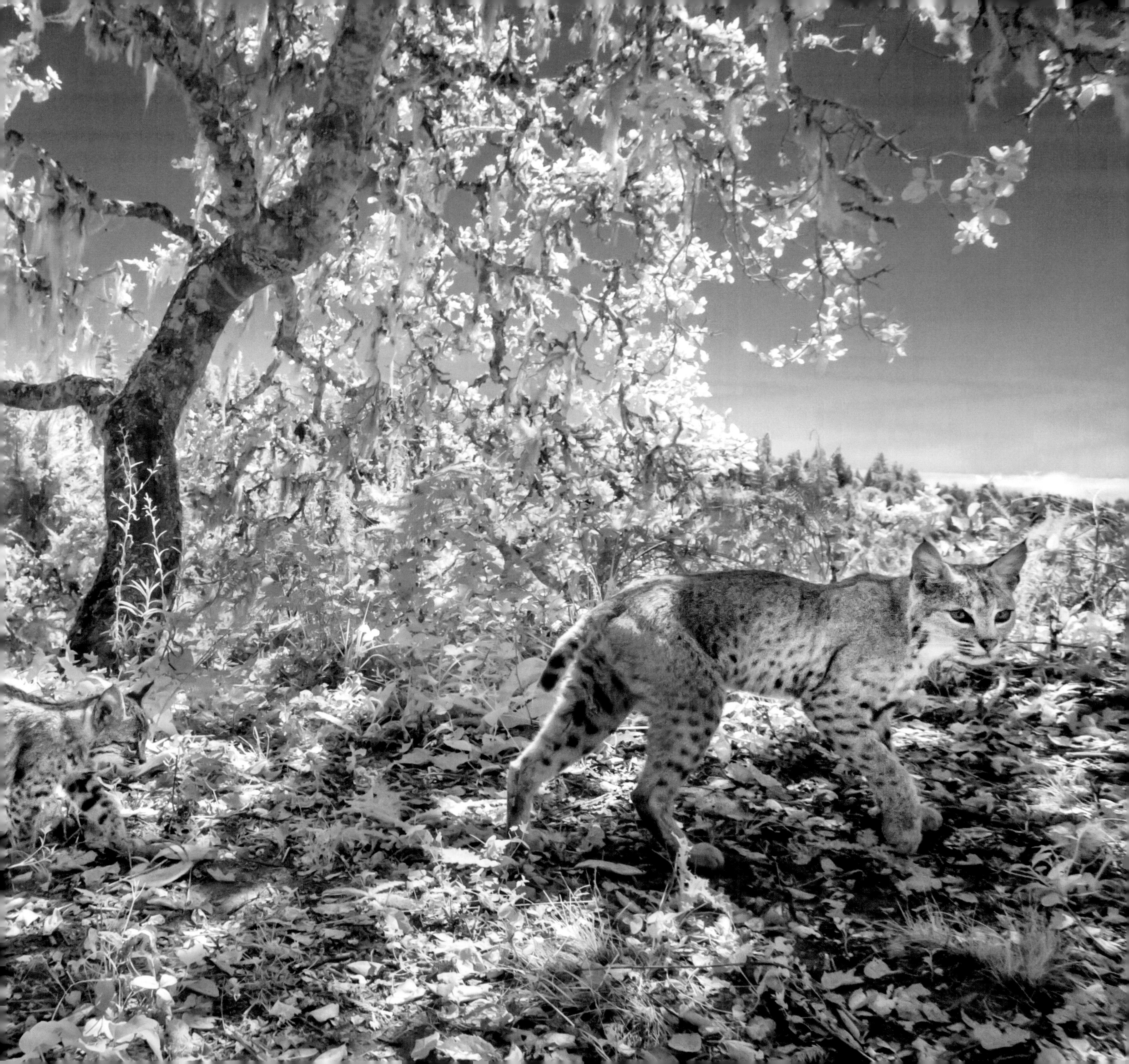

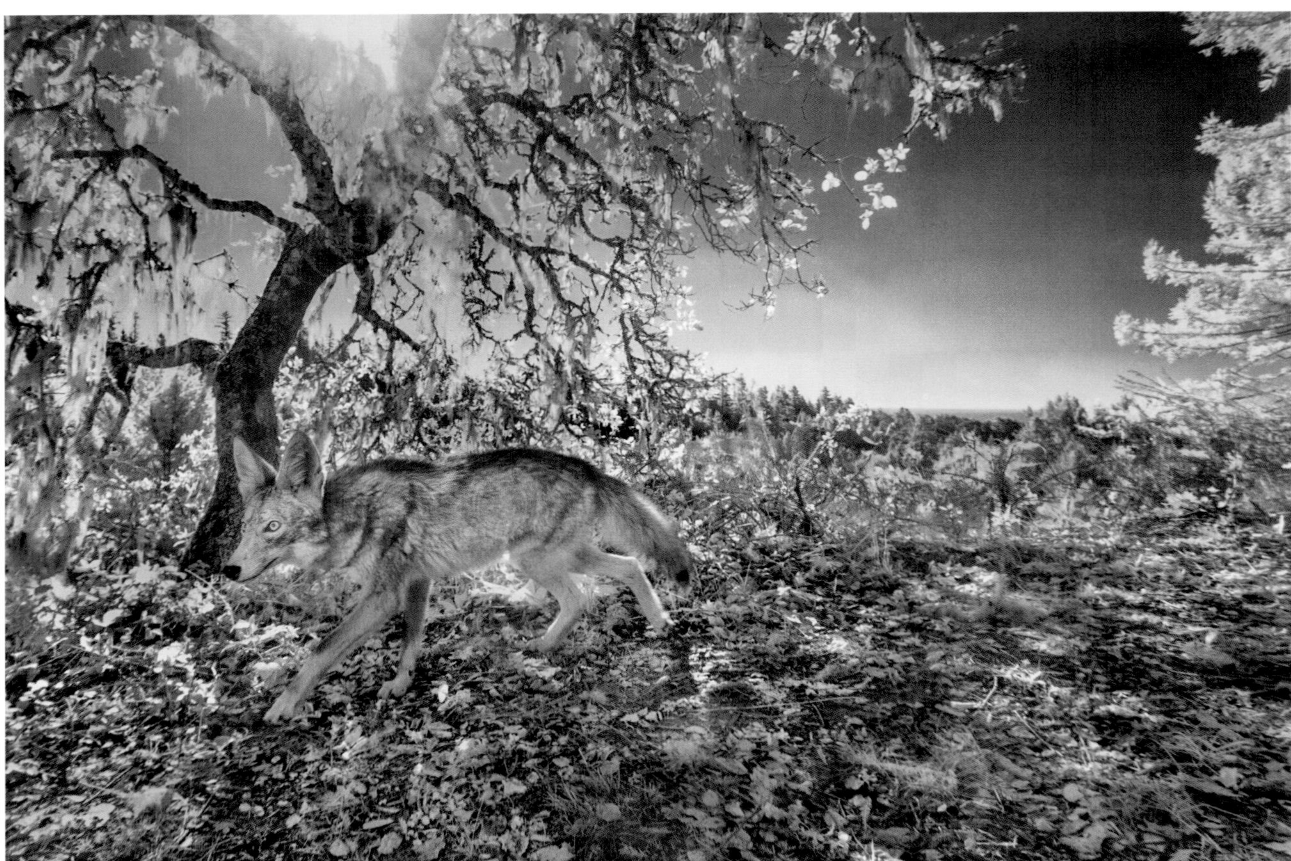

A keen coyote trots past the camera
trap on a sunny afternoon.

Coyote, Wilder Ranch State Park

A blacktail deer moves cautiously just after dark,
a time when mountain lions become more active.
Deer are their preferred prey.

Blacktail Deer, Wilder Ranch State Park

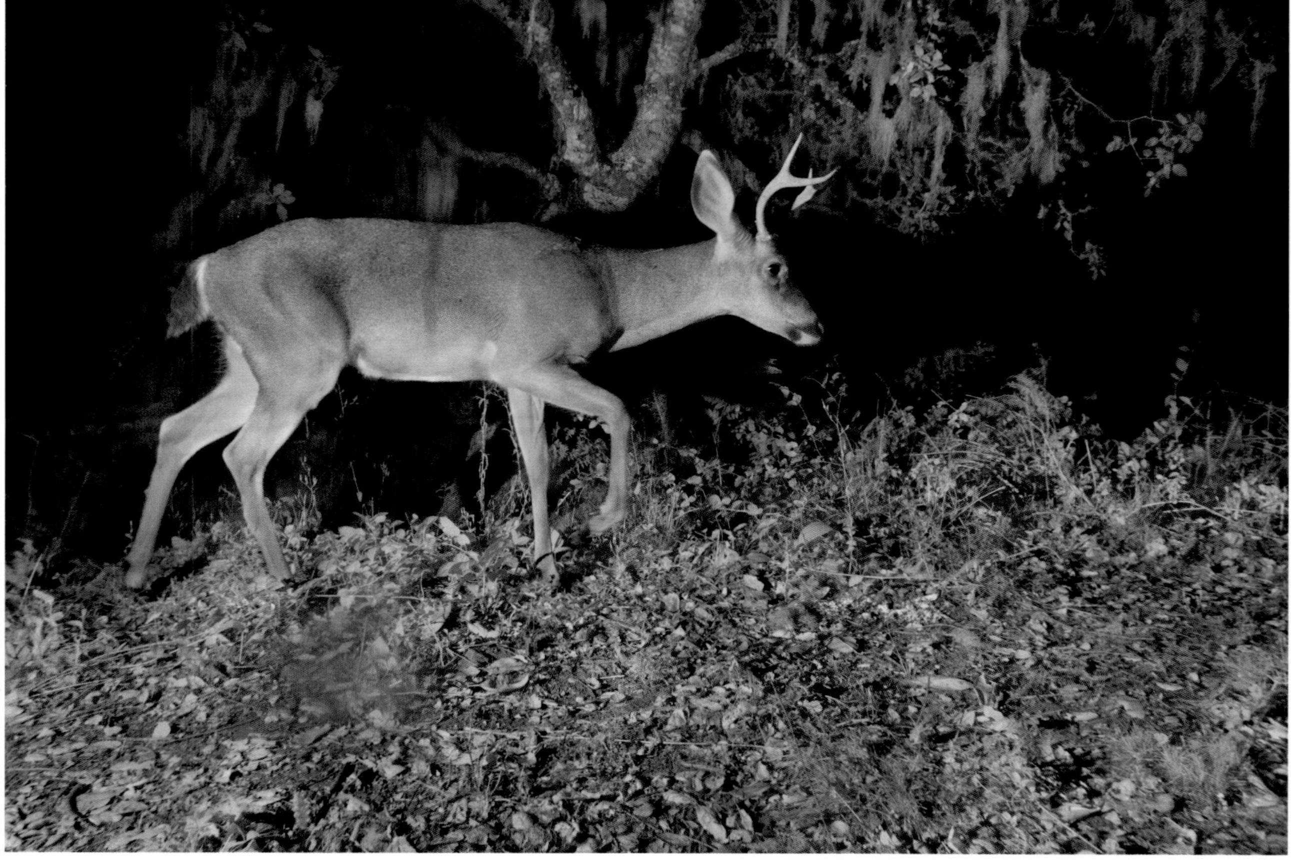

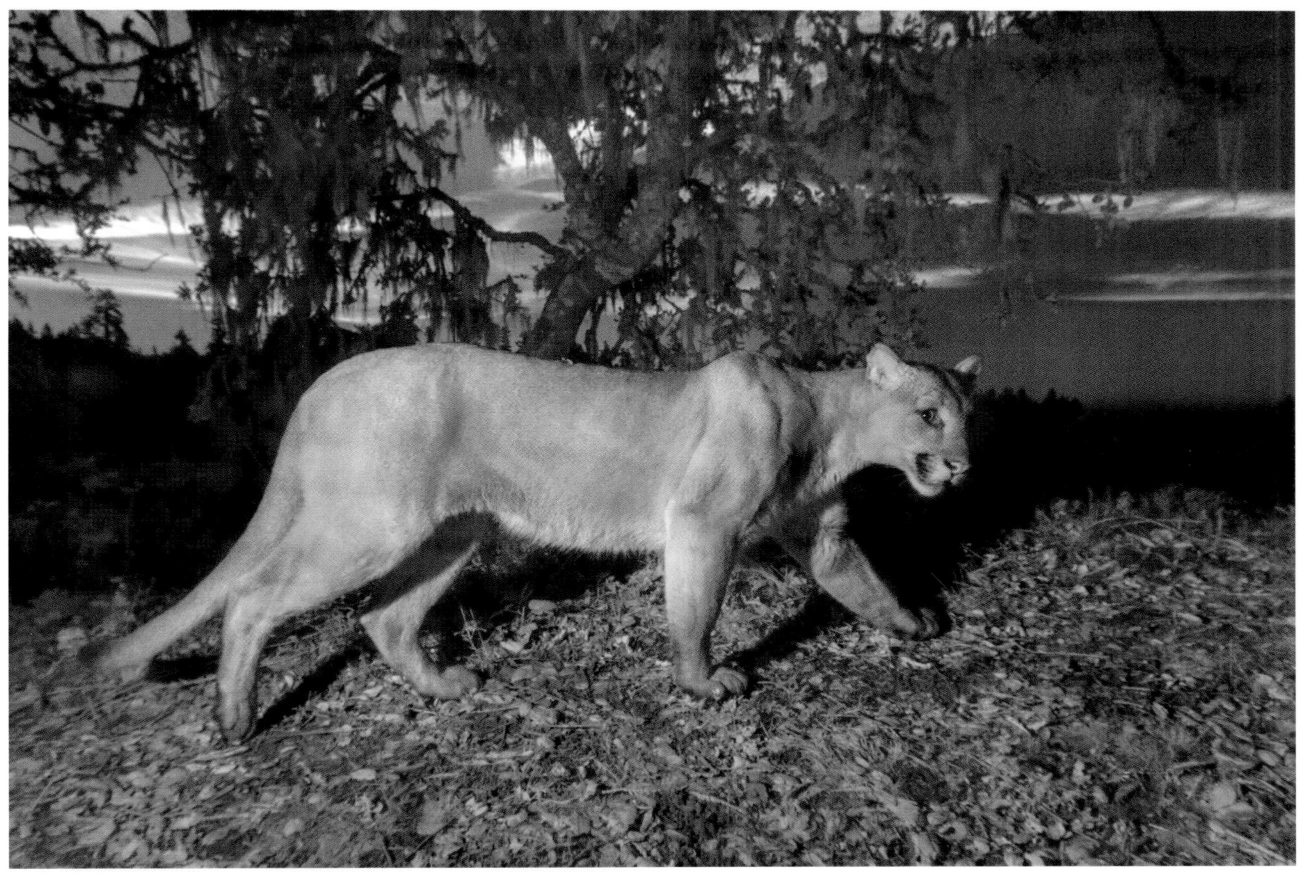

A male mountain lion's sideways glance indicates he has seen the camera, but dusk is near and hunting is on his mind.

Mountain Lion, Wilder Ranch State Park

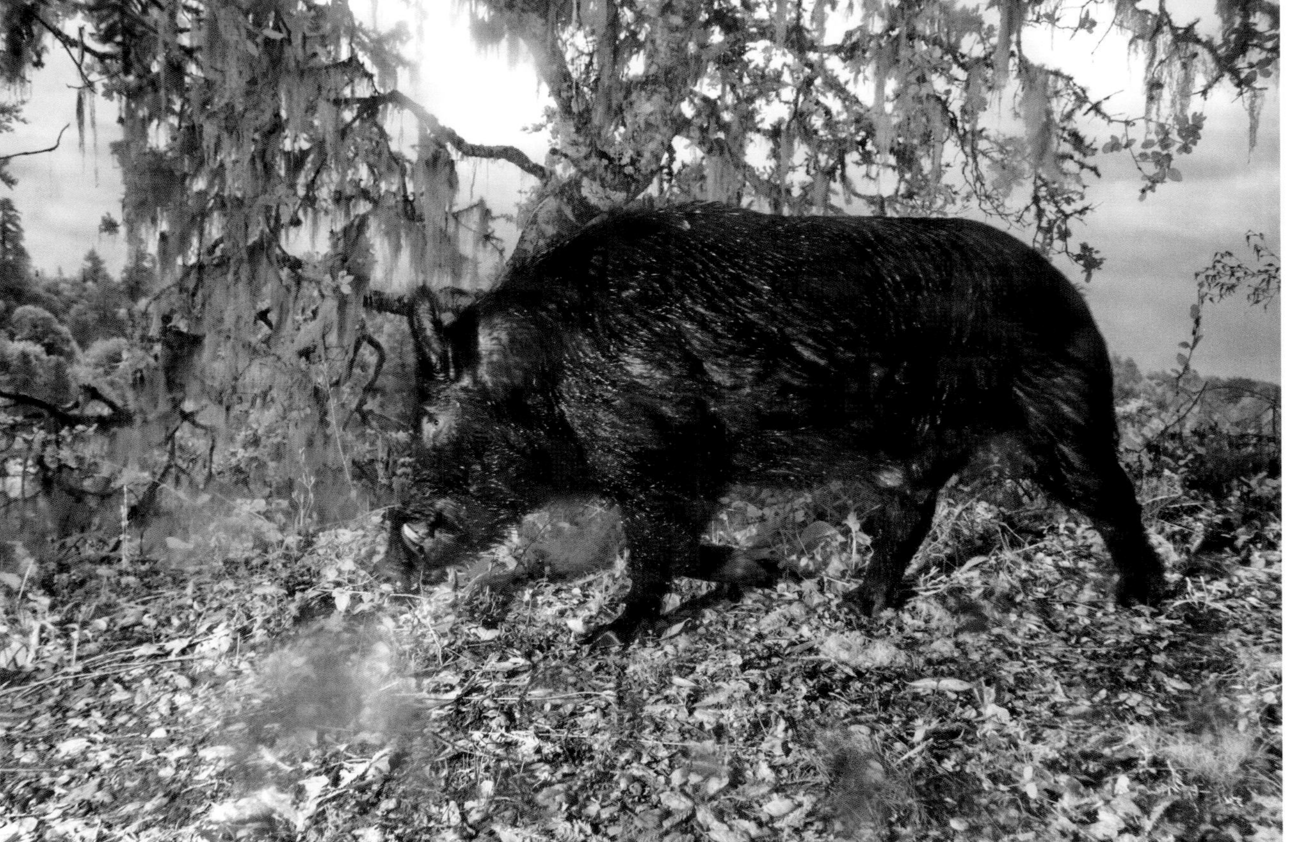

A massive feral pig weighing several hundred pounds searches for acorns and tubers. They are an ecological scourge in Monterey Bay. A single group of pigs can uproot acres of habitat in just a few nights.

Feral Pig, Wilder Ranch State Park

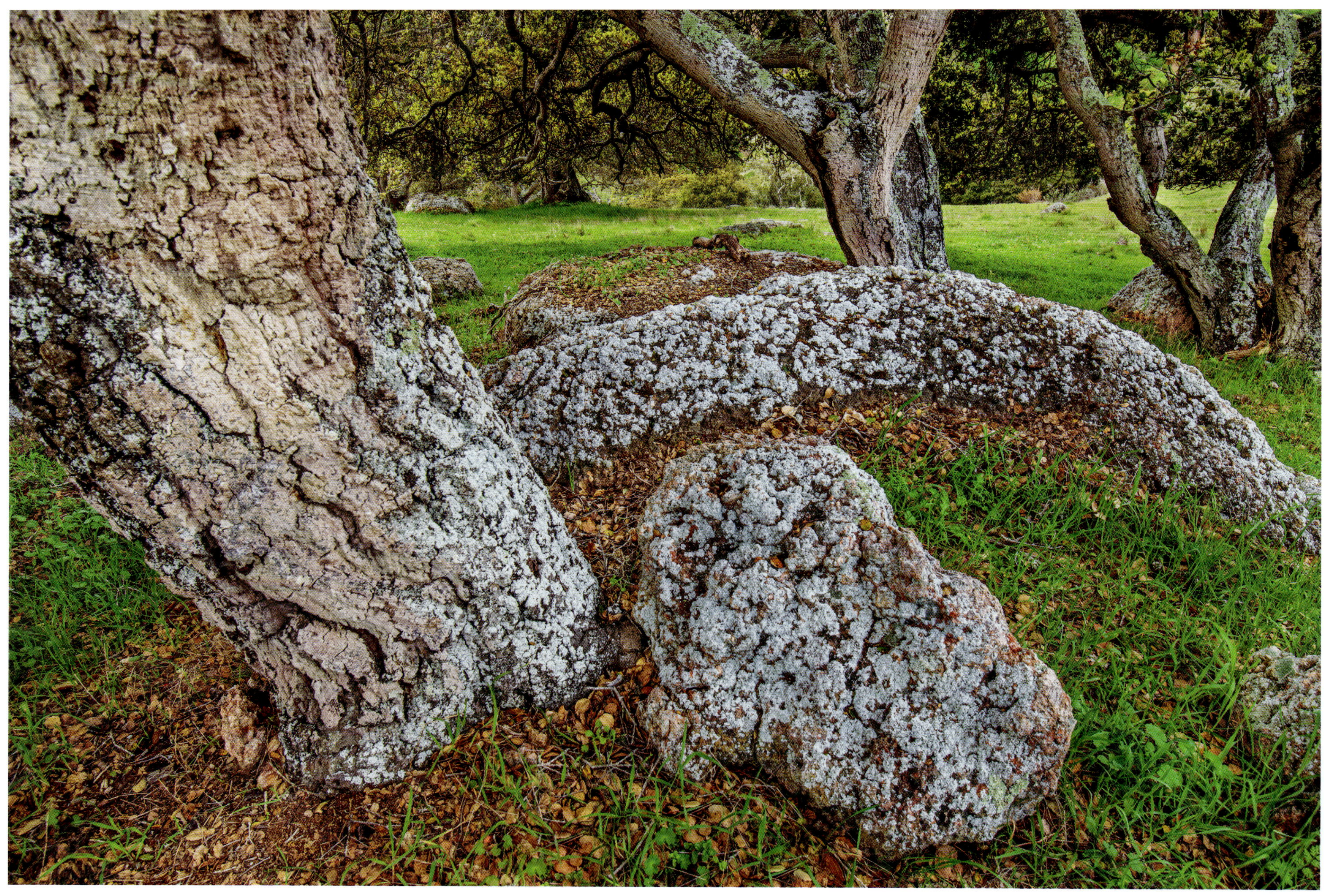

The weathered trunks of coast live oaks echo the worn granite boulders next to them on Rocks Ranch, named for the numerous outcrops that dot the landscape.

Coast Live Oaks, Rocks Ranch

opposite: Dry brush under an old oak flares up during a prescribed burn conducted by State Parks to reduce the buildup of forest fuel and encourage new plant growth, as was done in indigenous times.

Fire, Wilder Ranch State Park

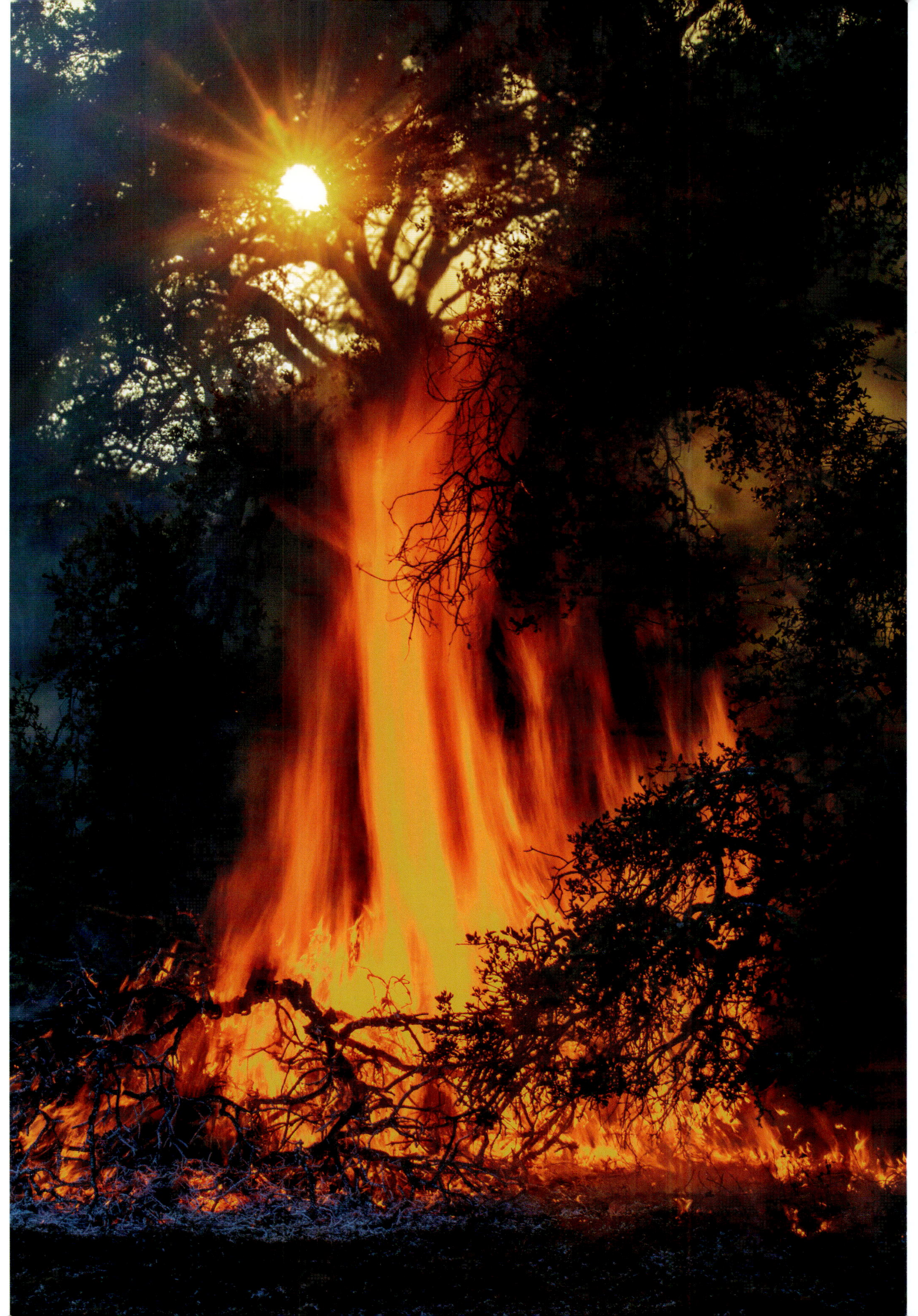

CHAPARRAL

The twisted trunks of brittle-leaf manzanitas form an impenetrable thicket of chaparral, an evergreen community of hardy plants. These mature shrubs live near a ridge that catches fog, which promotes the growth of lichen on their branches.

MANZANITAS, STAR CREEK RANCH

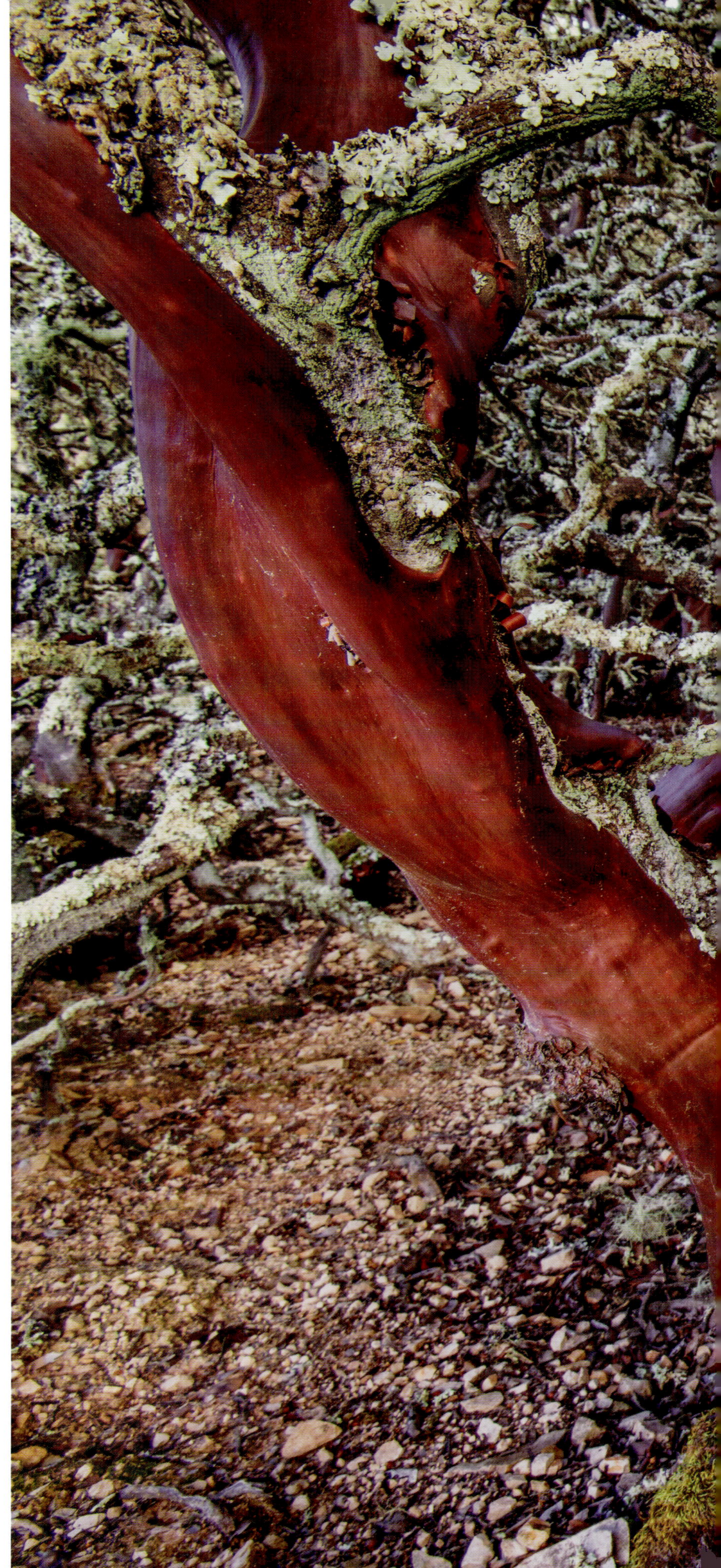

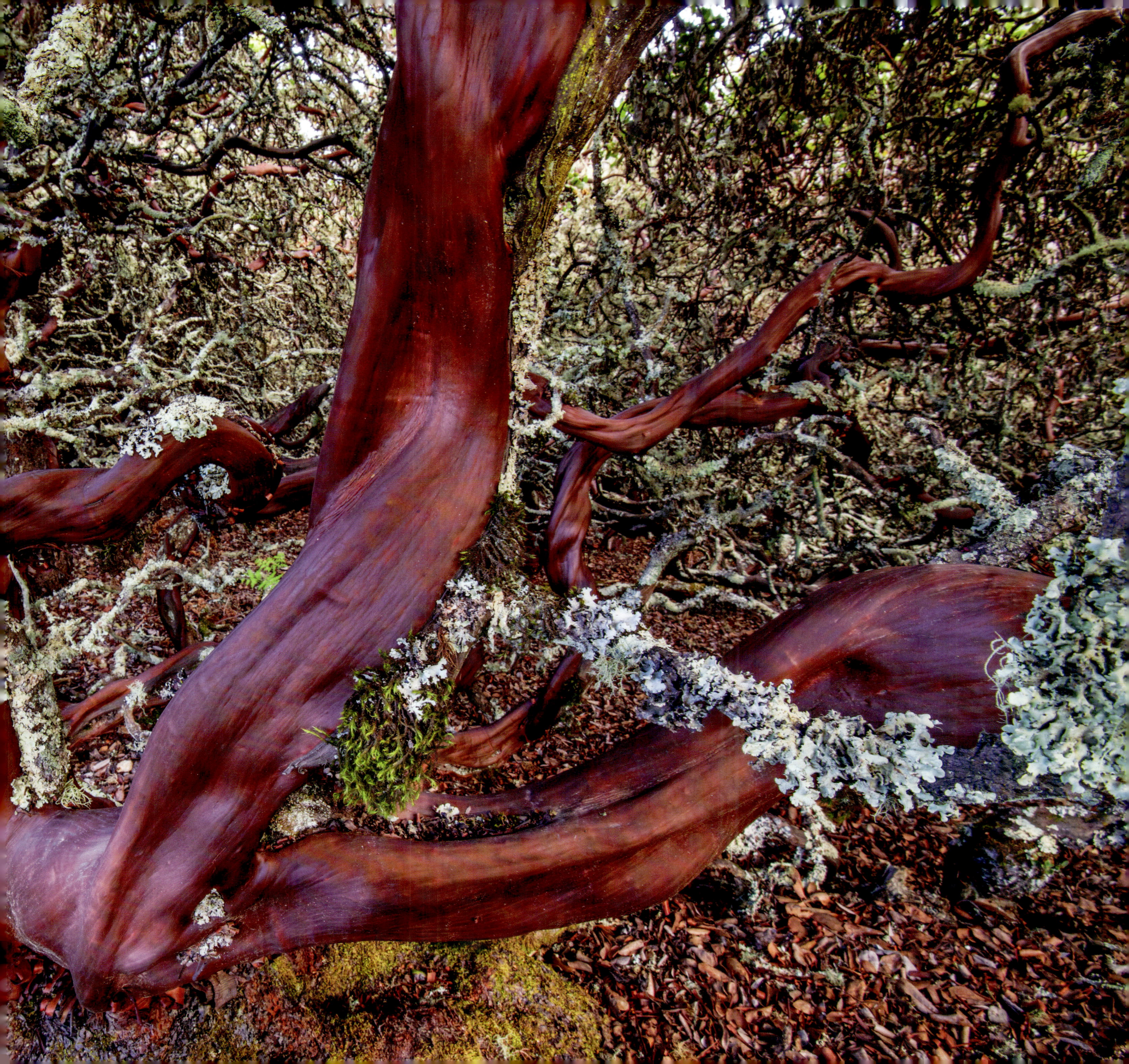

Downslope from a knobcone pine, ecologist Grey Hayes examines rare manzanitas
on the slopes of Chalk Mountain, a habitat valued for its unusual plant life.
A few months after this image was made, the 2020 CZU fire transformed this habitat.
To see what it looked like after the fire, check page 78.

ECOLOGIST WITH MANZANITAS, BIG BASIN REDWOODS STATE PARK

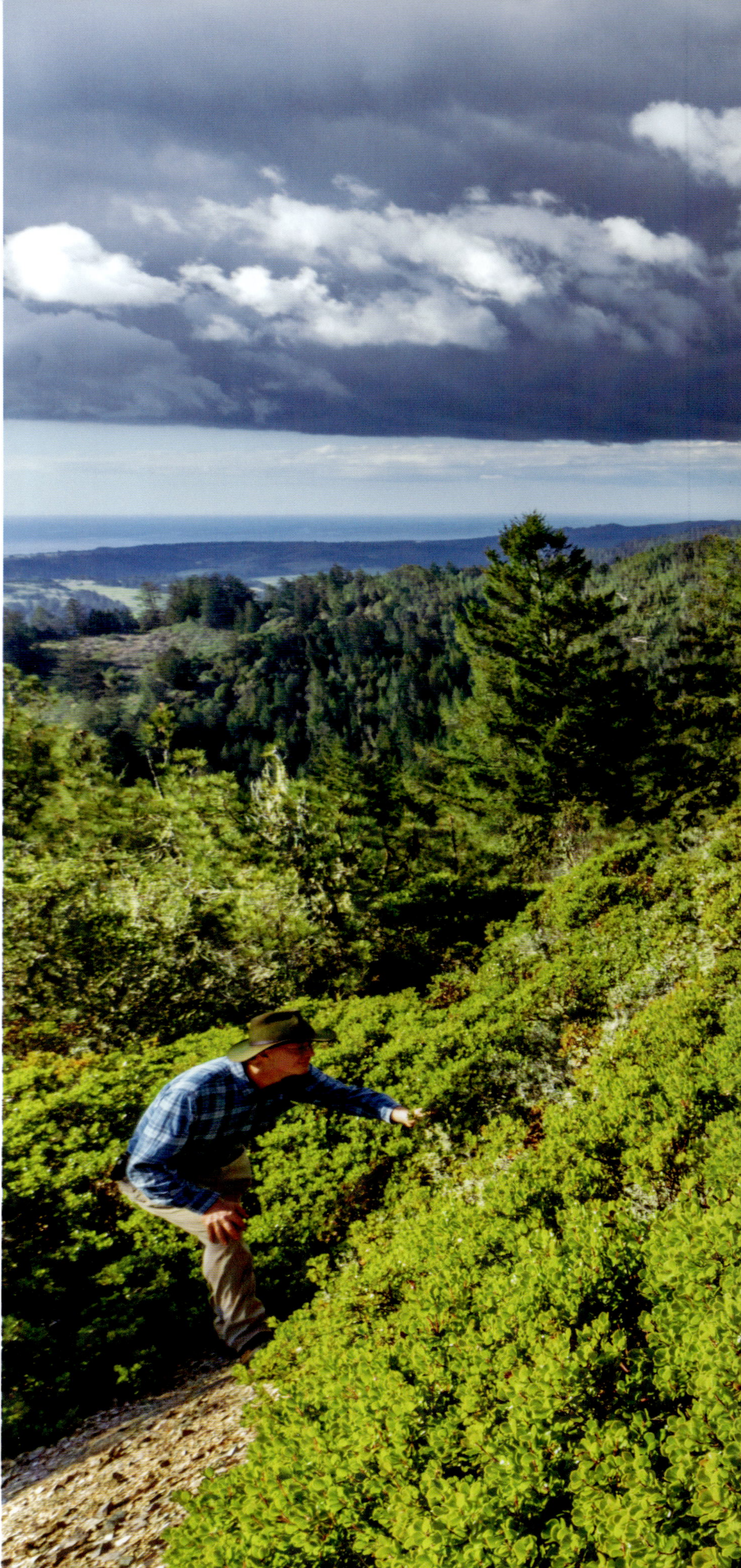

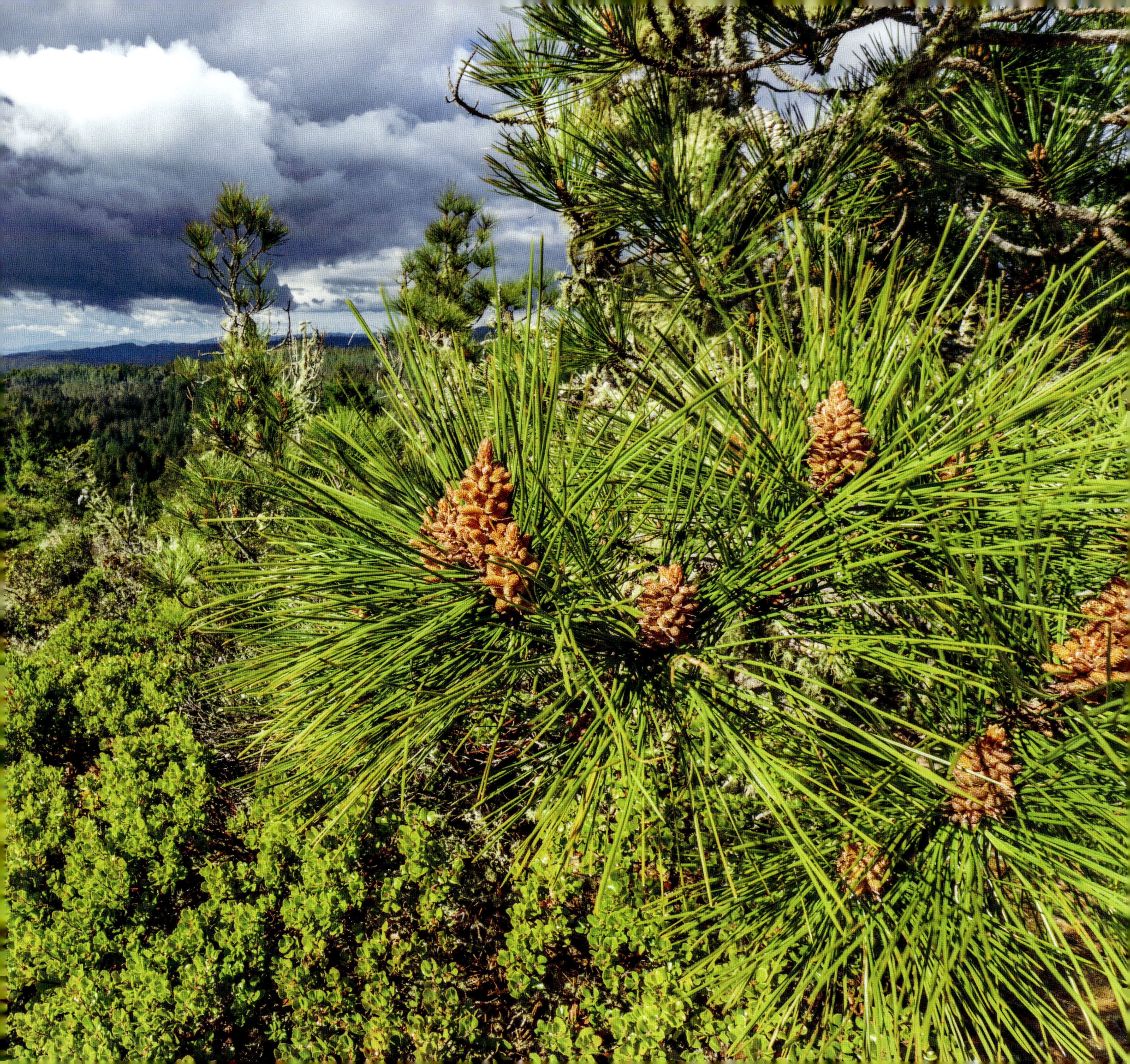

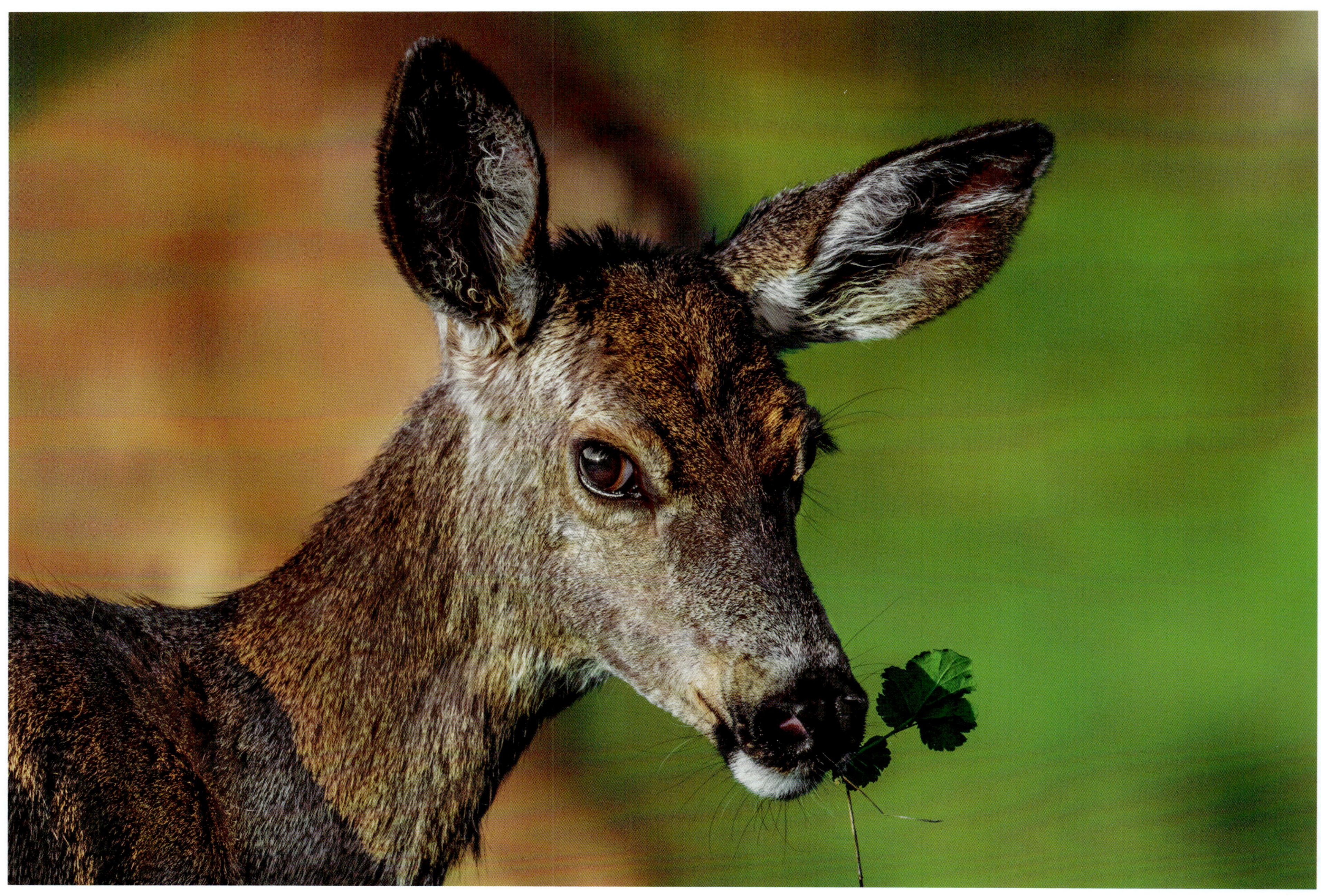

Blacktail deer are apex browsers across a wide range of habitats in the Monterey Bay, from deep forest to open grassland, with oak woodland and chaparral in between. They have expanded into suburban areas as well, where they have altered their behavior to fit into more confined territories.

BLACKTAIL DEER, RANCHO REFUGIO

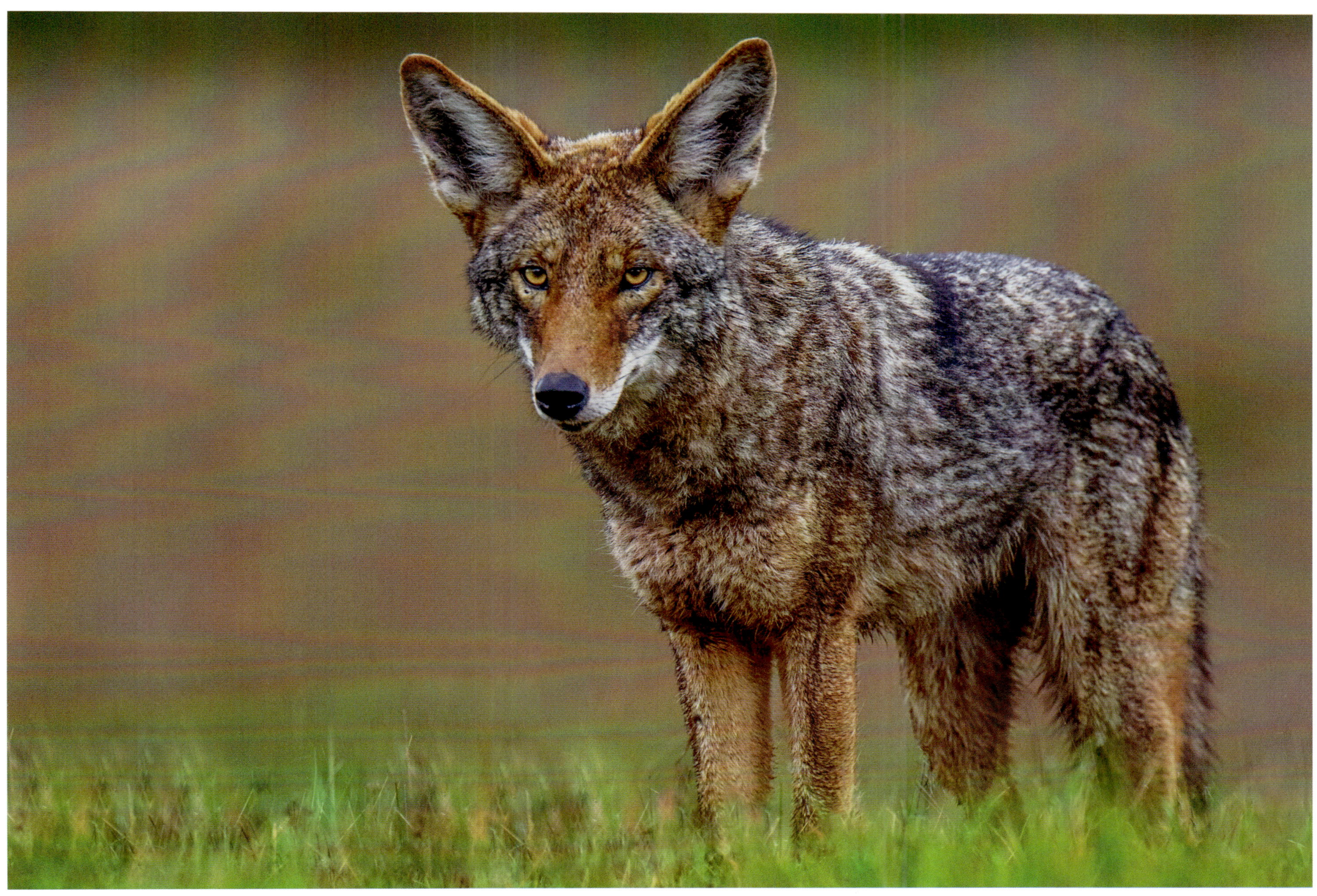

Coyotes are adept at adapting to new opportunities. They will eat anything from deer to fish to berries. They are flexible in their social organization and can live in packs or operate as individuals. After wolves disappeared from Monterey Bay, their niche enlarged, but since mountain lions rebounded, it appears coyote numbers may be decreasing in some areas, which benefits smaller predators such as gray foxes and bobcats.

COYOTE, RANCHO REFUGIO

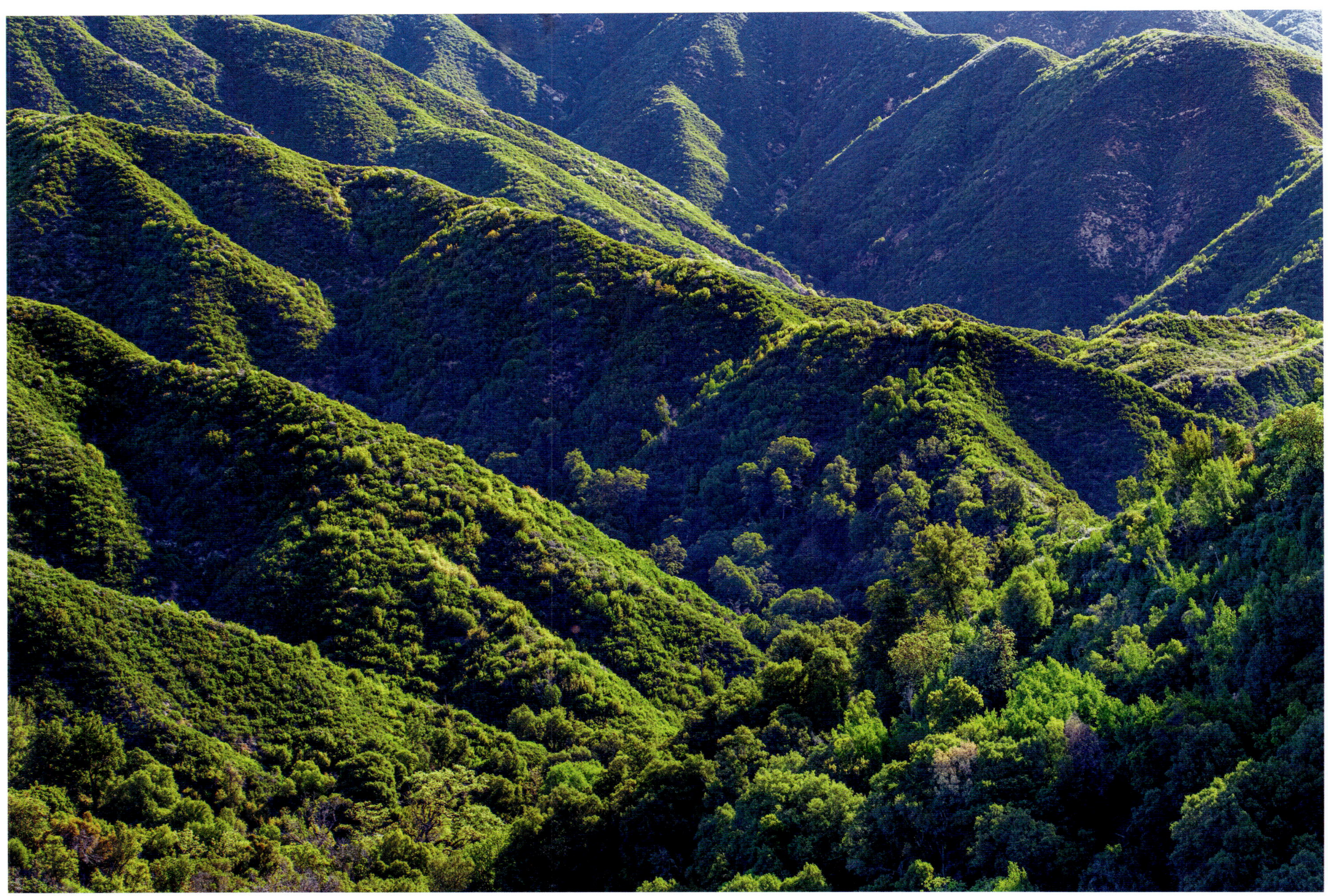

The chaparral-covered slopes in Big Sur's interior may look inviting from a distance, but up close they are a tight tangle of leathery leaves and rigid branches. The word "chaparral" is derived from a Spanish term for dense, thorny thickets. Fittingly, the leggings horseback riders wear to protect themselves from chaparral are called "chaps."

Chaparral, Los Padres National Forest

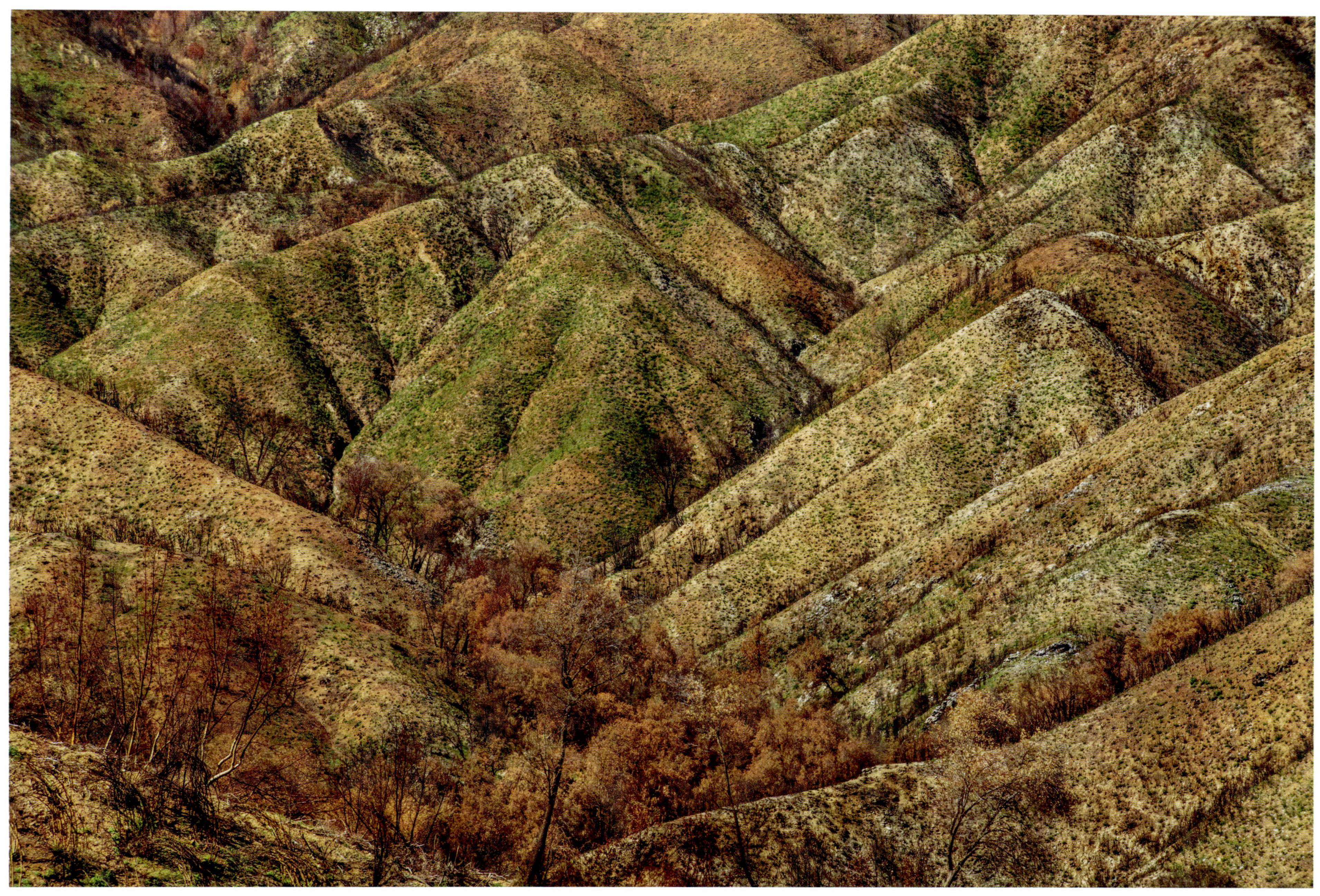

A massive wildfire in 2020 scorched 200 square miles of Big Sur backcountry, much of it chaparral. The following spring, the slopes show a flush of green as the vegetation begins to recover. Mature chaparral is often made up of shrubs of similar age and size that have grown back together since they last burned.

Burned Chaparral, Los Padres National Forest

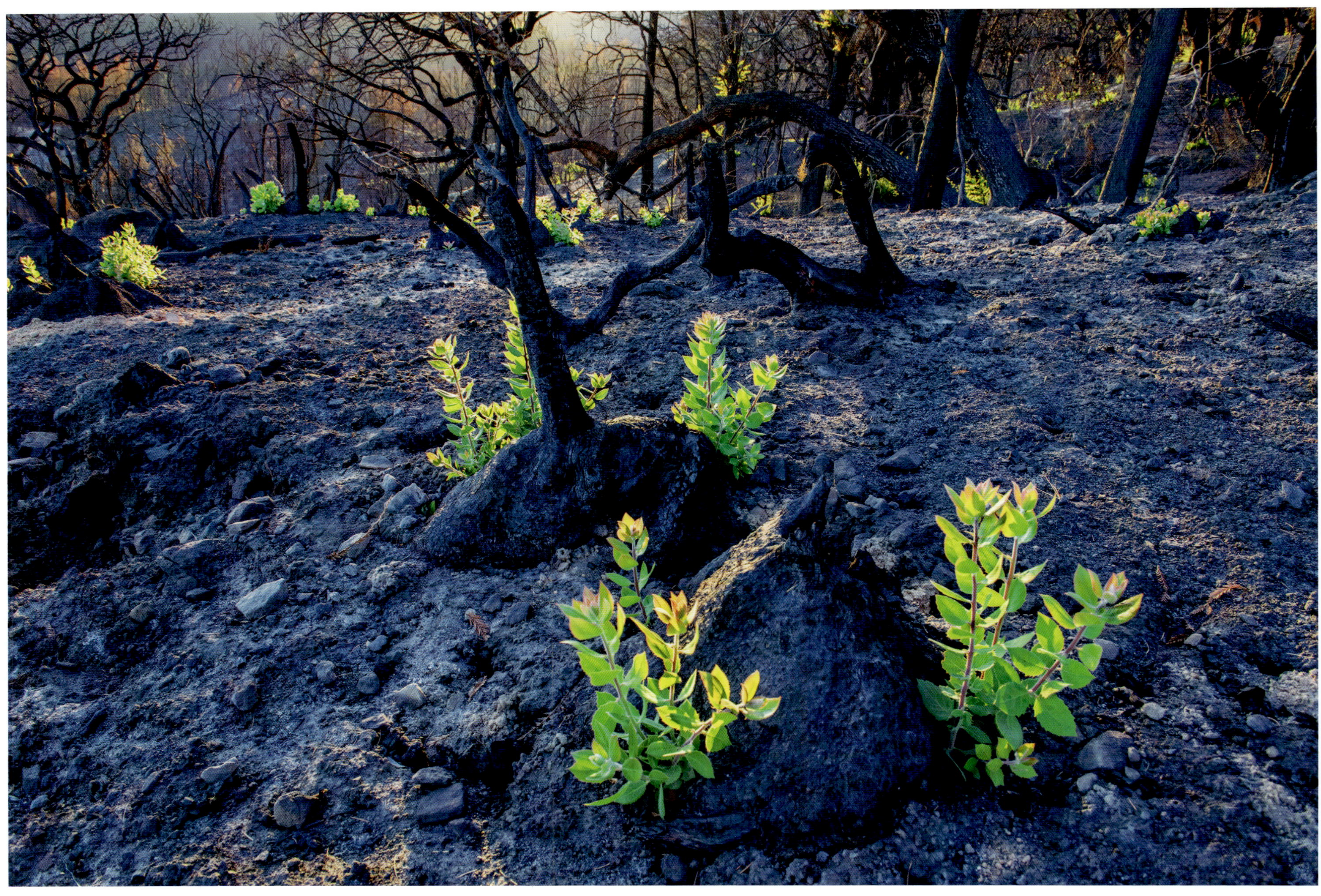

In a fire-blackened landscape fresh sprouts emerge from manzanita burls—ground-level, woody masses that are fed by a deep root system and help the plants regrow.

Manzanitas after Fire, Big Basin Redwoods State Park

opposite: Santa Cruz cypress cones reveal their seeds after a fire. This rare endemic tree has evolved with fire. It requires heat from a blaze to open the cones, releasing the seeds inside. A year later, a young seedling was seen growing under the dangling cones.

Santa Cruz Cypress Seeds, Bonny Doon | *Photo by Amy Patten*

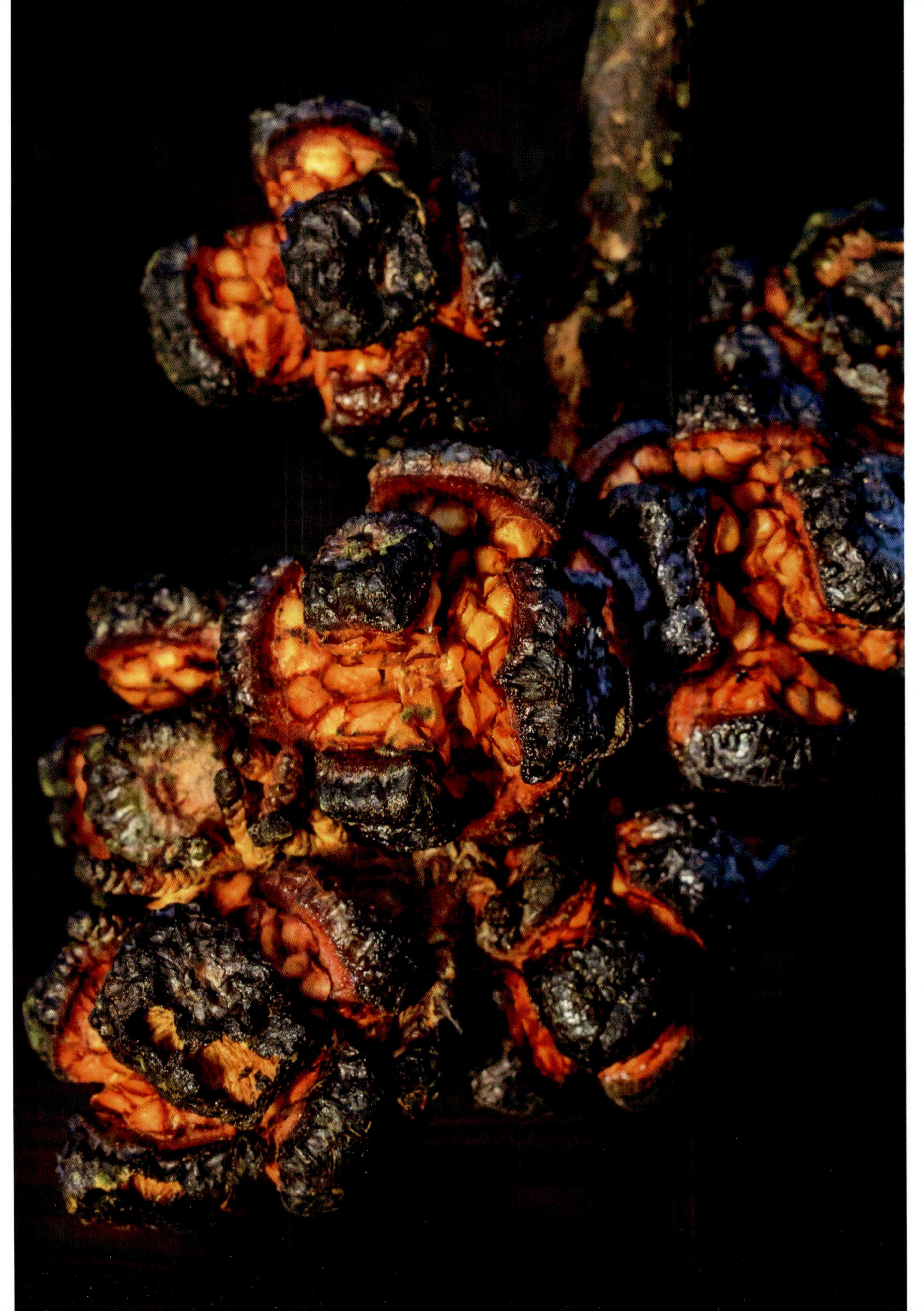

GRASSLAND

Coastal prairie is an endangered grassland habitat. Much of it has been converted for human use, from residential development to agriculture. Where coastal prairie still occurs, its plant composition is now a mix of native and non-native species. This image shows native California oat grass and spreading rush as well as non-native rattlesnake grass.

COASTAL PRAIRIE, RANCHO REFUGIO

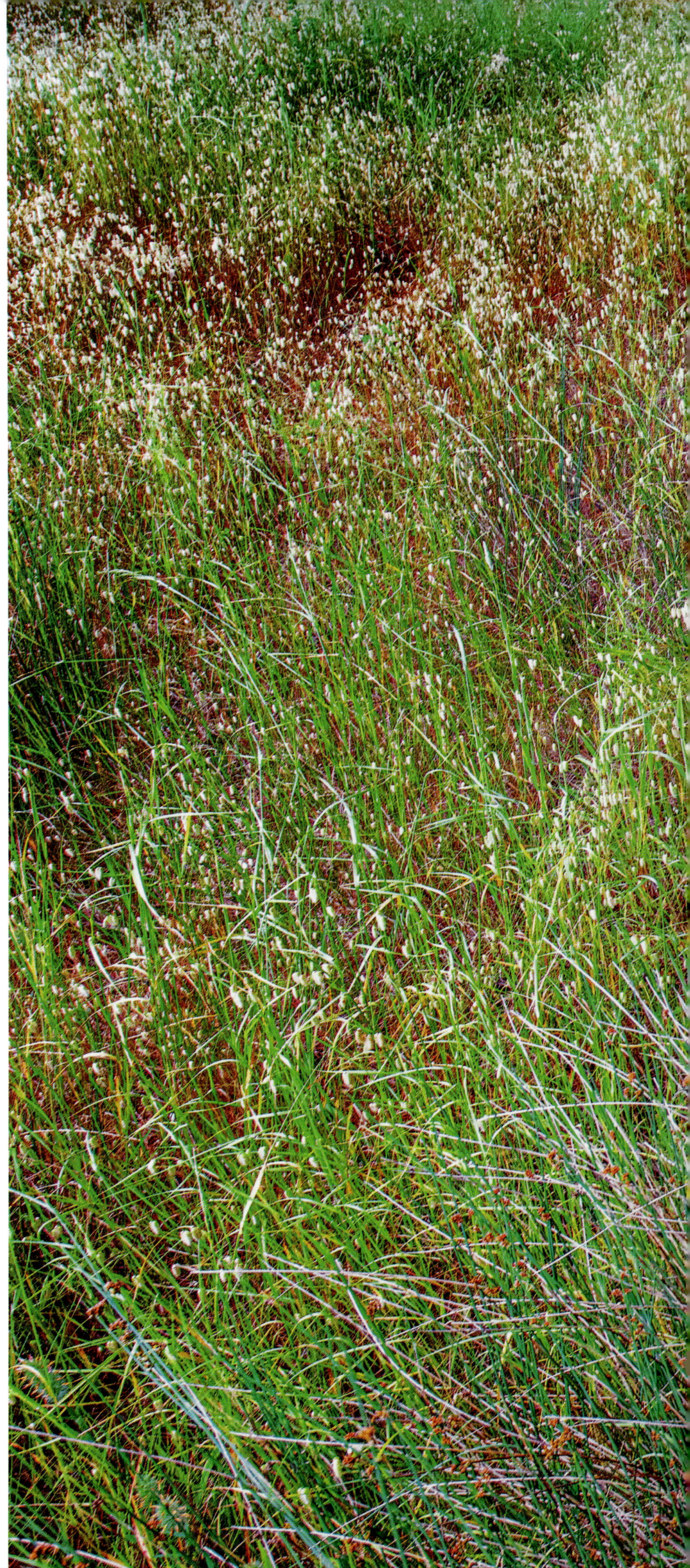

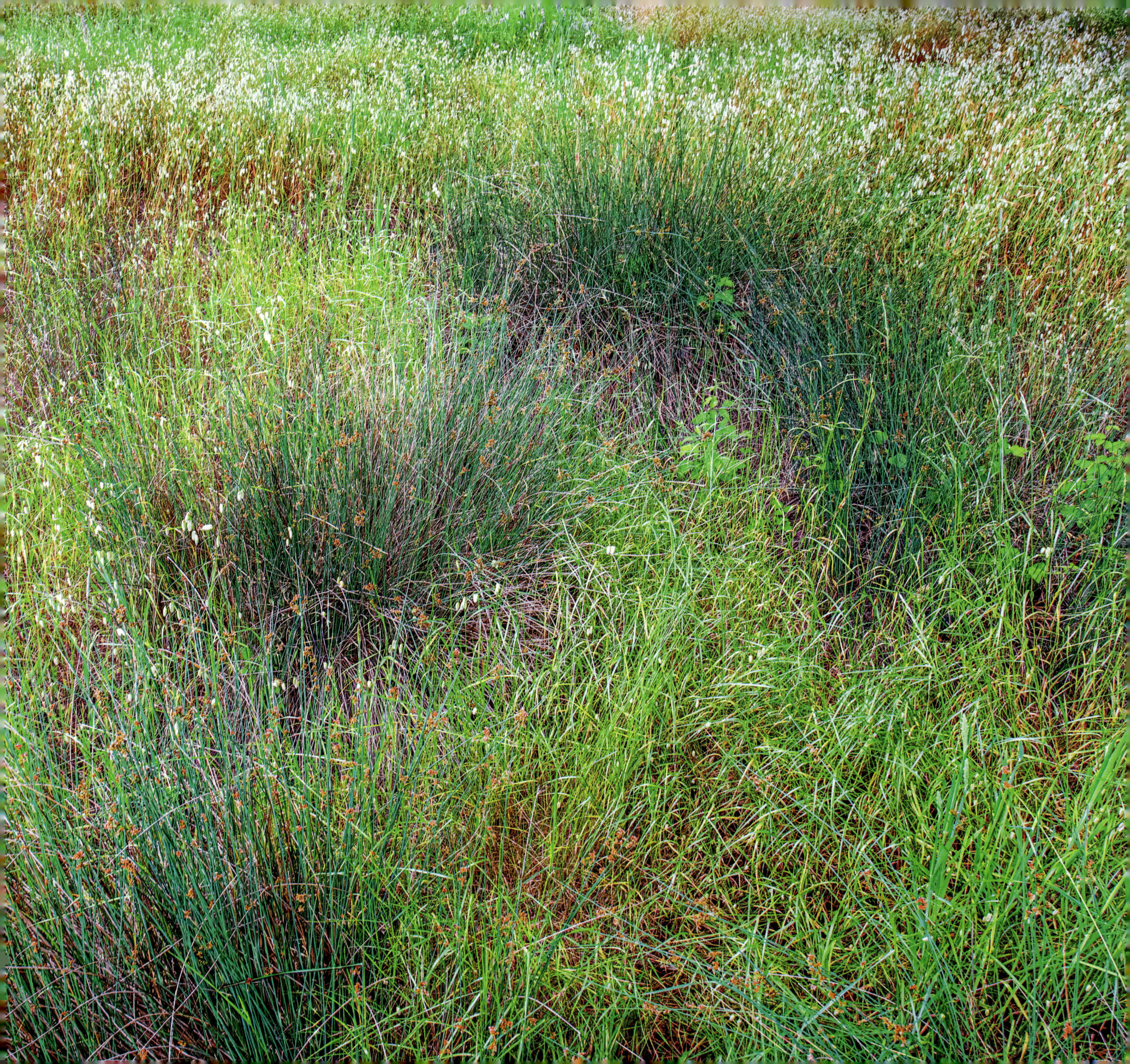

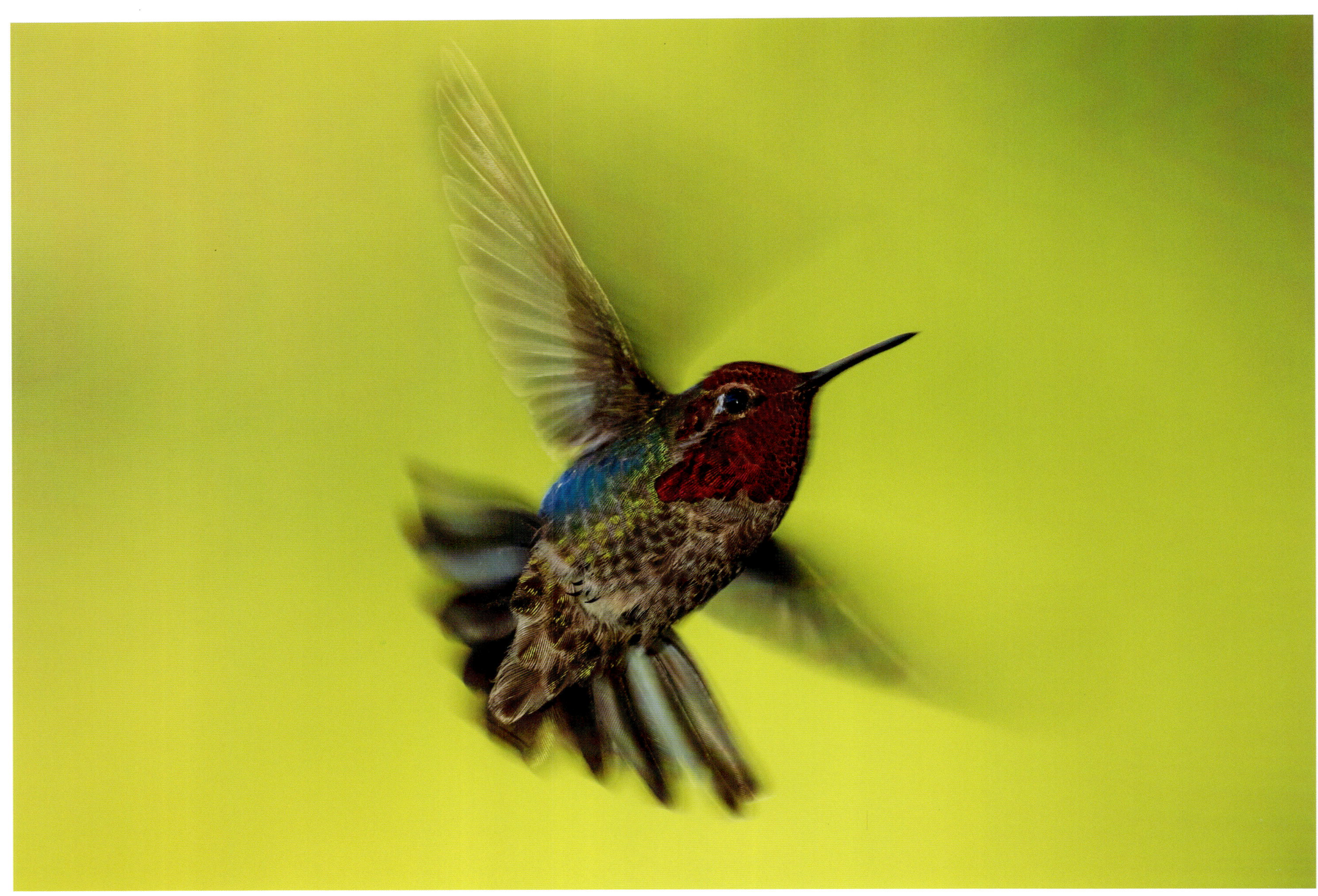

Anna's hummingbirds are year-round residents in Monterey Bay today, but in the early 20th century, they bred only in southern California and Baja. The planting of exotic flowering trees and gardens along the Pacific coast provided more nectar and nesting sites, enabling the tiny fliers to expand their breeding range as far north as British Columbia.

Anna's Hummingbird, Rancho Refugio

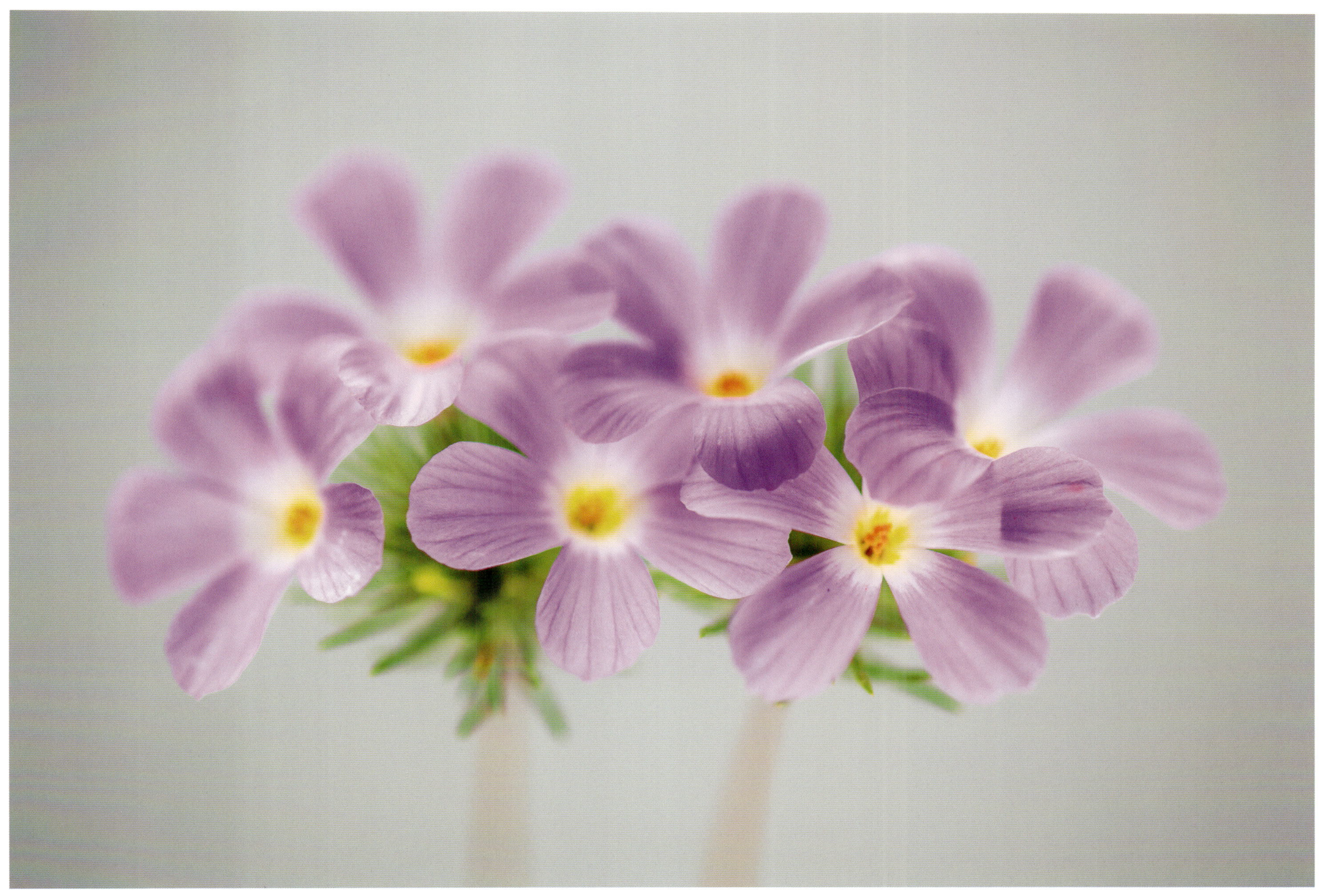

This rare and endangered wildflower is actually quite delicate and hard to find. Related varieties used to inhabit coastal prairies and other habitats around Monterey Bay, but its current range is unknown because it has disappeared from many places.

Large-flower Linanthus, UCSC Arboretum and Botanic Garden

FOLLOWING PAGES: Blue blazes of sky lupine carpet the grassy slopes of a ridge in the Santa Lucia Range.

Sky Lupines, Ventana Wilderness

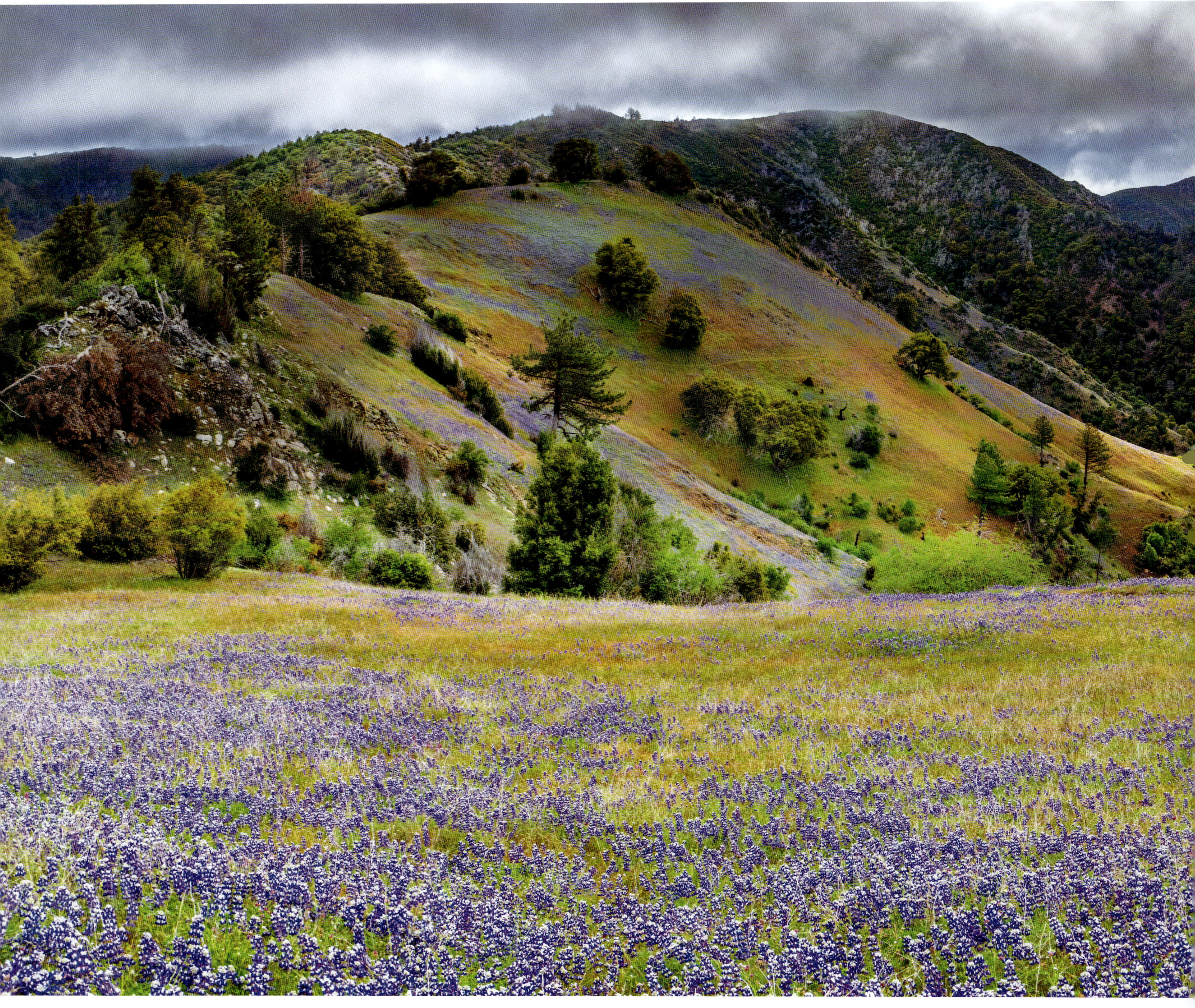

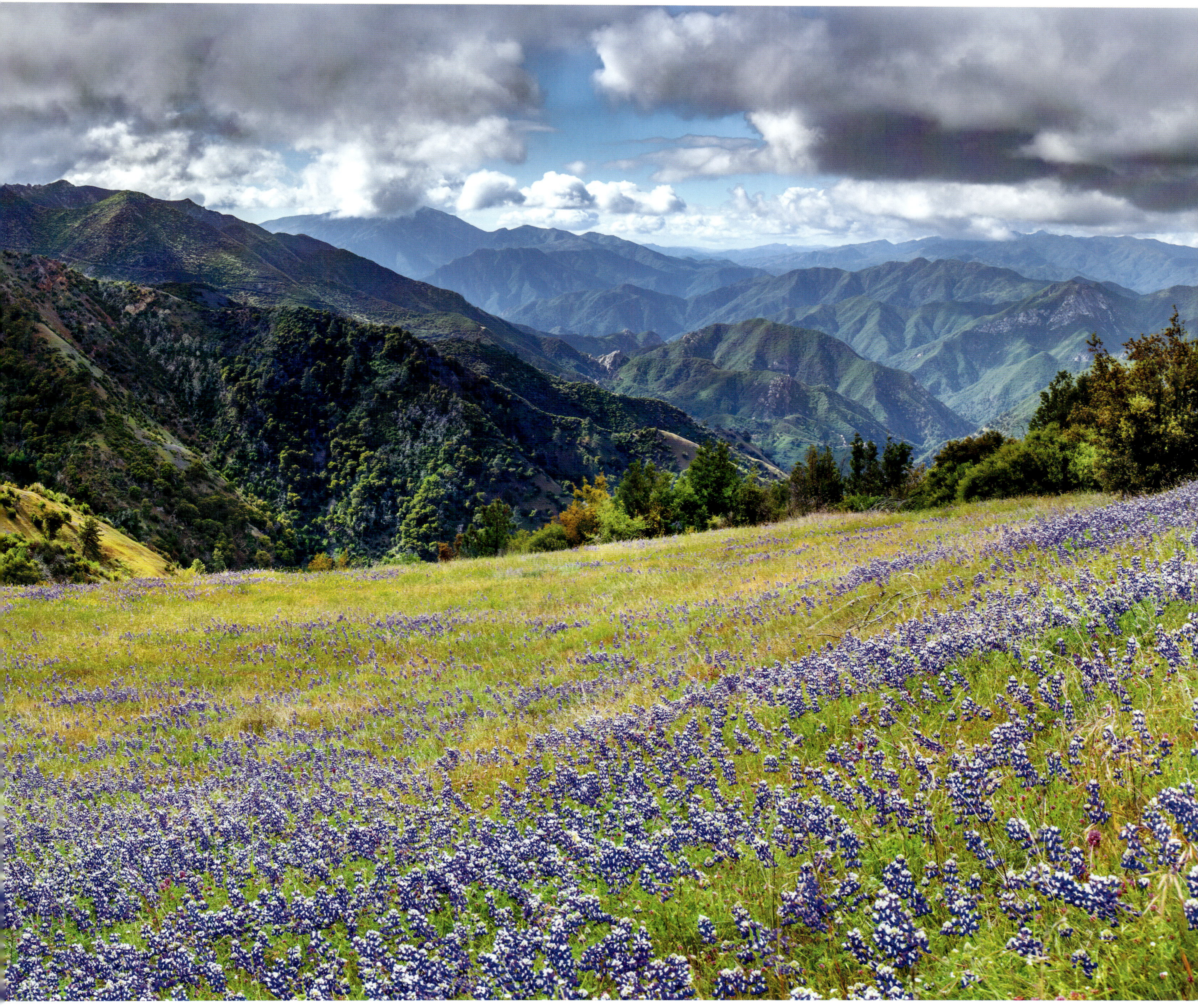

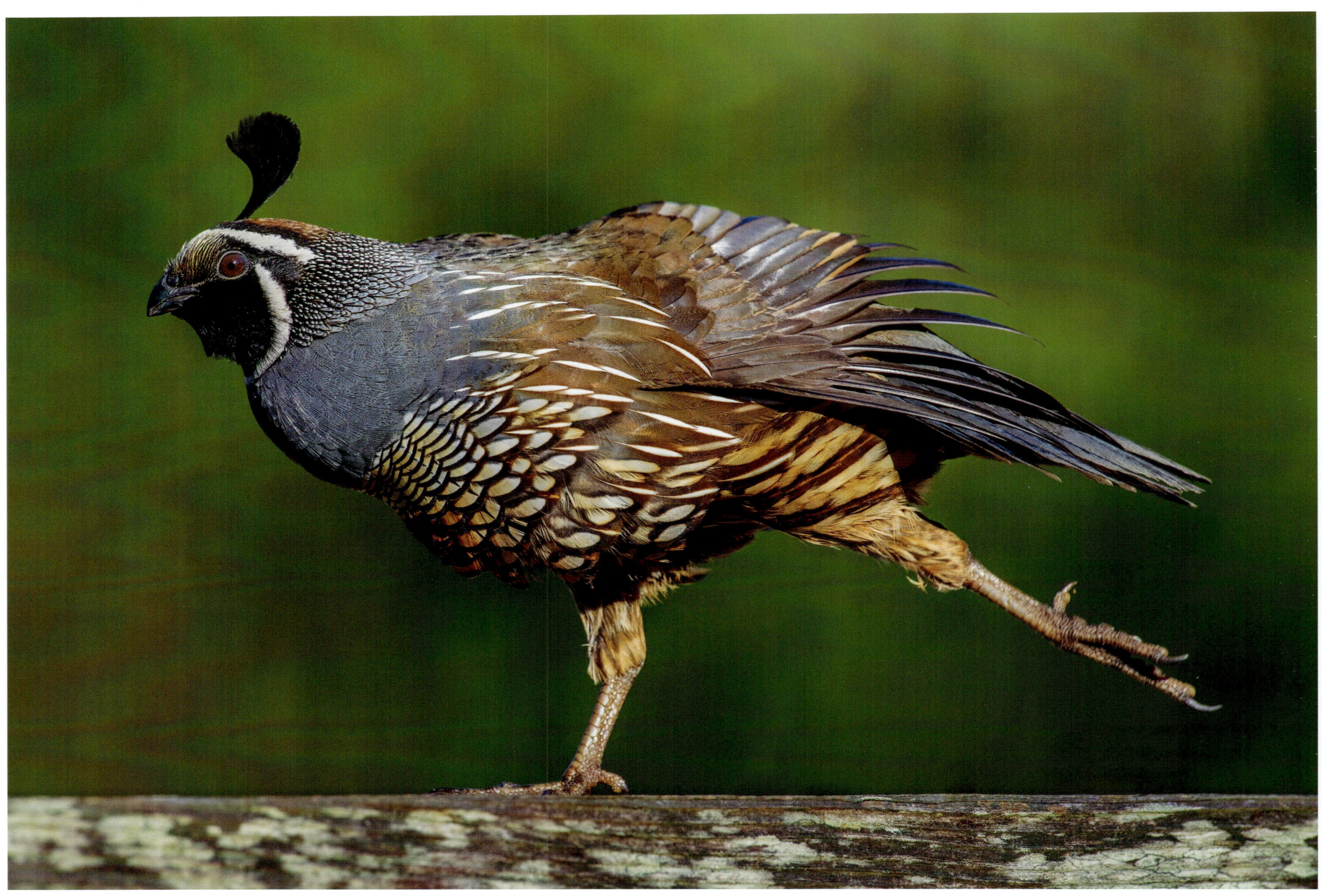

A handsome male California quail stretches while perched on a lookout post; his
family forages in tall grass nearby. California's state bird makes itself known in
Monterey Bay's dryland habitats, where its sharp "Chi-cá-go" cries are unmistakable.

CALIFORNIA QUAIL, RANCHO REFUGIO

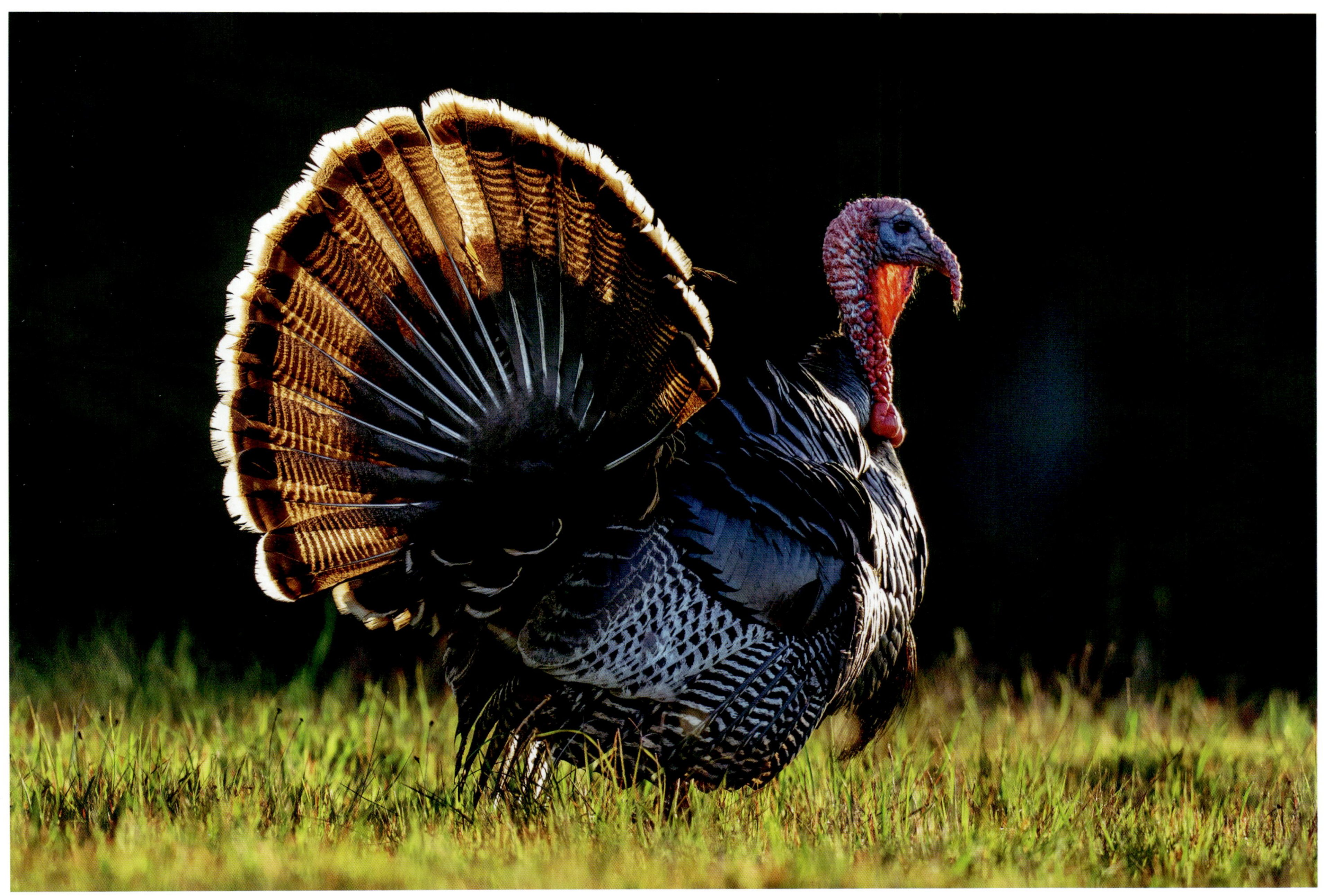

Wild turkeys were introduced to California from Texas as game birds, and now they are spreading rapidly around Monterey Bay and throughout the state. With their wide-ranging appetites for everything from seeds to roots to insects, they adapt easily to the bay's diverse habitats. In grasslands, they appear to have little competition from native species.

WILD TURKEY, RANCHO REFUGIO

The rugged Gabilan Range that parallels the eastern side of the Salinas Valley must be seen from the air to appreciate its expansive nature. South of the Pinnacles the range consists largely of grasslands, with few trees even in its valleys. Virtually all of it is privately held as ranchland.

AERIAL VIEW, GABILAN RANGE

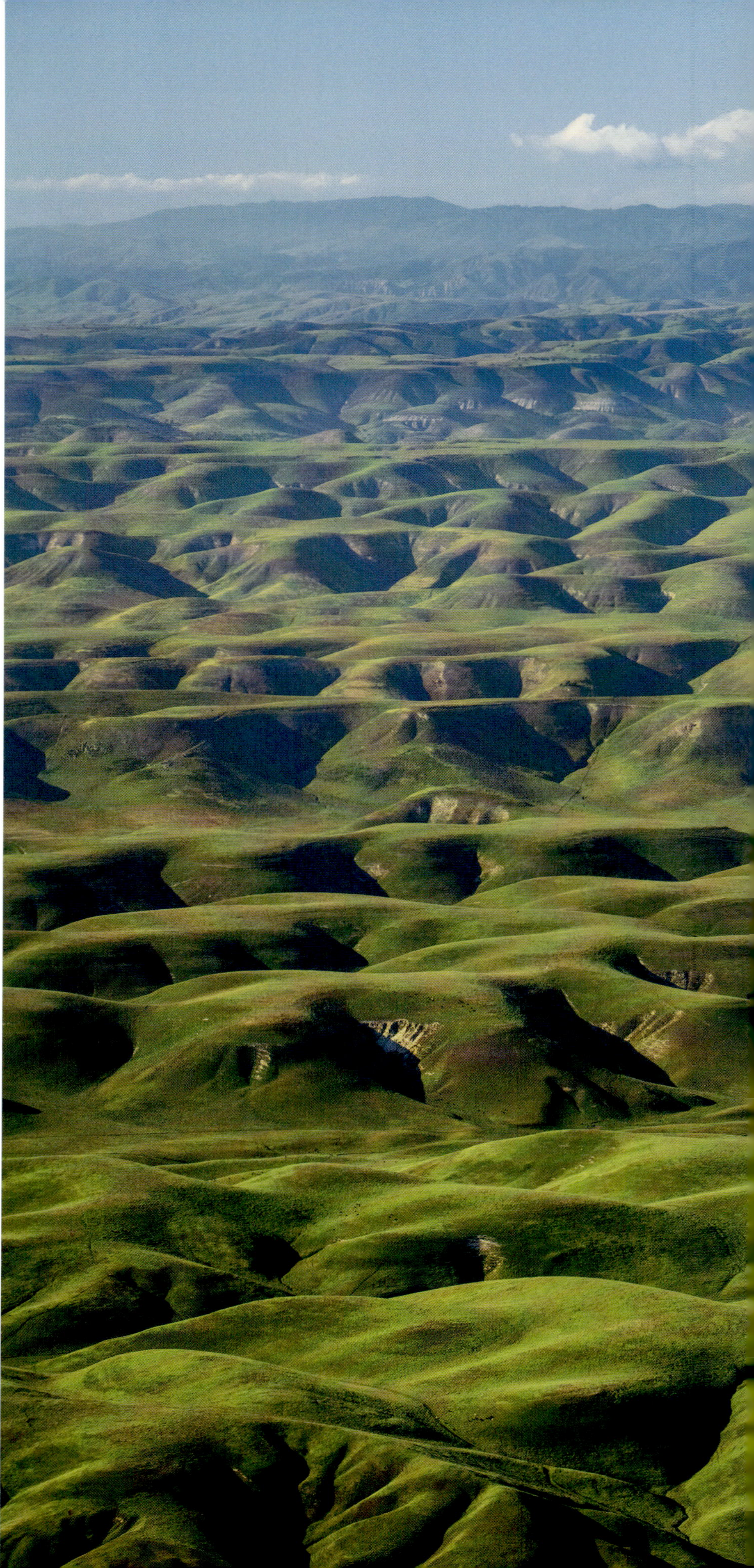

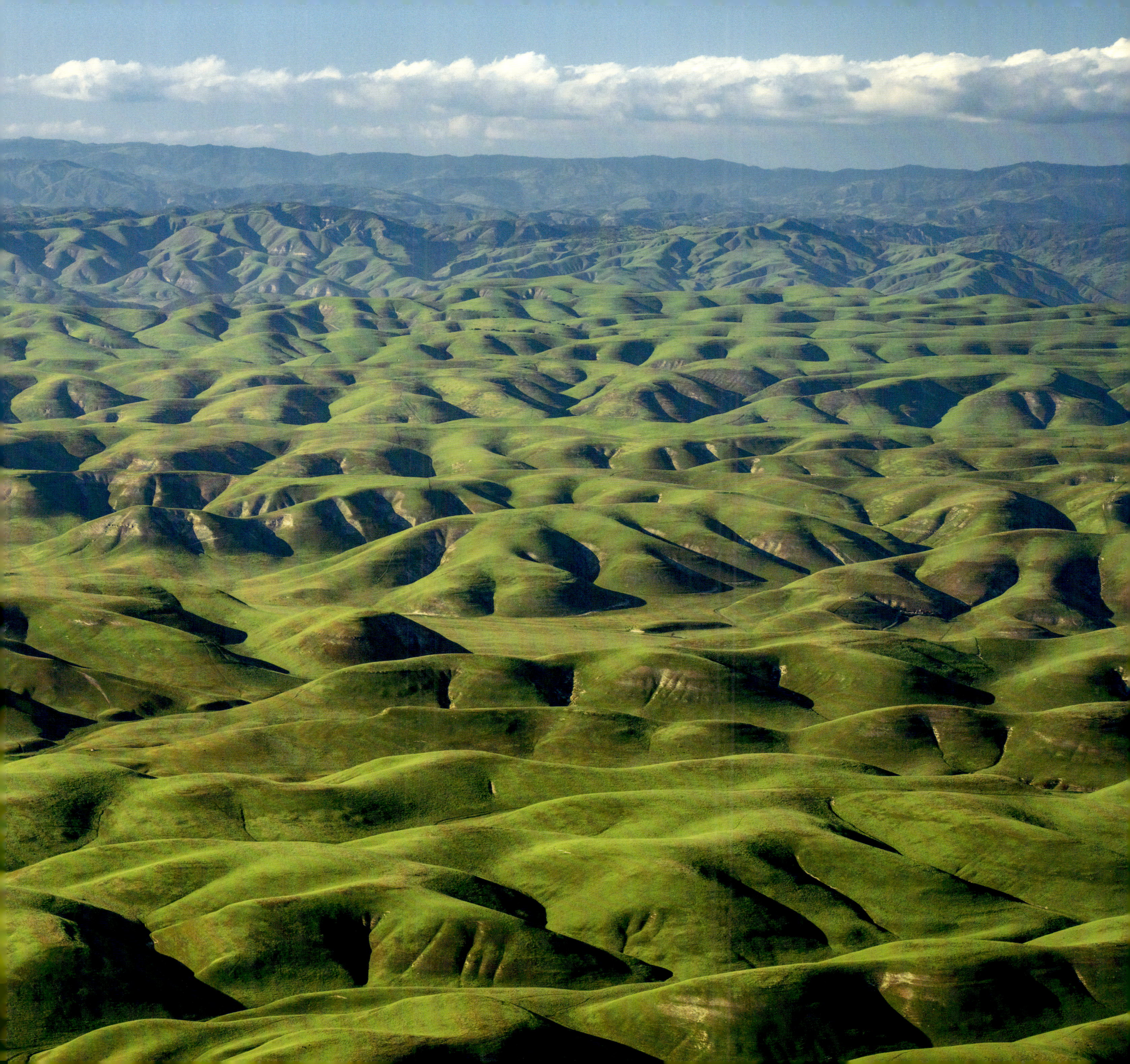

WETLAND

Free-flowing freshwater streams are precious aquatic arteries in Monterey Bay's onshore ecosystems, providing vital corridors that connect to the bay.

FALL CREEK, HENRY COWELL REDWOODS STATE PARK

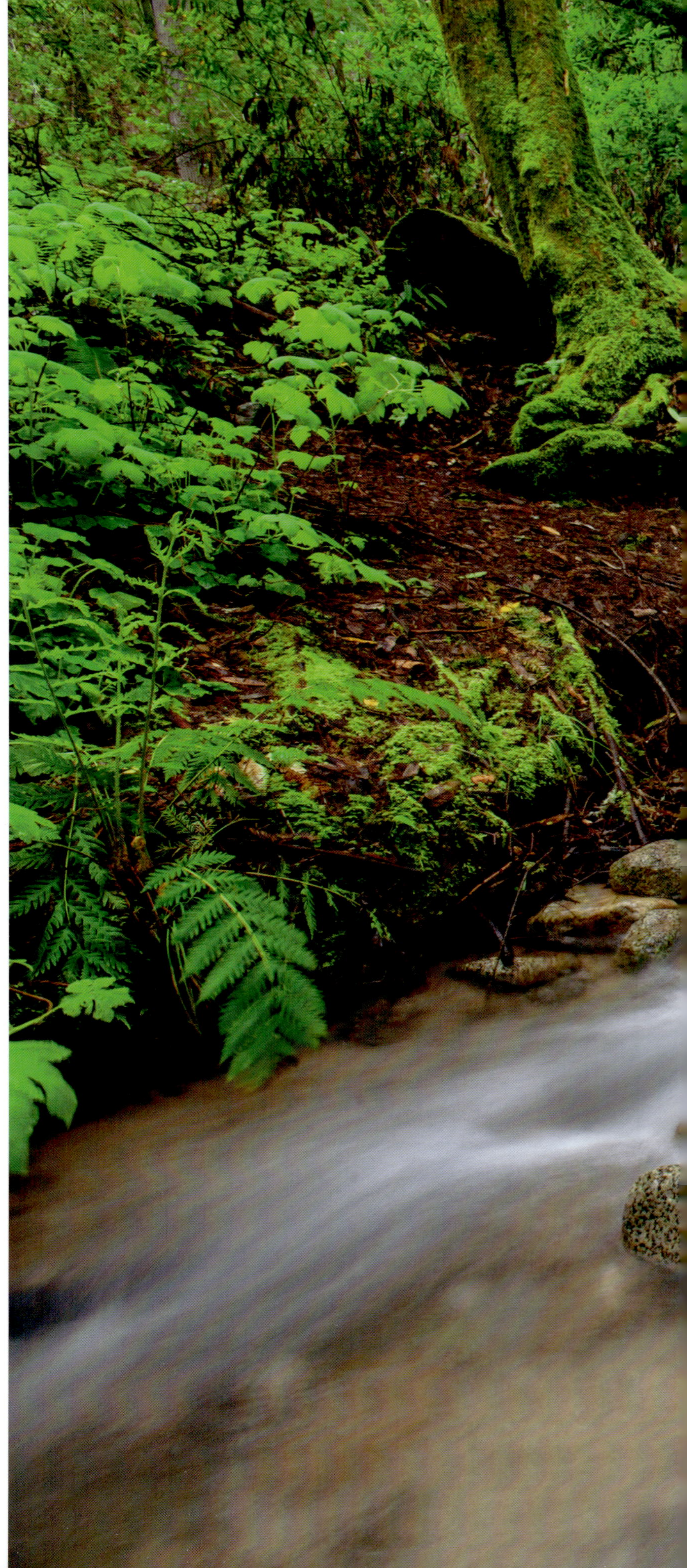

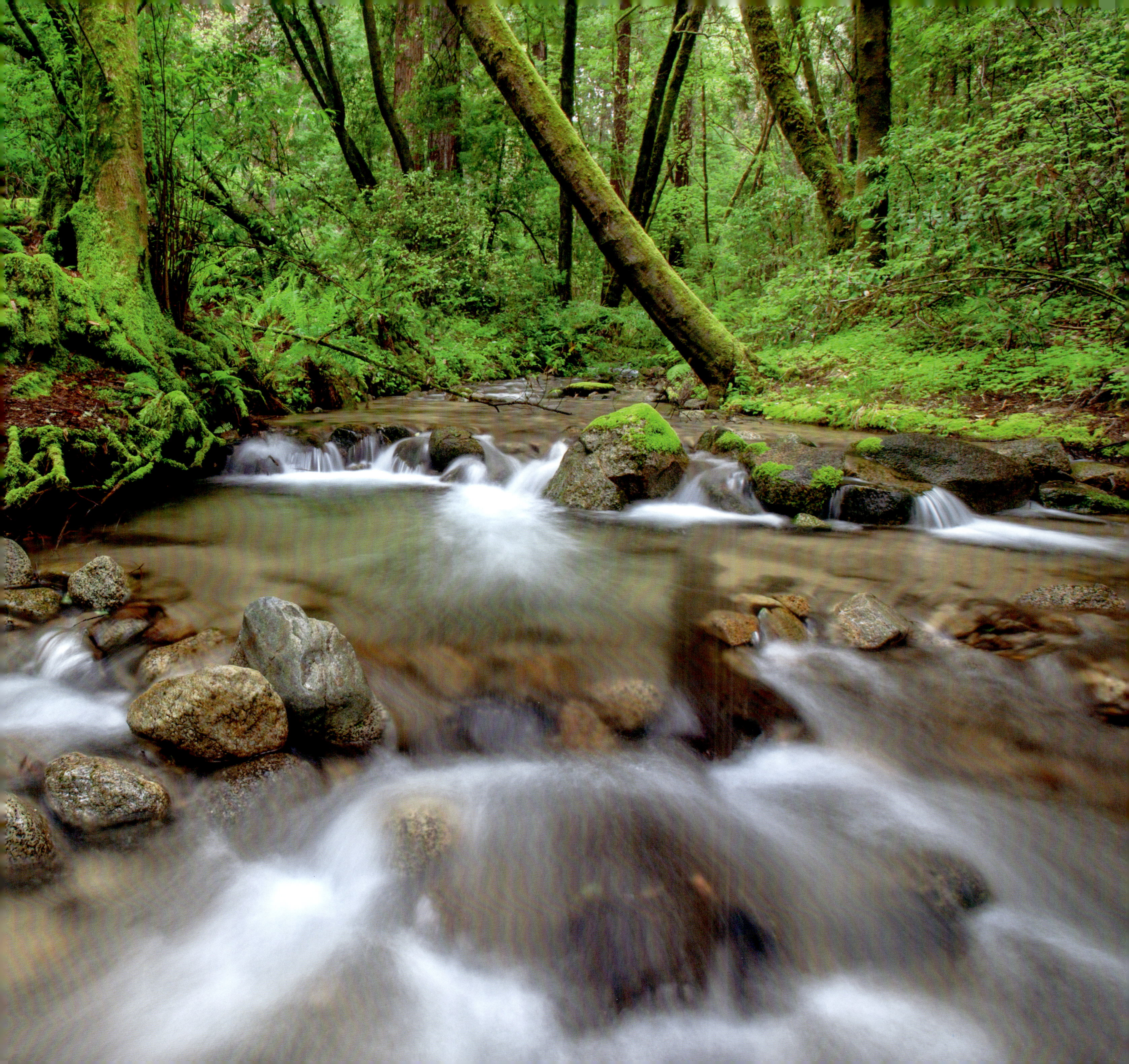

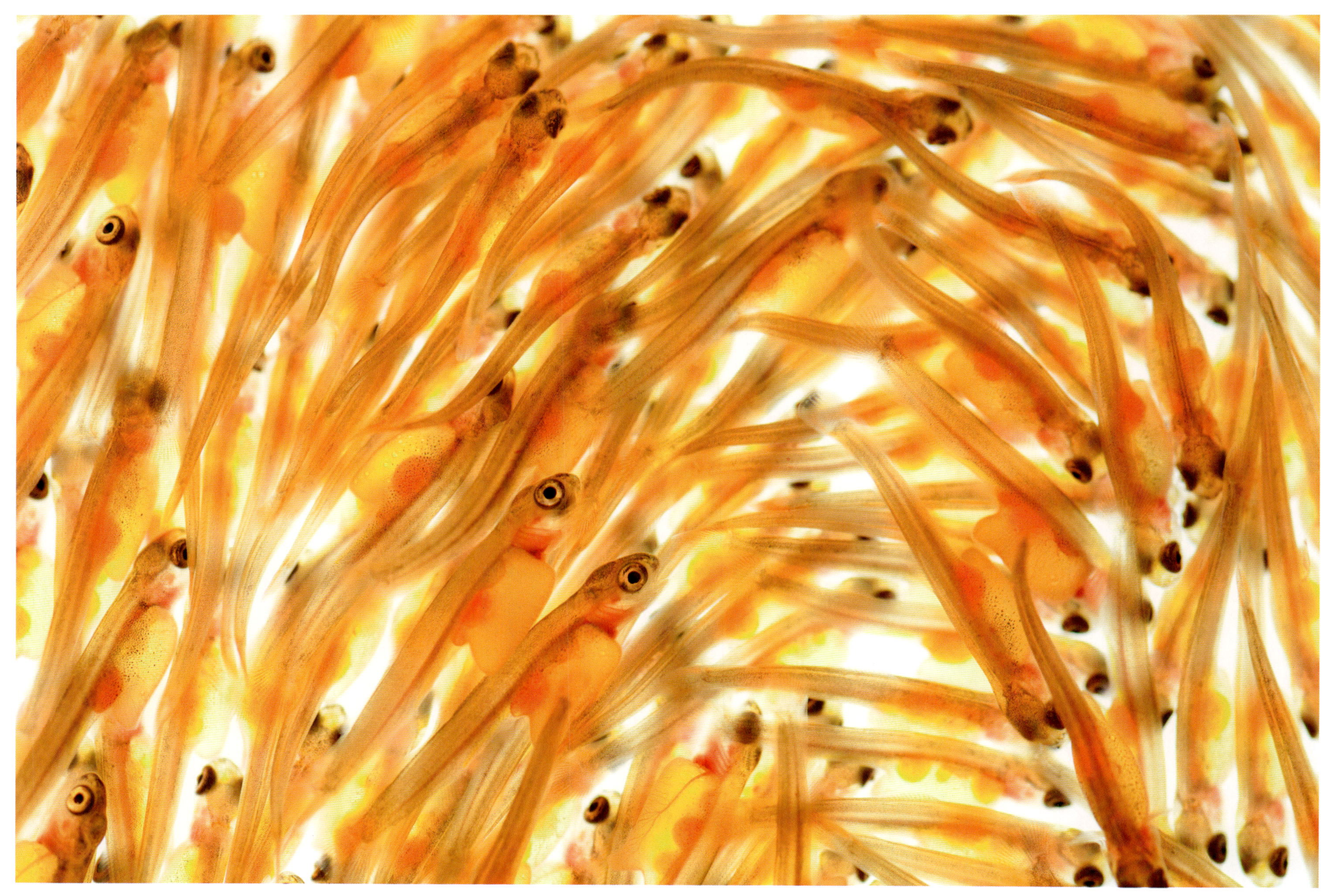

In the wild, steelhead fry are vulnerable; few survive to adulthood. On a tributary of
Scott Creek, the Monterey Bay Salmon and Trout Project hatchery nurtures fry until
they are big enough to be released safely to make their way downstream to the sea.

Steelhead Trout Fry, Swanton

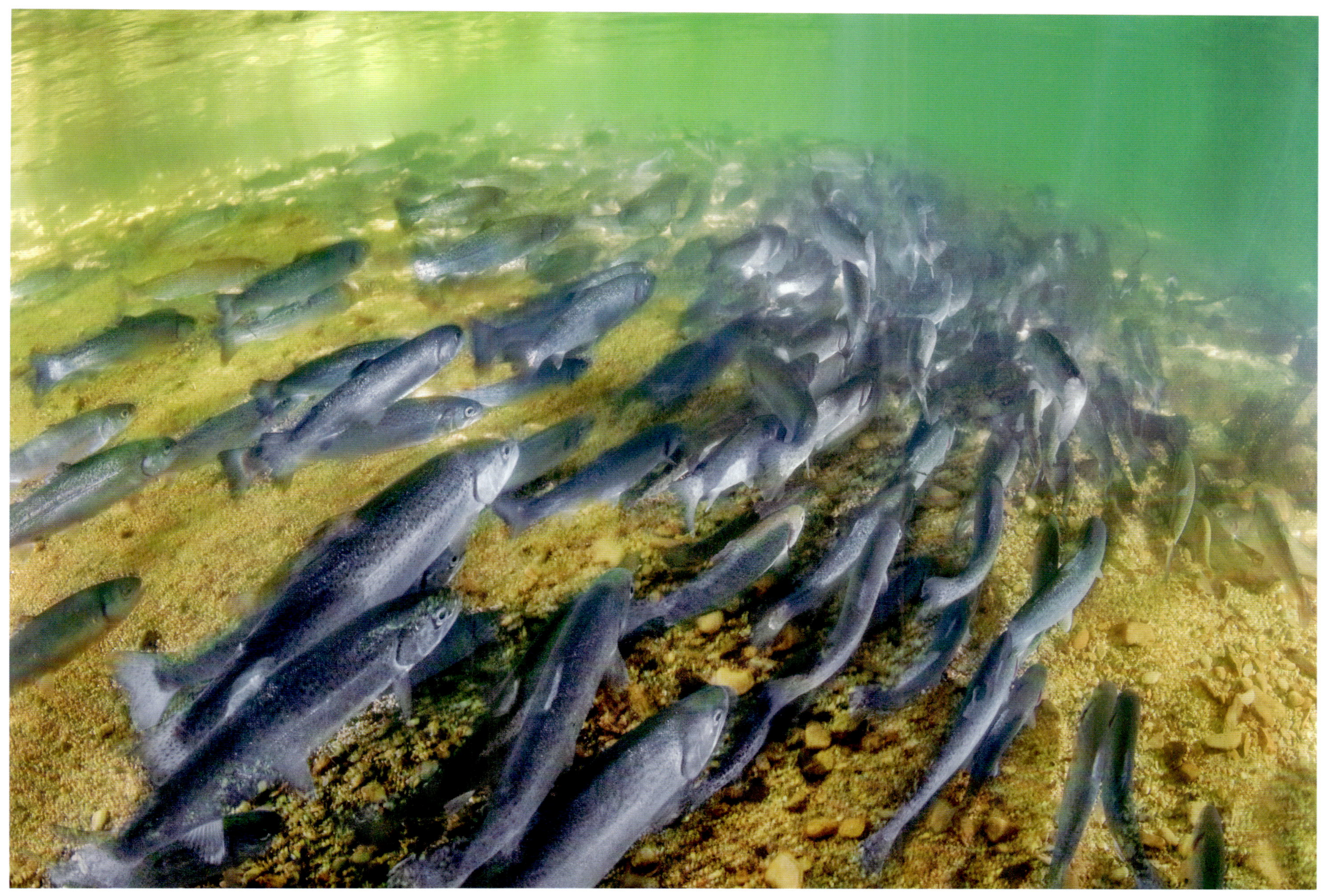

Steelhead, like salmon, are born in freshwater creeks. In a living linkage between land and sea, they swim to the ocean to mature and return to their native creeks to spawn. Their presence or absence is a good indicator of freshwater habitat quality.

Steelhead Trout, Scott Creek

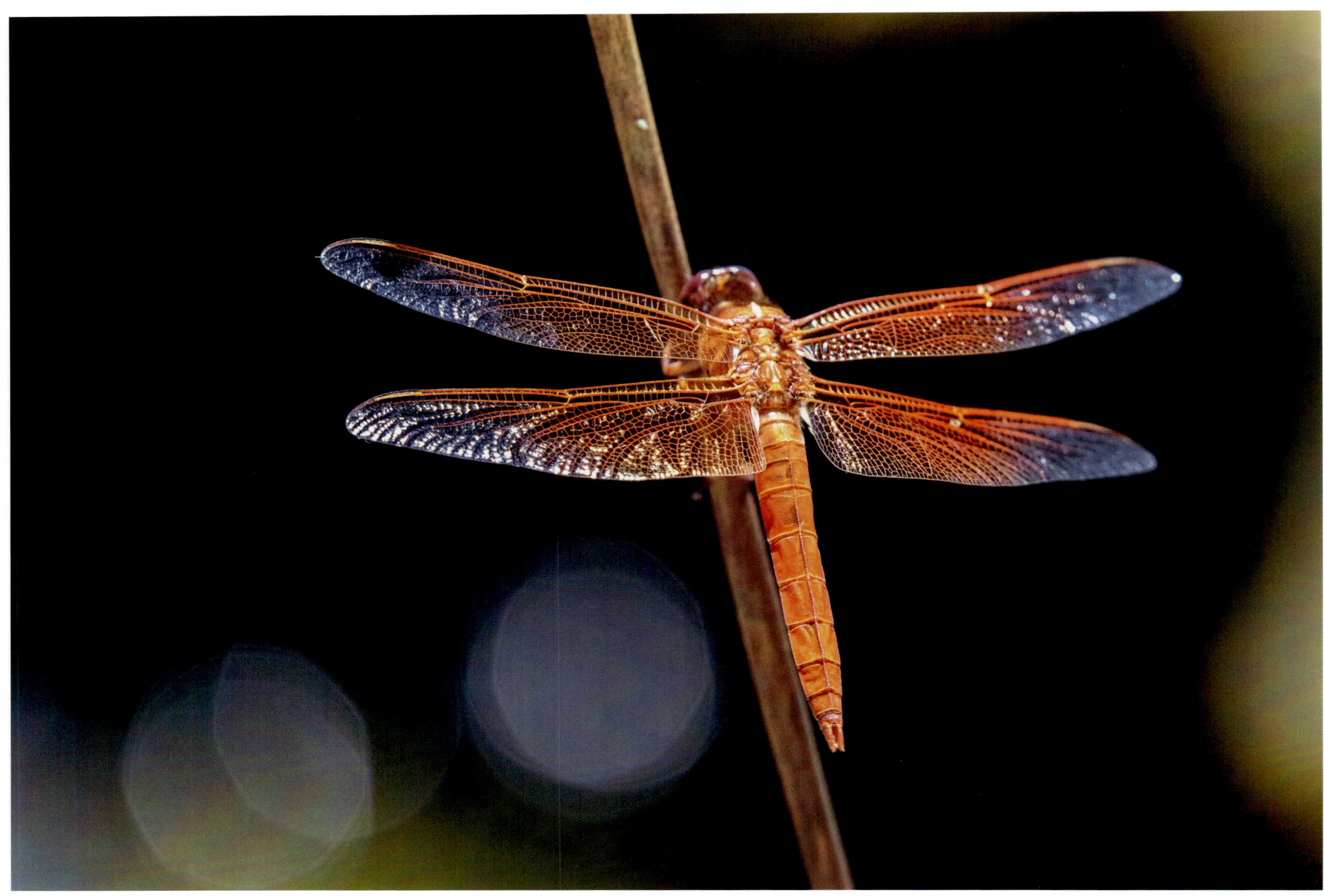

Beginning in spring, the large dragonflies known as "flame skimmers" are conspicuous around ponds and wetlands where they hunt insects and mate. Females dip their abdomens in water to release their eggs while flying. This male is perched to wait for prey. At least 29 species of dragonflies live around Monterey Bay. They are tracked by enthusiastic fans, who search for new species of "odes," the nickname for dragonflies and damselflies, from their Order name, Odondata.

Dragonfly, Rancho Refugio

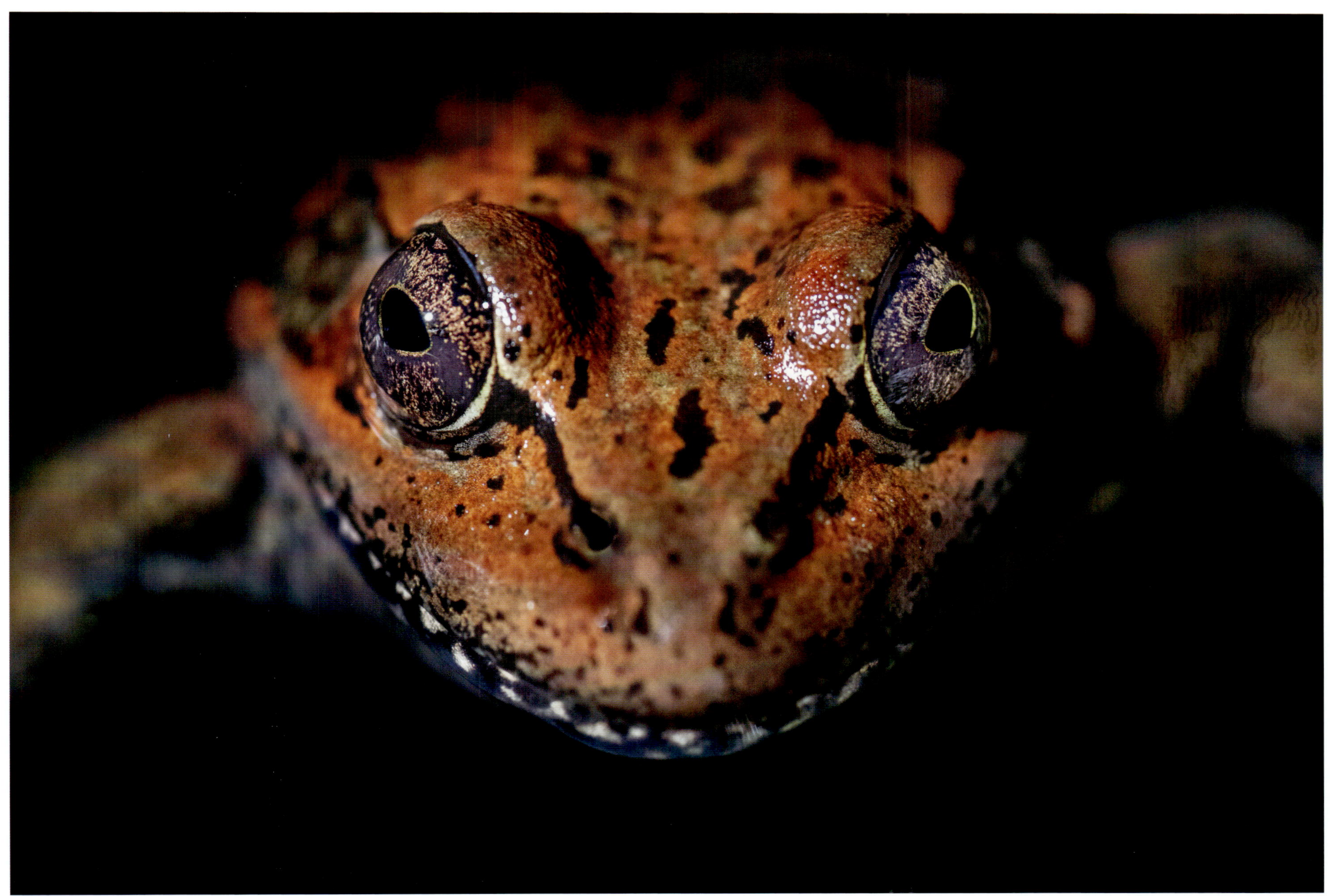

Only two frogs are native to Monterey Bay. One is the Pacific tree frog, or chorus frog—whose calls can be heard half a mile away. The other is the enigmatic red-legged frog, the largest native frog in the western United States. But they have a hard time coping with non-native bullfrogs that invade their breeding ponds and gobble up their tadpoles. Habitat loss from human activities has also depressed the population. Red-legged frogs are now an endangered species.

Red-legged Frog, Rancho Refugio

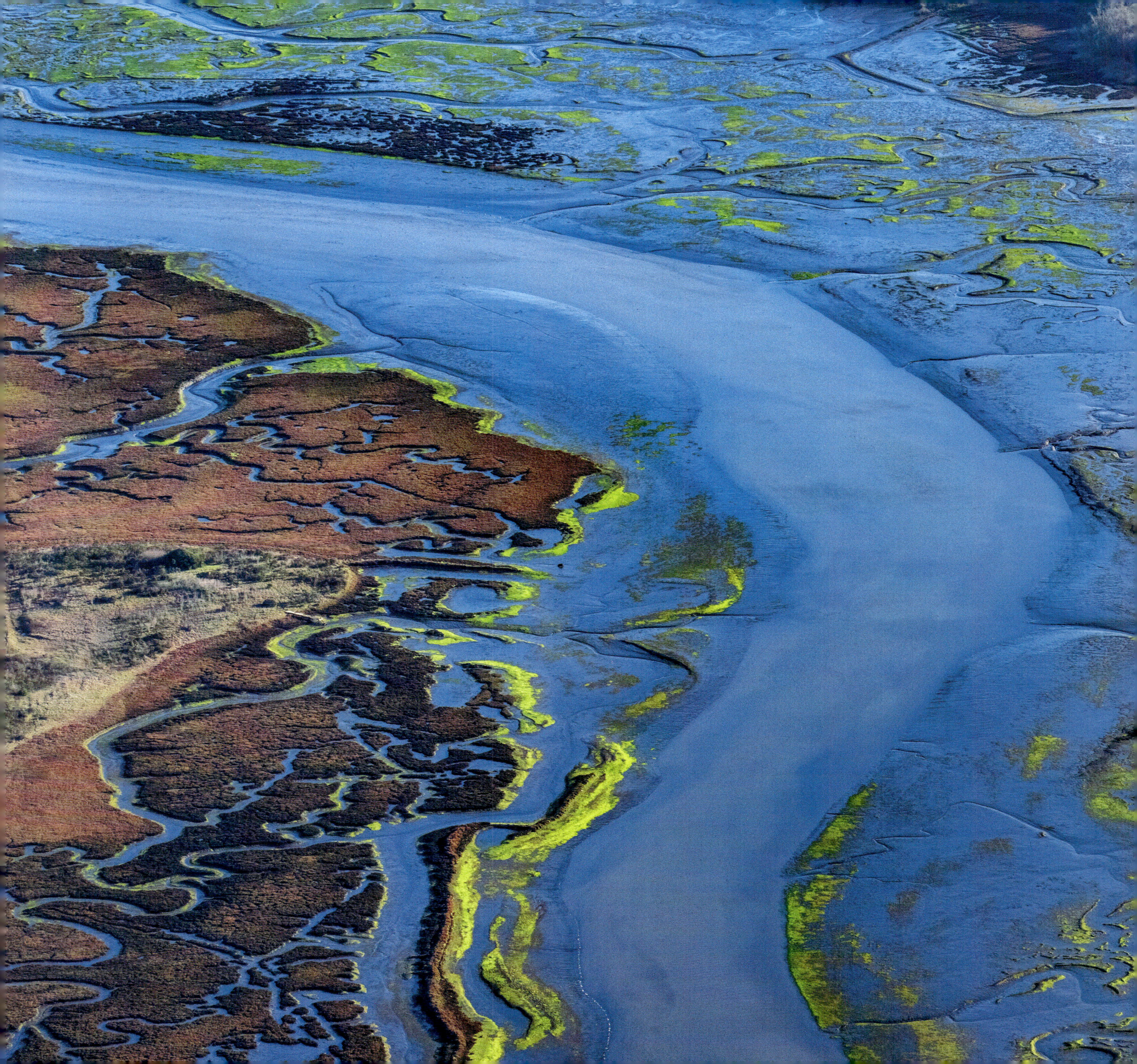

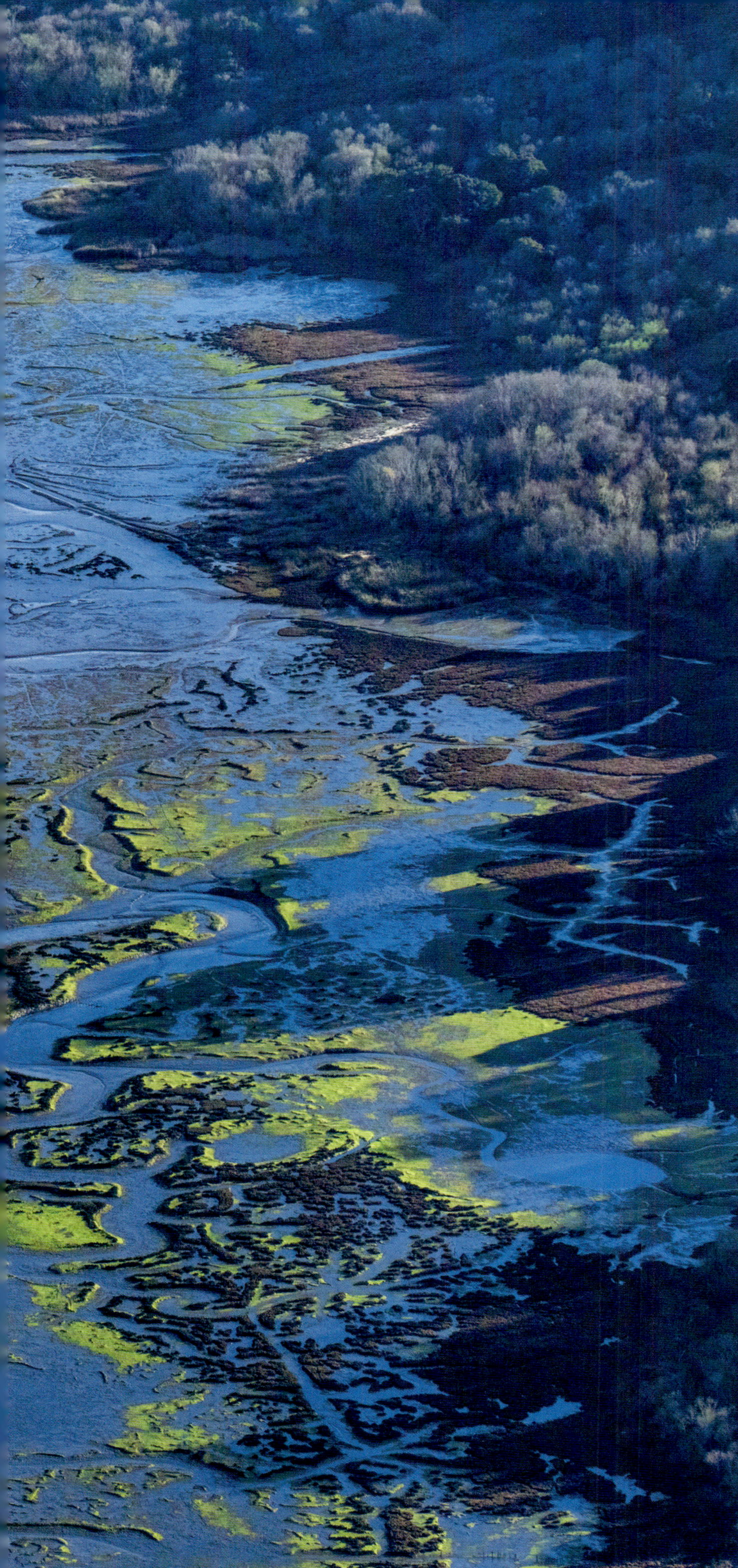

Low tide reveals the rich mudflats lining Elkhorn Slough's main channel and
the serpentine complexity of its tidal creeks. The most important wetland
in Monterey Bay is a refuge for harbor seals and sea lions by the hundreds,
multitudes of water birds, and rafts of sea otters. In partnership with the reserve,
the Elkhorn Slough Foundation has spearheaded crucial efforts to restore key
habitats around the slough. A current project involves adding sediment to a
subsided marsh that will make it more resilient to sea level rise.

AERIAL VIEW, ELKHORN SLOUGH NATIONAL ESTUARINE RESEARCH RESERVE

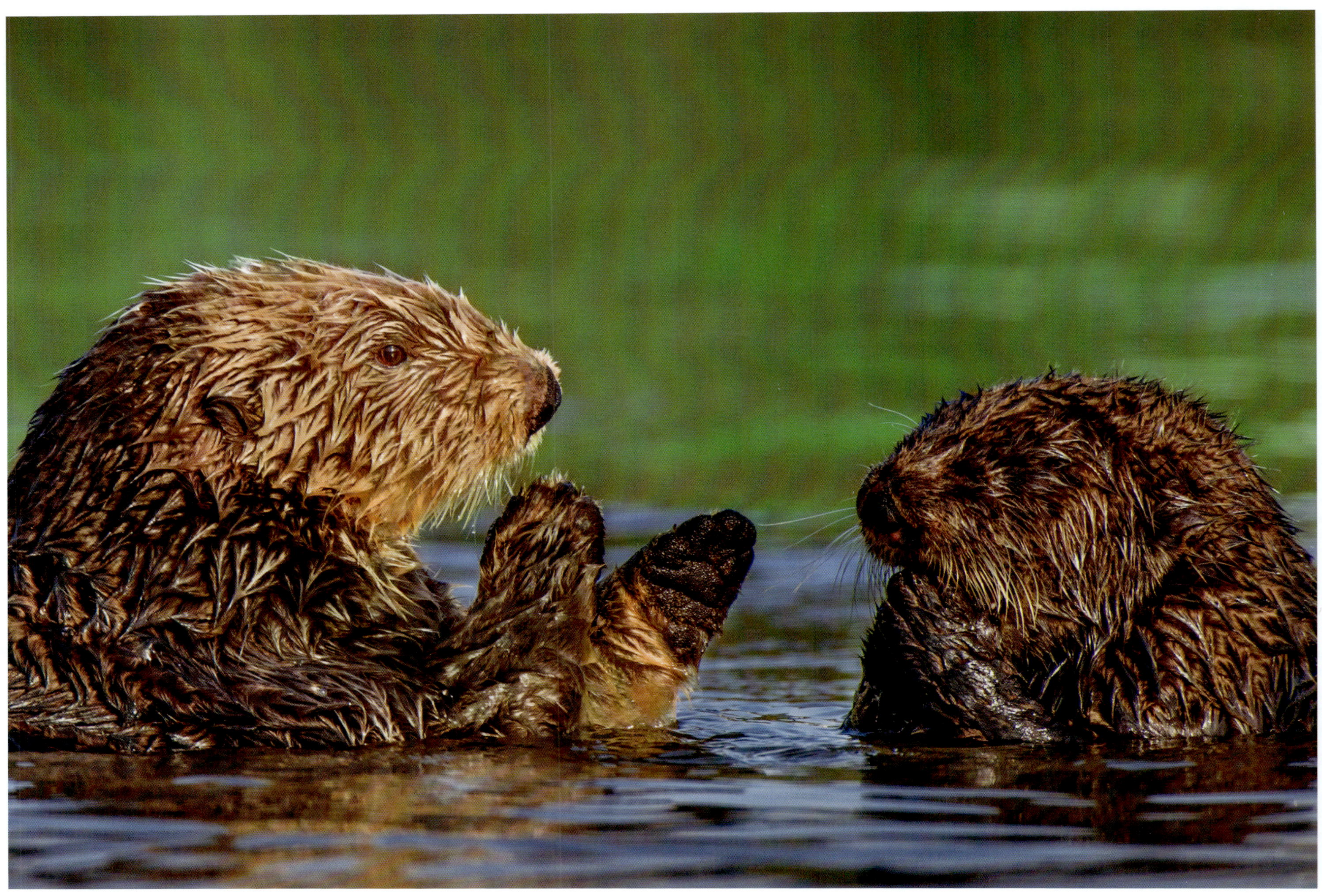

The largest population of sea otters along the California coast occurs in Monterey Bay because of its rich underwater habitats. Many use Elkhorn Slough as a nursery, like this female and her pup.

SEA OTTERS, ELKHORN SLOUGH NATIONAL ESTUARINE RESEARCH RESERVE

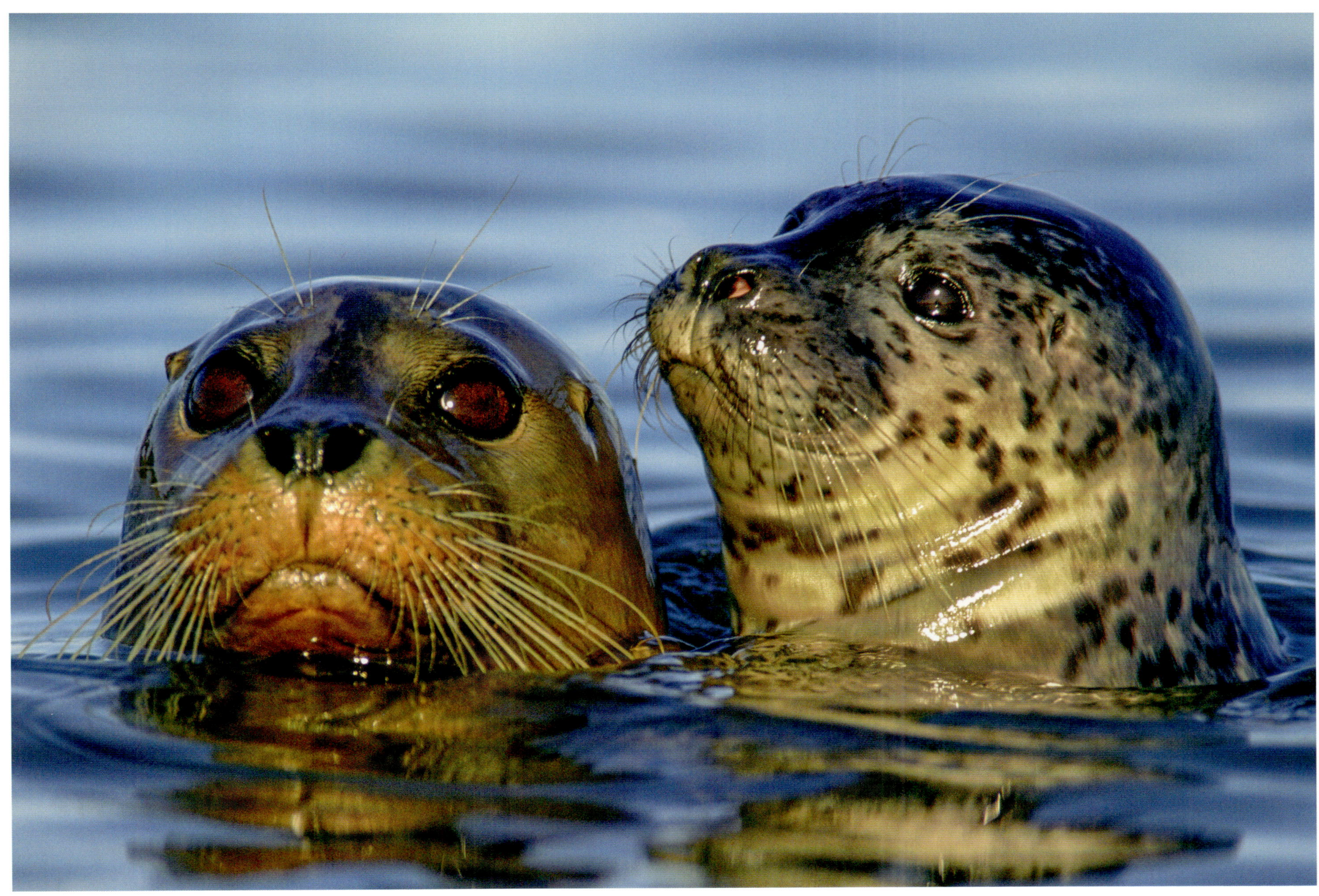

A harbor seal mother and pup surface in the backwaters of Elkhorn Slough. To protect their young from predators, mother seals raise their pups in groups with other mothers. In spring, the banks of the slough are lined with harbor seals basking in the sun.

HARBOR SEALS, ELKHORN SLOUGH NATIONAL ESTUARINE RESEARCH RESERVE

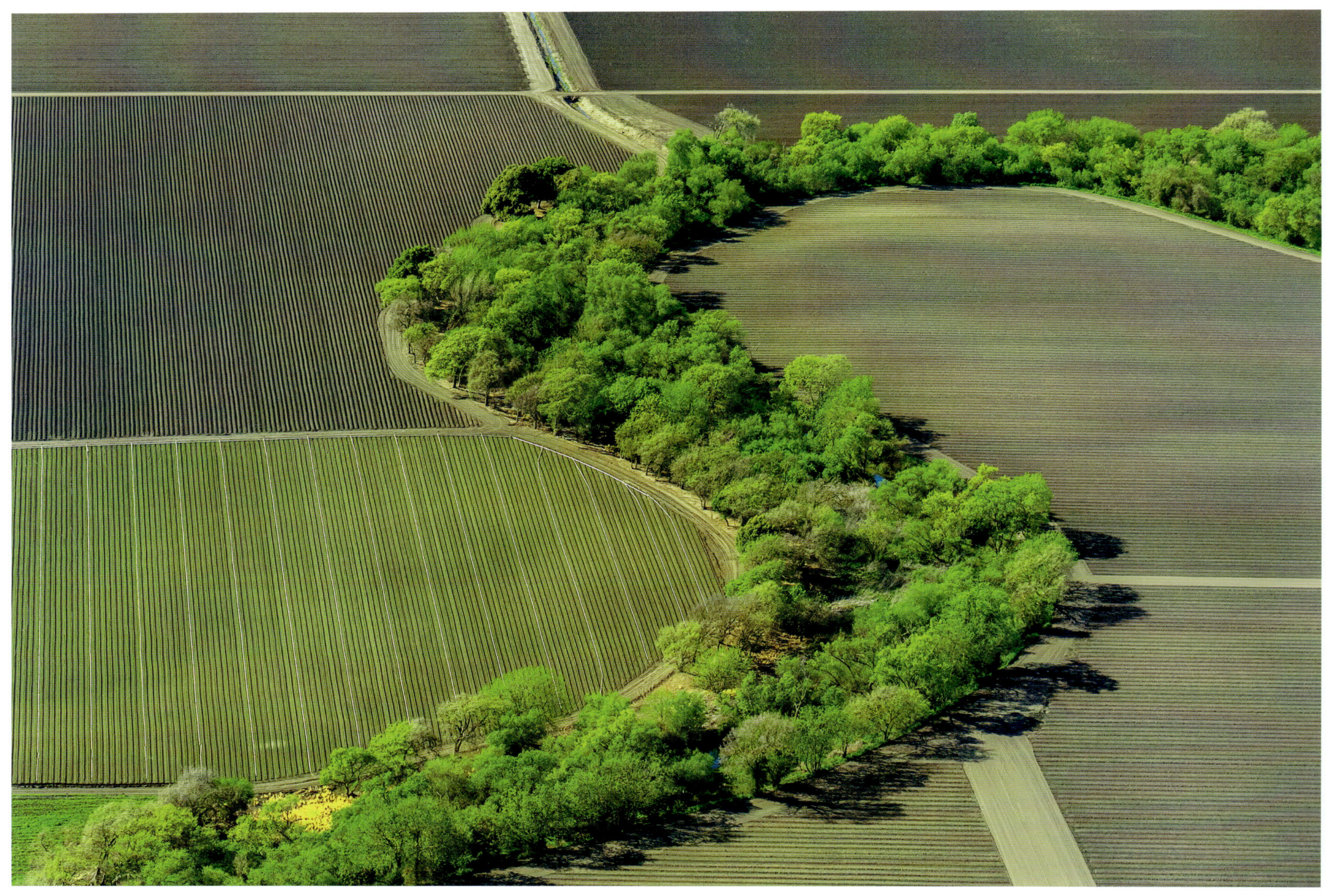

The Pajaro River once fed extensive wetlands, but those marshes have been drained, and the river is now hemmed in by levees. The barriers maximize the use of farmland at the expense of natural systems. Yet the river is still a vibrant ribbon of nature in a transformed landscape.

Aerial View, Pajaro River

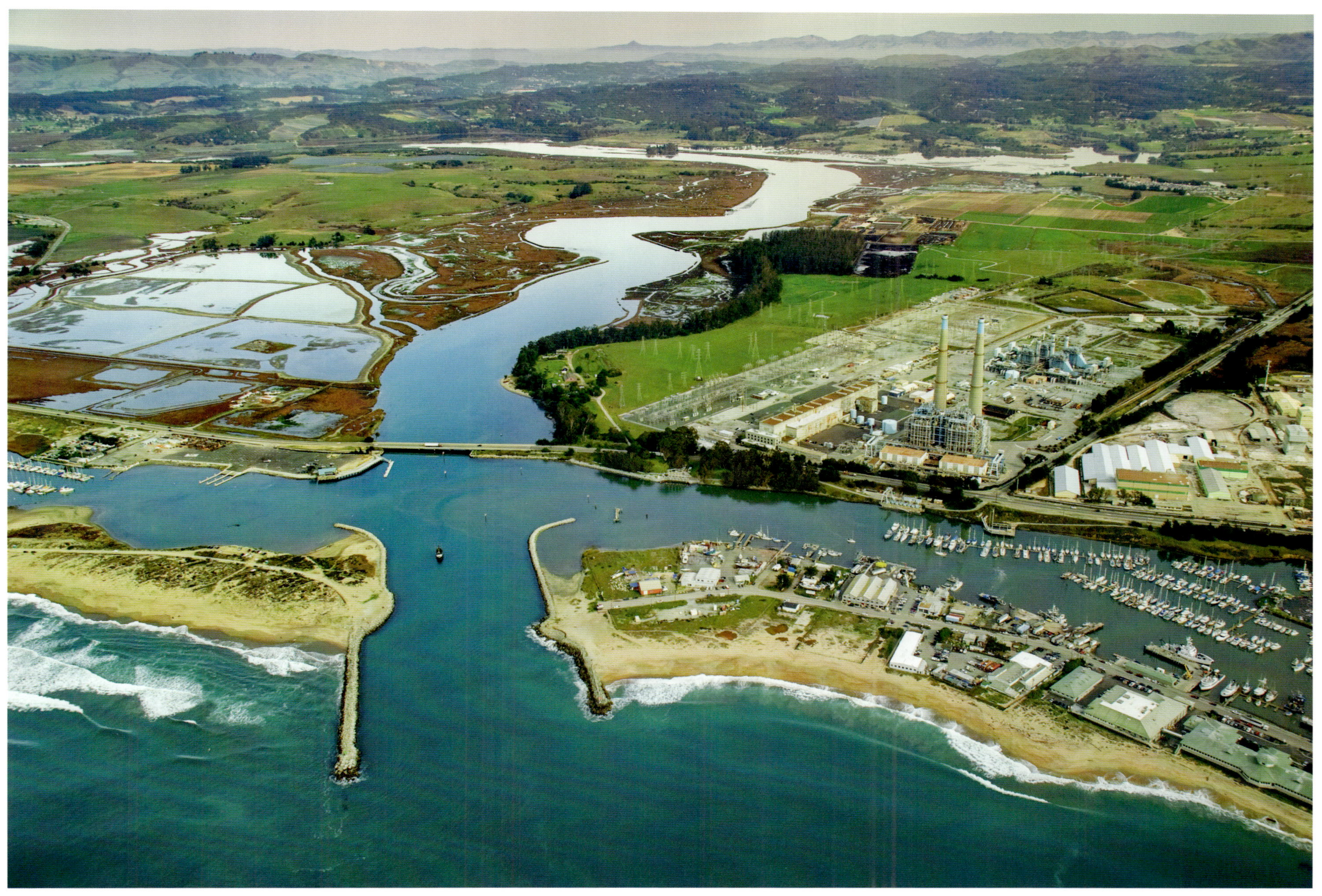

Moss Landing is an industrious place with a power plant, a highway, a fishing harbor, salt ponds, and farms along Elkhorn Slough. Yet it is also a sanctuary for marine wildlife. On the ground, the harbor shows a tenuous coexistence between sea lions lounging on docks next to fishermen preparing to head out to sea and kayakers floating past rafting sea otters.

Aerial View, Moss Landing Harbor

COAST

Evening light casts a warm glow on the Davenport bluffs, named for the man
who started a whaling operation here in the 19th century. These days, the bluffs
are a popular spot to watch gray whales migrating along the coast.

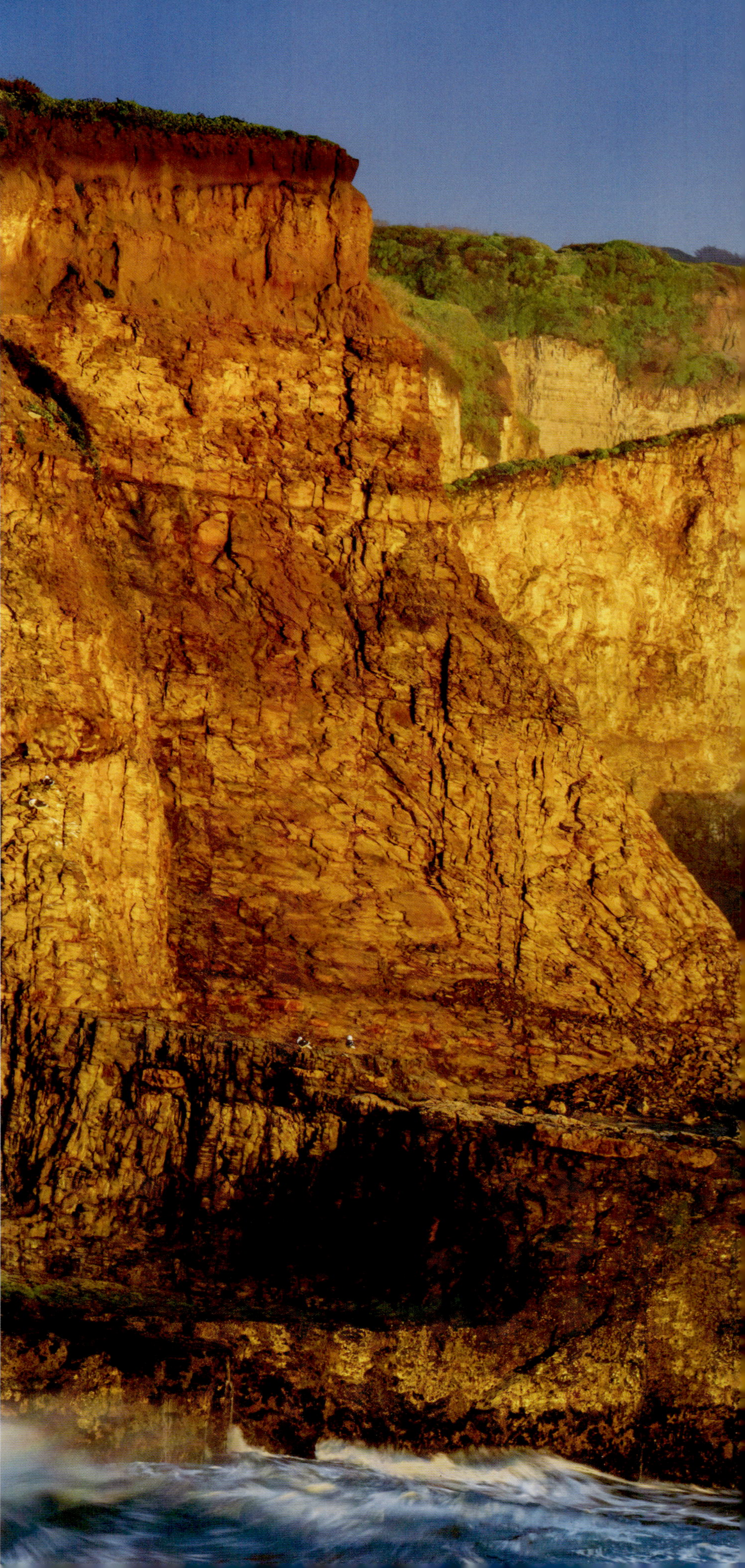

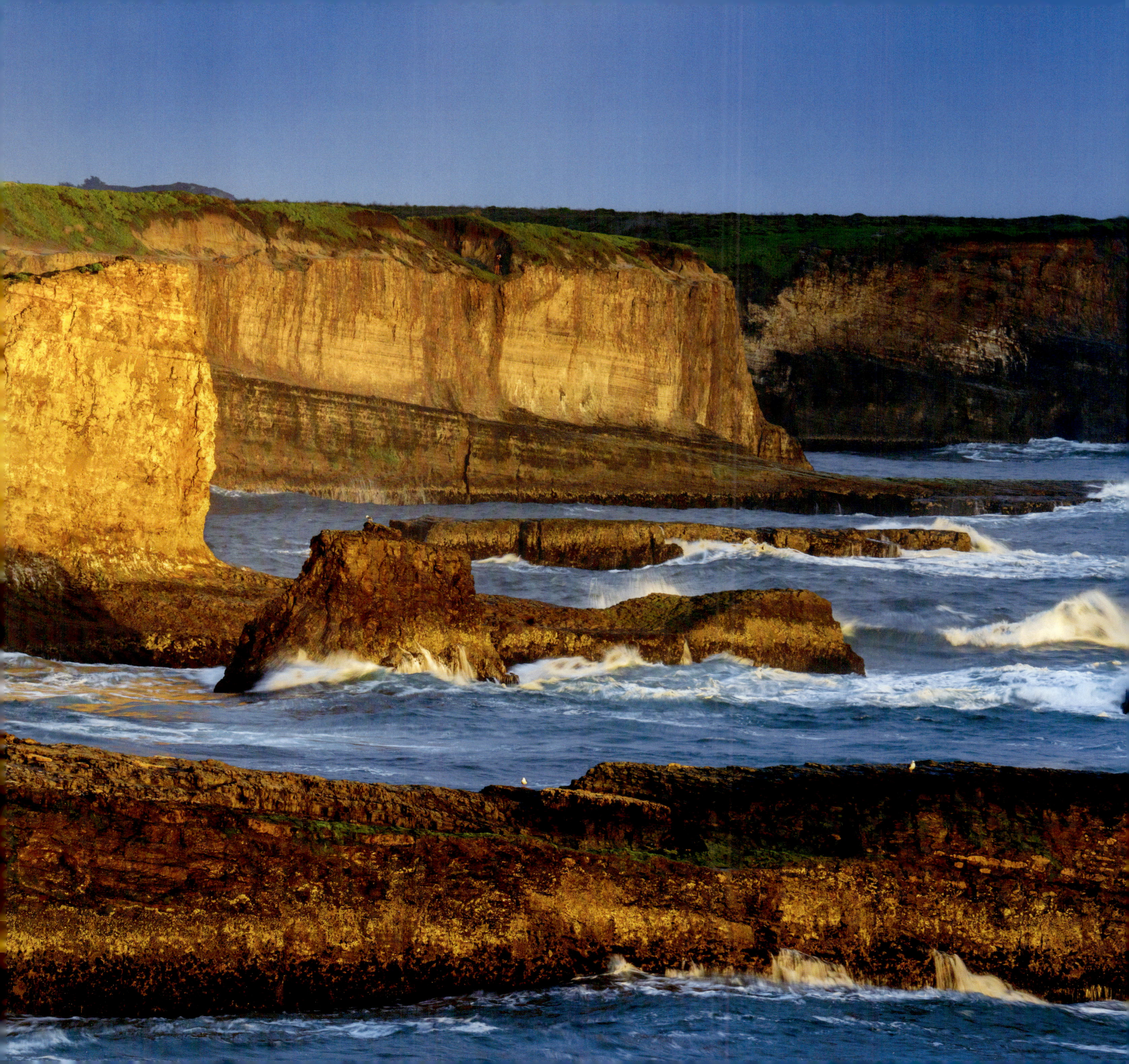

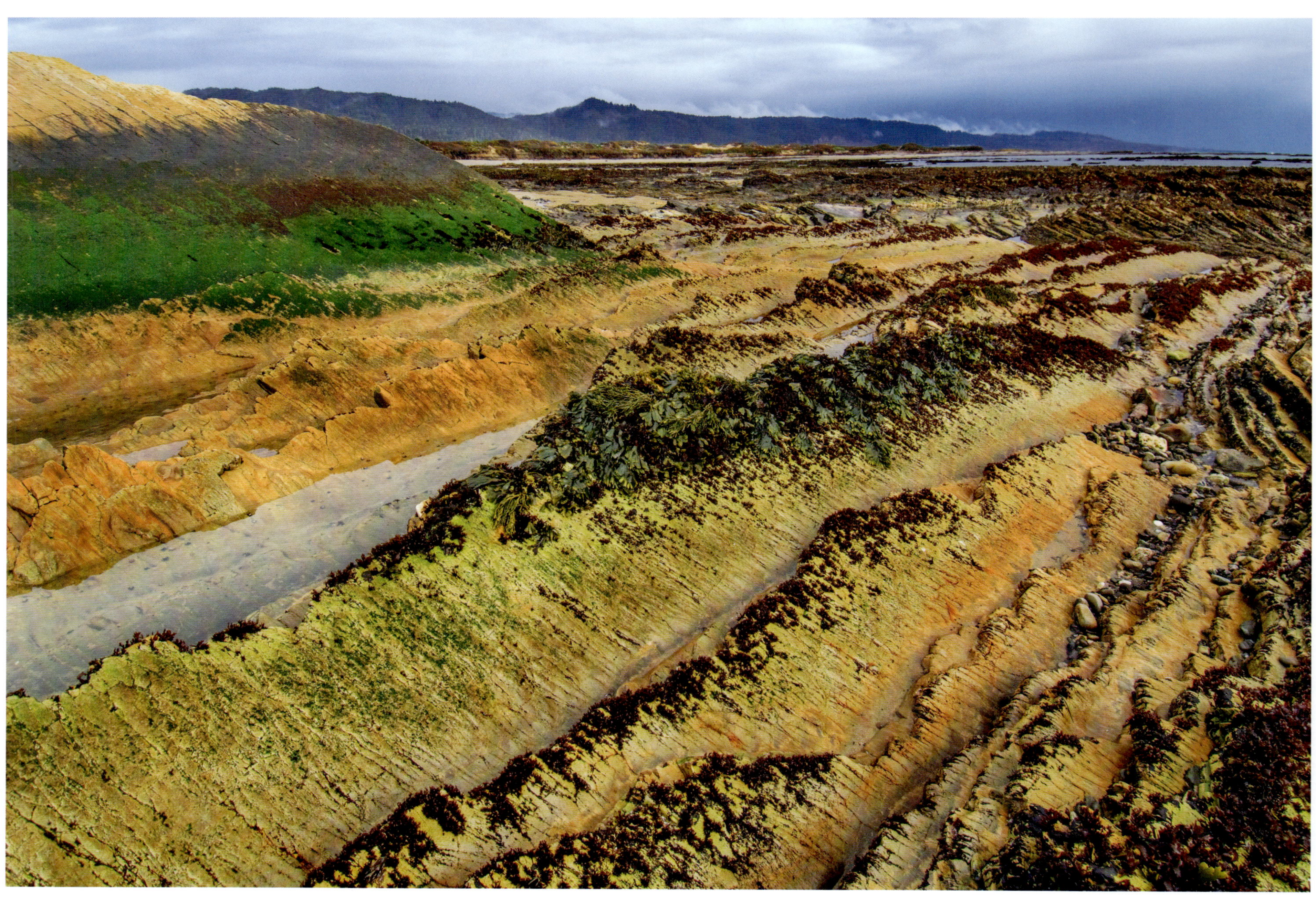

Algae-covered reefs exposed at low tide reveal the ledged layers of a mudstone formation at Año Nuevo Point. For many generations of indigenous people, this place was an important site for collecting rock chips to fashion into stone tools.

Reefs, Año Nuevo State Park

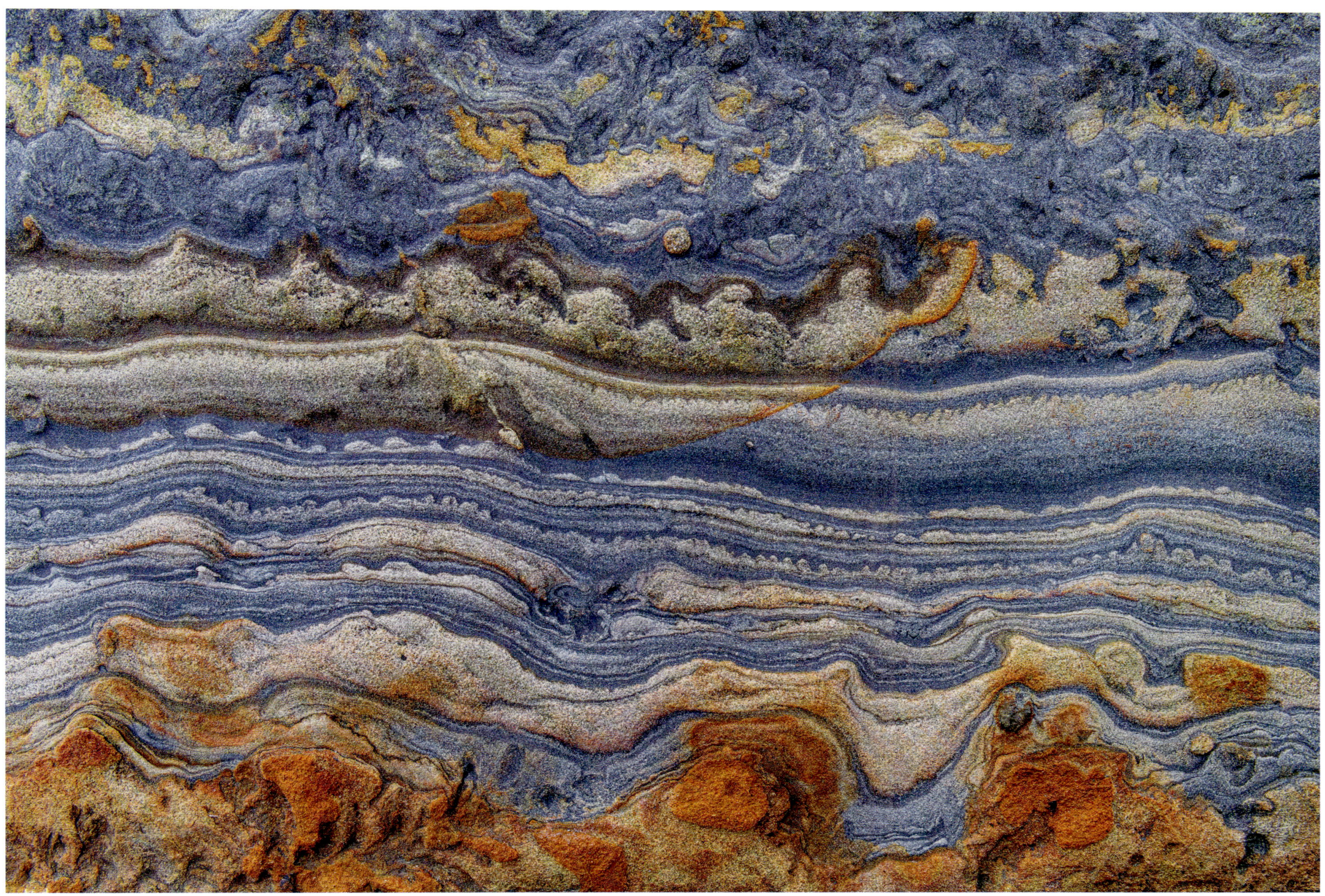

Multicolored patterns in bedrock at Point Lobos reflect its complex geologic history. These rock formations have inspired many photographers, including Ansel Adams, who lived just south of the reserve, and Edward Weston, whose name is memorialized in Weston Beach.

Rock Patterns, Point Lobos State Natural Reserve

following pages: Craggy offshore rocks support an abundance of marine life, but the creature that gave this place its name lives higher up on the bluffs in the dense thickets of chaparral: "Garrapata" is the Spanish word for "tick."

Coastline, Garrapata State Park

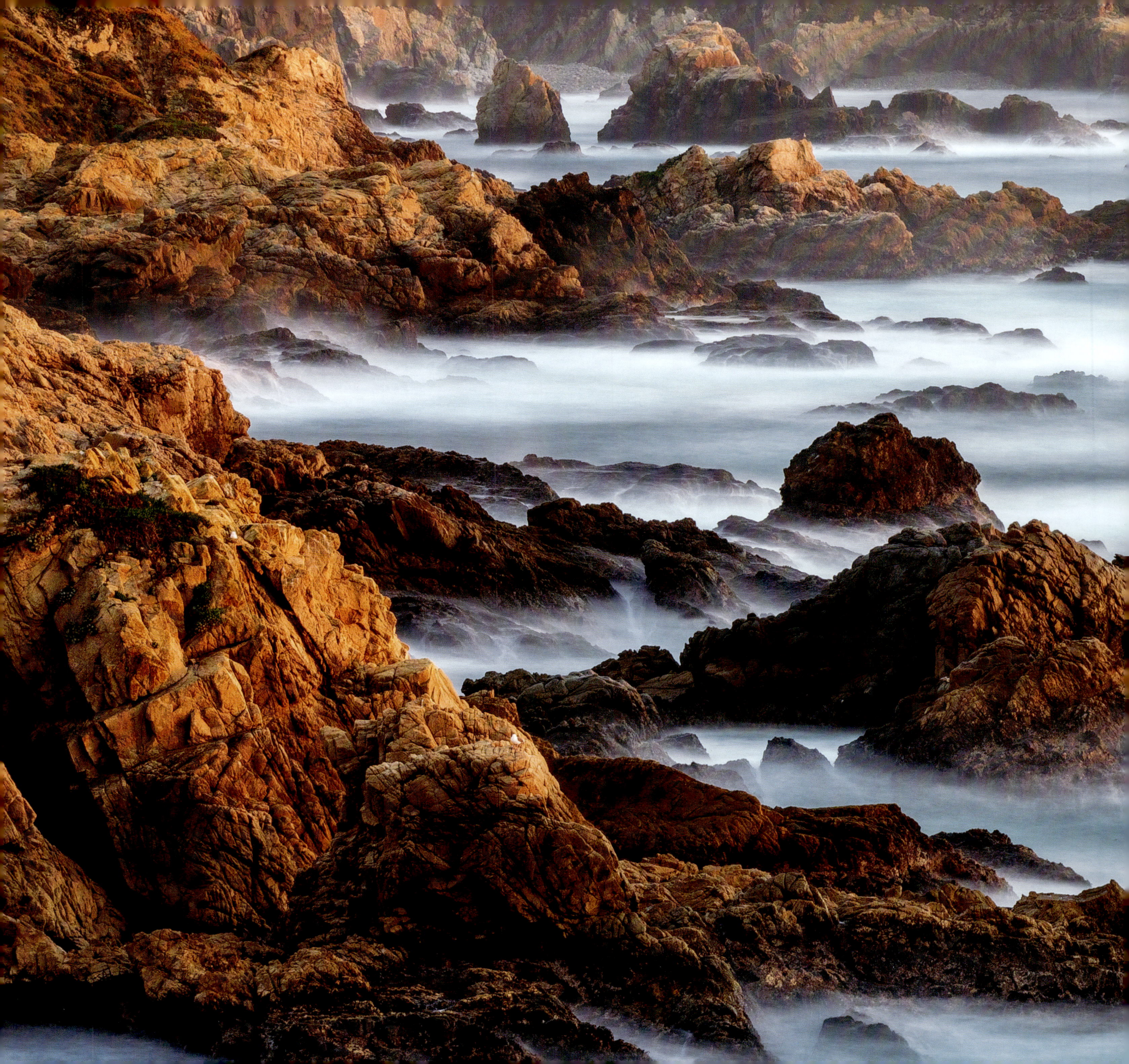

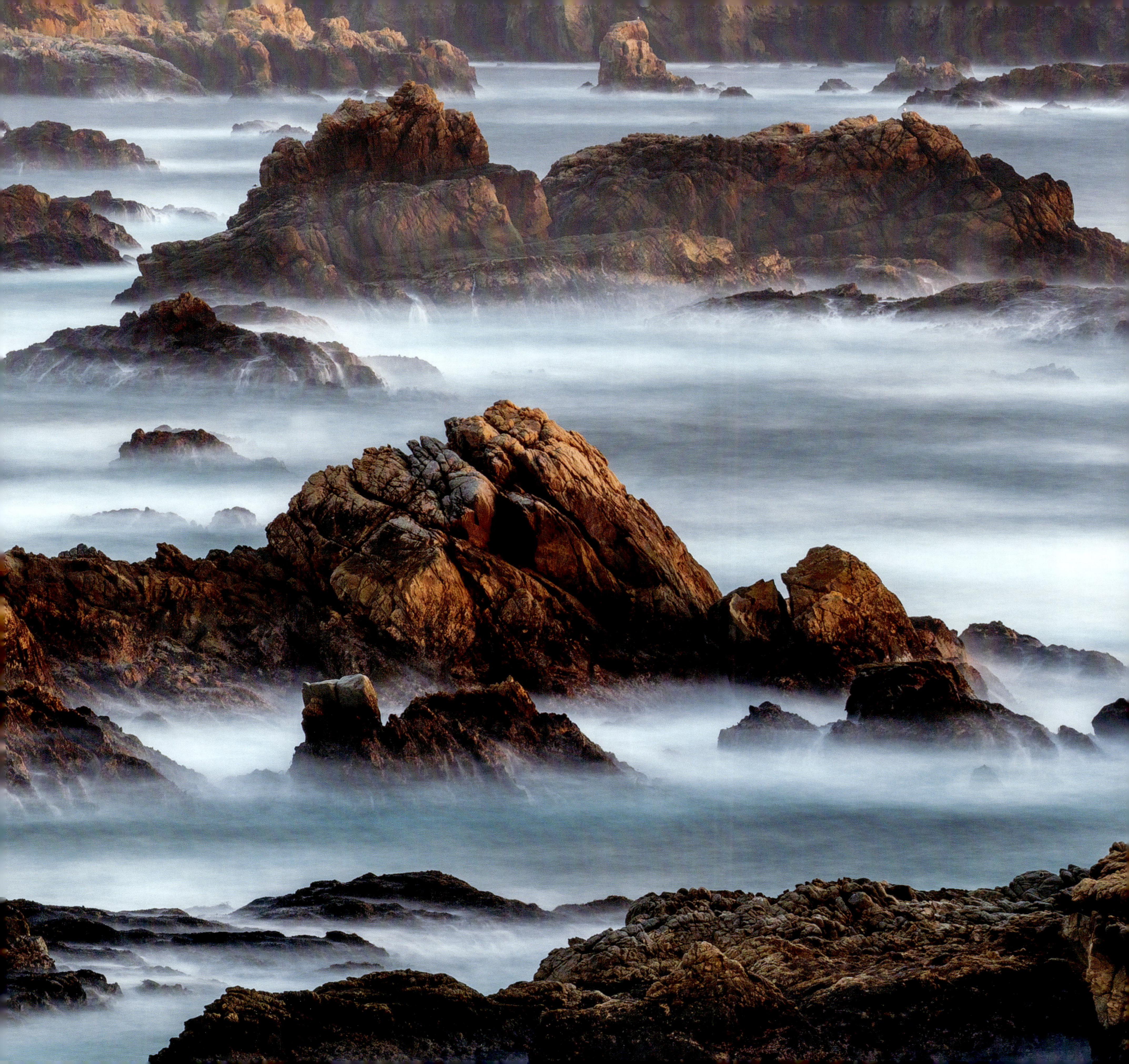

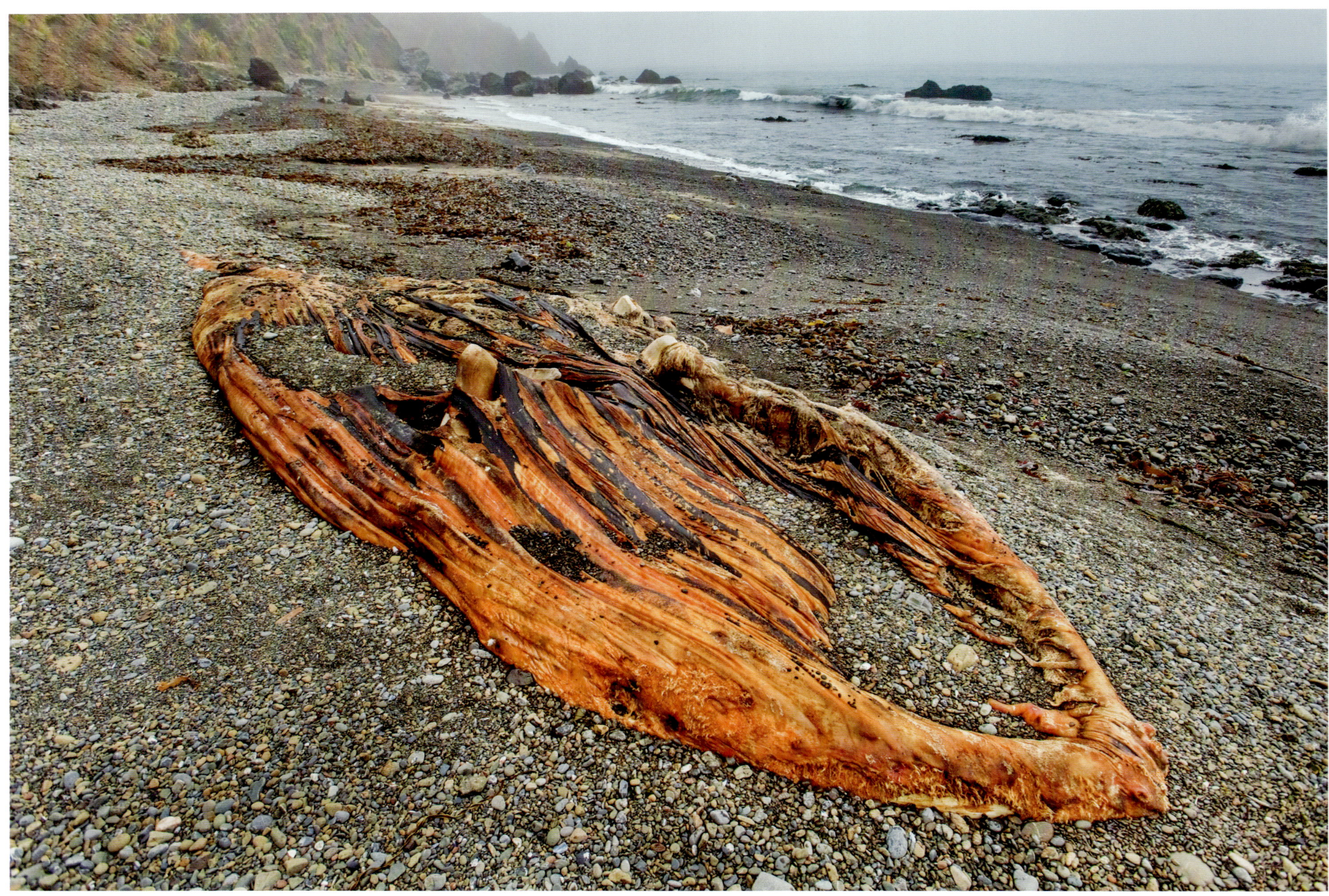

Whales have increased in numbers during the last few decades because of successful protective measures, and dead ones occasionally wash up on the shores of Monterey Bay. California condors used to forage on dead whales around whaling stations in the 19th century, but the condor population crashed in the 20th century due in large part to lead poisoning: They consumed carrion that contained lead ammunition, which killed the birds. Thanks to a California ban on lead bullets for hunting, condors are recovering. They now feed on beached carcasses like this one again—a sight not witnessed for more than a century.

Humpback Whale Remains, Big Sur

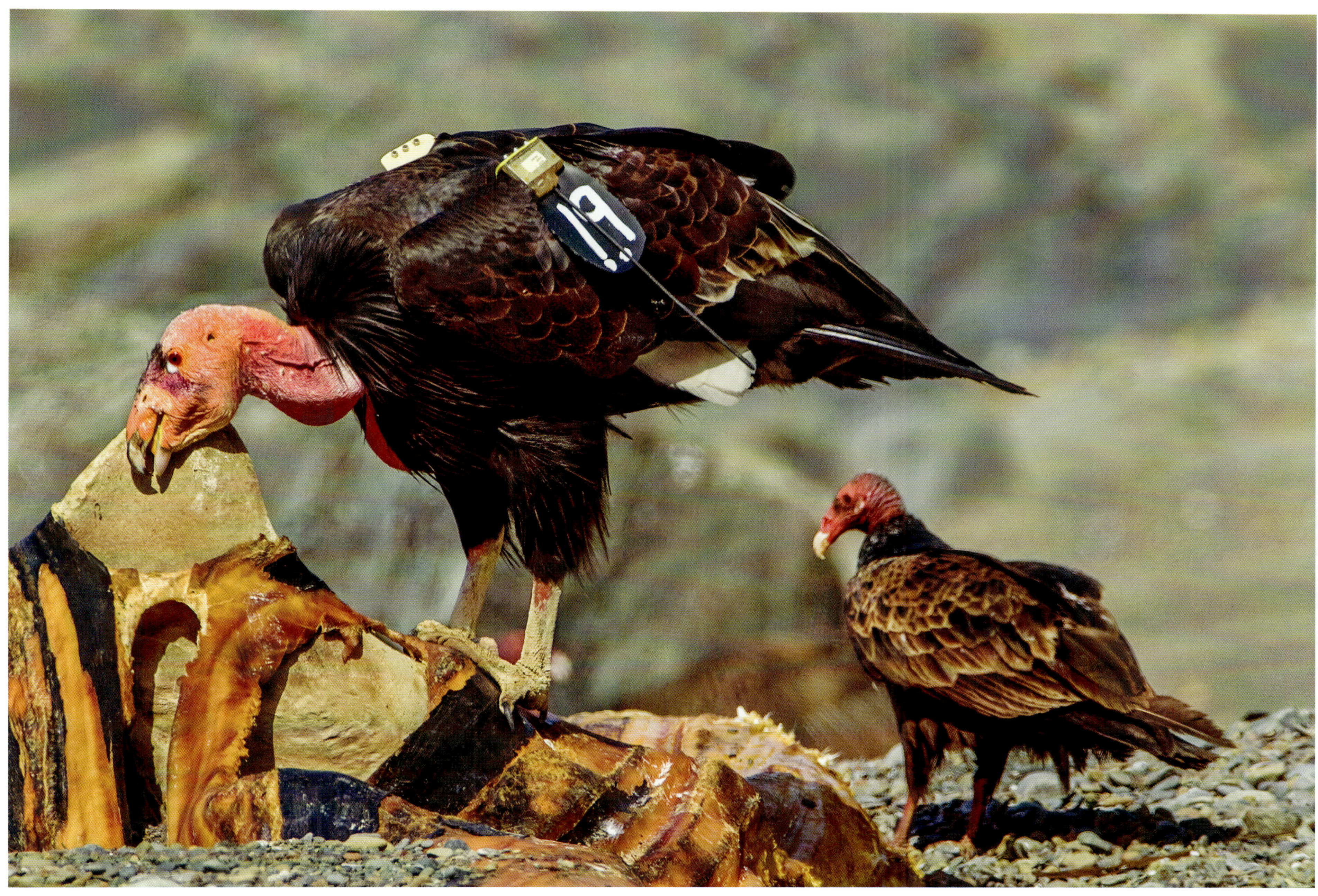

California condors have been rewilded in the Monterey Bay region—a historic comeback from near extinction. More than a hundred are now flying free between the Big Sur coast and the Pinnacles in the interior after an initial release of captive-born birds in 1992. The Ventana Wildlife Society has monitored the population for the past 25 years. A turkey vulture next to Condor #19, foraging on a dead humpback whale, provides scale. The gigantic condor is not only an icon for a prehistoric past but also a poignant symbol for a new future for wildlife in which every individual counts.

California Condor, Big Sur

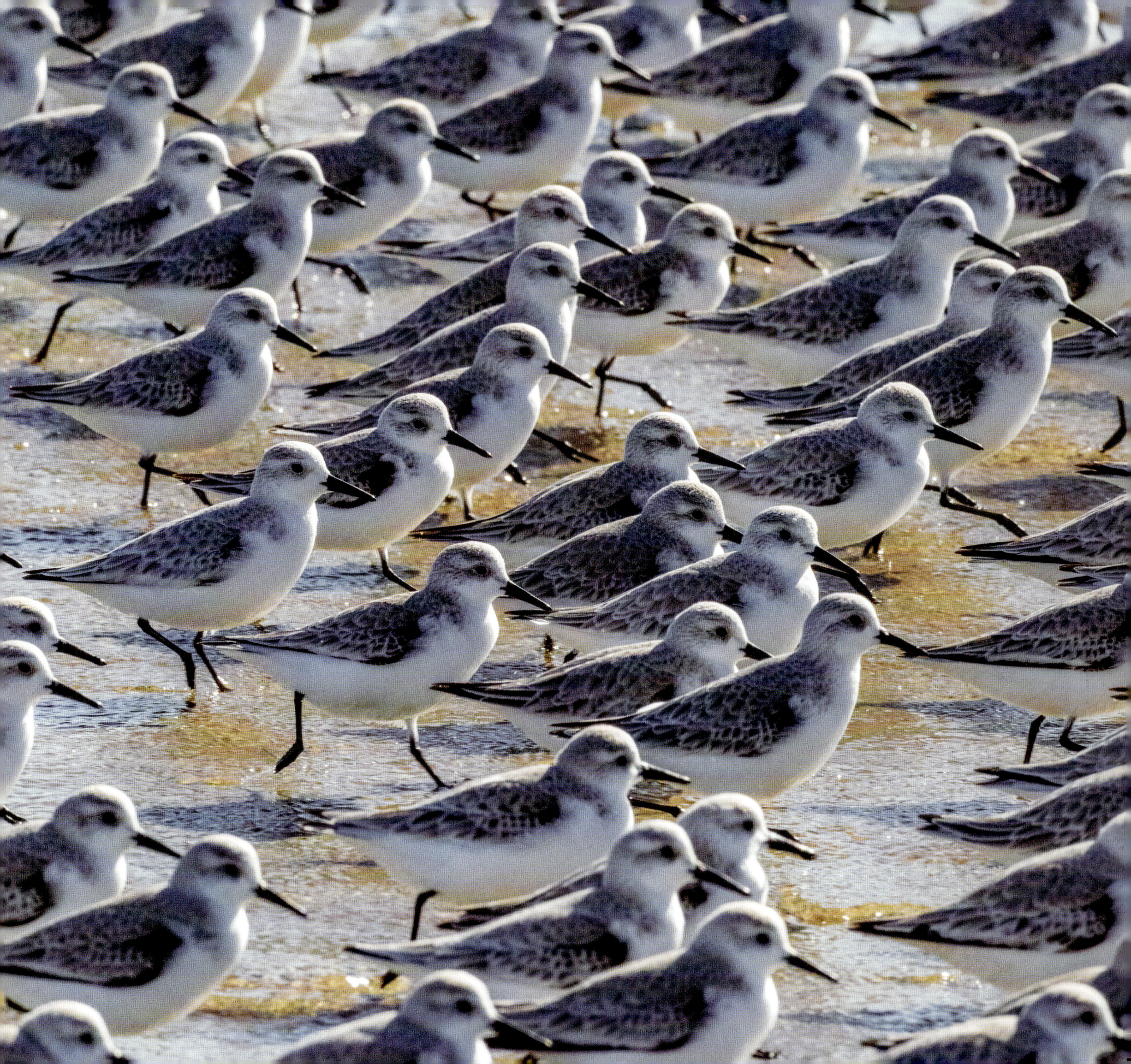

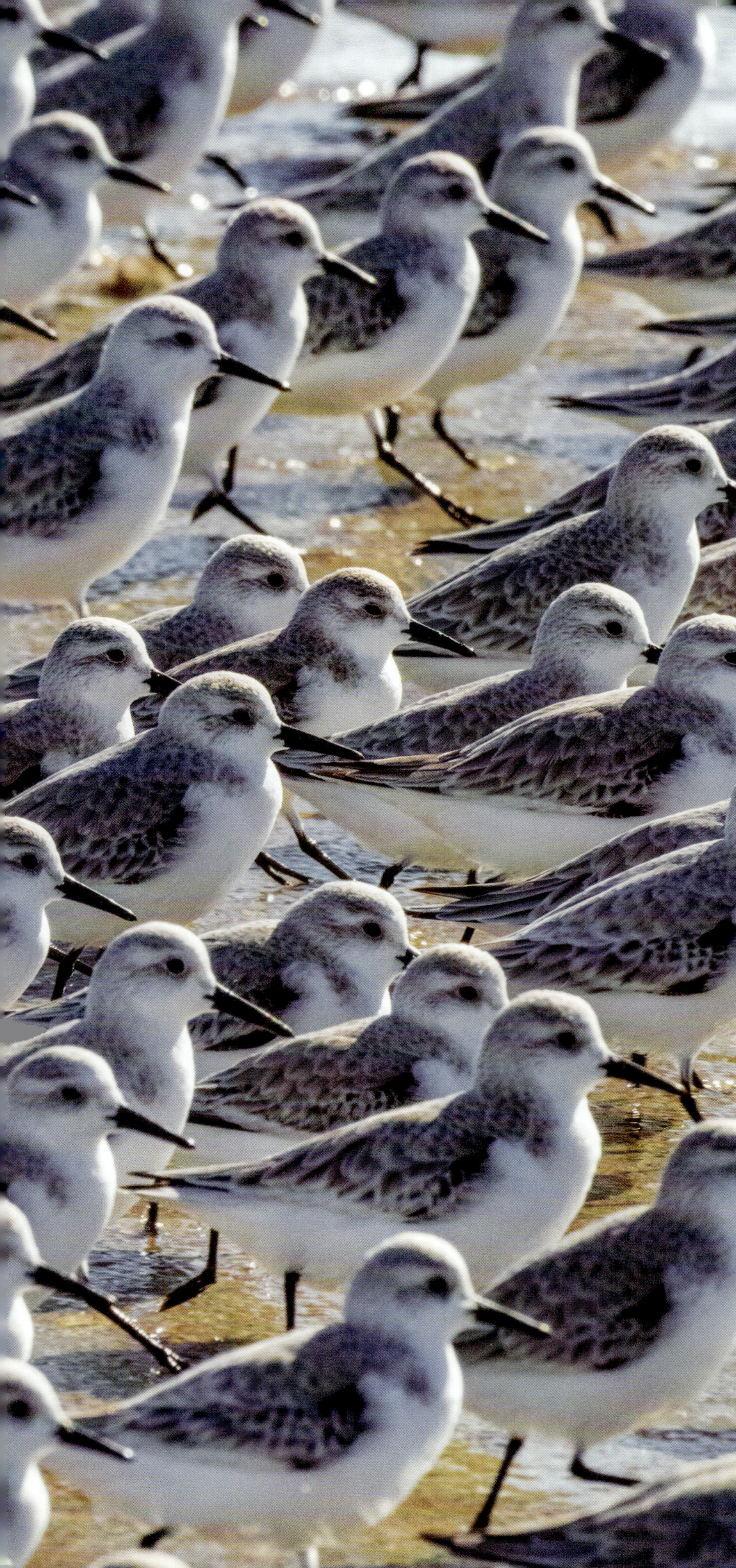

The world of sanderlings is only thirty feet wide but it spans the length
of continents. These diminutive shorebirds are tethered to the tideline,
running back and forth with the waves to forage for tiny crustaceans.
Hawaiians named sanderlings "huna kai." It's their word for the stuff
born of ocean and air—beautiful, but gone in a whiff—sea foam.

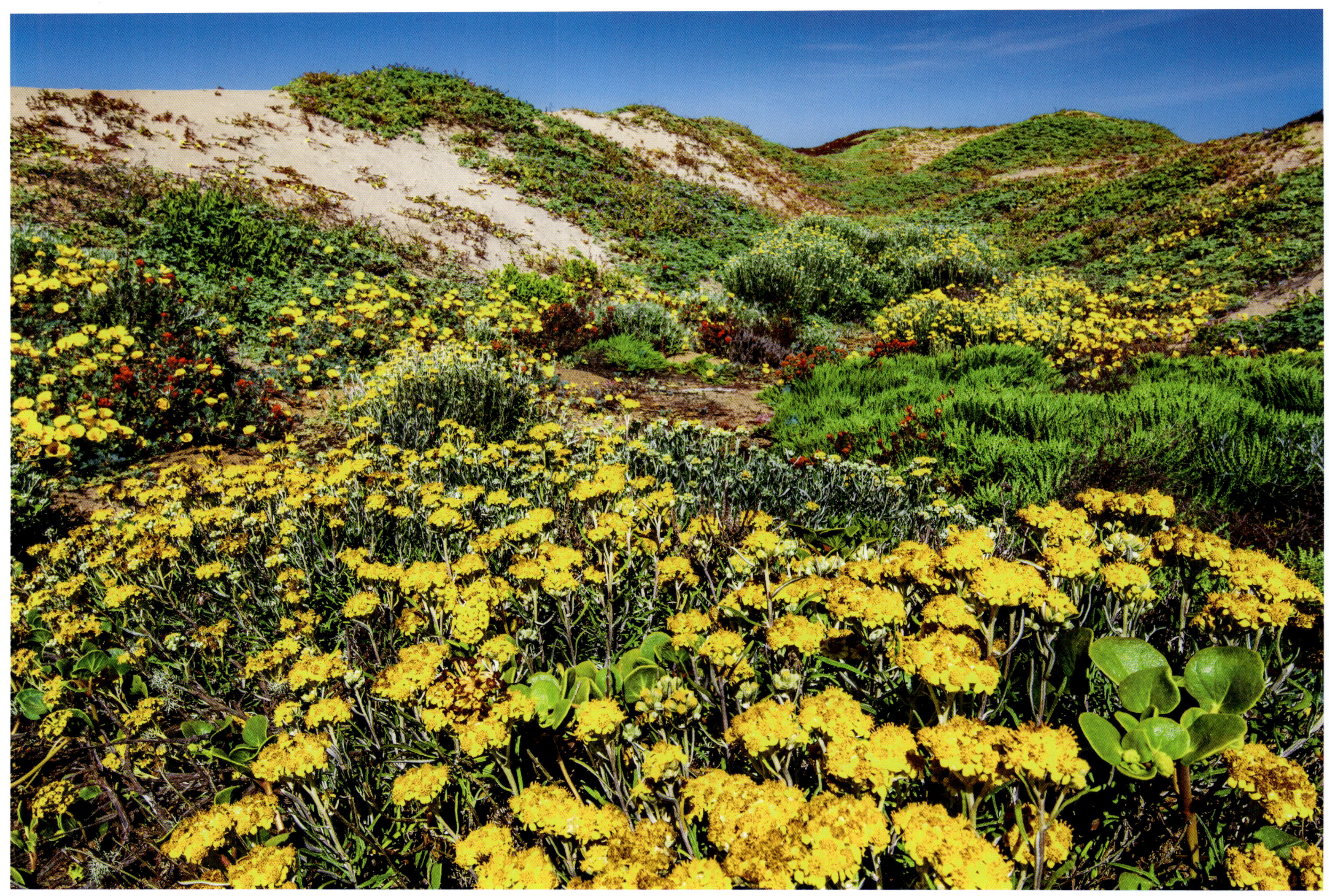

Many coastal dune-plant communities in Monterey Bay have been wiped out by development. The Salinas River dunes are a rare example of a more intact habitat, where a great variety of native plants bloom in a secluded swale, including yellow blossoms of seaside woolly sunflower and mock heather, red paintbrush, and the creeping vines of beach morning glory.

Wildflowers, Salinas River Dunes Natural Preserve

opposite: *Dudleya farinosa* is a hardy succulent that thrives on sea cliffs and sand dunes, where it is able to cope with wind, sun, and salt in the air. Yet it has no defense against poachers, who sneak into protected areas and make off with loads of them to supply the craze for succulent houseplants. This photograph was made at UCSC's Arboretum and Botanic Garden, an important native plant conservation center, where many confiscated *Dudleya* are cared for now.

Powdery Liveforever, UCSC Arboretum and Botanic Garden

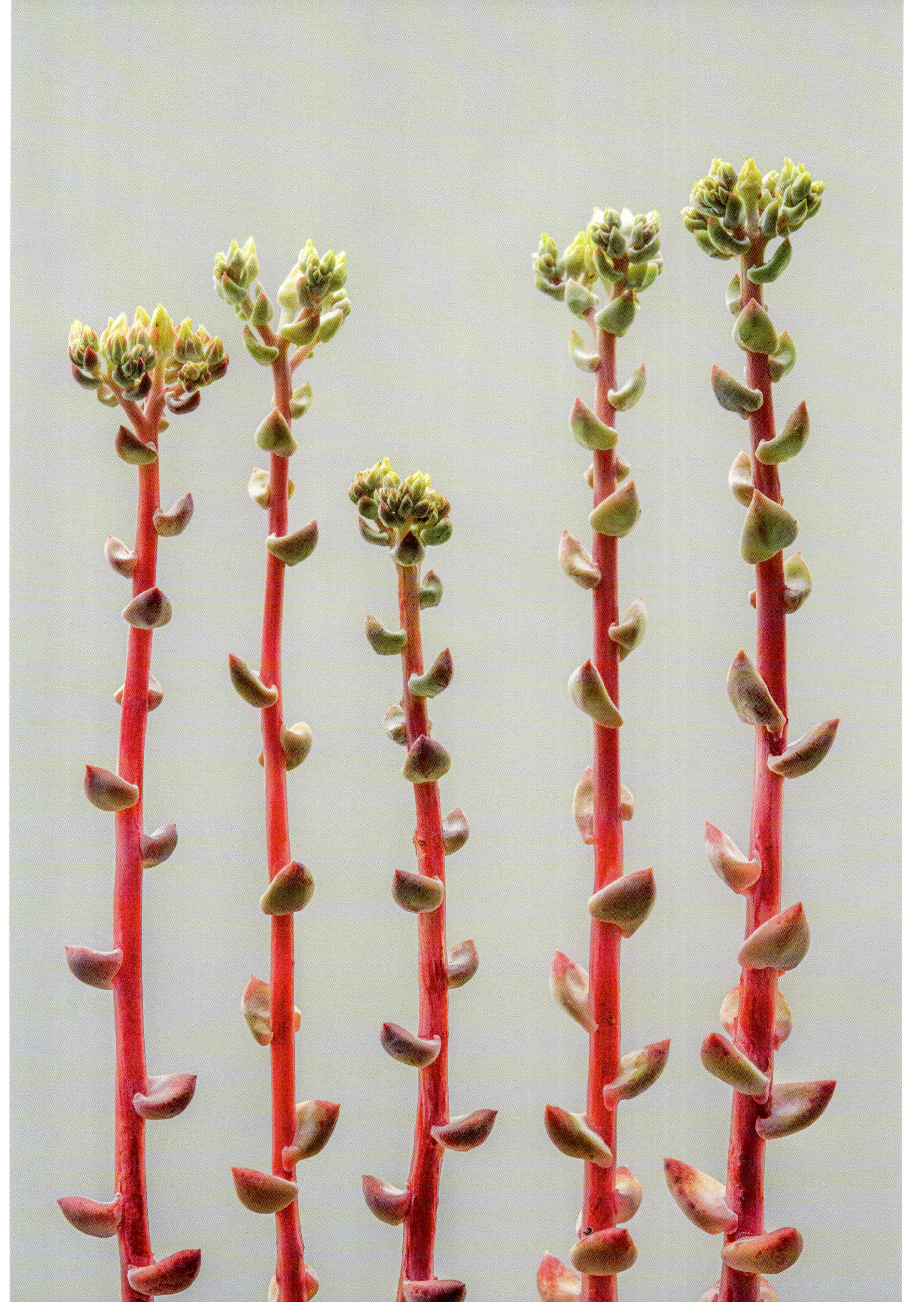

A century ago, the northern elephant seal was on the brink of extinction after
a period of intense exploitation. Less than 20 survived on Mexico's Guadalupe
Island off Baja. Soon after, they were protected, and elephant seals have
bounced back and repopulated several sites along the California coast.
Año Nuevo is now an epicenter for elephant seals and since the 1960s,
researchers from UC Santa Cruz have carried out the longest continuing study
of any animal in the world. Their research reveals that the largest of all seals spends
more than 90 percent of its time at sea submerged at depths of up to 8,000 feet,
making scientists question the physiological limits of mammals.

Elephant Seal, Año Nuevo State Park

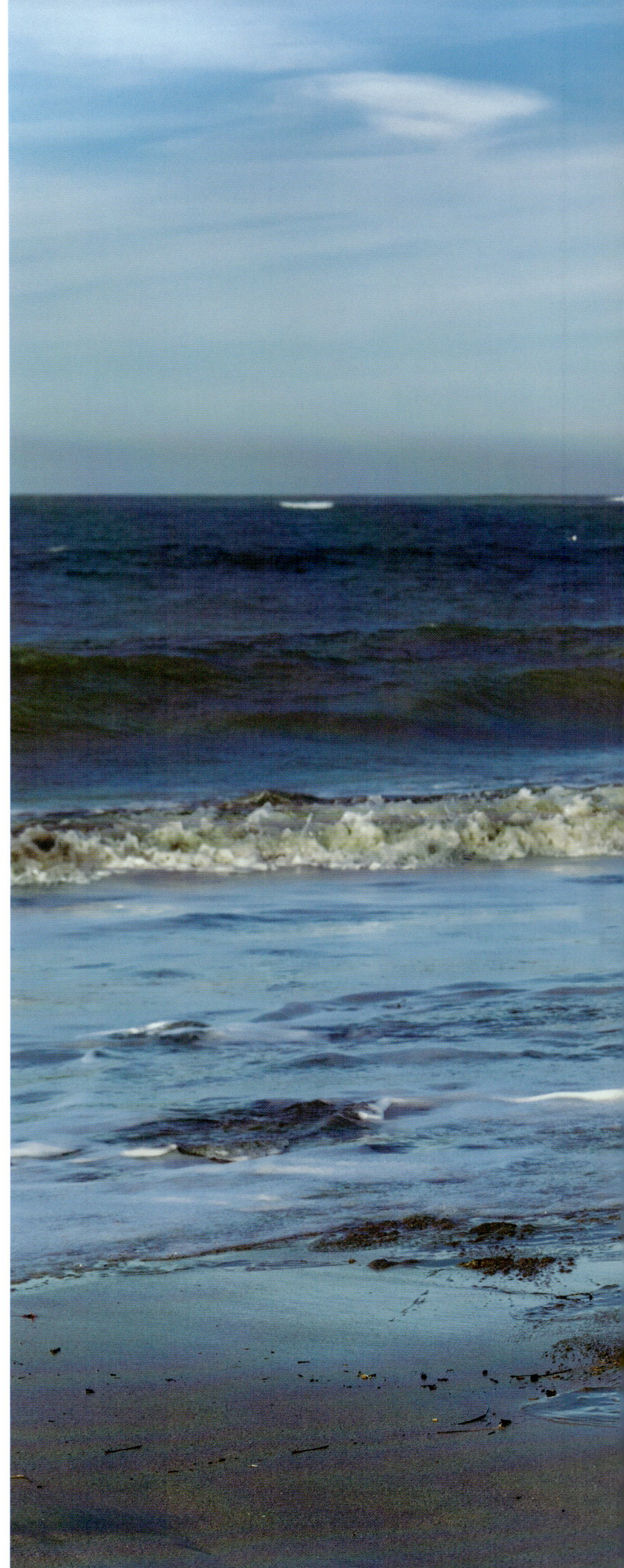

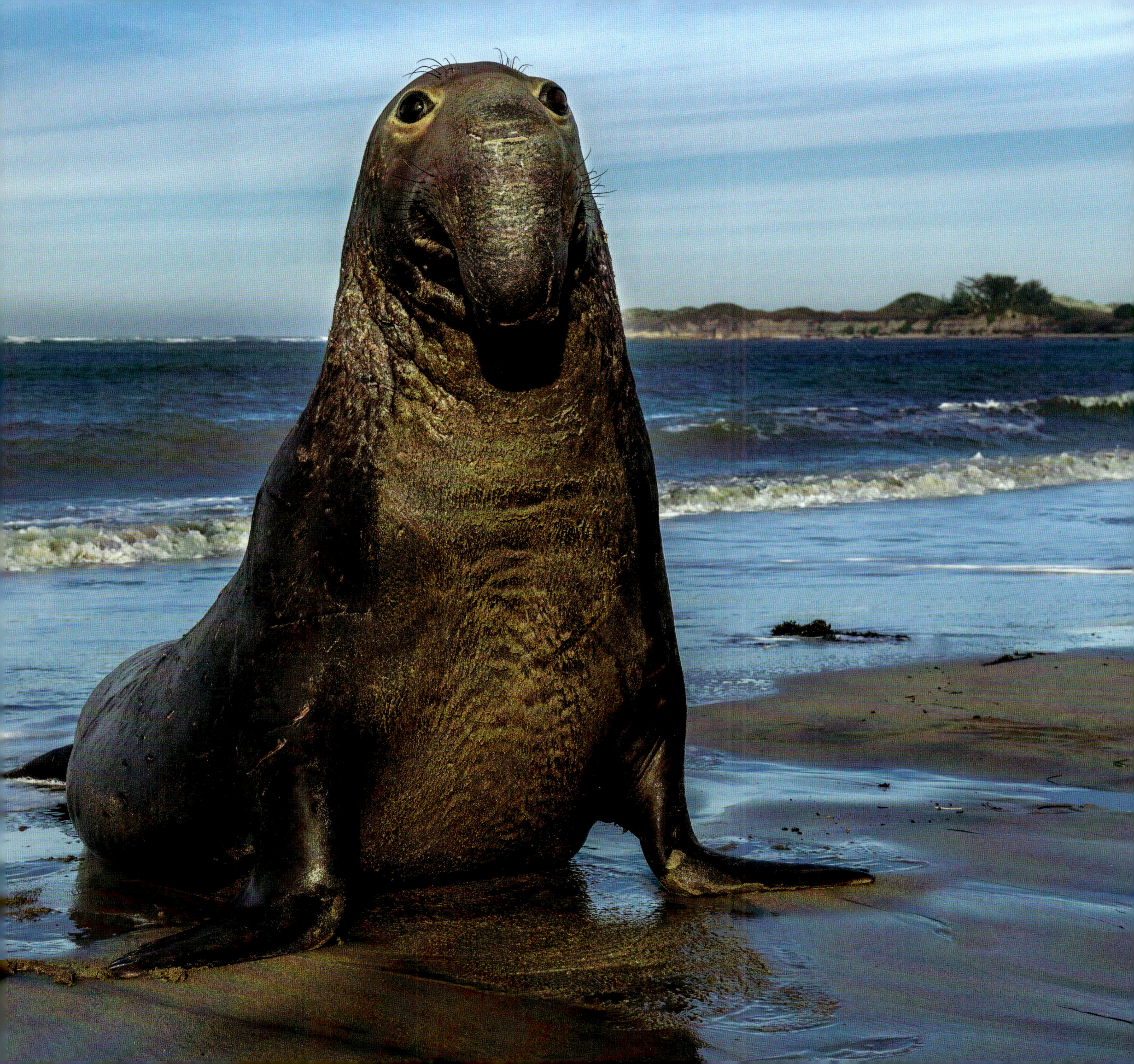

BETWEEN THE TIDES

California's intertidal zone is compressed in width, yet it stretches the length of the state. In Monterey Bay, coastal reefs and tidelands contain a rich mix of northern and southern species. The intertidal zone is an endangered habitat—and vulnerable to climate change.

REEFS AT DAWN, PIGEON POINT LIGHT STATION STATE HISTORIC PARK

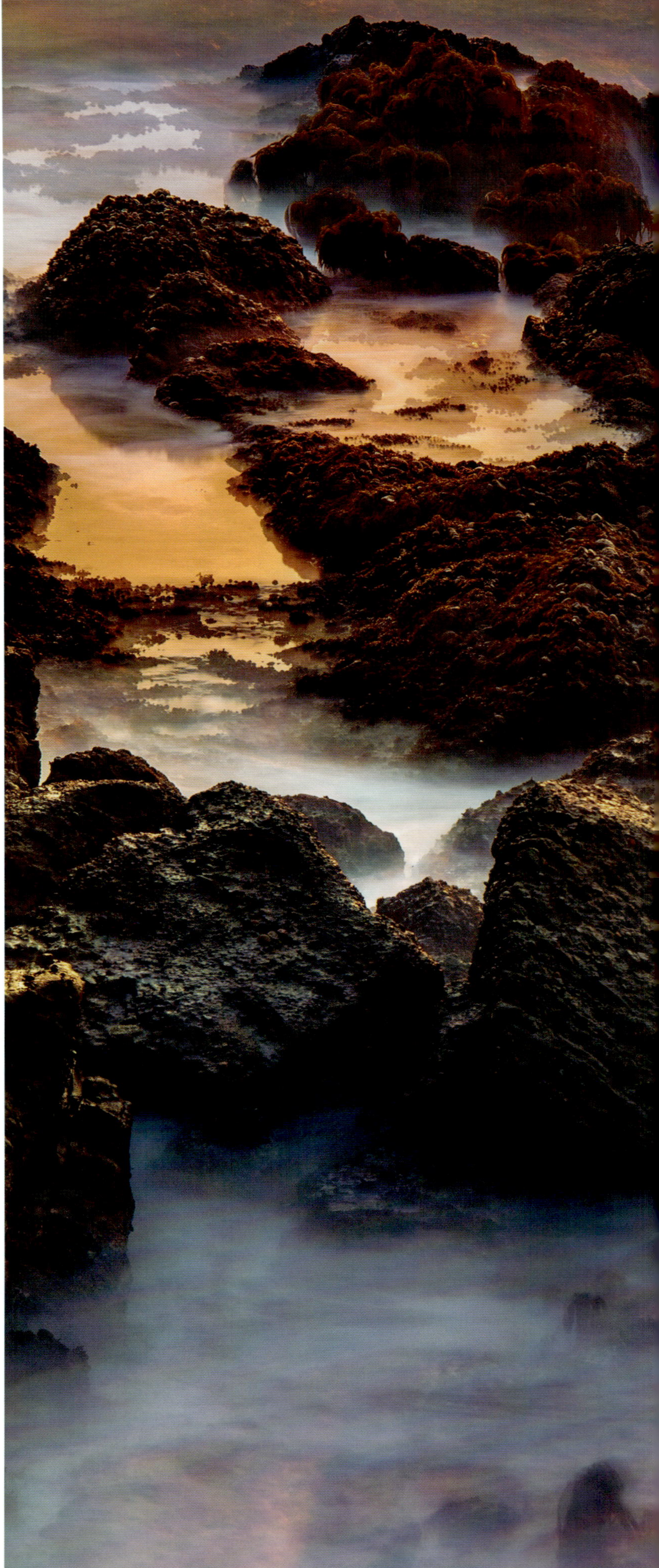

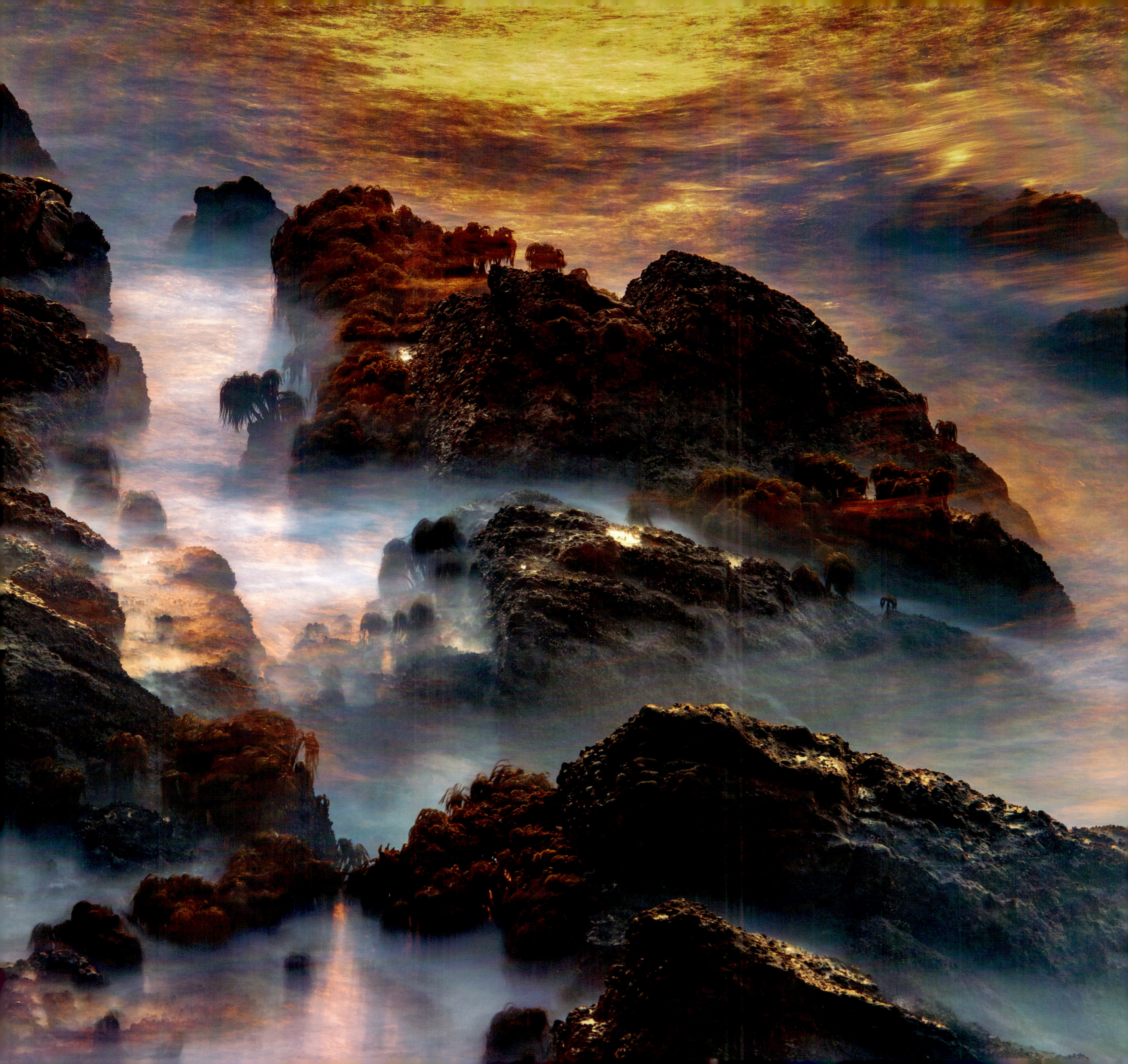

The Great Tide Pool was one of Ed Ricketts's favorite spots for collecting marine
specimens in the 1930s. He introduced many wonders of the marine world to
his friend John Steinbeck, who wrote this in his novel *Cannery Row*:
"The tide goes out imperceptibly. The boulders show and seem to rise up
and the ocean recedes leaving little pools, leaving wet weed and moss
and sponge, iridescence and brown and blue and China red.
On the bottoms lie the incredible refuse of the sea, shells broken
and chipped and bits of skeleton, claws, the whole sea bottom a fantastic
cemetery on which the living scamper and scramble."

**THE GREAT TIDE POOL, PACIFIC GROVE MARINE
GARDENS STATE MARINE CONSERVATION AREA**

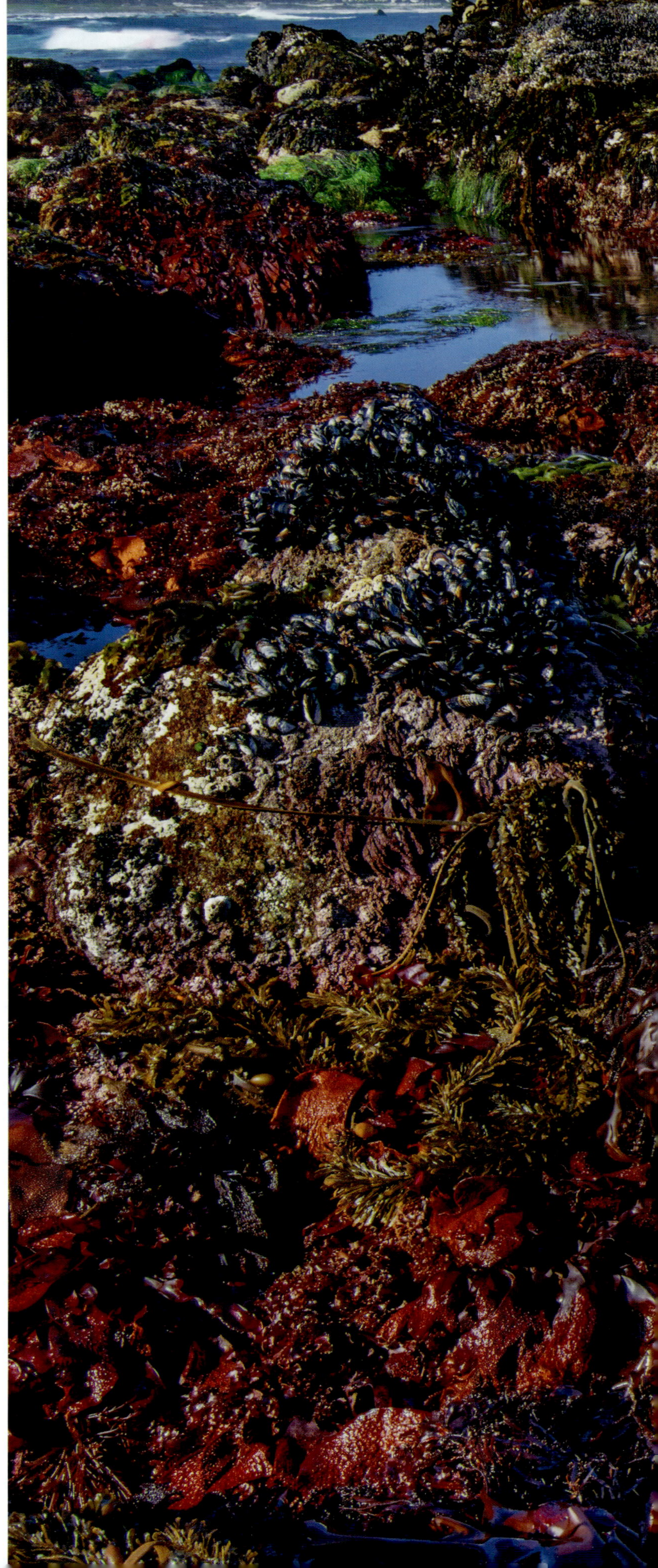

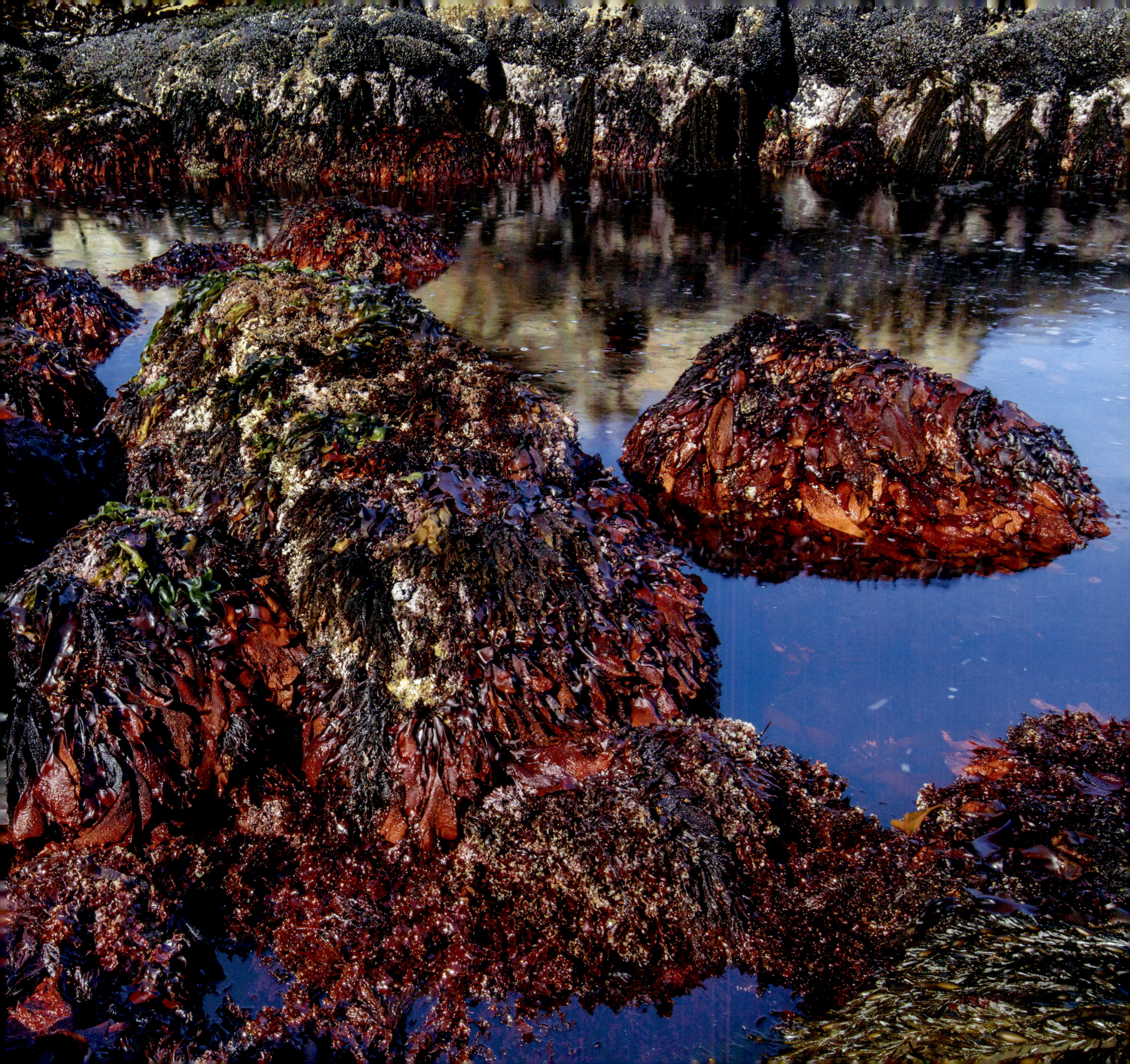

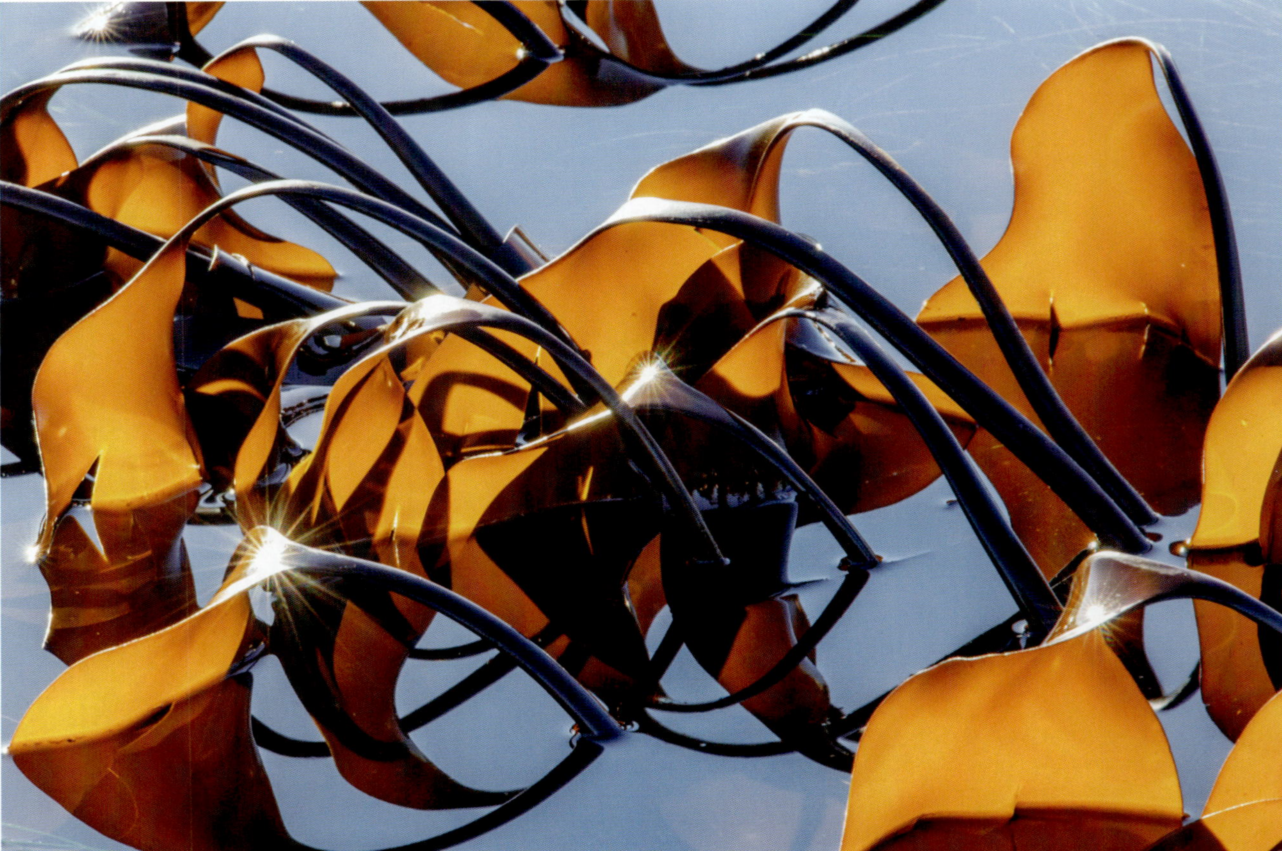

During extreme low tides, the translucent blades of stiff-stiped kelp surface at the edge of the subtidal zone where it grows on rocks. Cross sections of the stems, or stipes, can be aged like a tree, with each ring representing a year's growth.

KELP, DAVENPORT BEACH COUNTY PARK

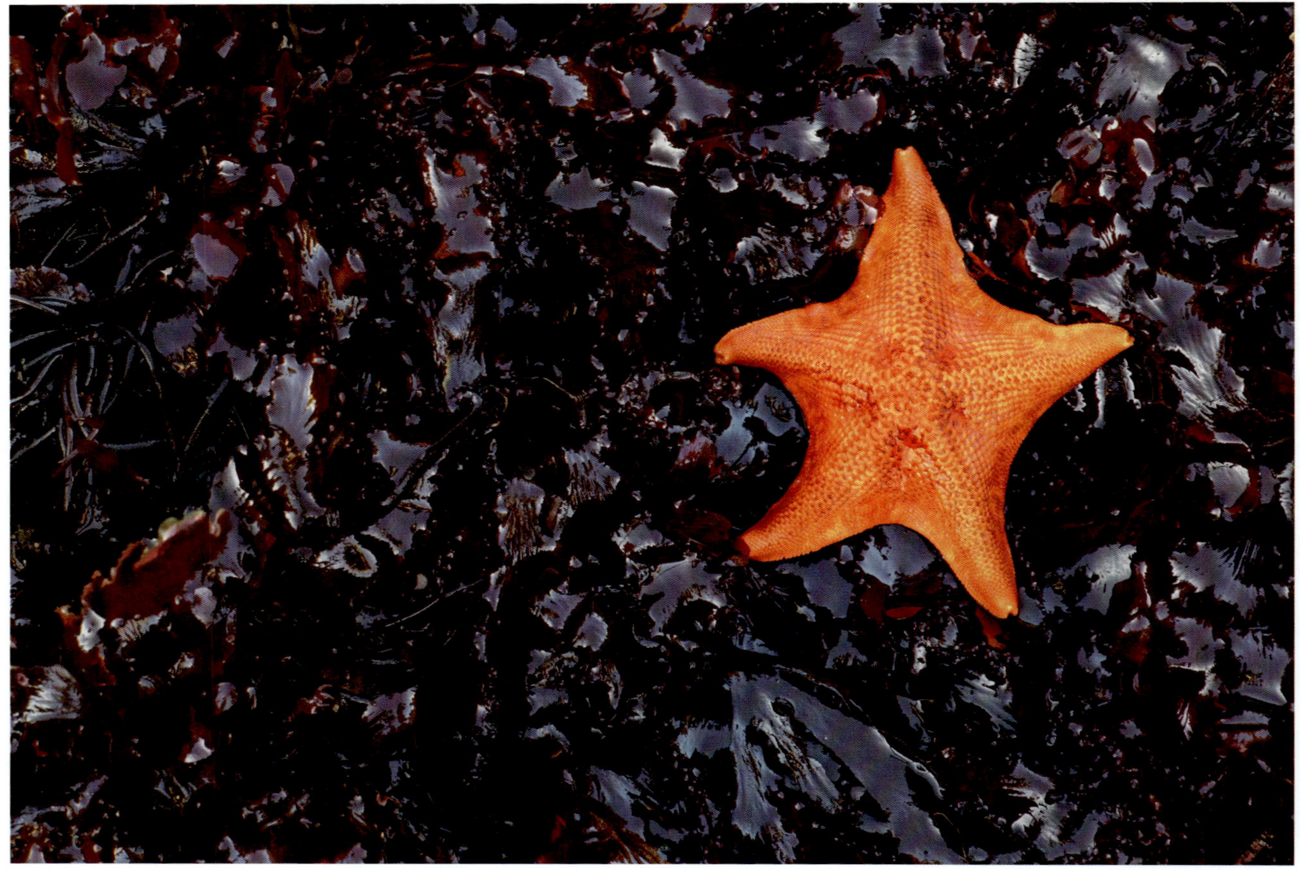

Named for the webbing between their arms that resembles a bat's wings, bat stars are scavengers that consume dead animals and algae from the seafloor. Although bat stars usually have five arms, they can have as many as nine. Eyespots at the end of each arm detect light, and tube feet on the underside are used to move and sense prey.

BAT STAR, PACIFIC GROVE MARINE GARDENS
STATE MARINE CONSERVATION AREA

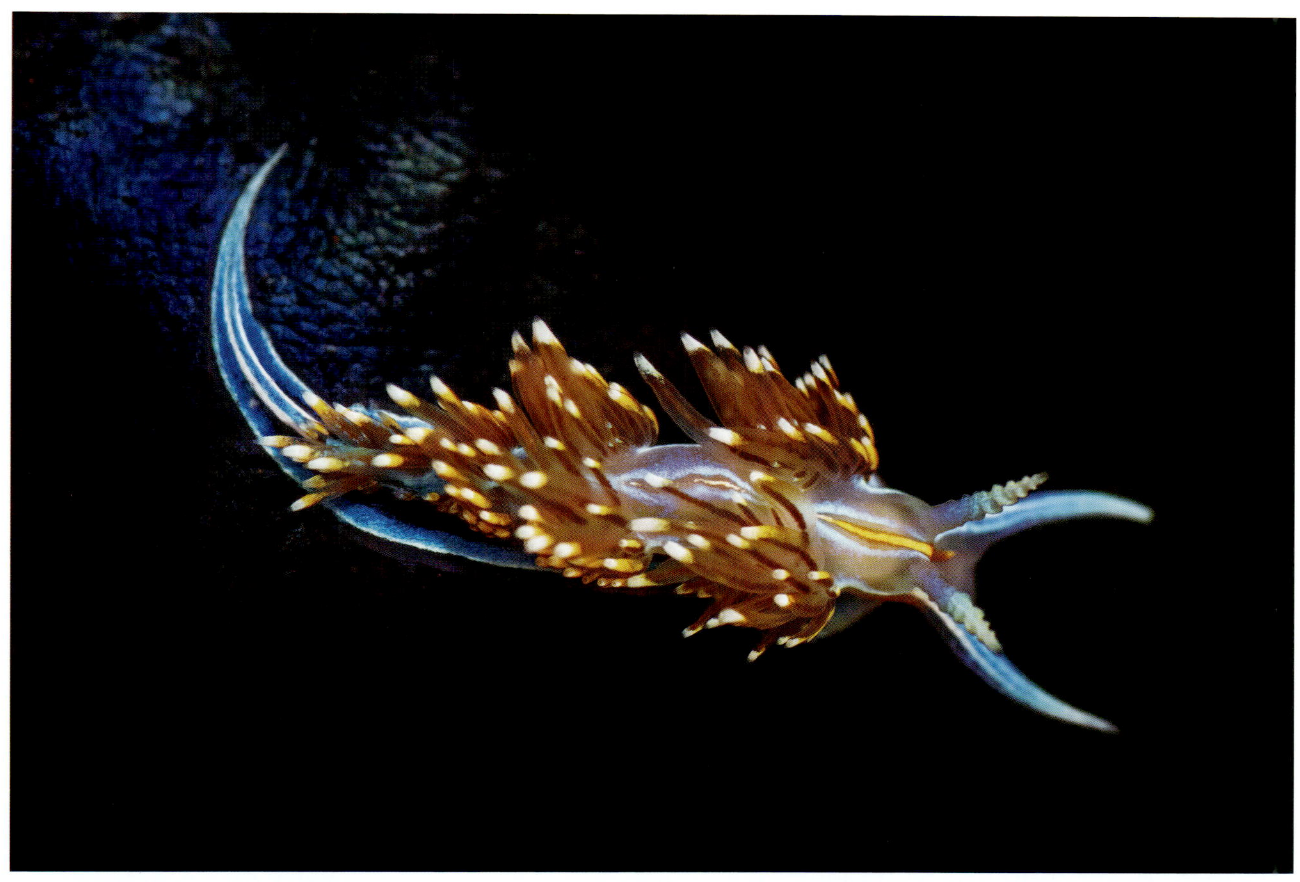

Festively patterned opalescent nudibranchs may look delicate, but they are formidable predators that feed on small anemones, jellyfish—and even each other. Impervious to the stinging cells of their prey, they can absorb those cells, store them in the white-tipped fringes on their backs, and then use them for their own defense.

NUDIBRANCH, DAVENPORT BEACH COUNTY PARK

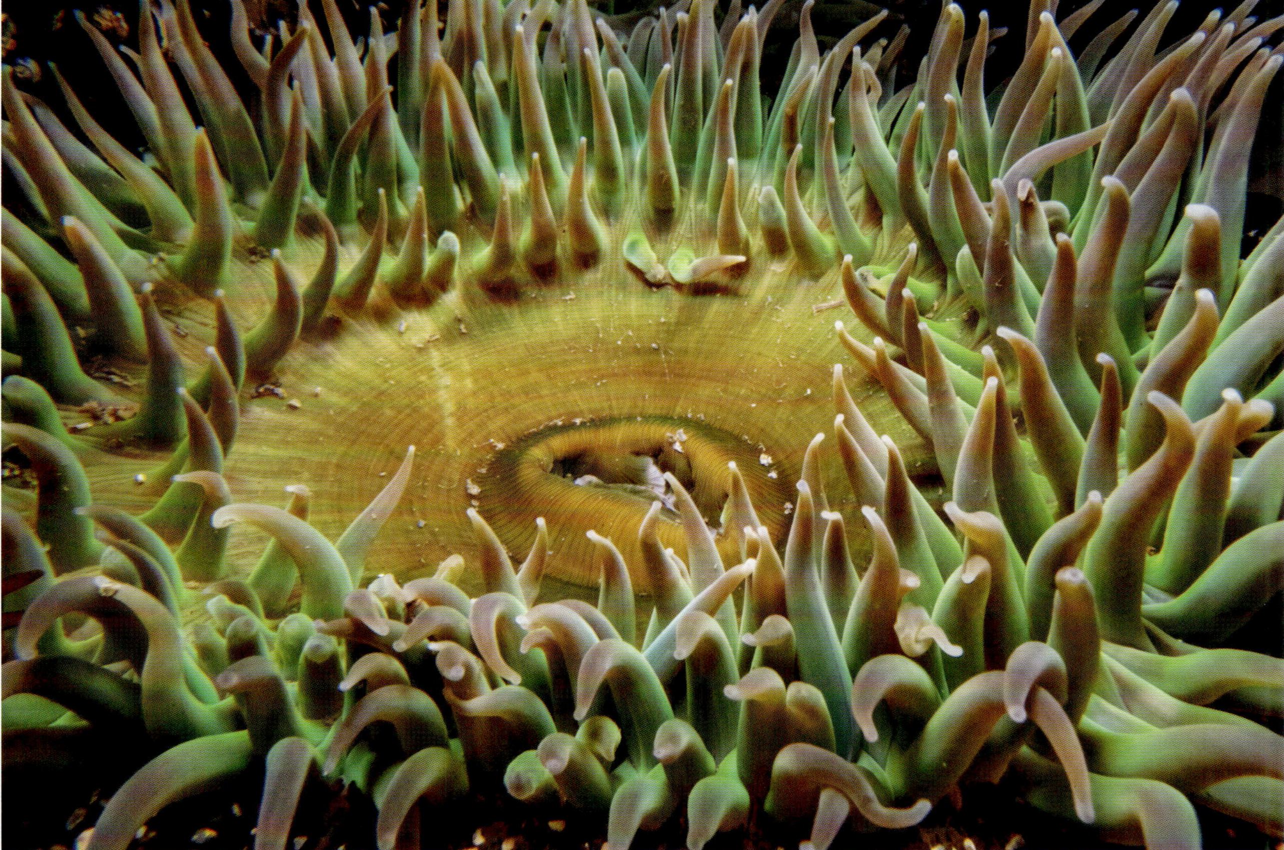

Green anemones are star attractions in Monterey Bay's tide pools. Algae and other microscopic creatures living in their tissues give them their distinctive green color.

**GREEN ANEMONE,
DAVENPORT BEACH COUNTY PARK**

FOLLOWING PAGES: The intricacy of life in a luminous tide pool reflects John Steinbeck's musings about interconnectedness: "All things are one thing and that one thing is all things— plankton, a shimmering phosphorescence on the sea and the spinning planets and an expanding universe, all bound together by the elastic string of time. It is advisable to look from the tide pool to the stars and then back to the tide pool again."

**TIDE POOL, POINT LOBOS STATE
NATURAL RESERVE**

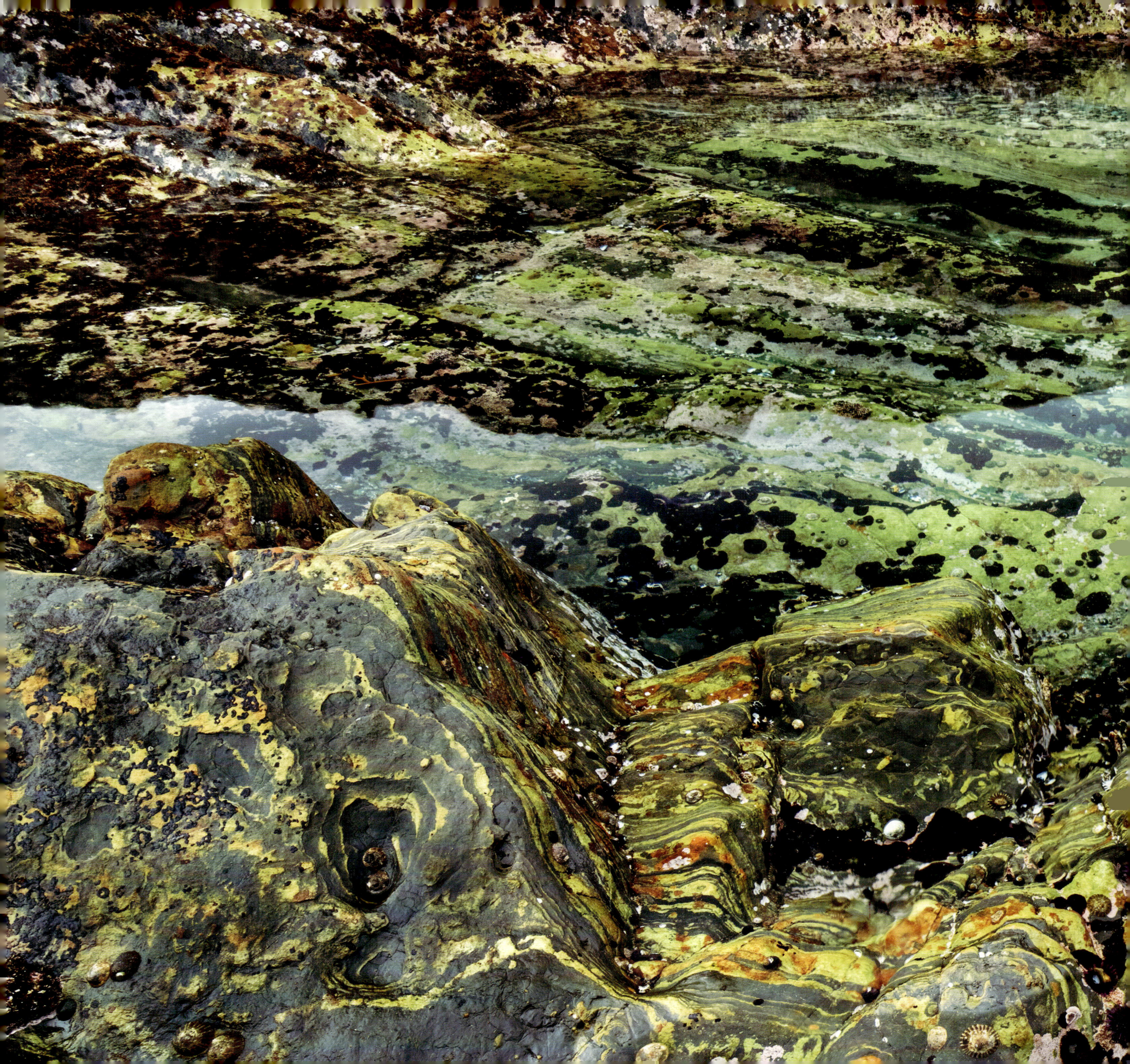

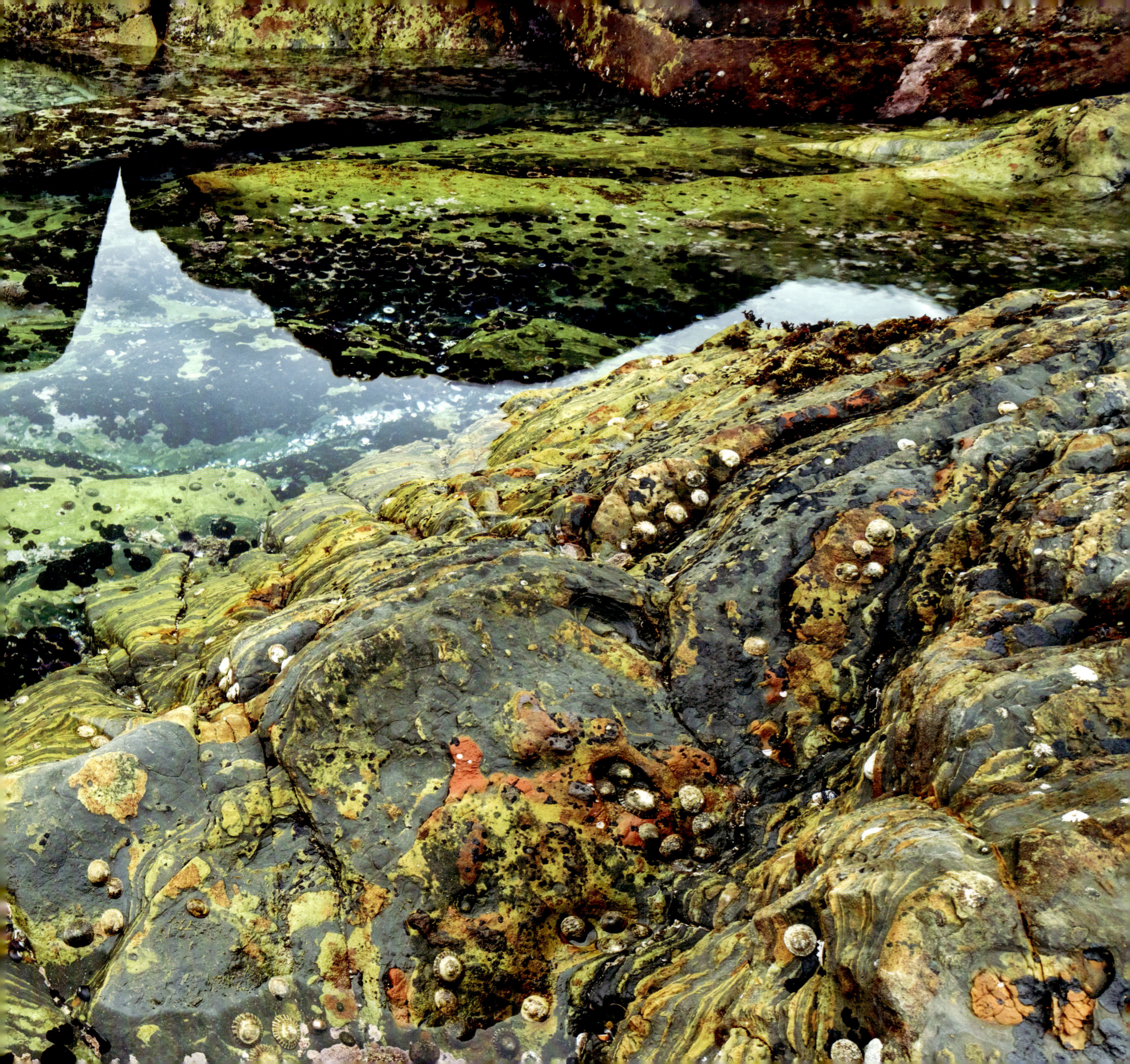

SHALLOW SEA

Blue rockfish weave through swaying strands of bull kelp. Less than a decade ago,
giant kelp forests along the California coast were hit hard by the double blow of
a multi-year marine heat wave and an explosion in sea urchin populations.
The urchins devoured kelp and the forests began to disappear. But here off Point Pinos,
a reef that was scraped bare by sea urchins and then abandoned by them is now being
recolonized by bull kelp—a hopeful sign that a new forest may take hold.

**BULL KELP AND BLUE ROCKFISH, PACIFIC GROVE MARINE
GARDENS STATE MARINE CONSERVATION AREA** | *Photo by Patrick Webster*

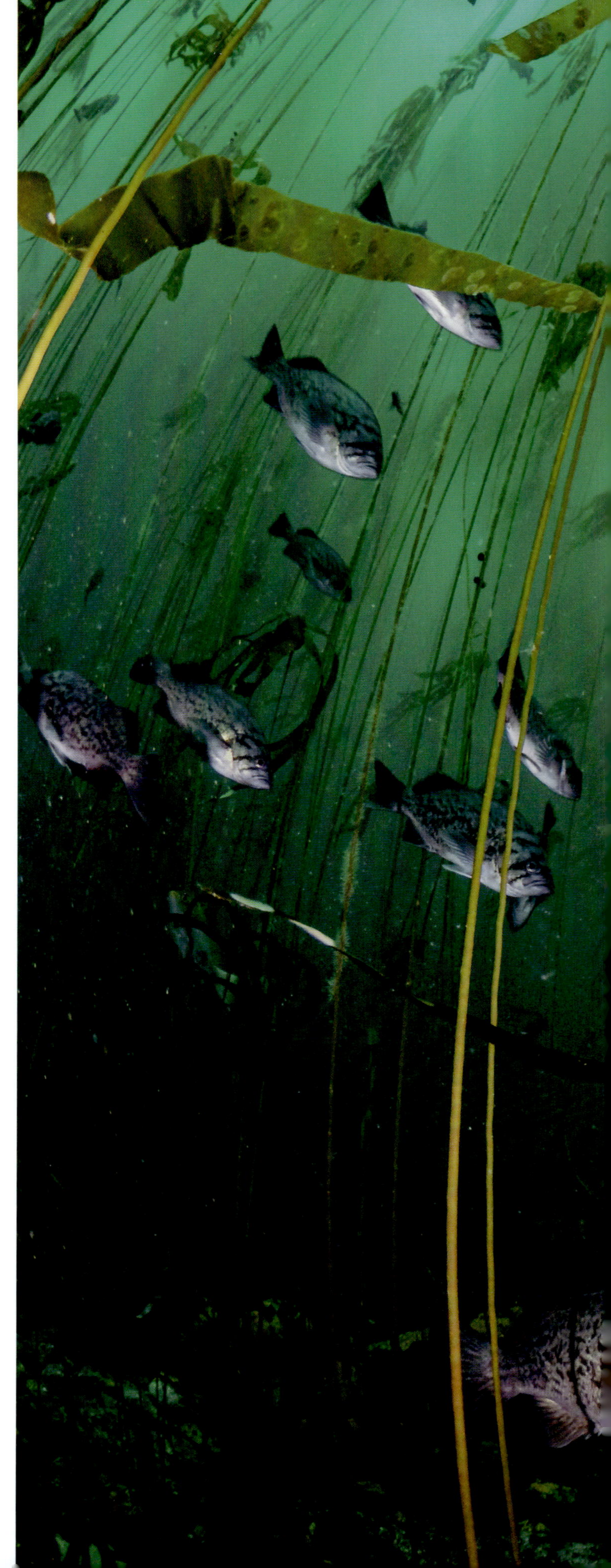

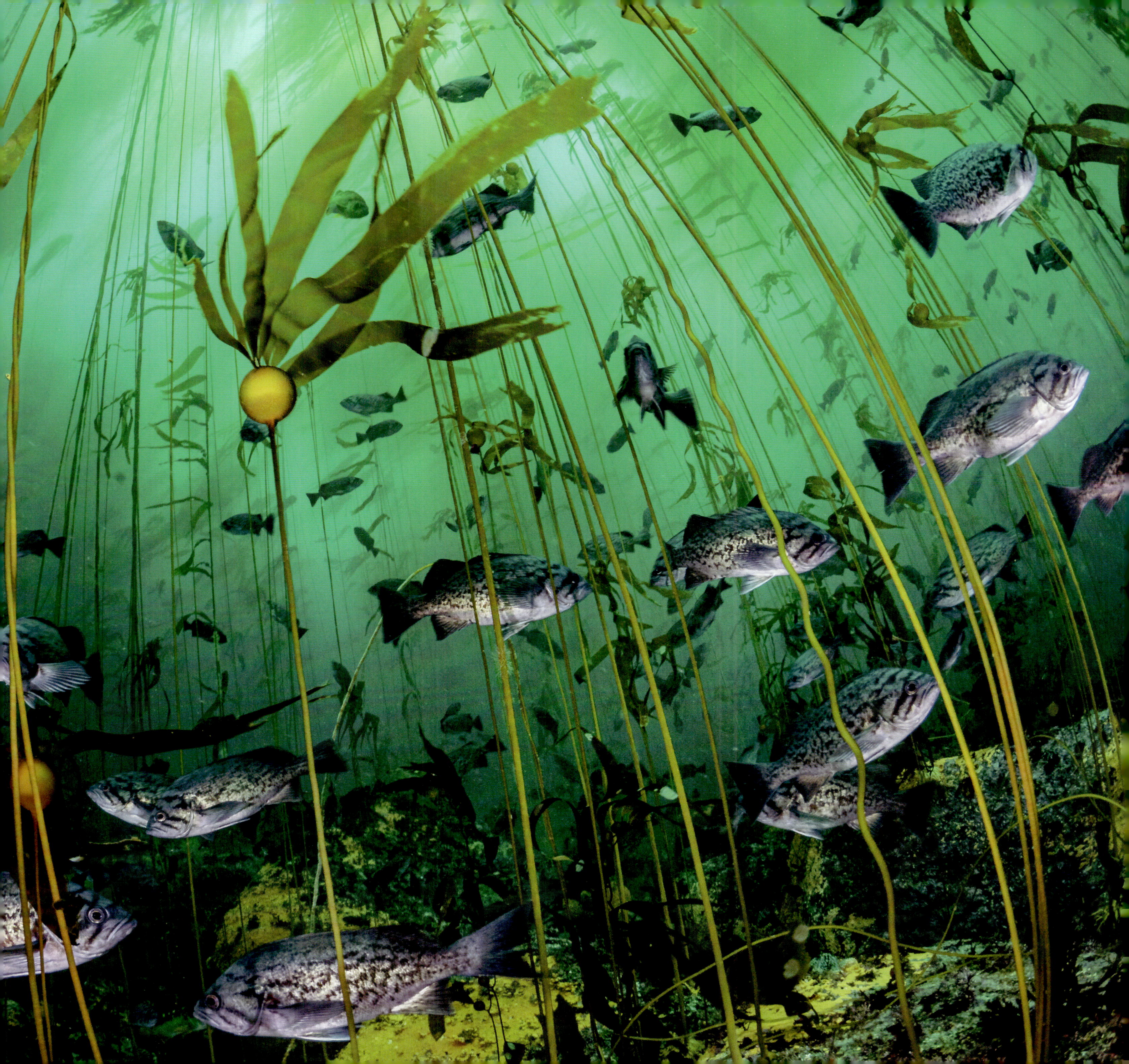

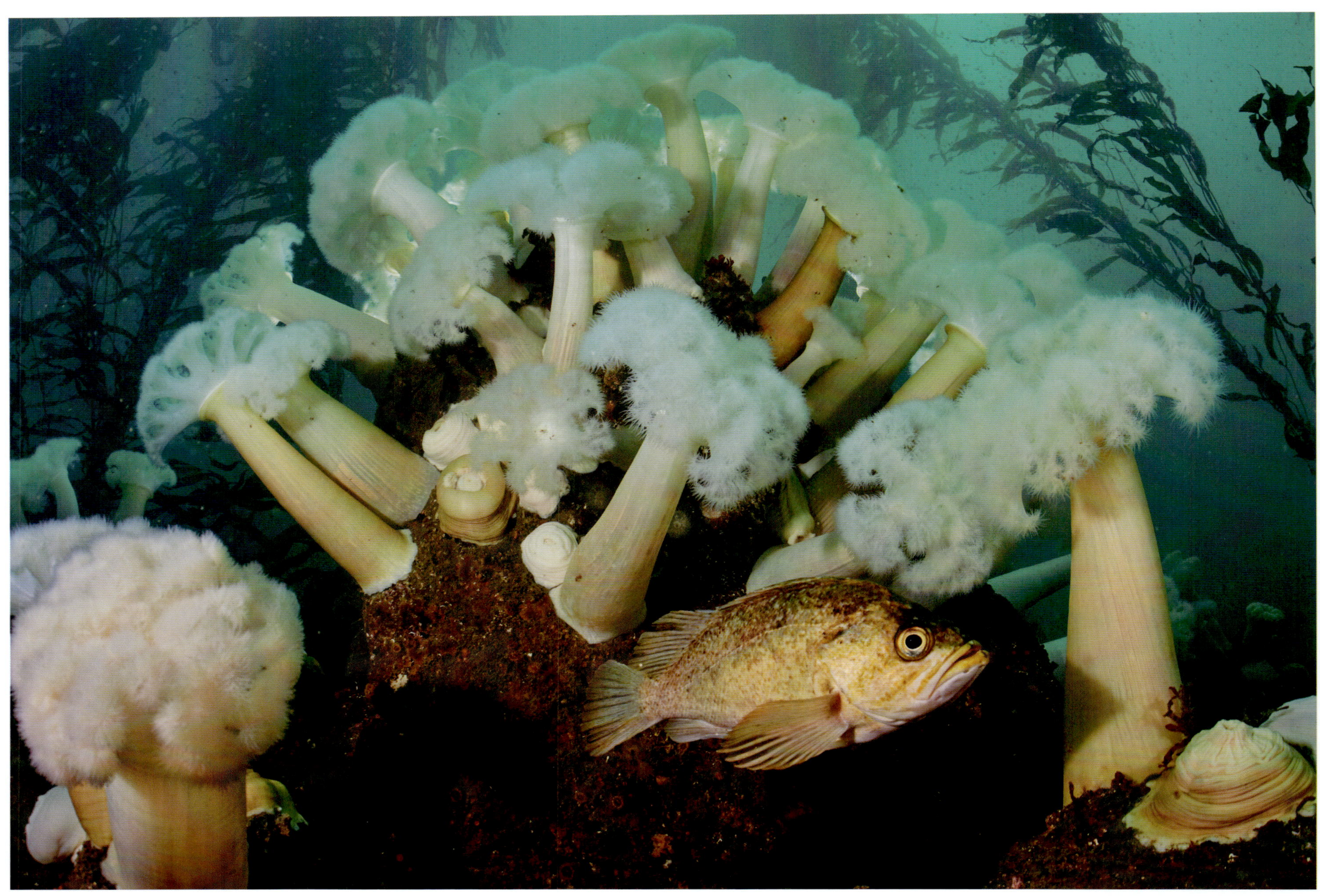

A kelp rockfish swims past a fantasy forest of white-plumed anemones growing on rocks offshore from Monterey's San Carlos Beach. The plumes on these 15-inch-tall polyps are stinging tentacles used to capture zooplankton and other small creatures.

White-plumed Anemones, Monterey Bay National Marine Sanctuary | *Photo by Justin Hofman*

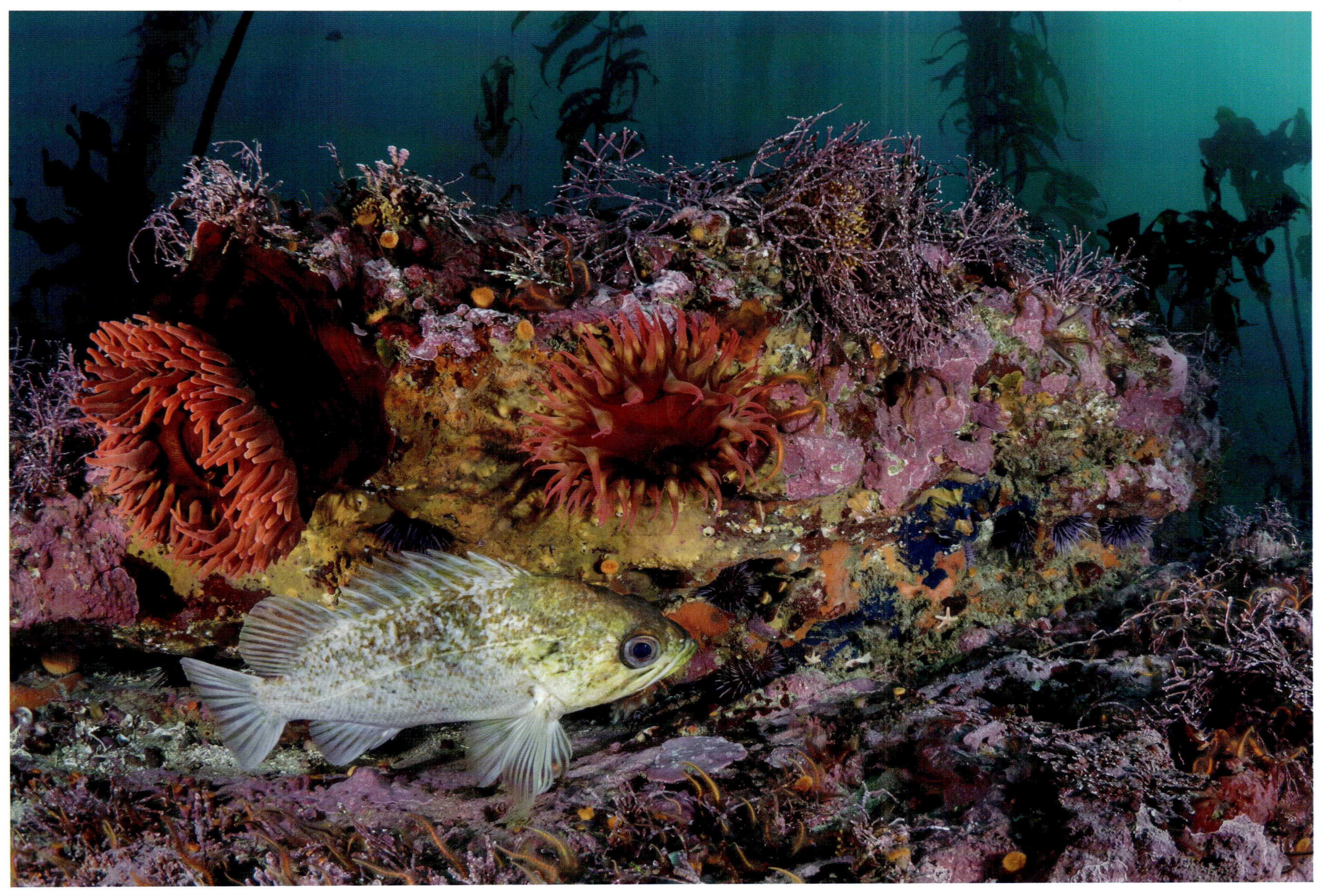

From intense competition for rocky real estate, this kelp forest reef is crowded with encrusting organisms: algae, bryozoans, sponges, tunicates, hydroids, worms, barnacles, and anemones. A solitary kelp rockfish cruises by this rainbow of life.

KELP FOREST REEF, POINT LOBOS STATE MARINE RESERVE | *Photo by Kate Vylet*

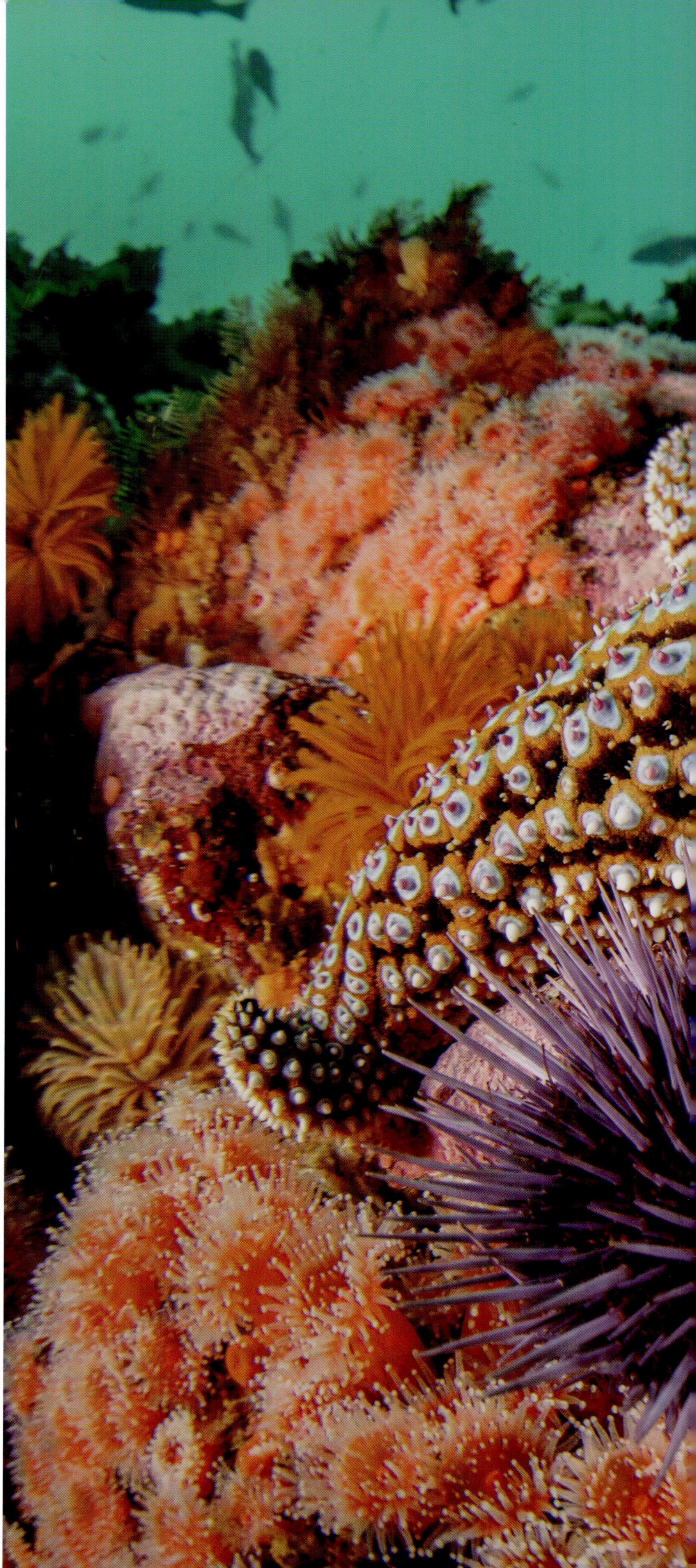

A giant sea star drapes its spiny arms over a reef of kaleidoscopic
sea life, where a purple sea urchin nestles next to a two-inch-long Hilton's
aeolid nudibranch—a frilly red-and-white sea slug with a pugnacious temperament.

REEF LIFE, CARMEL PINNACLES STATE MARINE RESERVE | *Photo by Jon Anderson*

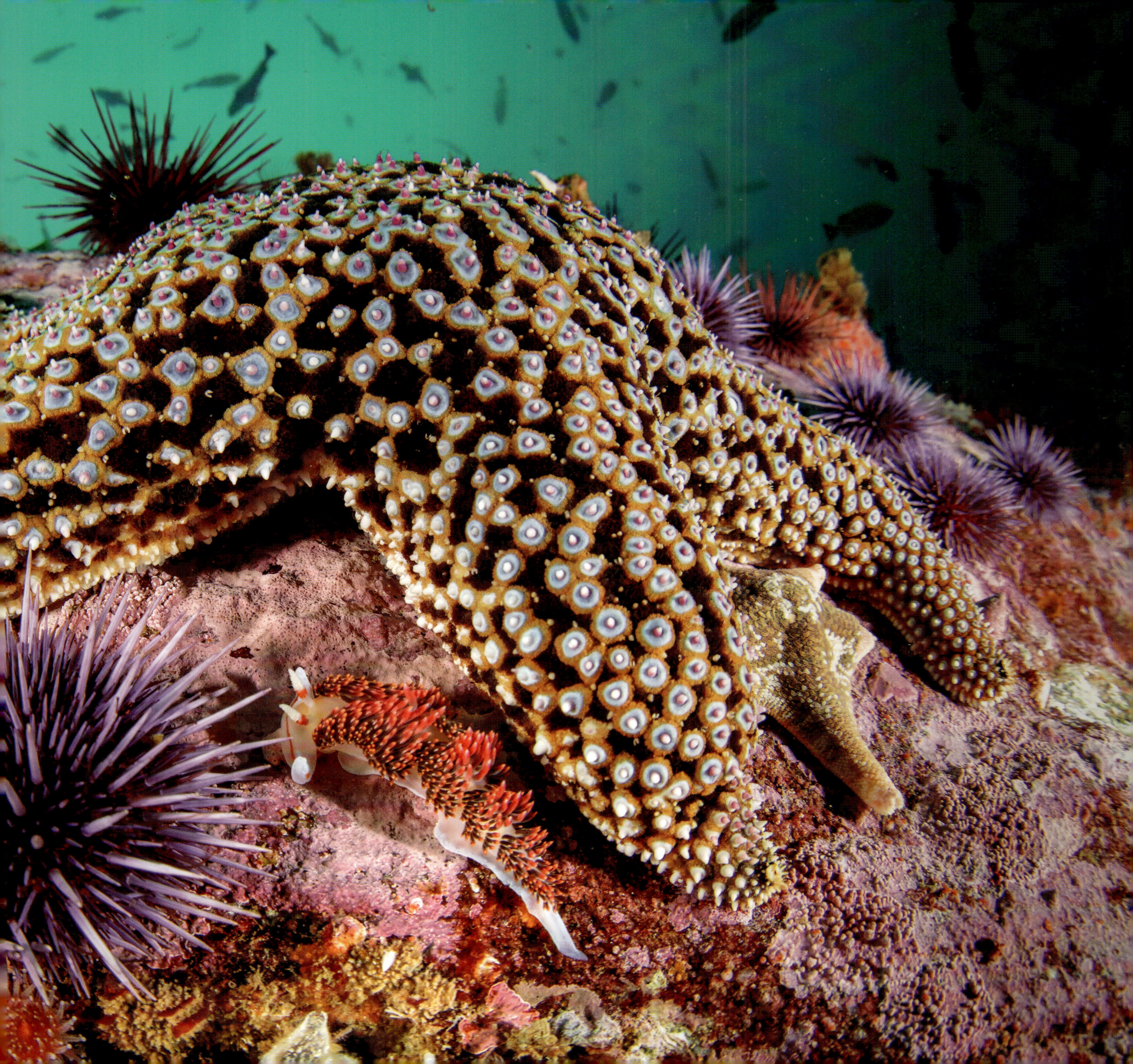

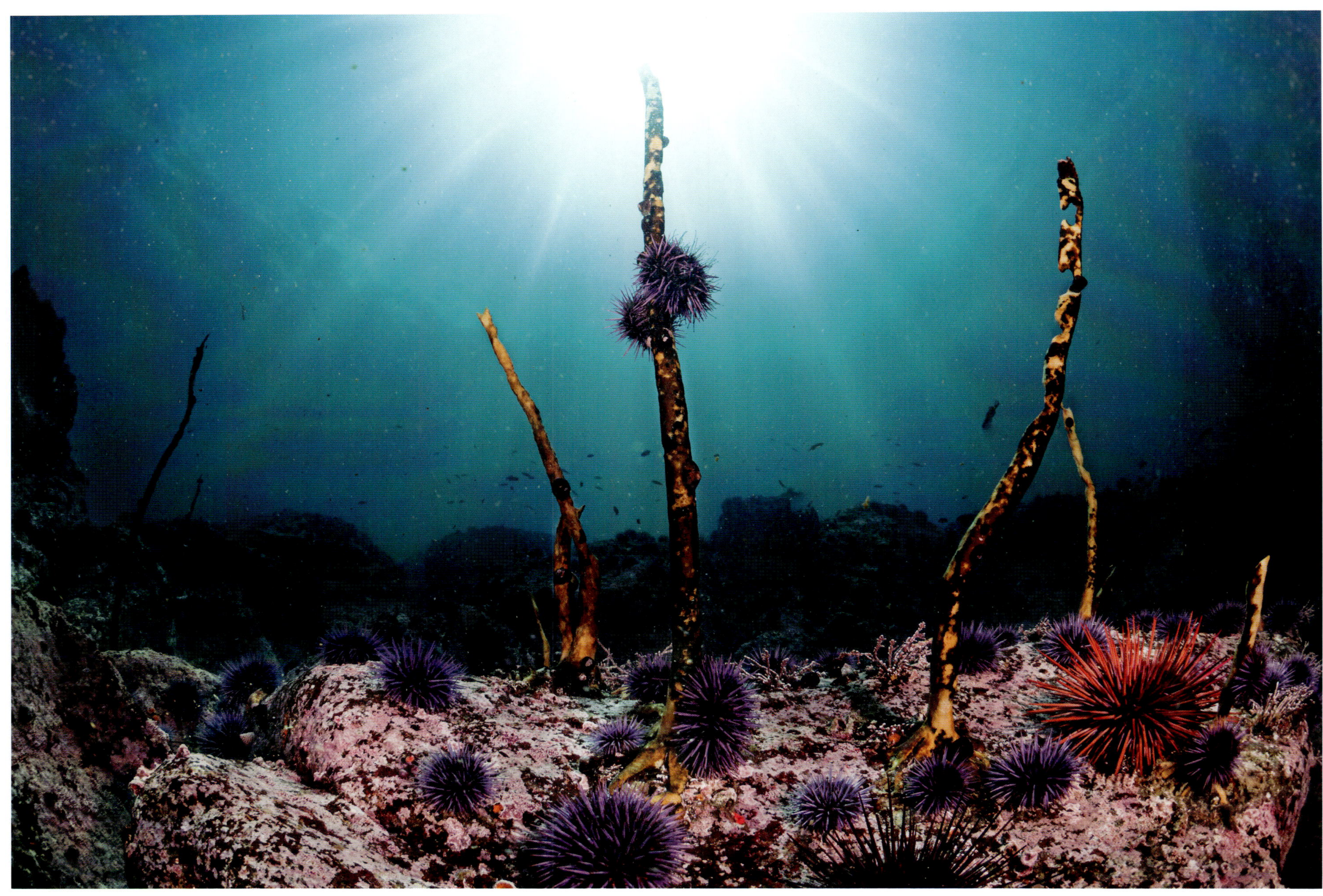

Understory kelps have been stripped bare by purple and red sea urchins, creating an "urchin barren" where little else survives. After they have exhausted their kelp food supply, the urchins eventually become so nutritionally starved that sea otters—an important predator—won't eat them. But the near-dead "zombie" urchins are still viable and may revive when giant kelp reappears.

URCHIN BARREN, CARMEL BAY STATE MARINE CONSERVATION AREA | *Photo by Patrick Webster*

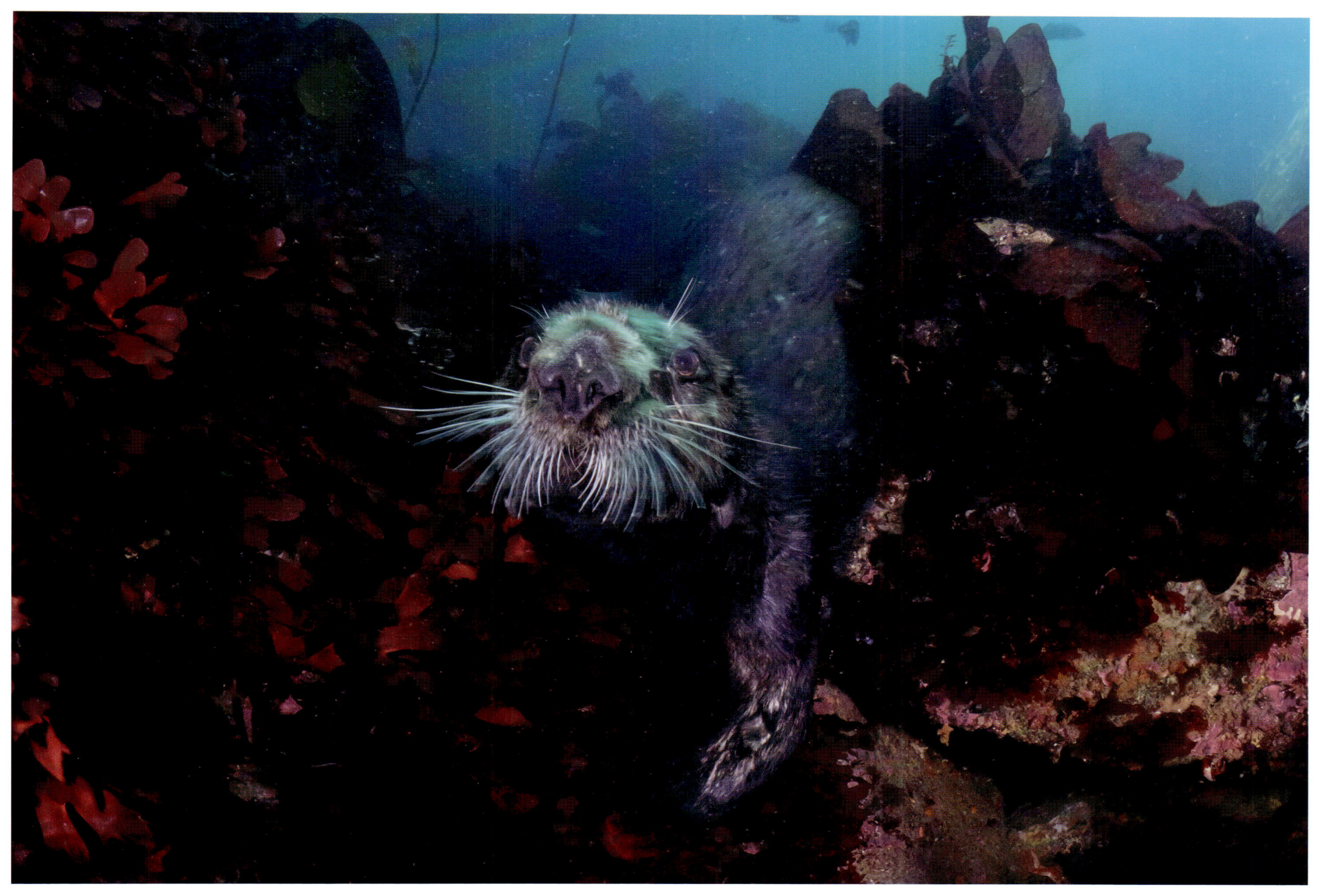

Guardians of kelp forests, sea otters feed on sea urchins, which adds balance to the ecosystem.
After urchin populations boomed, sea otters began to consume them and since then, otter
populations have increased—a predator-prey shift that may enable more kelp beds to regenerate.

Sea Otter, Point Lobos State Marine Reserve | *Photo by Kate Vylet*

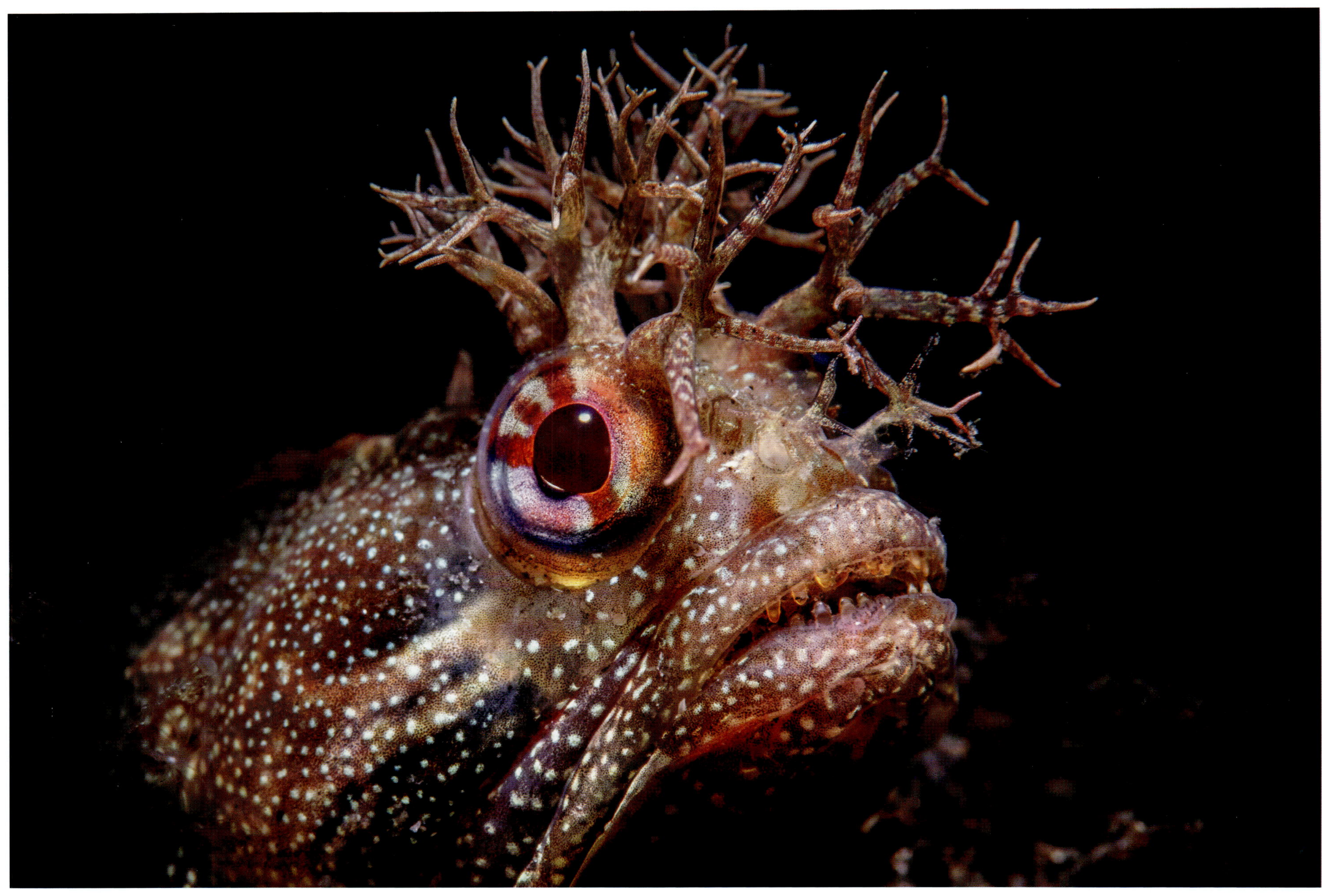

A two-inch-long fish with a fearless personality, the yellowfin fringehead sports a crown of multi-branched appendages called "cirri," which serves as camouflage. Curious and defiant, it peers out from its hiding place in a rocky hole.

Yellowfin Fringehead, Edward F. Ricketts State Marine Conservation Area | *Photo by Jon Anderson*

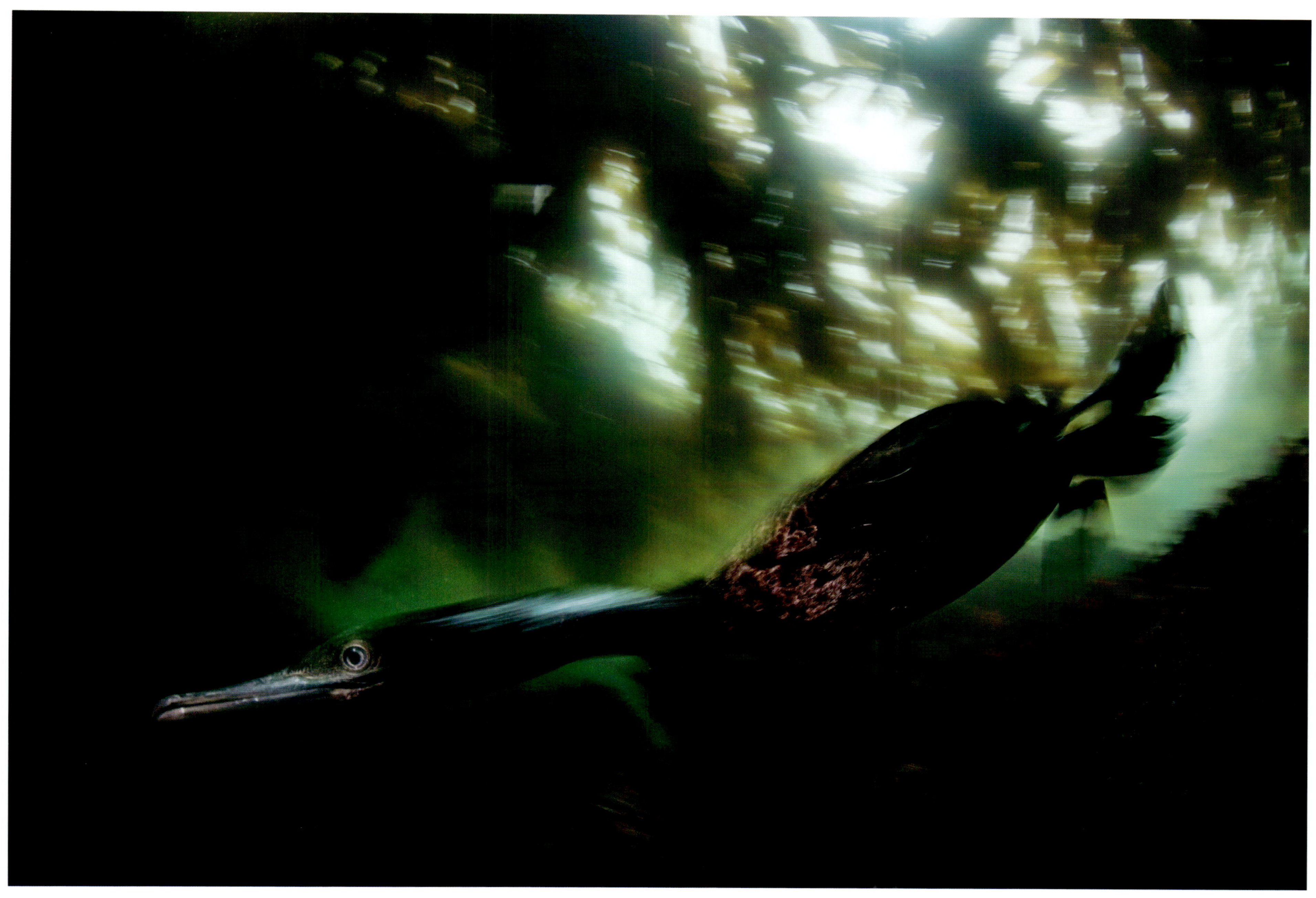

During the summer Brandt's cormorants take over Monterey's Coast Guard jetty where they nest.
Underwater, these sleek seabirds dart through the kelp as they hunt for small fish such as señorita wrasse,
blacksmiths, and young rockfish.

Brandt's Cormorant, Edward F. Ricketts State Marine Conservation Area | *Photo by Joe Platko*

OPEN OCEAN

Common dolphins come into Monterey Bay from the south
during summer months. They are acrobatic and wonderful to watch
when they appear in small groups, but when they gather in superpods of
thousands of individuals, they become a truly spectacular sight.

COMMON DOLPHINS, MONTEREY BAY NATIONAL MARINE SANCTUARY
Photo by Chase Dekker

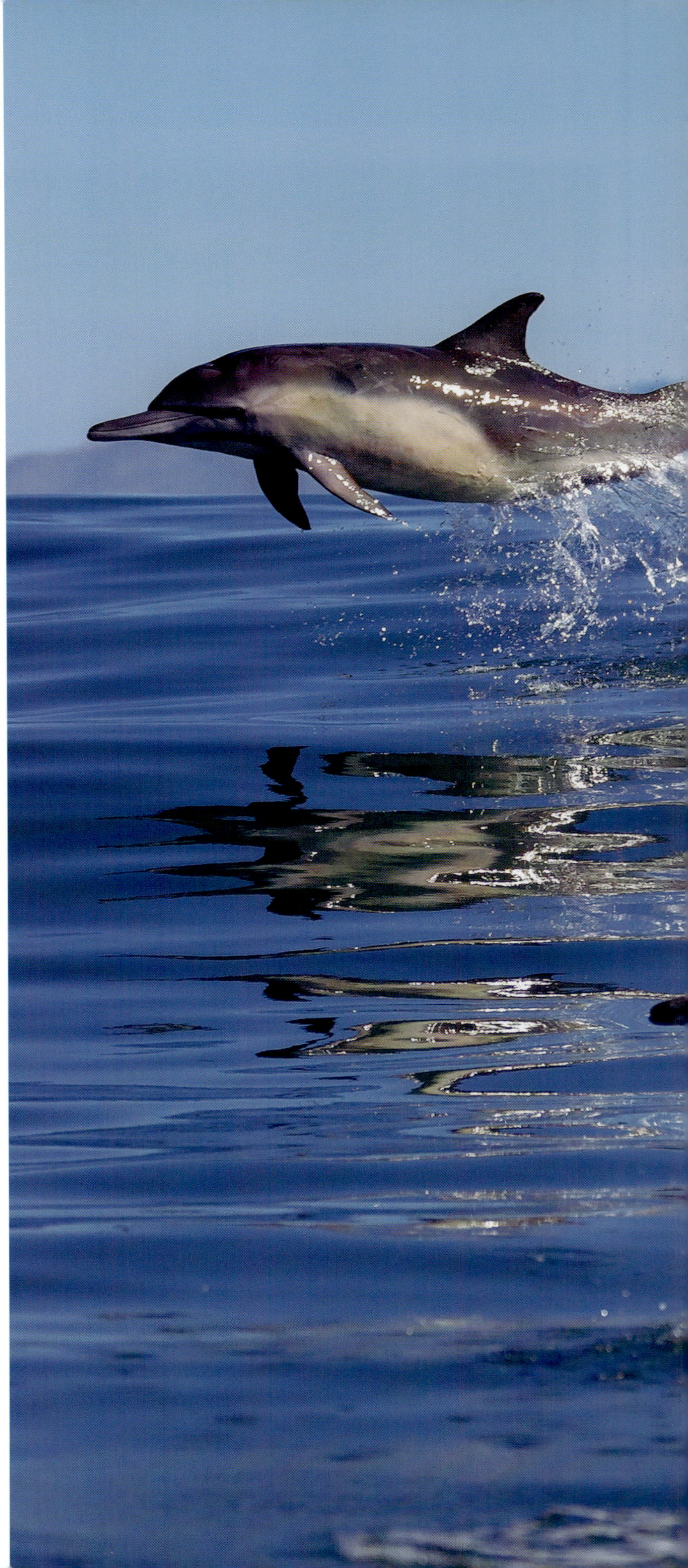

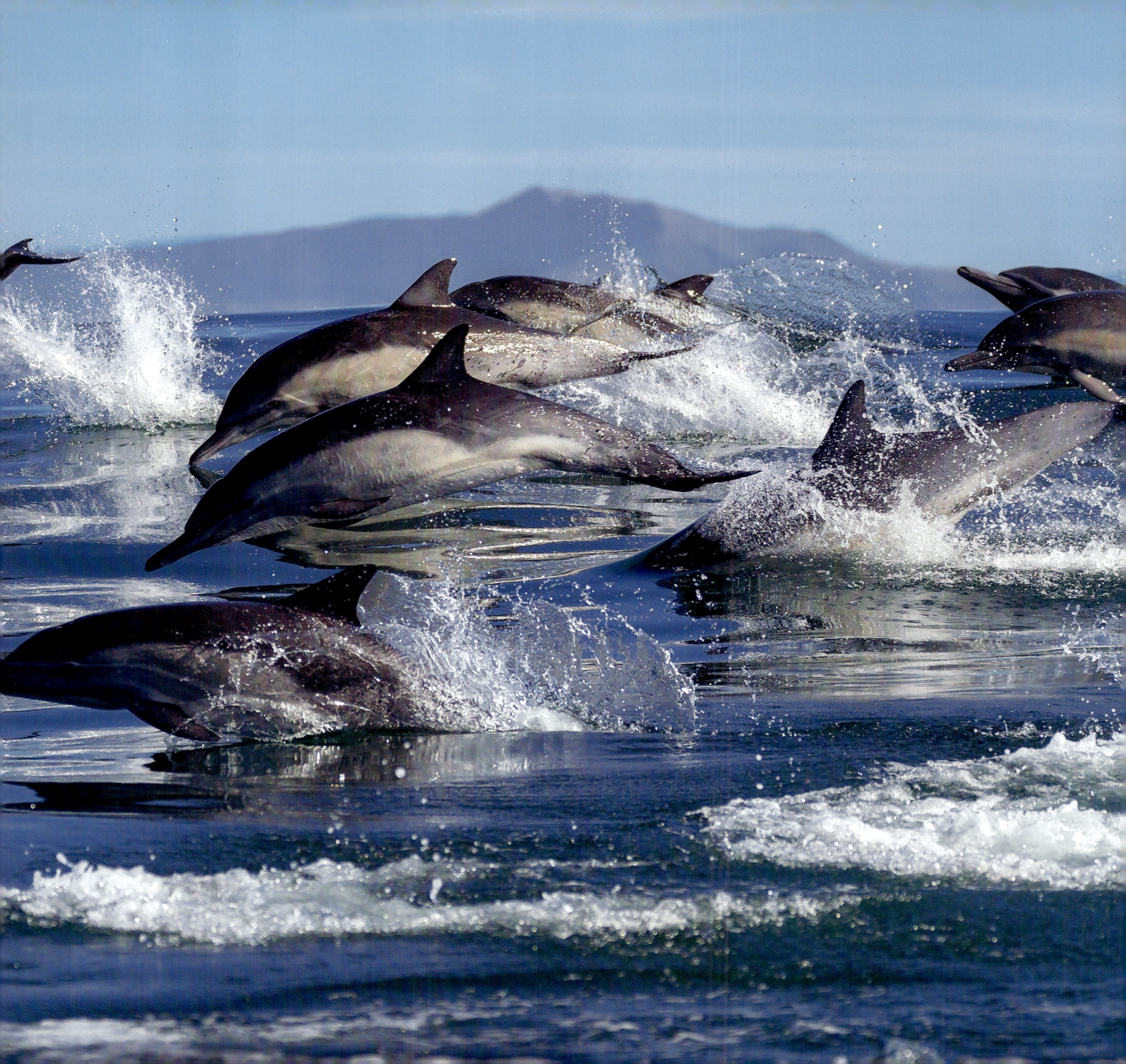

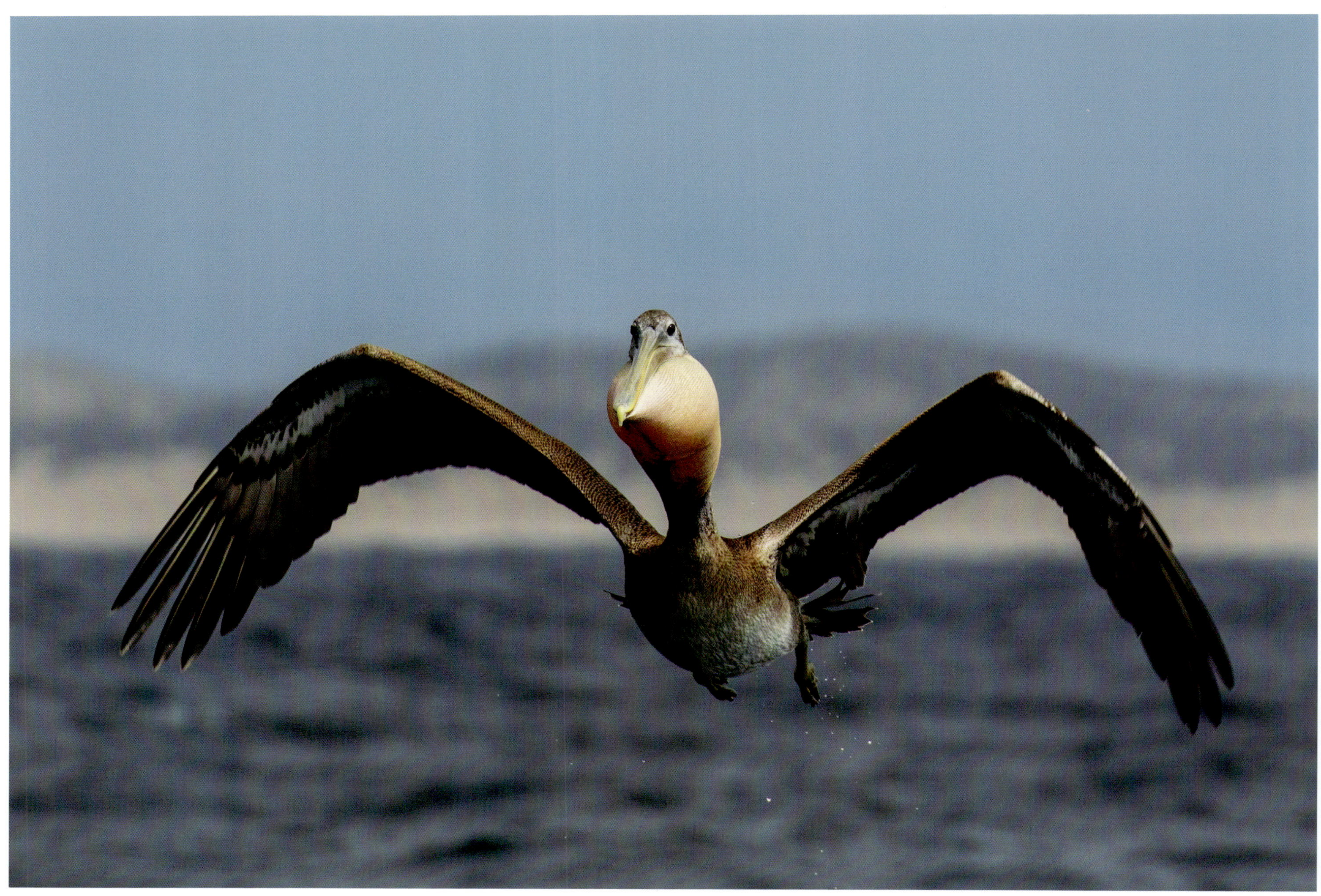

Brown pelicans are gulpers. They grab fish during shallow dives and drain the water from their expandable pouches when they come back up for air. Monterey Bay supports thousands of brown pelicans, but they no longer nest here. Point Lobos used to host a breeding colony, but it collapsed during the 1950s due to the poisonous effects of DDT, and the birds have not resettled there since. These days, adults fly down to the Channel Islands and Baja California to reproduce before returning to the bay, but perhaps one day they will start breeding here again.

BROWN PELICAN, MONTEREY BAY NATIONAL MARINE SANCTUARY | *Photo by Jodi Frediani*

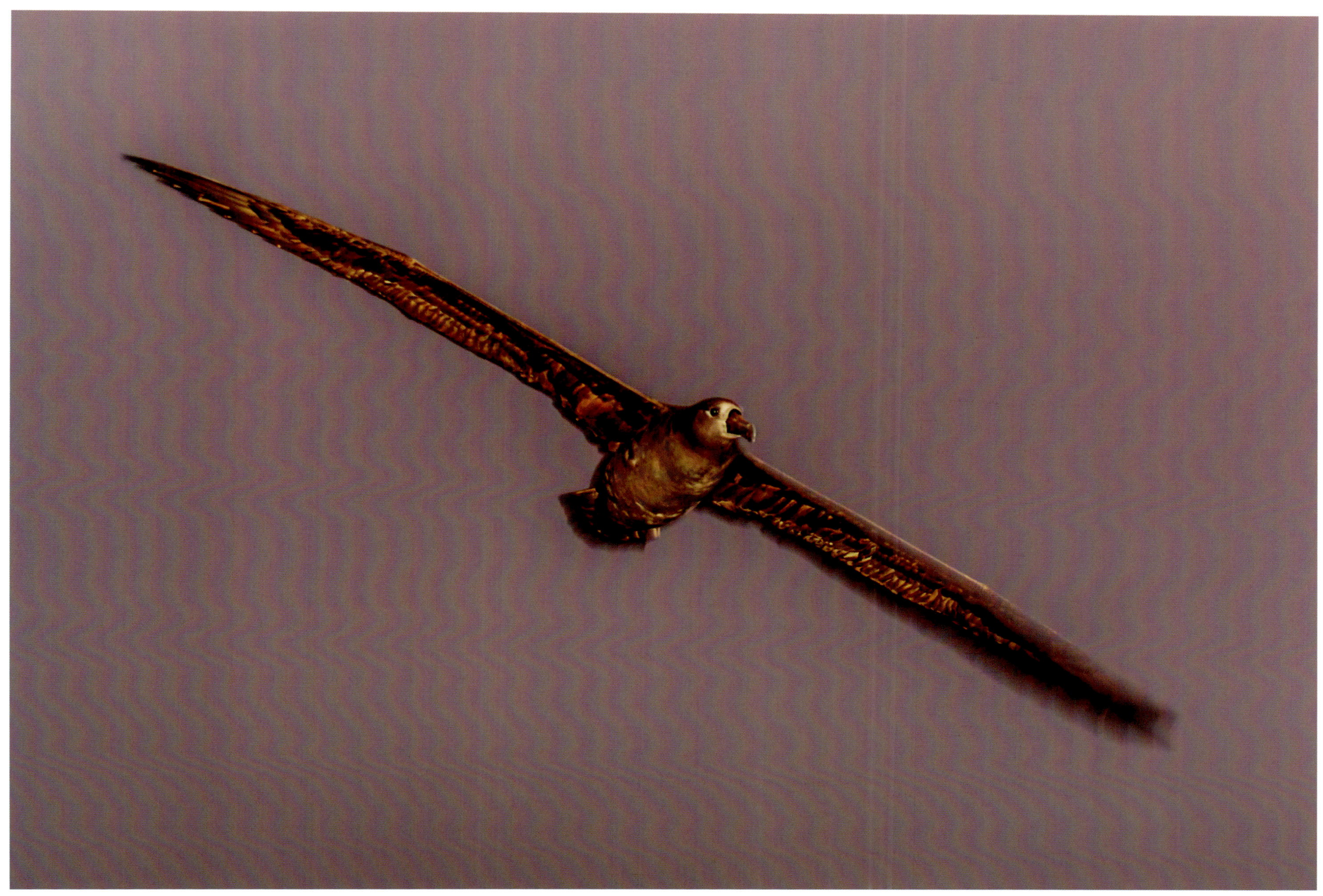

Albatrosses are legendary birds of the open ocean and seldom come close to mainland shorelines. But because of the deep-sea environment in the Monterey Canyon, albatrosses can be seen here within 15 miles of the beach. Black-footed albatrosses fly all the way from Hawaii's Leeward Islands to Monterey Bay to forage on fish and squid in midsummer.

Black-footed Albatross, Pacific Ocean

following pages: Sooty shearwaters come to Monterey Bay to fatten up before they embark on an epic oceanic journey back to islands near New Zealand where they nest.

Sooty Shearwaters, Monterey Bay National Marine Sanctuary

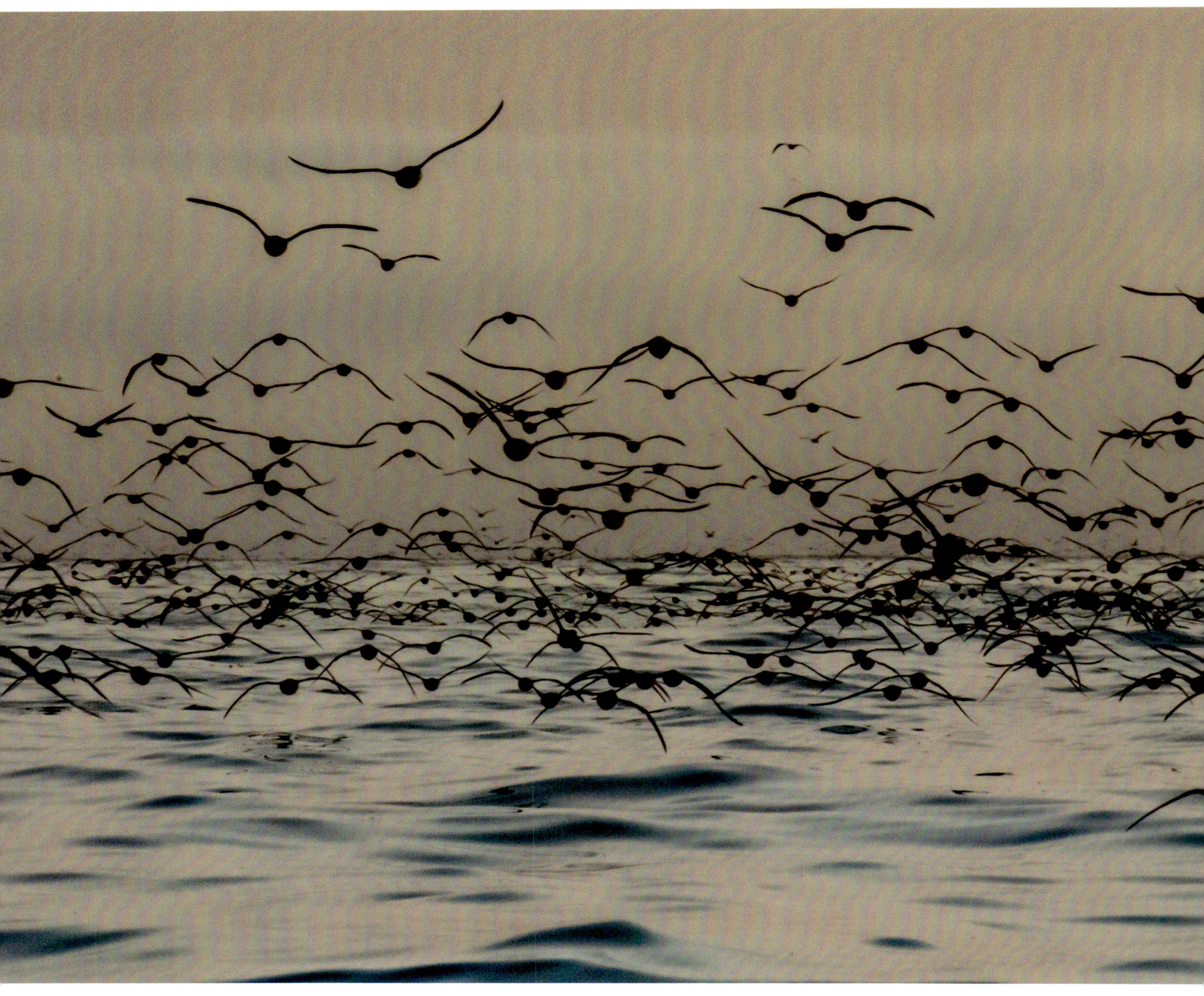

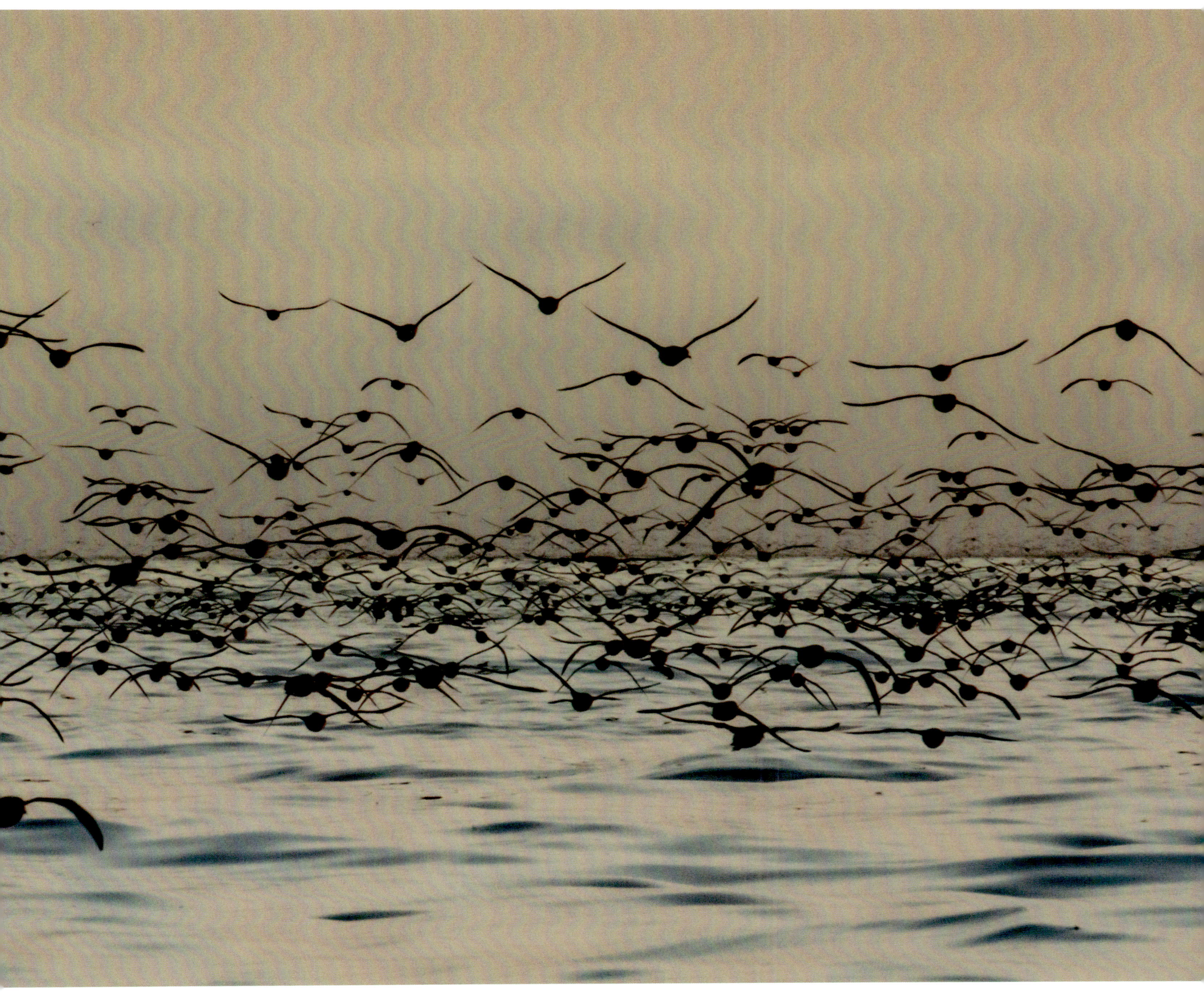

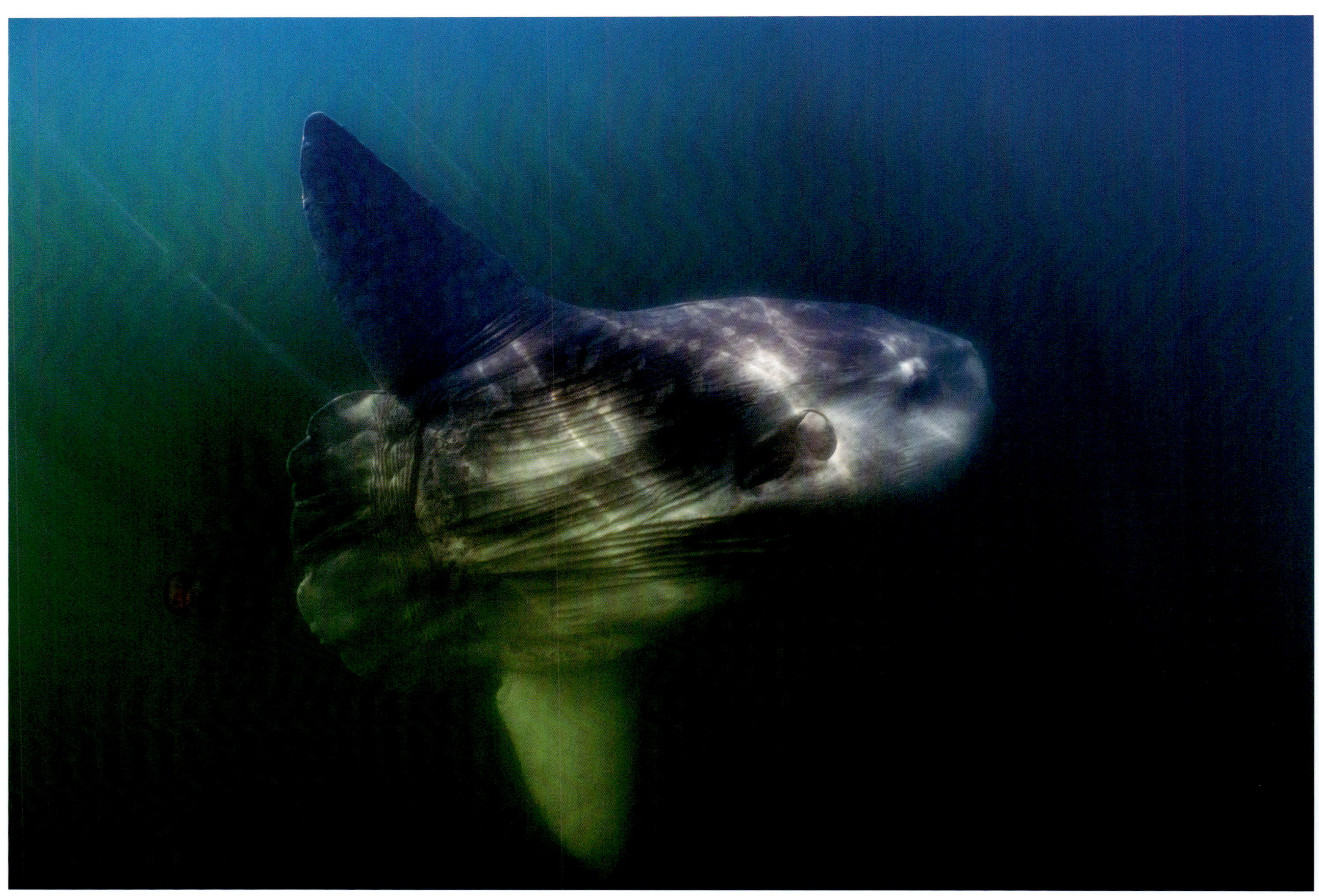

The *Mola mola*—or ocean sunfish—is an improbable looking fish with a huge flattened head six feet long, two rudder-like fins, and almost no tail. Its common name, sunfish, comes from its habit of sunbathing at the surface.

Mola mola, Monterey Bay National Marine Sanctuary | *Photo by Ralph Pace*

OPPOSITE: Market squid are prolific but live less than a year, and they die after they breed. During one summer week, large congregations came up to the edge of the Monterey Canyon off Monastery Beach where they mated and laid eggs. This individual, which had just reproduced, flashed its color-producing chromatophores then sank into the depths.

Market Squid, Point Lobos State Marine Reserve | *Photo by Joe Platko*

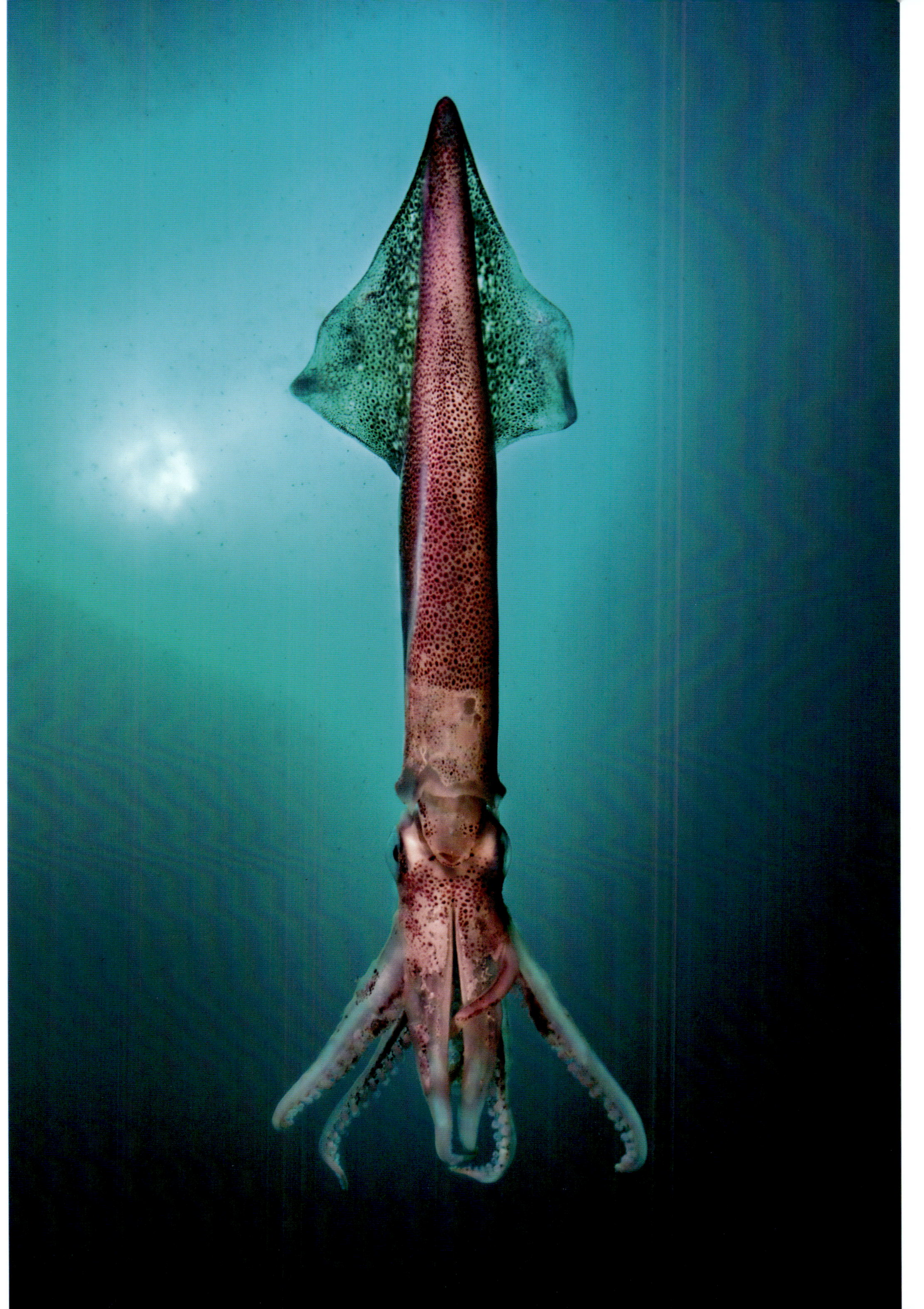

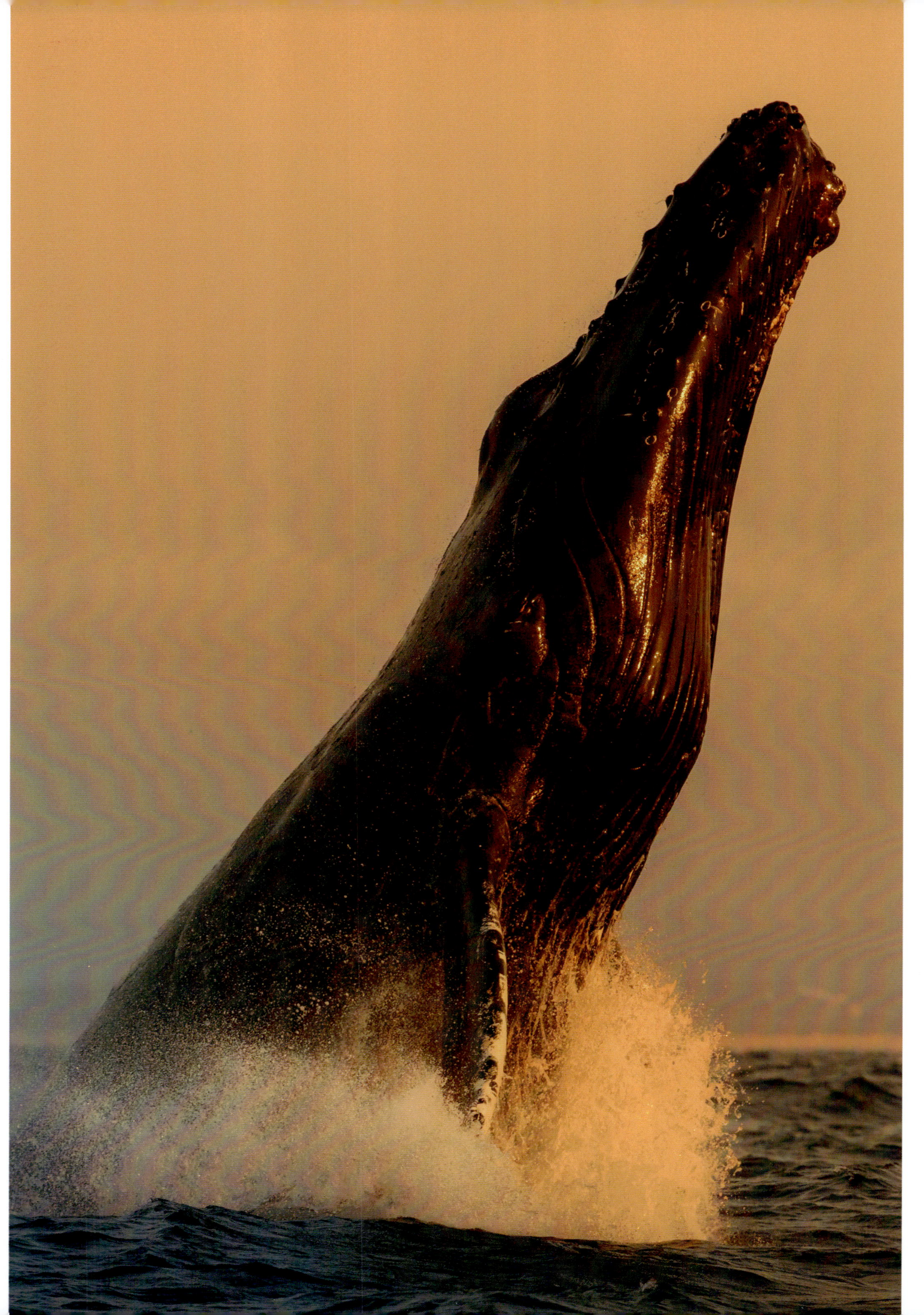

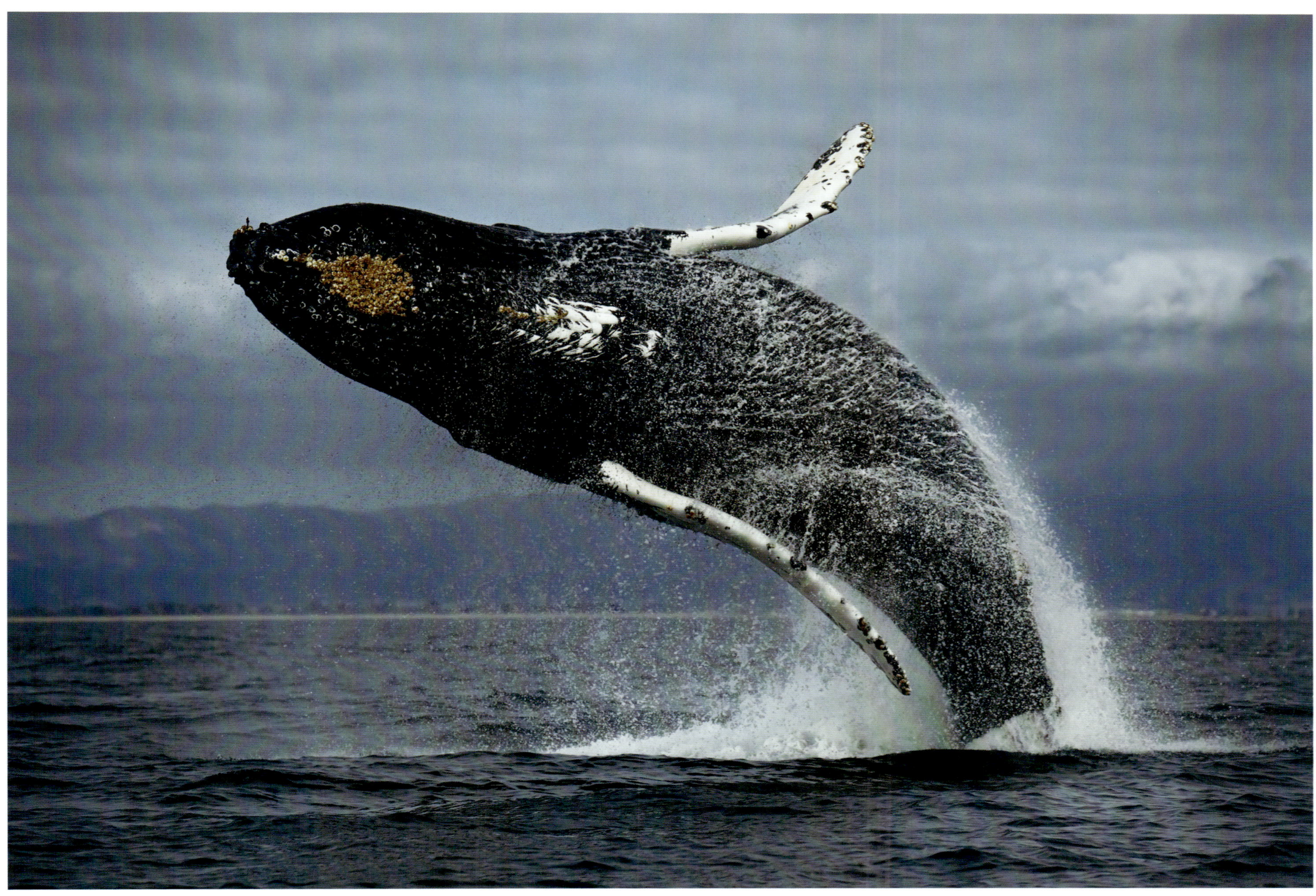

Why whales breach is a question with many answers. Is it a display of exuberance? Does it serve physical needs, like getting rid of barnacles and other body parasites? Is it a way to communicate with other whales nearby? That theory has been proposed by researchers who noted humpback whales breach more often during their mating season. Yet humpback whales come to Monterey Bay to feed, not to mate, and they breach here in spectacular fashion. The world of whales is full of mysteries, and we watch them in awe.

HUMPBACK WHALES, MONTEREY BAY NATIONAL MARINE SANCTUARY | *Photos by Chase Dekker*

INTO THE DEEP

This bloody-belly comb jelly, six inches long, is a new species first described from Monterey Bay. It probably preys upon smaller bioluminescent animals in depths from 1,000 to 3,300 feet. Because the color red is nearly invisible in the deep, its crimson belly helps hide the glow of creatures it has just eaten—which could otherwise alert the jelly's own predators. The deep-sea world of Monterey Bay is full of unique forms of life still being discovered by researchers at the Monterey Bay Aquarium Research Institute (MBARI) and captured by cameras on robotic submersibles.

BLOODY-BELLY COMB JELLY, MONTEREY BAY NATIONAL MARINE SANCTUARY
Photo by MBARI

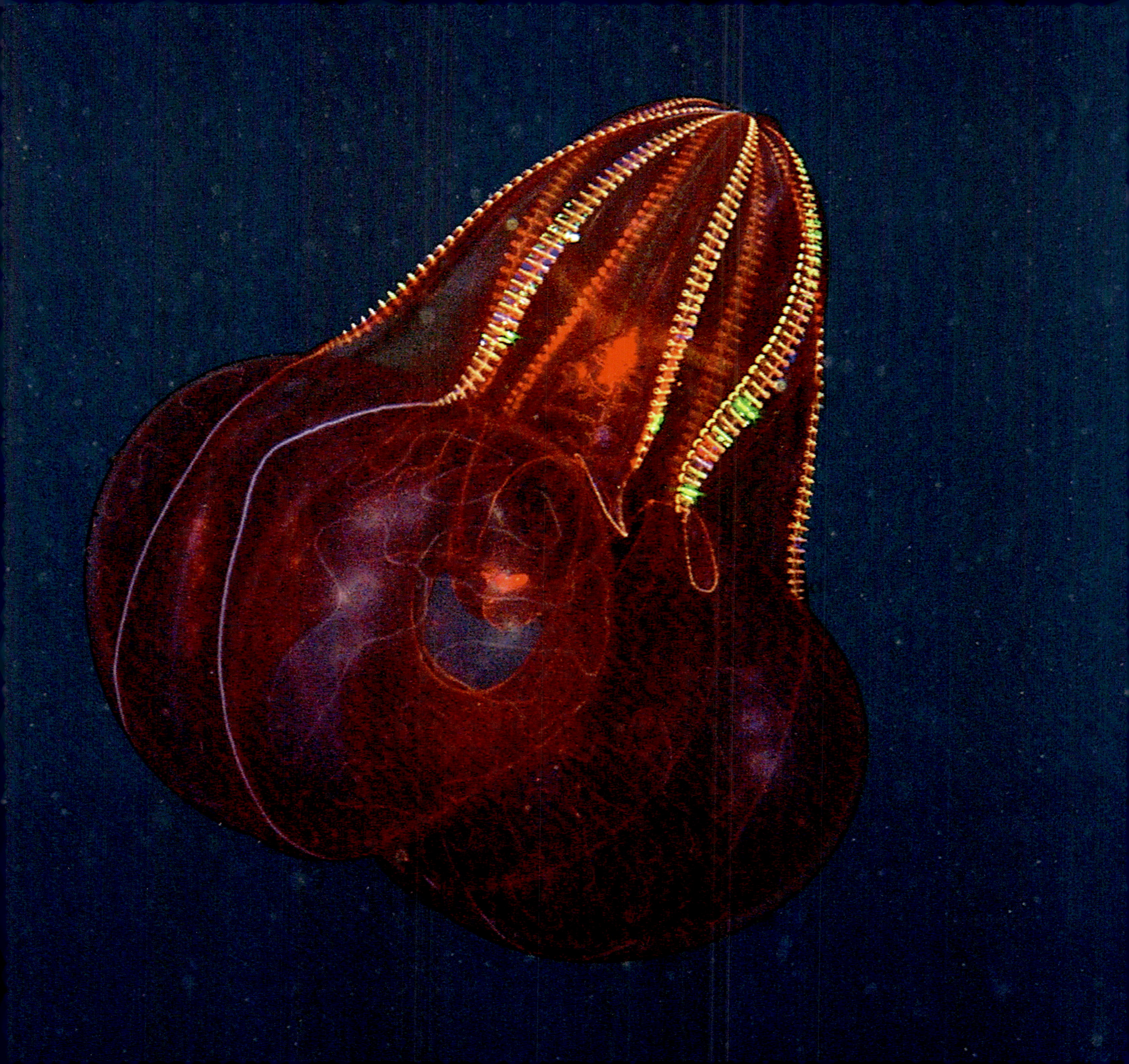

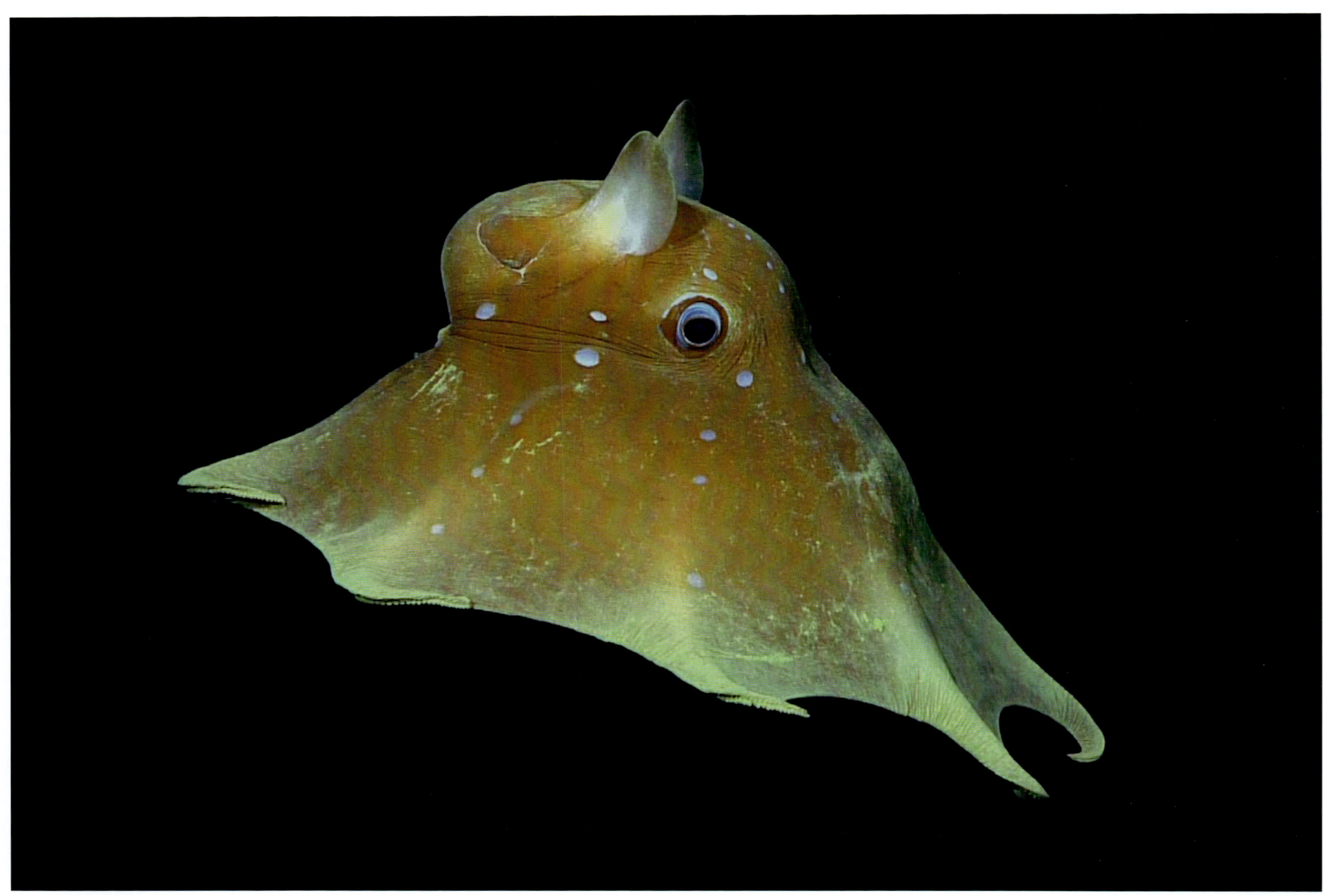

Webbing between its arms makes this 20-inch-wide octopus look like an umbrella as it drifts at depths of up to 7,500 feet. Small fins on its rounded mantle resemble ears, but they actually help it swim, which it does by pulsing like a jellyfish. MBARI's robotic submersibles often spot the flapjack octopus resting on the muddy floor of the Monterey Canyon.

FLAPJACK OCTOPUS, MONTEREY BAY NATIONAL MARINE SANCTUARY | *Photo by MBARI*

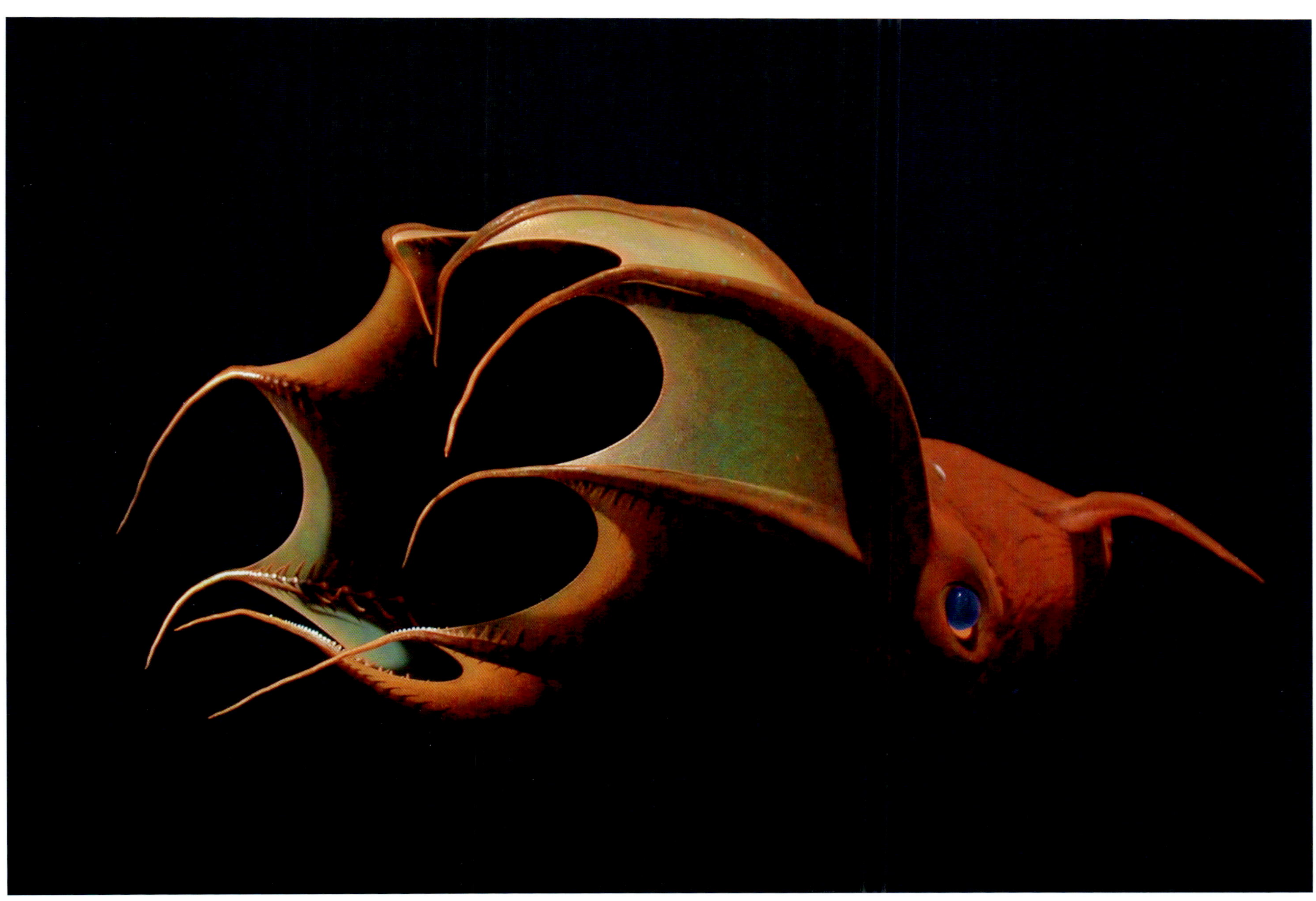

With a cloak-like web stretching between its arms, the vampire squid earned its name by appearance, not behavior, when it was discovered a hundred years ago. This 12-inch-long animal is actually not a squid, and scientists have placed it in its own unique group. Like many creatures living at depths of 3,000 feet, its primary food is "marine snow," the shower of organic material that falls from the upper waters to the seafloor.

Vampire Squid, Monterey Bay National Marine Sanctuary | *Photo by MBARI*

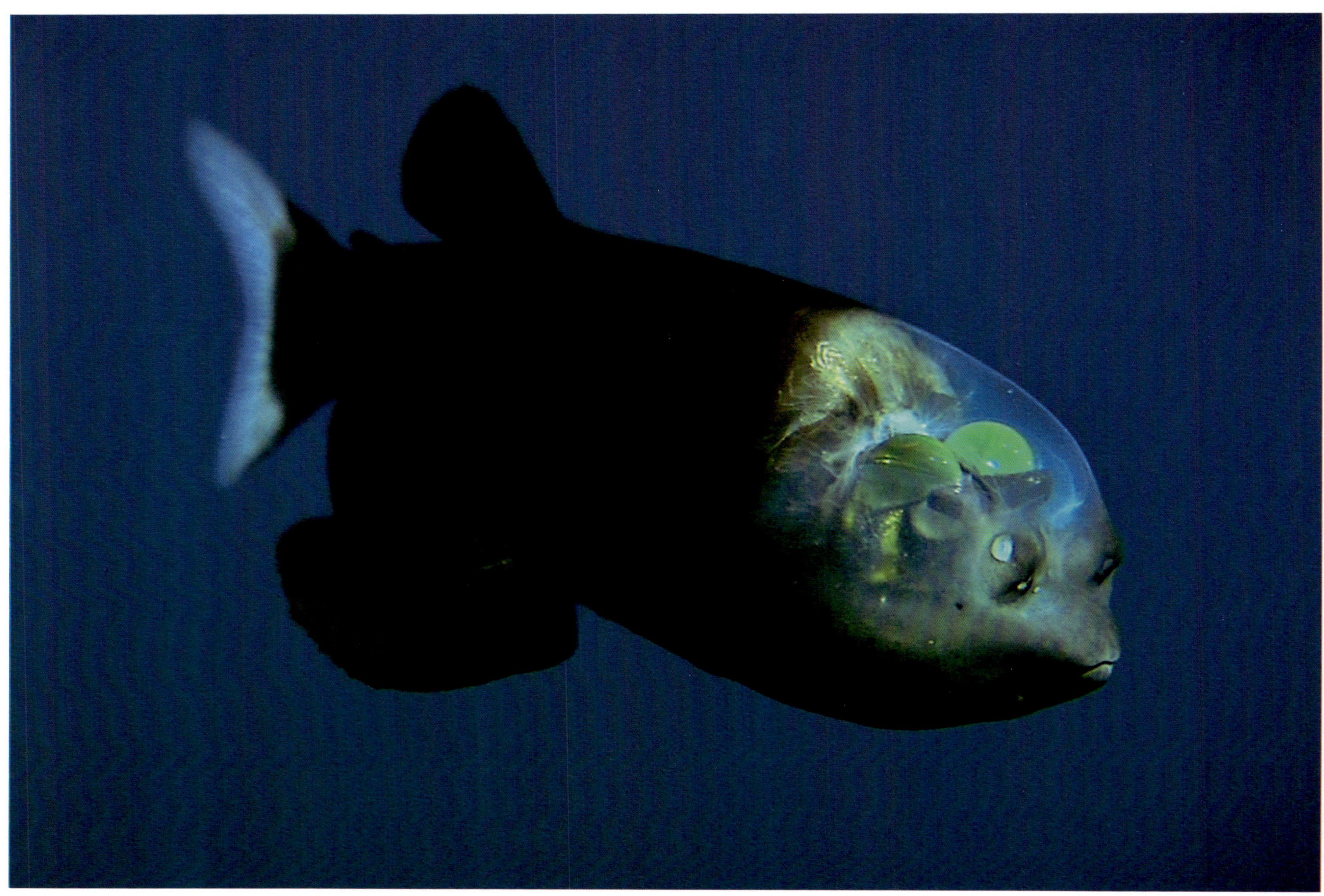

The barreleye fish can see through its own forehead. Its tubular eyes, capped with bright green lenses, rotate within the transparent, fluid-filled shield on its head. The eyes point upward when it searches for food overhead and point forward to align eyes and mouth when it's ready to eat. Two dark spots above its tiny mouth detect scent. Just six inches long, it lives at depths below 2,000 feet. Researchers think the barreleye steals food from siphonophores and is protected from their stinging cells by the shield over its eyes.

Barreleye Fish, Monterey Bay National Marine Sanctuary | *Photo by MBARI*

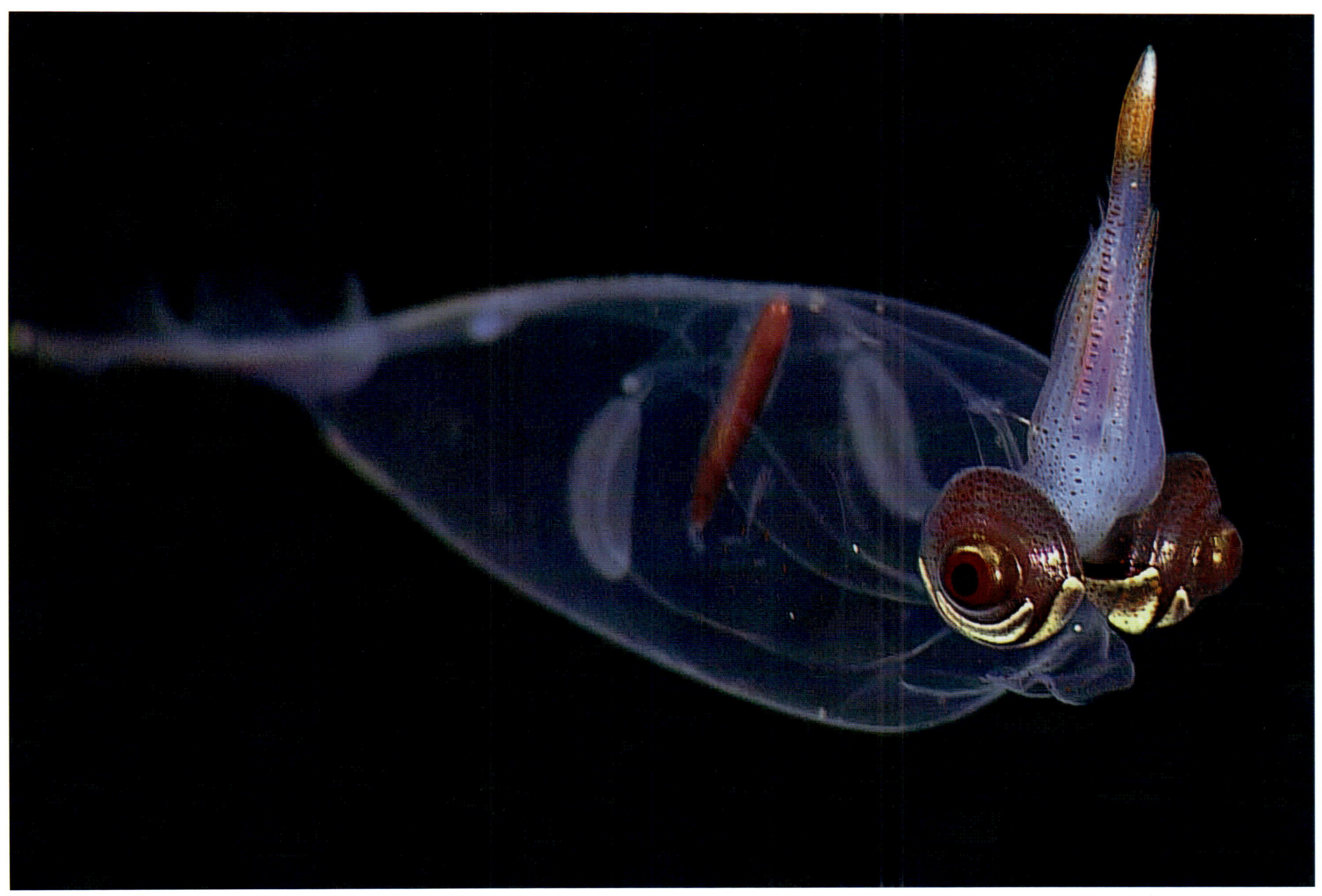

With huge eyeballs bulging from its head and golden, light-emitting organs under its eyes, this 20-inch-long cockatoo squid can hang motionless in the water column between 650 and 3,200 feet deep, waiting for prey. Named for the peaked tentacles on its head that resemble the raised crest of a cockatoo, this squid's transparent body is filled with ammonia, which helps it float.

Cockatoo Squid, Monterey Bay National Marine Sanctuary | *Photo by MBARI*

This inch-long bomber worm—
a new species first found in Monterey
Bay—lives in the midnight zone of the
deep sea, swimming vigorously just above
the seafloor at depths below 8,800 feet.
To startle predators, it can release bomb
sacs of fluid that explode with a burst of
green bioluminescence. Each worm carries
eight bombs behind its head—
and can regenerate new ones.

Shining Bomber Worm, Monterey Bay National Marine Sanctuary

Photo by Karen Osborn

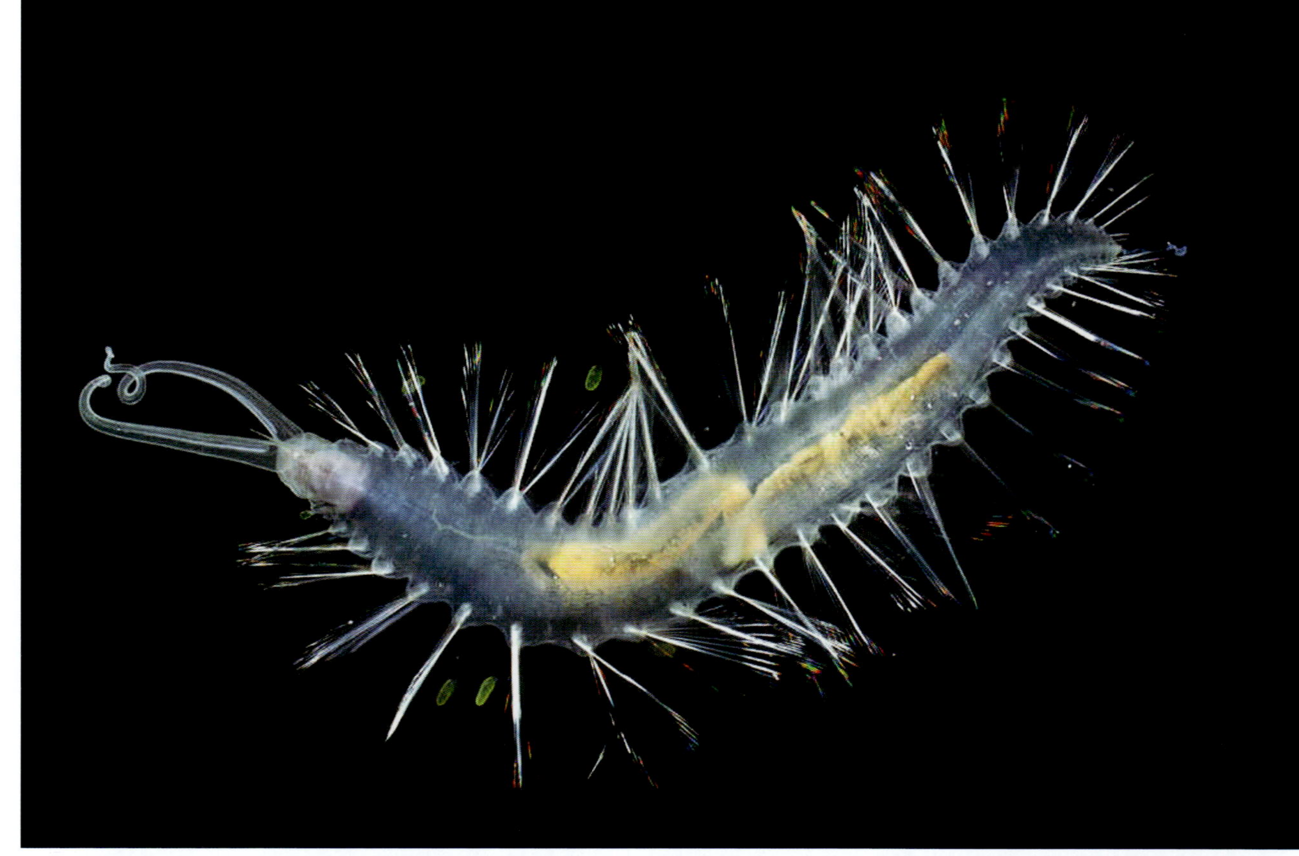

The long, coiling bodies of siphonophores are
made up of clusters of cells that clone themselves
thousands of times and work together as a single
organism. Individual segments specialized for
feeding, locomotion, and defense are linked
together by a long stem. They live in the depths
of the open ocean, using their many tentacles to
capture crustaceans and small fish. Siphonophores
related to this one have been measured at lengths
of more than 120 feet—longer than a blue whale.

Siphonophore, Monterey Bay National Marine Sanctuary

Photo by MBARI

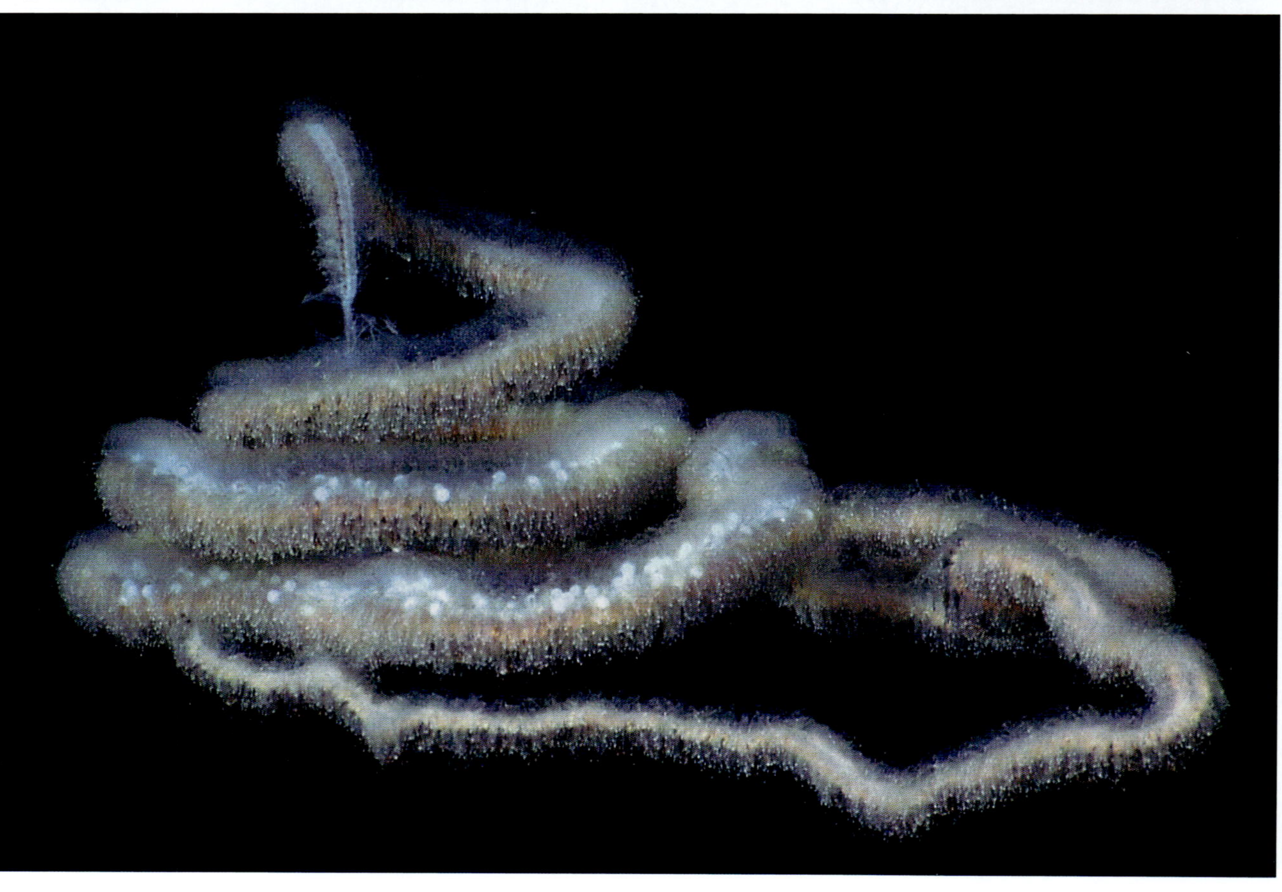

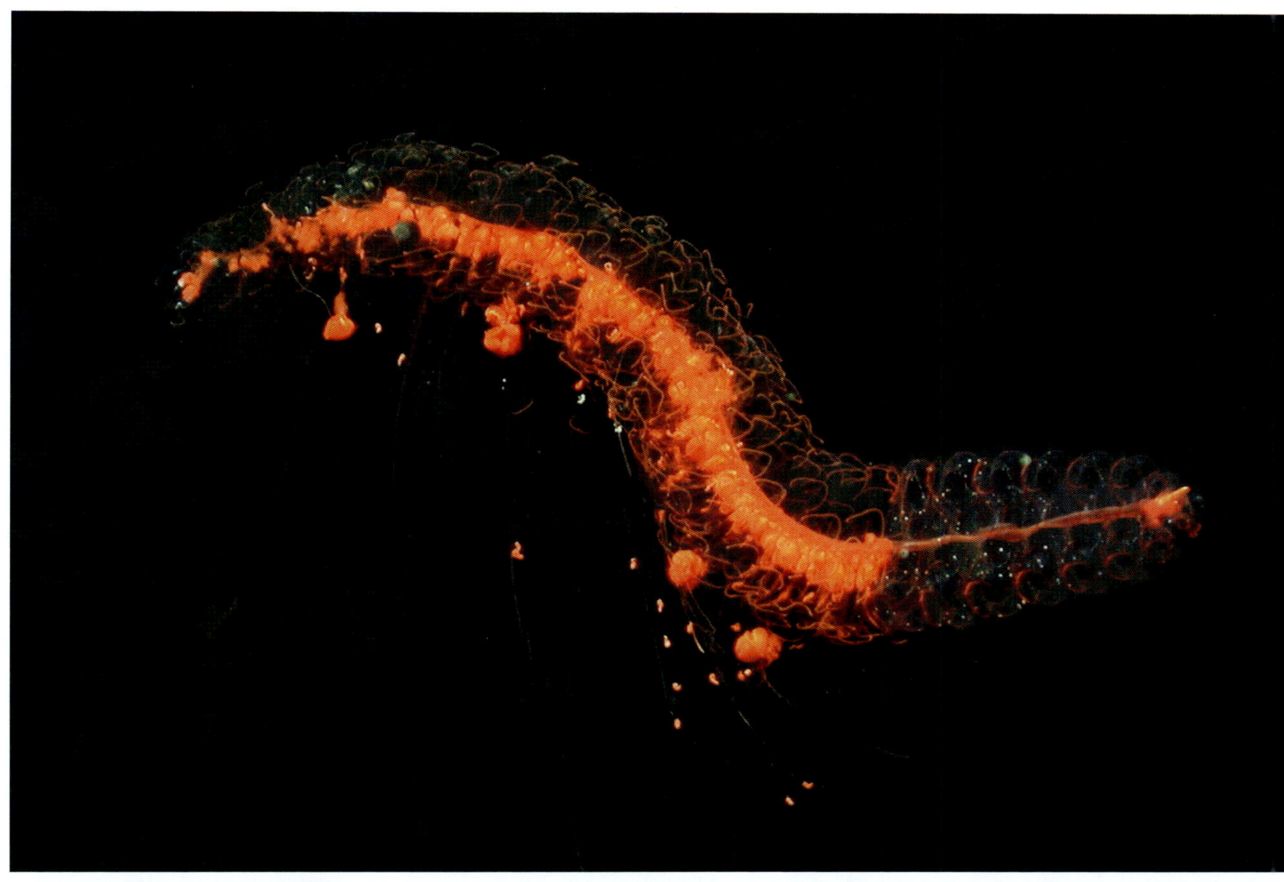

A rainbow of siphonophores has been discovered in the bay's dark depths, including this new species, just 12 inches long and found between 1,500 and 5,000 feet deep. When threatened, it can cast off bioluminescent body parts to confuse a predator. Most siphonophores are exceedingly fragile and break apart at the slightest touch, making them difficult to study under controlled conditions. Cameras on MBARI's robotic submersibles have captured these delicate drifters in action, providing illuminating views of their behavior in the wild.

RED SIPHONOPHORE, MONTEREY BAY NATIONAL MARINE SANCTUARY

Photo by MBARI

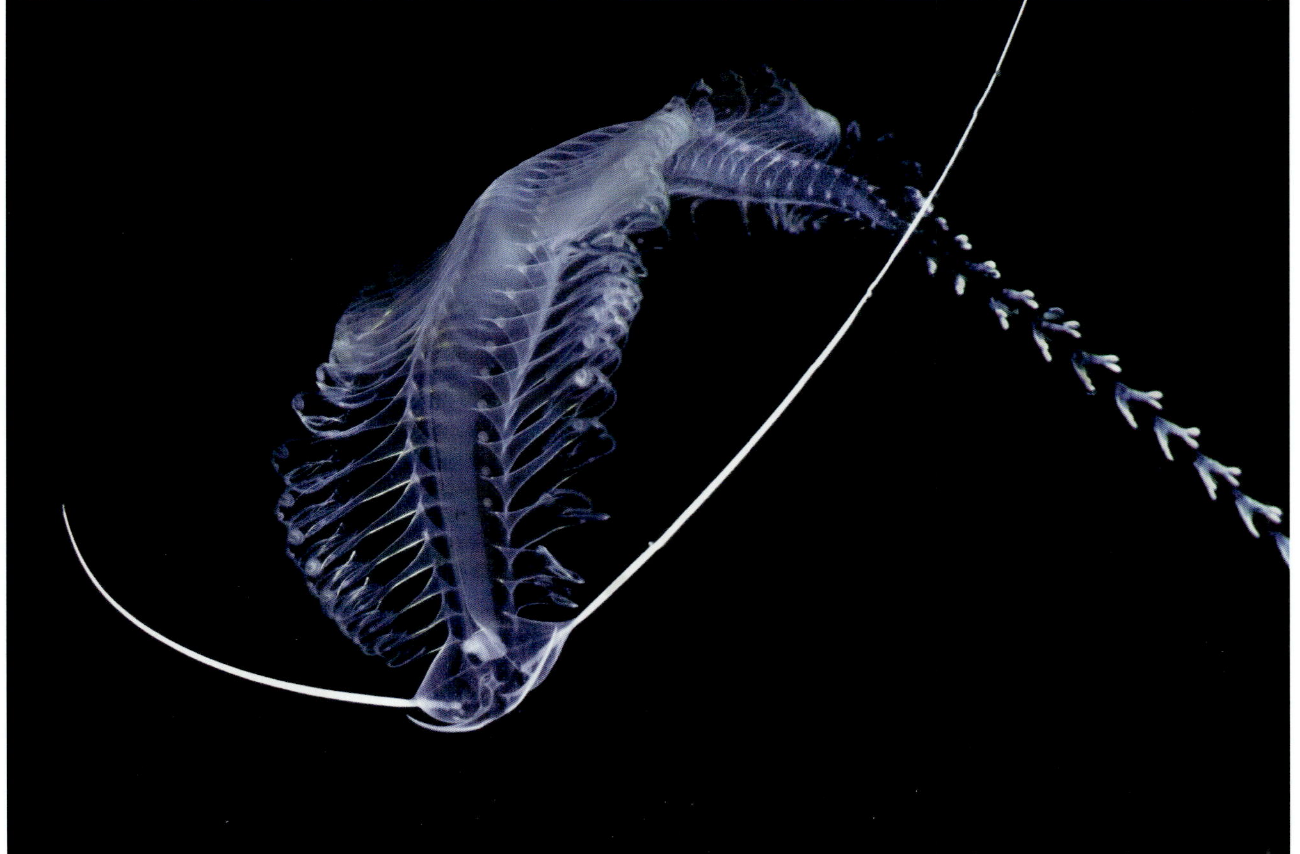

The gossamer worm is always on the move. Its graceful swimming techniques are mesmerizing to watch, but scientists are interested in it for other reasons too. A flexible body plan enables it to use different modes of propulsion to swim efficiently. This tiny worm could inspire new designs for a range of medical and engineering applications.

GOSSAMER WORM, MONTEREY BAY NATIONAL MARINE SANCTUARY

Photo by MBARI

This wildly colorful jelly looks like a fireworks display in the night sky.
Unusual for jellies, the differences between sexes are obvious. Males, like this one,
have orange gonads; the female's eggs are pale and round. One of a handful of jellies
that bear live young, females brood offspring inside their one-inch-wide bells until
the young are ready to pulse off and live on their own. These tiny
jellies are found at depths between 3,000 and 13,000 feet.

Psychedelic Jelly, Monterey Bay National Marine Sanctuary
Photo by MBARI

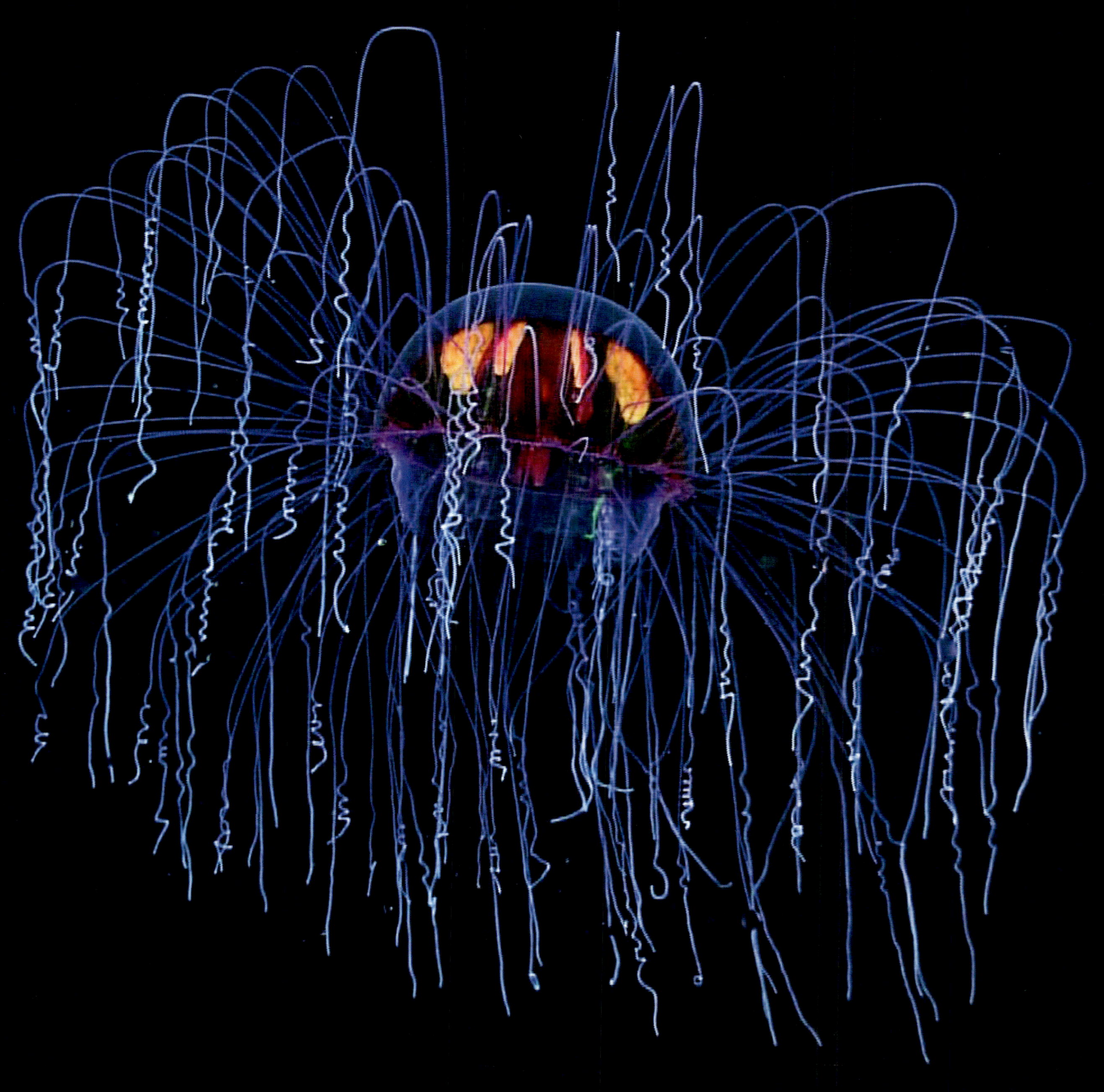

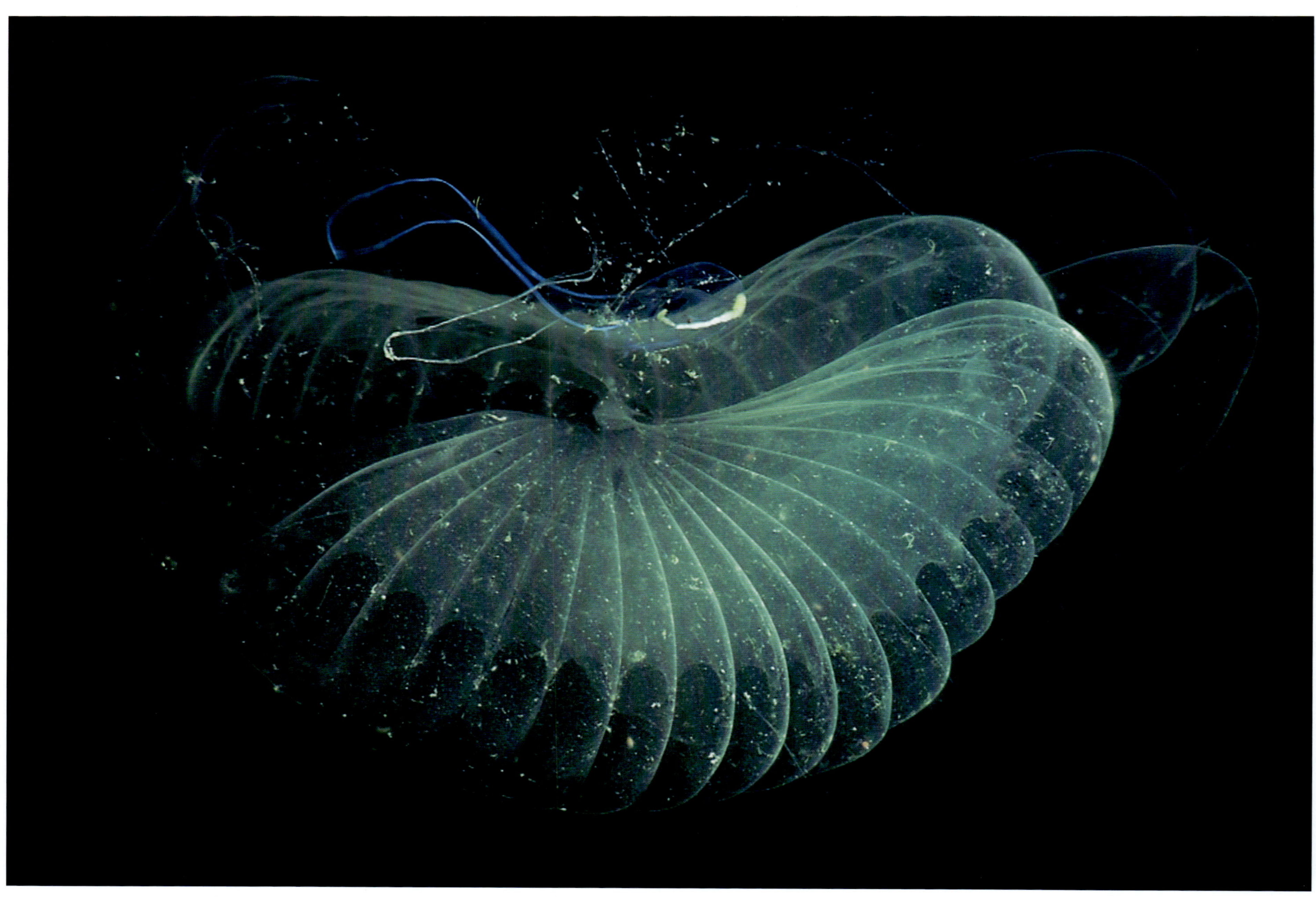

Giant larvaceans are small, only the size of a finger, but extremely prolific; collectively they filter all of Monterey Bay's water between 300 and 1,000 feet deep in less than two weeks. Larvaceans construct transparent mucus "houses" around themselves, then beat their tails (shown with a blue edge in this image) to pump seawater through the structures, trapping organic matter they can eat. When their mucus houses get clogged with debris, they shed them and build new ones. The cast-off mucus transports more carbon to the deep ocean floor than any other plankton—including algae, bacteria, and other drifting animals.

GIANT LARVACEAN, MONTEREY BAY NATIONAL MARINE SANCTUARY | *Photo by MBARI*

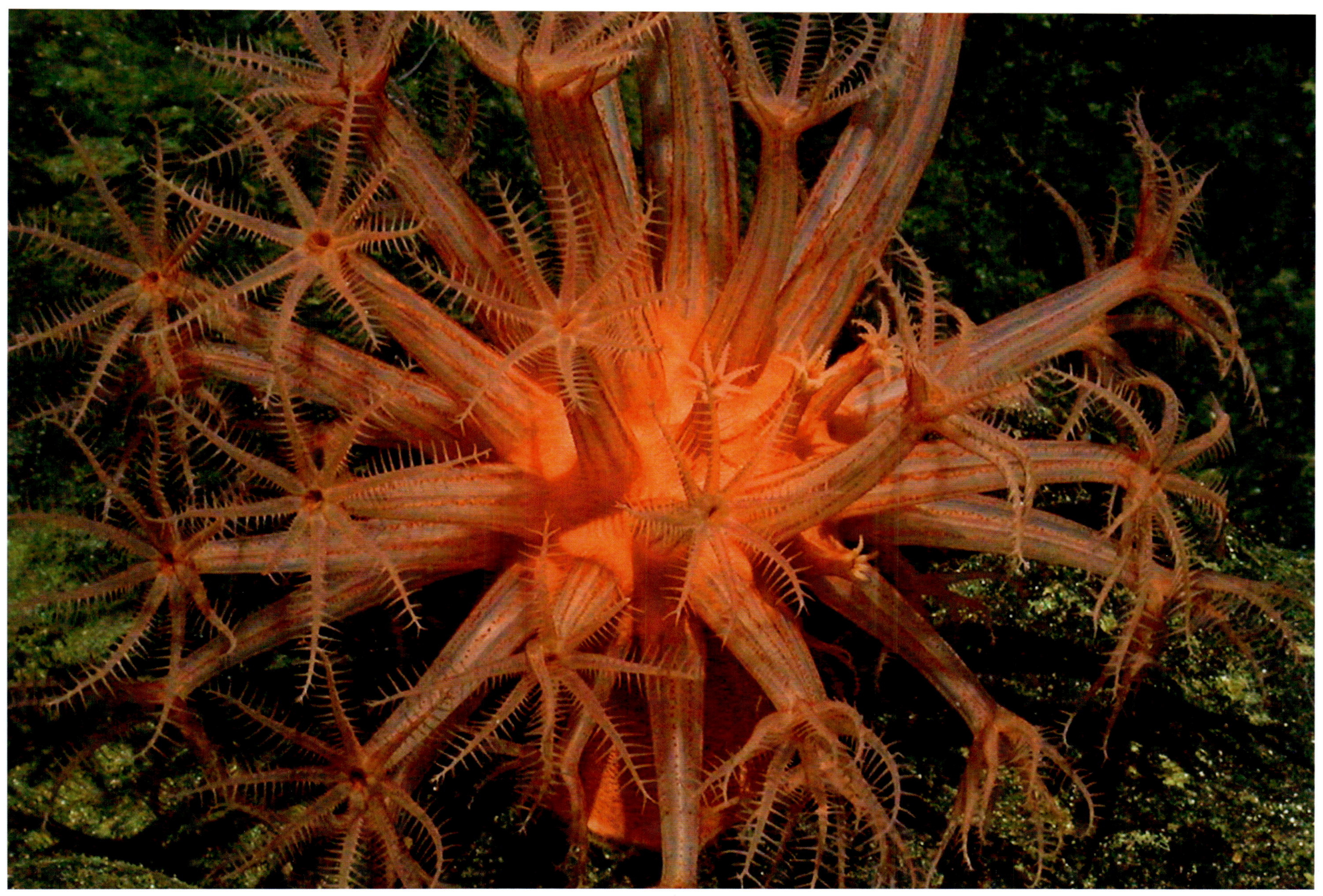

When closed up tight, this deep-sea soft coral, six inches wide, looks like an orange mushroom. But here, with its tentacles outstretched to feed, it looks like a fluffy dandelion head about to seed. It lives at depths from 700 to 4,000 feet. Stinging cells in its tentacles capture tiny animals drifting by. Bottom-feeding catsharks sometimes lay their egg cases on its stalks.

Mushroom Coral, Monterey Bay National Marine Sanctuary | *Photo by MBARI*

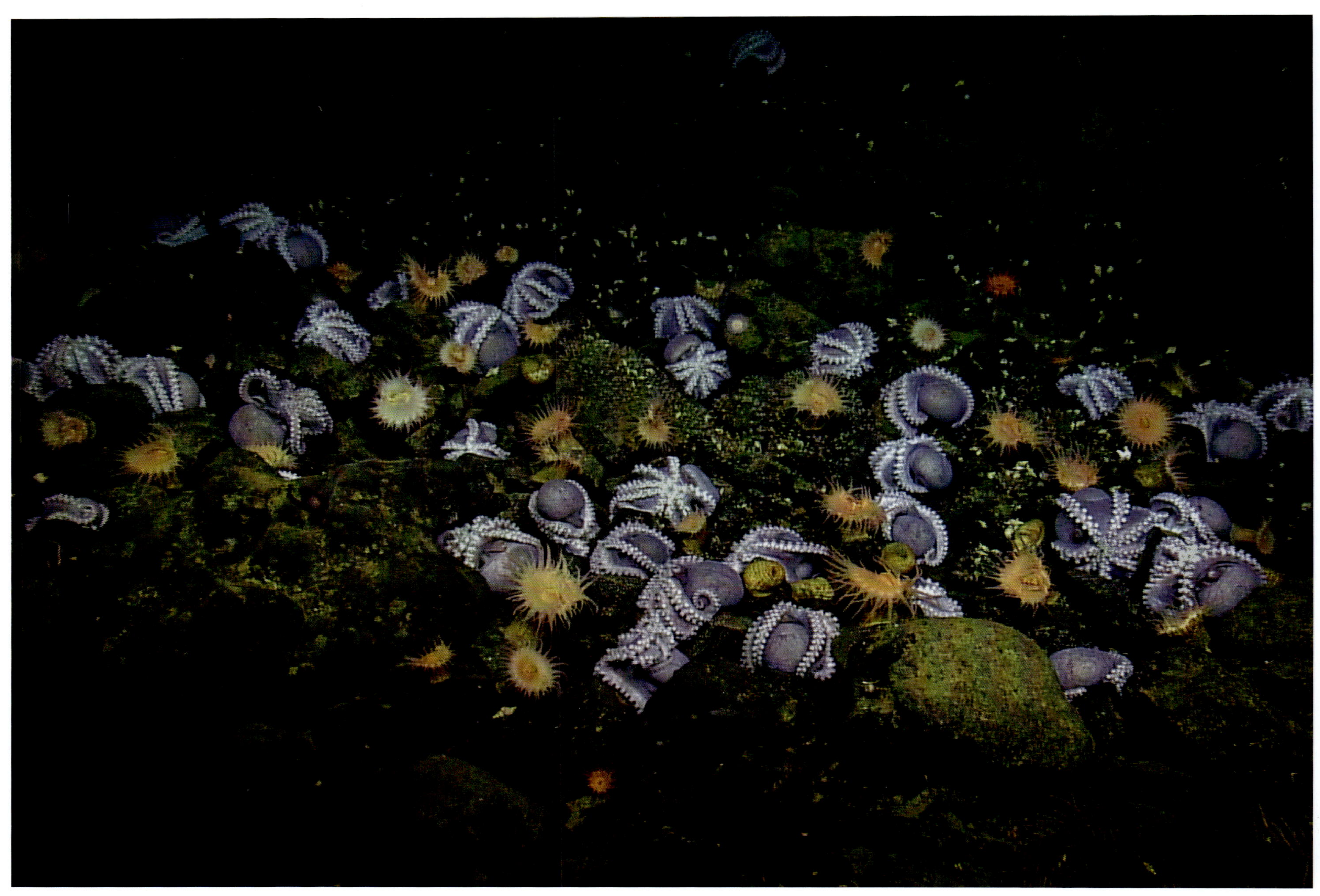

At a depth of nearly 10,000 feet, researchers discovered more than a thousand deep-sea octopuses in a gathering that had never been seen before. Brooding females were tucked into rocks with their arms flipped outward to cover their bodies and eggs. Since the discovery of this "Octopus Garden," researchers have returned and seen babies inside eggs along with several hatchlings, suggesting that this rocky reef near the Davidson Seamount could be an important nursery.

OCTOPUS GARDEN, MONTEREY BAY NATIONAL MARINE SANCTUARY | *Photo by NOAA/Ocean Exploration Trust*

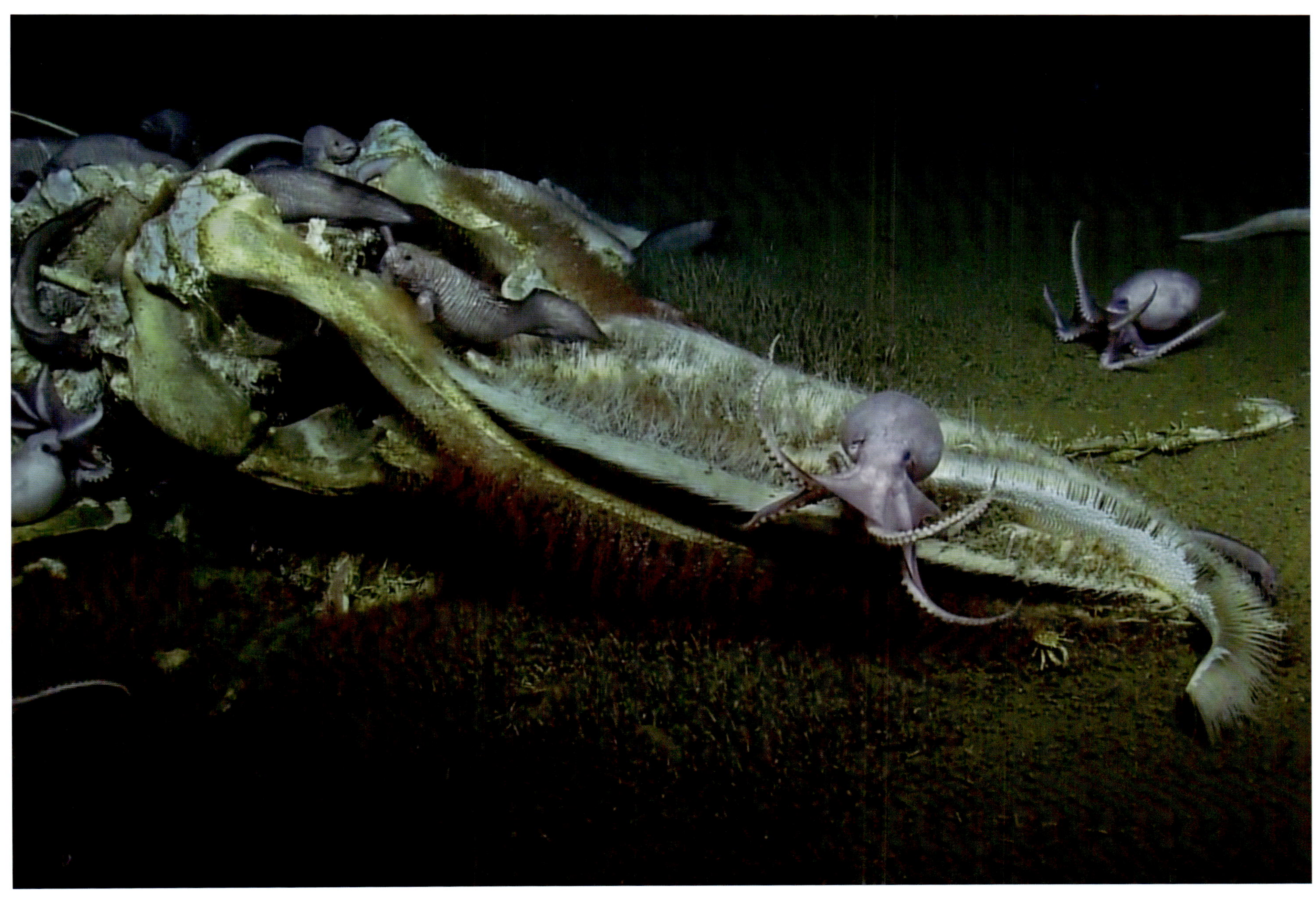

When a whale dies at sea, its body sinks to the seafloor where it becomes a unique ecosystem—
and a bonanza for deep-sea life. Octopus, eelpouts, and other scavengers consume the whale's soft tissue
then invertebrates colonize the skeleton. *Osedax* worms dissolve the bones and metabolize the lipids.
When researchers found this gray whale skeleton 10,630 feet down on the Davidson Seamount,
only some of the flesh remained.

WHALE FALL, MONTEREY BAY NATIONAL MARINE SANCTUARY | *Photo by NOAA/Ocean Exploration Trust*

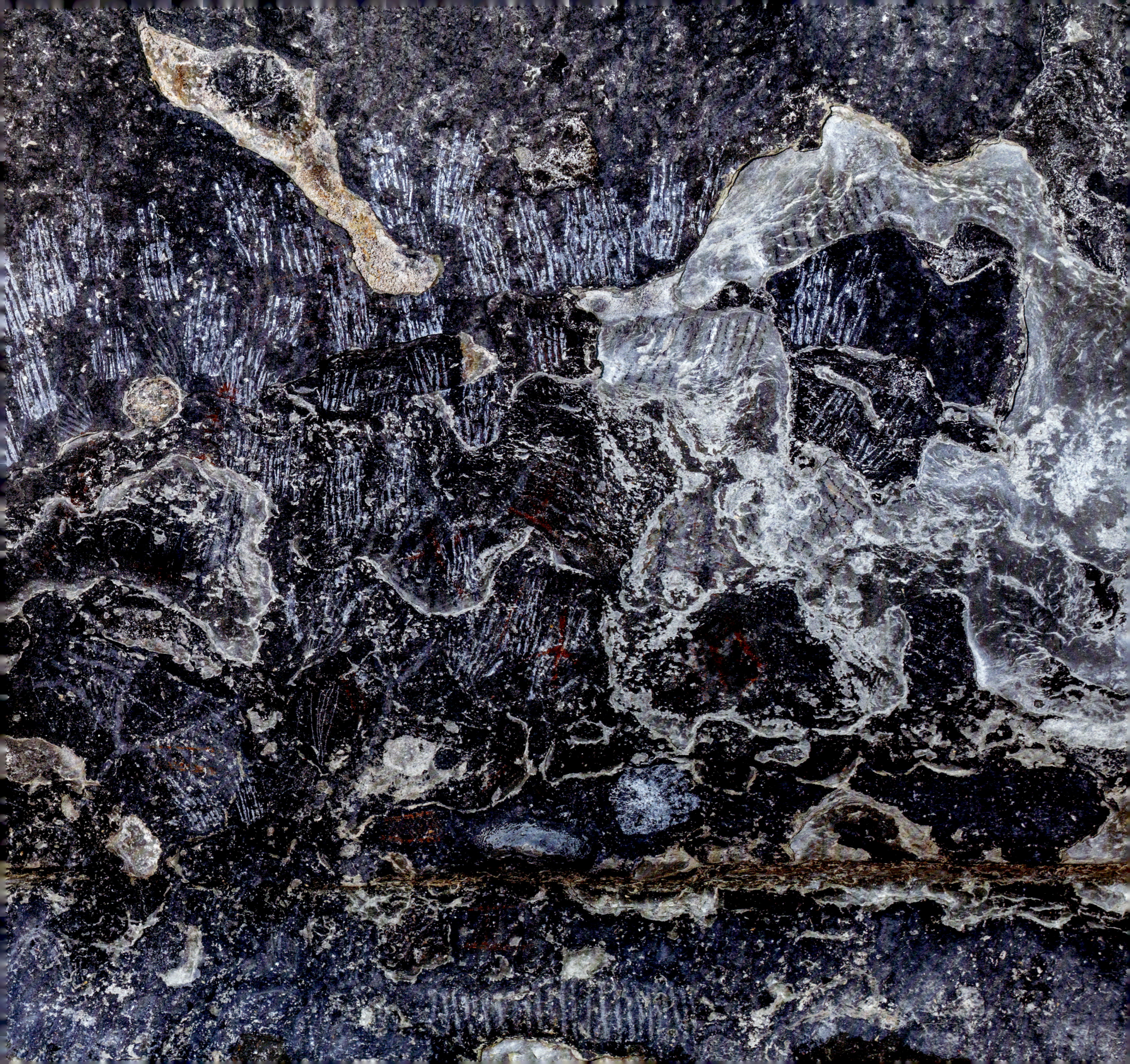

FOOTPRINTS

LIVING WITH THE BAY

The earth does not belong to man, man belongs to the earth.

—Chief Seattle

A buckeye seed, an old oak tree, a forgotten redwood, a soil secret, a lost species found. What can we learn from them about the connections between people and nature in the Bay of Life?

Along a secluded coastal creek in the northern part of Monterey Bay, a grove of buckeye trees still thrives next to a former Native American village site. The trees are a living reminder of their long association with the people who once lived here. Buckeye seeds the size of chestnuts were processed and eaten when acorns were scarce. Raw seeds, which are toxic, were ground up and spread in streams to stun fish so they could more easily be caught.

Not far from this orchard of buckeyes is a large coastal shell mound that contains a continuous record of daily life over a period of almost 8,000 years. The depth of human history accumulated in this one place is humbling. Hidden inside the mound are untold stories about indigenous people and their connections with the land. Huge amounts of shells reveal the bounty that people once harvested near the shoreline: mussels and scallops, black turban snails and red abalone, crabs, and many others. Mixed in are the bones of land and marine mammals, fish, and seabirds, including those of a now-extinct flightless duck—a giant relative of the surf scoter.

For people living off the land and sea, Monterey Bay was a place of plenty. The landscapes treasured for their biodiversity today were a rich mosaic of foodscapes for indigenous people in the past. The region was populated by different tribes speaking distinct languages, from Awaswas to Rumsen to Esselen. This cultural complexity was supported by the natural abundance of the bay. Año Nuevo and Santa Cruz were hotspots of intertidal resources. The wetlands of Elkhorn Slough and Pajaro Valley were valued for their wildlife and the tule reeds used for building huts and rafts. Favored places in the southern part of Monterey Bay included Carmel Valley and Morgan Hill, which had extensive oak woodlands with blue, valley, interior, live, and black oak species— all major producers of acorns, a staple food for millennia.

Hunting and gathering was a way of life for thousands of years, but the people who settled around Monterey Bay also became dedicated gardeners of nature. Food plants were carefully tended to increase their productivity as were patches of plants important for basketmaking. Fire was used as a powerful tool to rejuvenate the land. It was often set after the harvest of seeds in the fall, improving living conditions for people, plants, and animals alike. The regularity of these burns is still traceable in tree rings today. This lifeway, fine-tuned to local conditions over countless generations, came to an abrupt end after Spanish colonizers arrived in the 1770s to establish missions. Although the mission era itself lasted only 50 years, it marked the beginning of massive cultural and environmental changes. The deep connections between indigenous people and their land were severed. But the people are still here.

Not far from the shell mound with its layers of history, we joined a ceremonial gathering of Amah Mutsun people. There

Painted handprints pattern the walls of a secluded cave where Esselen people once gathered for sacred ceremonies.

Esselen Rock Art, Ventana Wilderness

were elders and families with small children and teenagers too. They all came back to a place where their ancestral neighbors had once lived. A dam had recently been removed from a nearby coastal creek, enabling salmon to swim upstream again into a watershed they had been denied for many decades. It was a new opportunity for the fish and an occasion for people to reconnect with the land.

Ceremonies to call salmon home to the streams where they spawn have been performed for ages by indigenous people up and down the Pacific coast, but it had not happened here for more than 200 years. Led by drumbeats against the backdrop of the bay, a group of dancers adorned with the plumage of local birds entered a sacred circle, and an ancient connection was restored.

Amah Mutsun Chairman Valentin Lopez, a charismatic leader in the cultural revival of his people, spoke. We heard him say this: "Our ancestors knew that before they made any changes, it had to be good for seven generations. We need to bring back their wisdom." We can only hope that the changes we are able to make in our lifetime will benefit both people and salmon so they can thrive together again.

A majestic old oak on a hillside above the Salinas Valley is a silent witness to changes that have occurred here since domesticated animals began to spread to this part of Monterey Bay in the late 1700s. The Spanish and Mexican colonial economies were based on introducing livestock to the landscape, and the animals proliferated in great numbers. By 1860 Monterey County had more sheep than any other county in the United States—nearly 300,000, along with 100,000 cattle. It was a short-lived bounty.

The replacement of large native mammals like elk and pronghorn antelopes with livestock had far-reaching ecological impacts. Many exotic plants were introduced as well, and the balance between native and non-native vegetation changed dramatically. Over time, ranches became less productive, and by the end of the 19th century many were giving way to more profitable farms. Today ranching in the valley has largely been replaced by intensive agriculture, but it persists in the hills.

We sat down with Steve Dorrance at his ranch on the slopes of Mount Toro with commanding views over the Salinas Valley and the Monterey Bay. He shared stories about his love for the land and its wildlife—from mountain lions and condors to tiger

salamanders and burrowing owls. He also explained that his 4,300-acre ranch could sustain only 200 head of cattle in the best of times now, and that the meager income from ranching alone would not support a family. The potential value of his ranch to a property developer was enormous, but he did not want to sell it. "This ranch is our core asset," he told us. "This is what matters to the family. So we will sacrifice everything else we have to keep this operation that was started in our family."

He signed a conservation easement with The Nature Conservancy that provides his family with some financial security and enables him to maintain a ranch where livestock can coexist with wildlife. Steve's decision ensures that an important habitat and a prominent natural landmark visible to everyone who lives in or passes through the Monterey Bay will be protected forever.

In the foothills above the Pajaro Valley, at the edge of the San Andreas Fault, stands an ancient redwood tree with massive elbowed limbs that thrust out from the main trunk. It is a solitary survivor from the logging era that wiped out most of the old redwoods in the Monterey Bay region. Perhaps tree fellers passed this one by because its elbows made it less than prime timber.

In the early 1800s, the logging of primeval redwoods in the Santa Cruz Mountains was arduous manual work involving axes and handsaws. The mid-century Gold Rush triggered great demand for timber that was met first with new mechanized tools and later with steam-powered sawmills, which led to industrial-scale clear-cuts. The small town of Boulder Creek became one of the largest lumber centers in California in the 1880s, with two dozen sawmills operating within five miles. Another logging spike occurred after the San Francisco earthquake and fire of 1906, when huge quantities of wood were needed to rebuild the city—and redwood was prized for its fire resistance and durability.

When the McCrary family started their Big Creek Lumber Company in Swanton in 1946, there were few big trees left to log in the area, and people were skeptical about the viability of making a living off timber. Yet the McCrarys persisted and ended up pioneering an approach to harvesting second-growth redwoods that has set standards within Monterey Bay and beyond. Clear-cutting was still allowed when they started, but the McCrarys began to practice harvesting trees selectively, based on their insight that redwoods grow faster when you nurture them properly and consider the forest as a whole.

Running a timber company in Monterey Bay today is not easy. The margins are thin and getting thinner all the time. Much of Big Creek's timberland burned during the 2020 fires, and that imposes another major challenge. But the McCrarys have always taken the long view, as befits a family of foresters whose livelihood depends on the life cycle of ancient trees.

"We weren't here because we were trying to move in and make a profit and leave," says company president Janet McCrary Webb, against a backdrop of fire-scarred, big trees near her home. "We were here because we wanted to stay here and make it sustainable."

For organic farmer Dick Peixoto, it's all about the soil. "We farm the soil, and the soil grows the crops," he says, pointing to the fields where it all started for him. The lands he farms are in the Pajaro Valley, where the soil has been enriched for thousands of years by riverine deposits from the Gabilan Range. Much of the Pajaro Valley was once wetlands but after the Gold Rush, settlers began to convert them to farmlands to raise crops for California's burgeoning population. Grains and potatoes gave way to fruit trees and sugar beets and eventually to the wide variety of row crops grown today.

Dick's grandfather came to Watsonville from Portugal's Azores in the early 1900s and farmed potatoes, as his family had done in their homeland. Dick's father sold fertilizers and pesticides to farmers. Dick himself started growing crops conventionally, but in the mid-1990s he switched to organic farming. His grower-shipper business, Lakeside Organic Gardens, is now the largest family-owned organic operation of its kind in the United States.

A potent combination of soil, water, and climate have made the Pajaro Valley a prime place for agriculture. The cooling effect of fog enables farmers here to grow crops through the summer months that can't be grown anywhere else in the country. "A lot of people from warmer areas would love to have a house in the fog," Dick says. "But we have a limited amount of soil that we are constantly battling to keep from being paved over because it is in the fog belt. Urban sprawl is a big threat to the future of farming." Dick feels as strongly about giving back to his community as he does about farming the soil. "As a business owner, it's not really just about profit," he says. "It's about creating wealth in your community, creating wealth for your employees, creating wealth for everybody around you."

In 1778 French explorer La Pérouse commented about the abundance of marine mammals in Monterey Bay. Whales, he wrote, were everywhere. Soon after, the exploitation began. For several decades, the main commerce along the California coast involved hunting otters, seals, and whales for fur, oil, or meat. The slaughter only came to an end when virtually all local populations of marine mammals were wiped out.

Sea otters were thought to be long extinct when a raft of them was spotted in a remote part of Big Sur in 1938. It was a startling rediscovery that made it into the pages of *LIFE* magazine. The comeback of marine mammals to the bay since then has been a historic turnaround. Every year now, thousands of elephant seals gather at Año Nuevo where 50 years ago there were none. A female known as G1885 heaves herself out of the water to join the masses on the beach. On her back is a sophisticated instrument attached by researchers from the University of California, Santa Cruz. It tracks where she goes, how deep she dives, and when she eats. After it's retrieved, researchers gain intimate insights into her life at sea, and the information becomes part of a database accessed by scientists around the world.

A new knowledge economy is blossoming around Monterey Bay, which has become an epicenter for marine science because of its biodiversity and the systematic protection of the bay. This wealth of knowledge builds on a tradition that began with pioneers like ecologist Ed Ricketts, who influenced John Steinbeck and inspired the founders of the Monterey Bay Aquarium. Today more marine scientists live and work here than in any other place in the world.

"Monterey Bay is the best-studied patch of deep ocean on the planet," says MBARI Senior Scientist Bruce Robison. "And yet we're still finding new things every time we go out." Knowledge nourishes action, and the work of Monterey Bay's formidable marine brain trust energizes efforts to conserve oceans far beyond the bay. While Bruce Robison stares at a computer screen connected to an ROV that reveals another deep-sea wonder, whale watchers on the surface of the bay shriek with delight when a huge humpback surfaces in front of their boat. Every day new experiences affirm the ability of the Bay of Life to astonish the human mind.

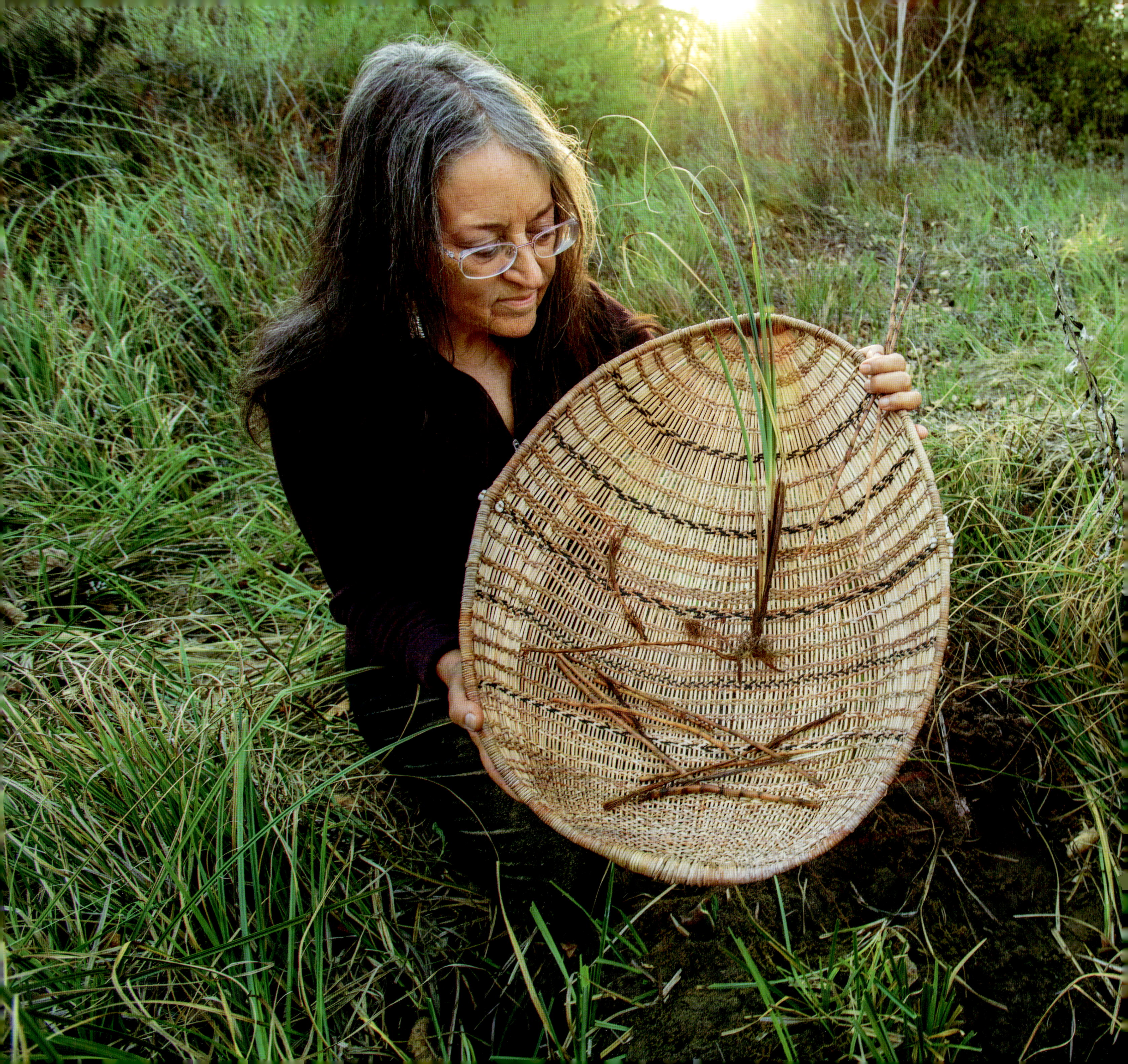

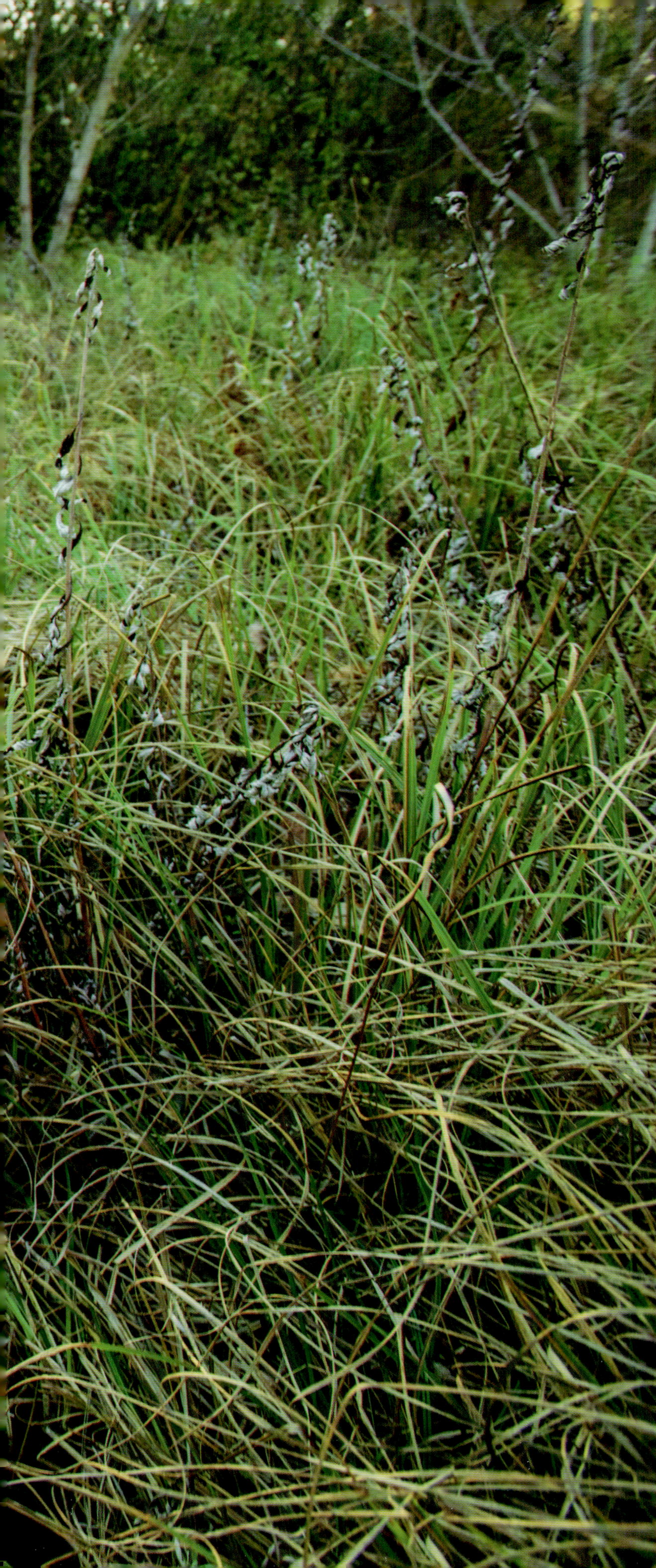

TENDING
THE BAY

Linda Yamane has devoted her life to reviving the cultural traditions
of her Rumsen Ohlone people. A renowned basket weaver, she has an
intimate understanding of traditional baskets, which were essential
tools in daily life. Her basket holds freshly harvested white-root sedge,
a material prized for weaving. It grows in a sheltered place along the
Carmel River where she tends the wild plants seasonally.

Rumsen Basket Weaver Linda Yamane, Carmel River

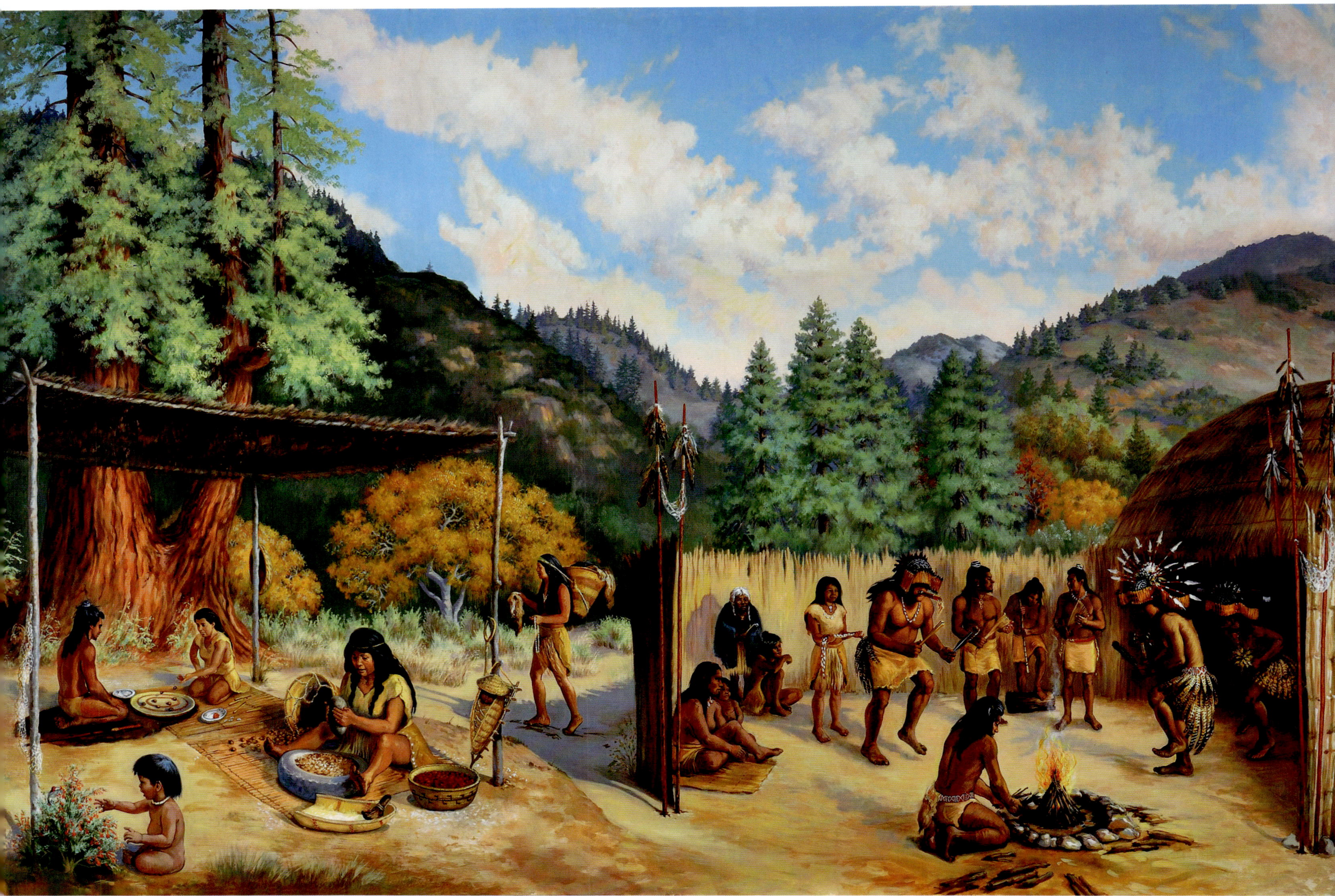

This recreation of daily life in Quiroste Valley near Año Nuevo is based on eyewitness accounts from the first European visitors in 1769 and interviews with descendants of the people who lived near here. The hills behind the village show the effects of regular burnings conducted to enhance habitats for food plants and animals.

DANCING AT QUIROSTE | *Mural by Ann Thiermann*

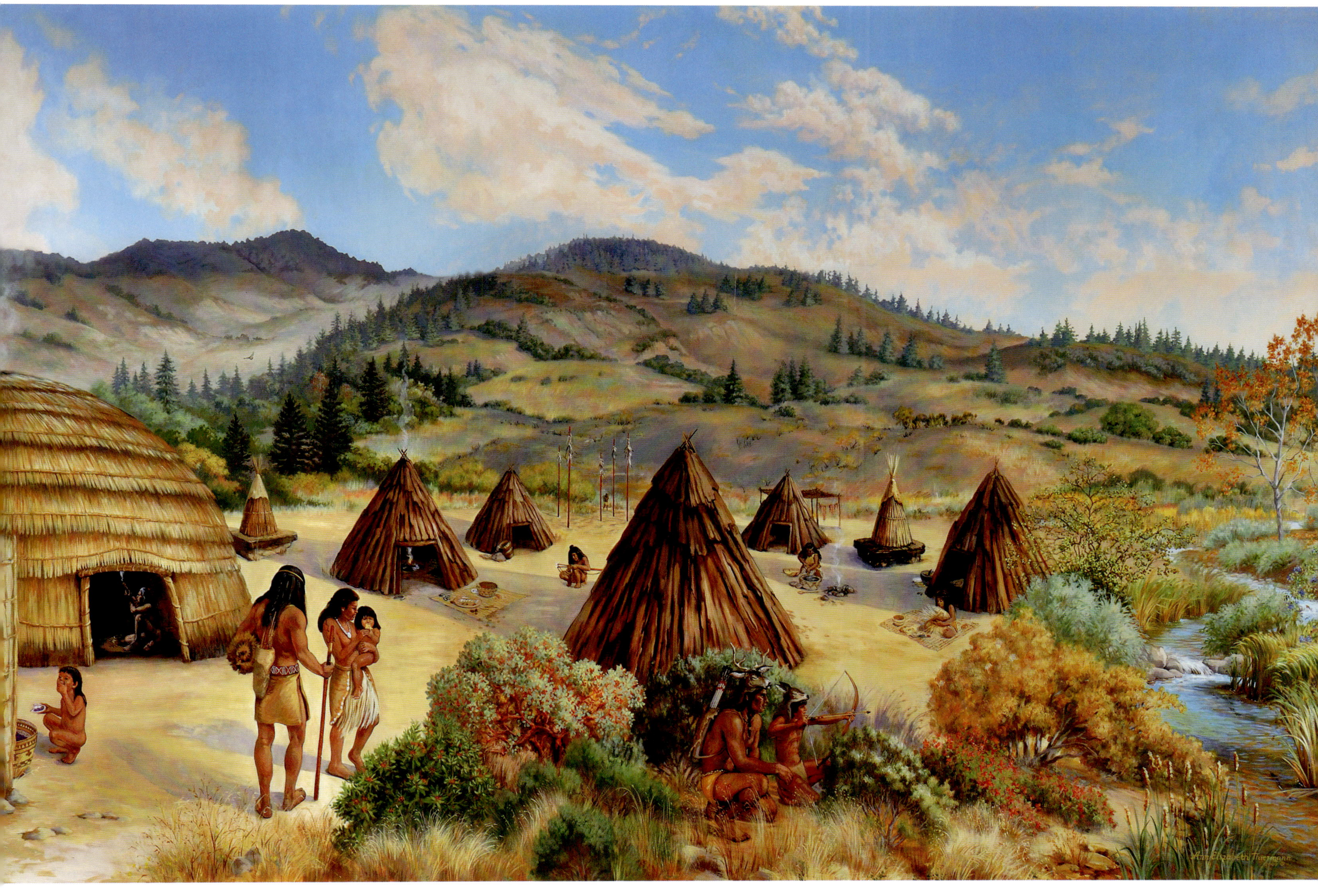

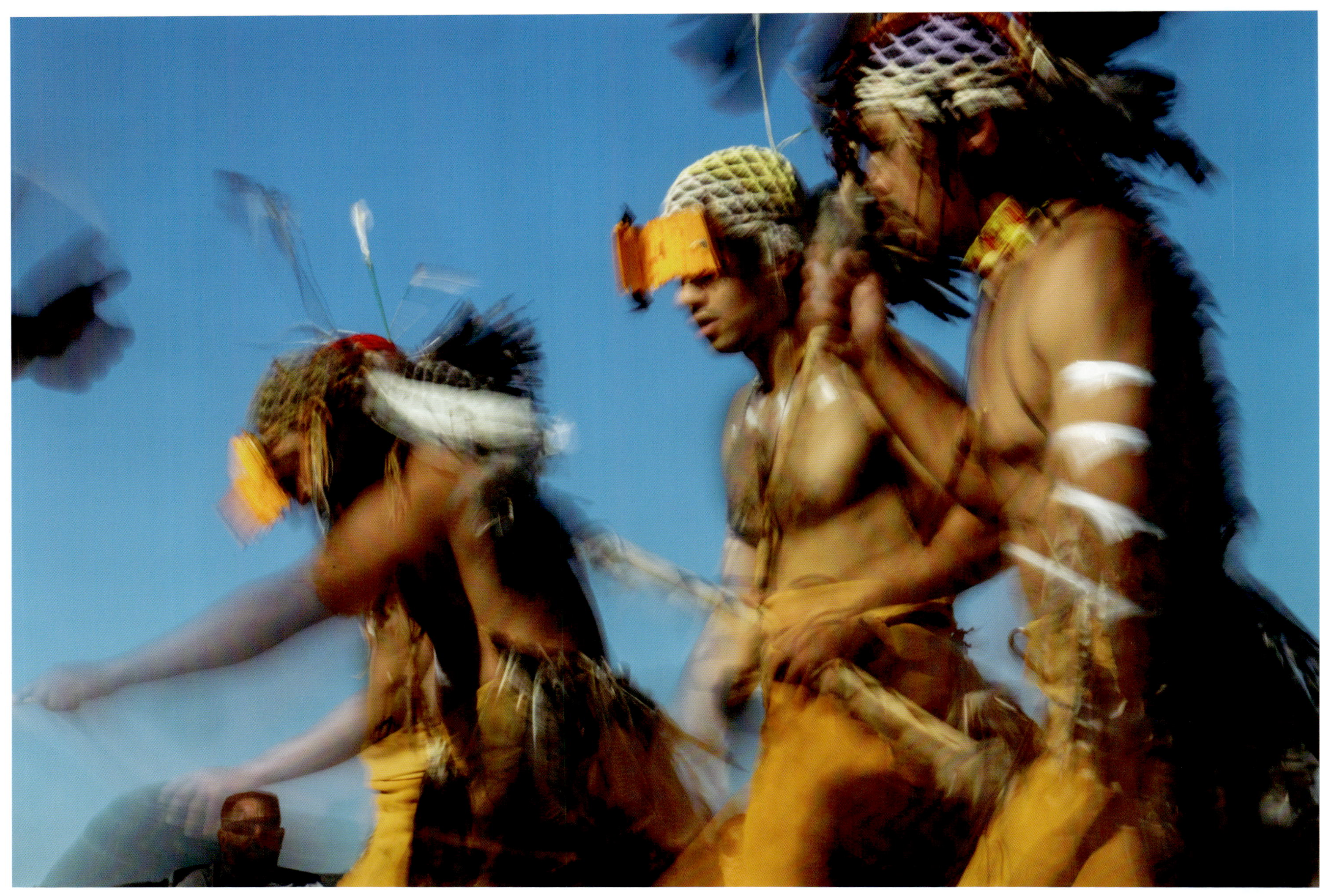

Amah Mutsun dancers (right to left) Arthur "Chico" Lopez, Alexii Sigona, Esak Ordoñez, and Steven Pratt perform at a ceremony to call salmon home to a coastal stream where they spawn. Cultural practices are being revived by a younger generation of Native Americans as they reconnect with their heritage.

Amah Mutsun Dancers, Wilder Ranch State Park

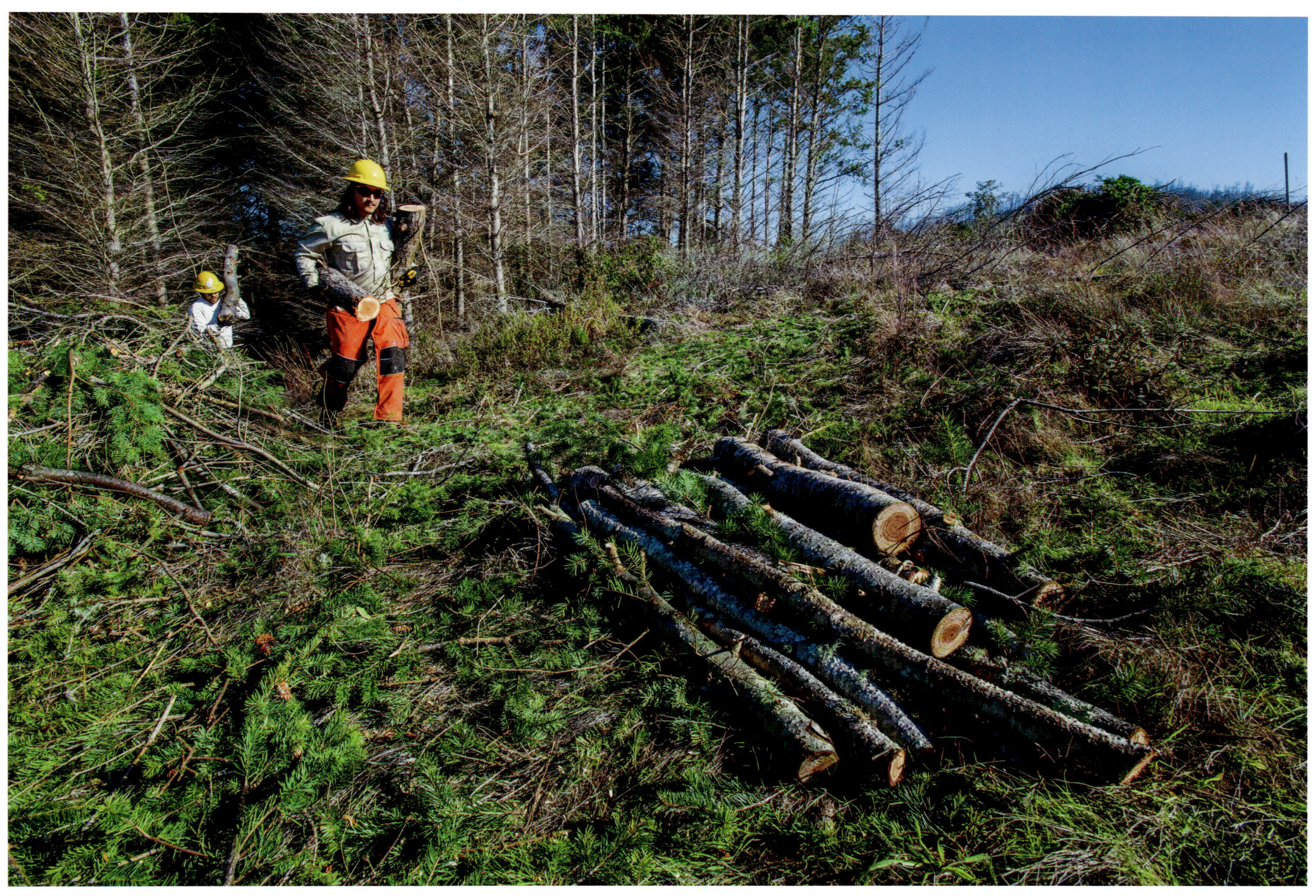

Land stewards Esak Ordoñez and Gabriel Pineida rehabilitate an ancestral landscape by cutting trees and brush from a former Quiroste village site (depicted on pages 204–205), now a cultural preserve within Año Nuevo State Park. Here, tribal members from the Amah Mutsun Land Trust collaborate with park managers and archaeologists to reintroduce traditional land-management practices.

Amah Mutsun Land Stewards, Quiroste Valley Cultural Preserve

EXPLOITING THE BAY

Exploitation of marine resources intensified during the second half of the 19th century. It included massive takes of abalone that were dried on racks across from Whaler's Cove, as seen here in 1905. The products were shipped to San Francisco and beyond.

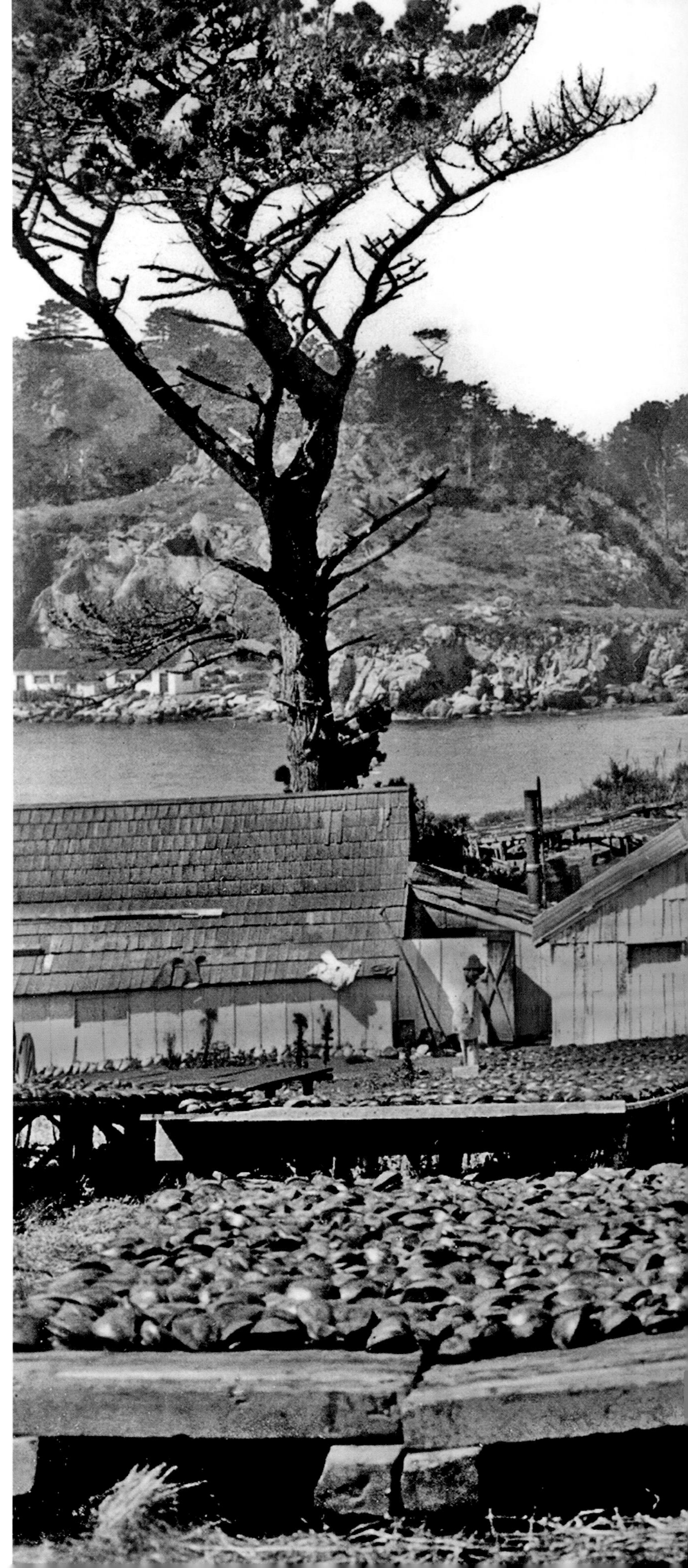

Photo by C. K. Tuttle / Pat Hathaway Photo Collection

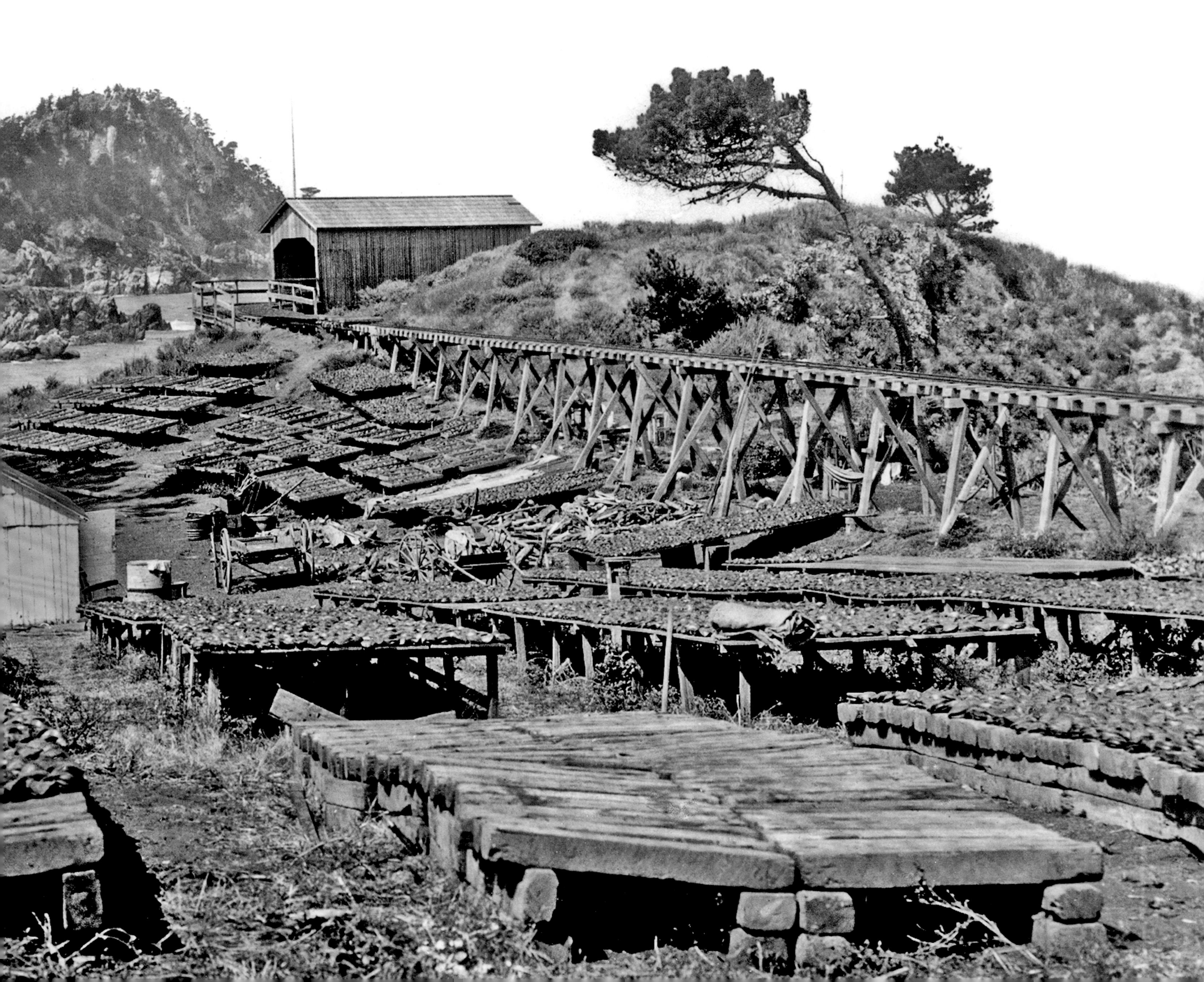

Well-dressed citizens watch whalers flense a humpback whale on McAbee Beach in the 1880s. Shore-based whaling began in Monterey in 1851 and spread to Carmel, Moss Landing, Davenport, and Pigeon Point. By the time this photo was made, the industry was already in decline because local whale populations had been largely exterminated.

HUMPBACK WHALE FLENSING, MONTEREY

Photo by C. K. Tuttle / Pat Hathaway Photo Collection

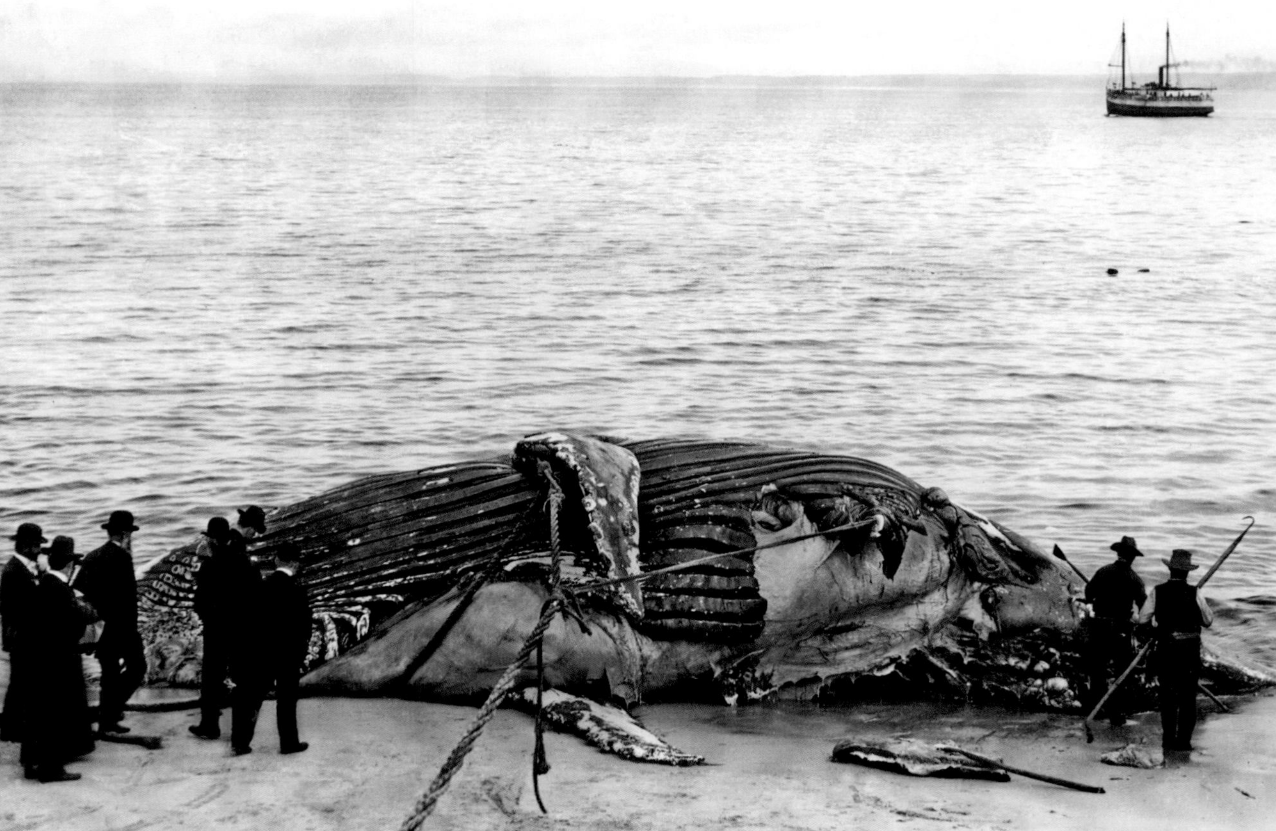

Sardine fishing boomed in the early 1900s, and canning factories soon lined the waterfront in Monterey. But due to decades of overfishing, the sardine population collapsed in the 1940s, which led to the demise of Cannery Row—made famous by John Steinbeck's novel of the same name.

SARDINE CANNING FACTORY, MONTEREY

Photo by Donn I. Clickard / Pat Hathaway Photo Collection

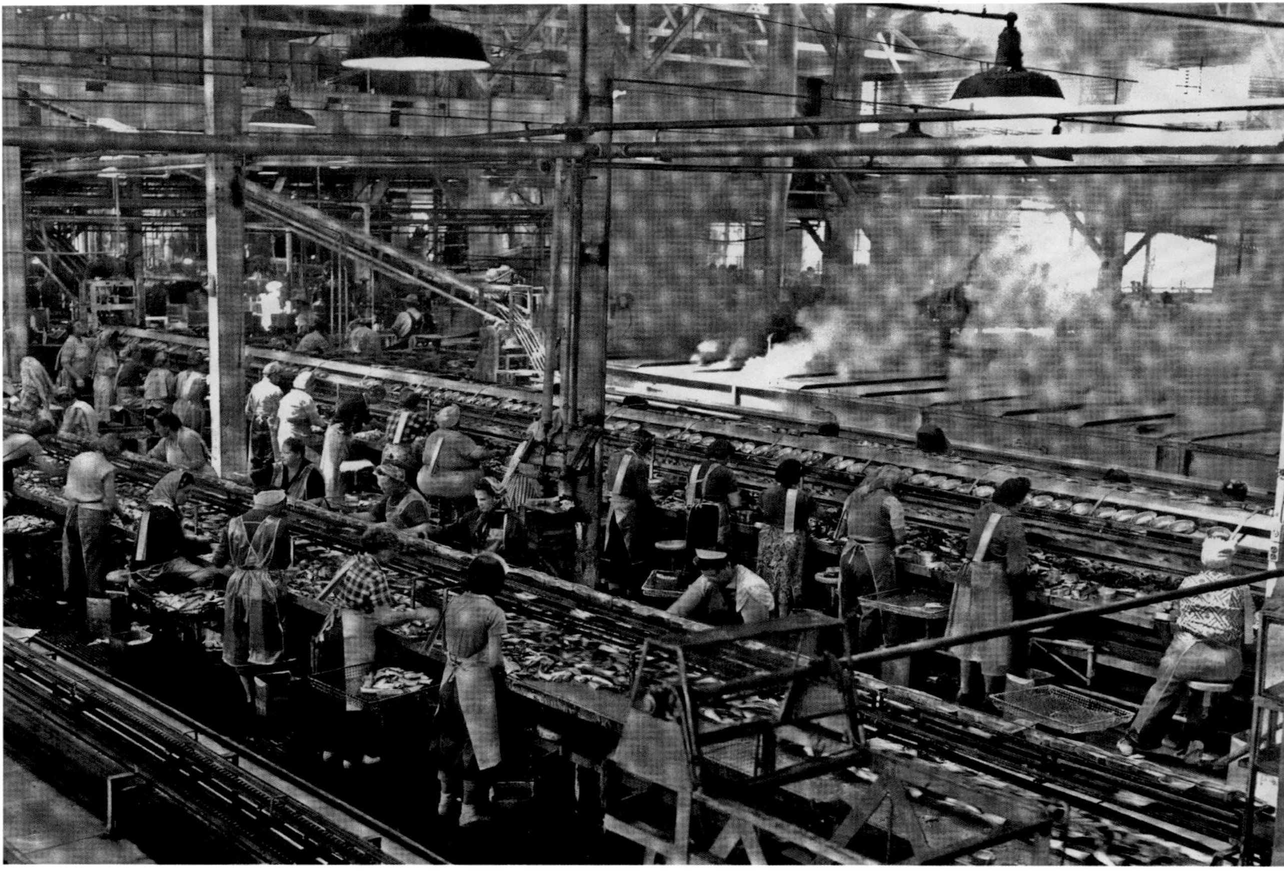

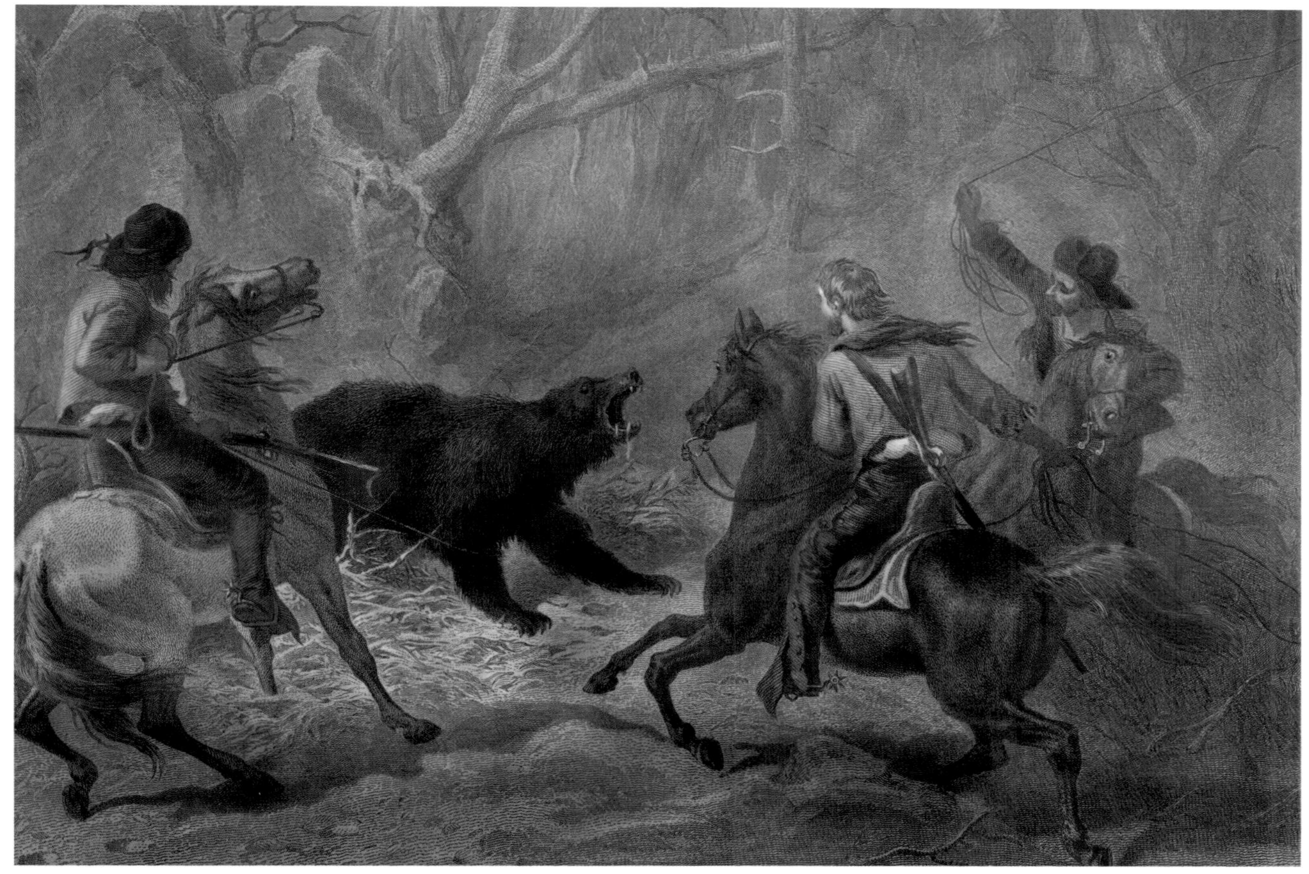

Grizzly bears were once common and their numbers briefly increased after livestock proliferated in the early 1800s. When shore-based whaling began, they were seen around carcasses along the coast, though their numbers plummeted soon after because of indiscriminate killings. The last grizzly sighting in the Santa Cruz Mountains was in 1887. The bears held on longer in the rugged Santa Lucia Range, but today they are extinct in California. Ironically, the state still features a grizzly bear on its flag.

GRIZZLY BEAR SURROUNDED BY VAQUEROS
Etching by Felix Darley / The Bancroft Library

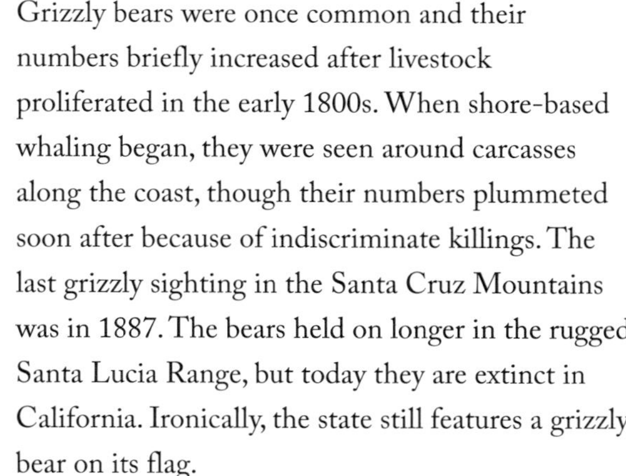

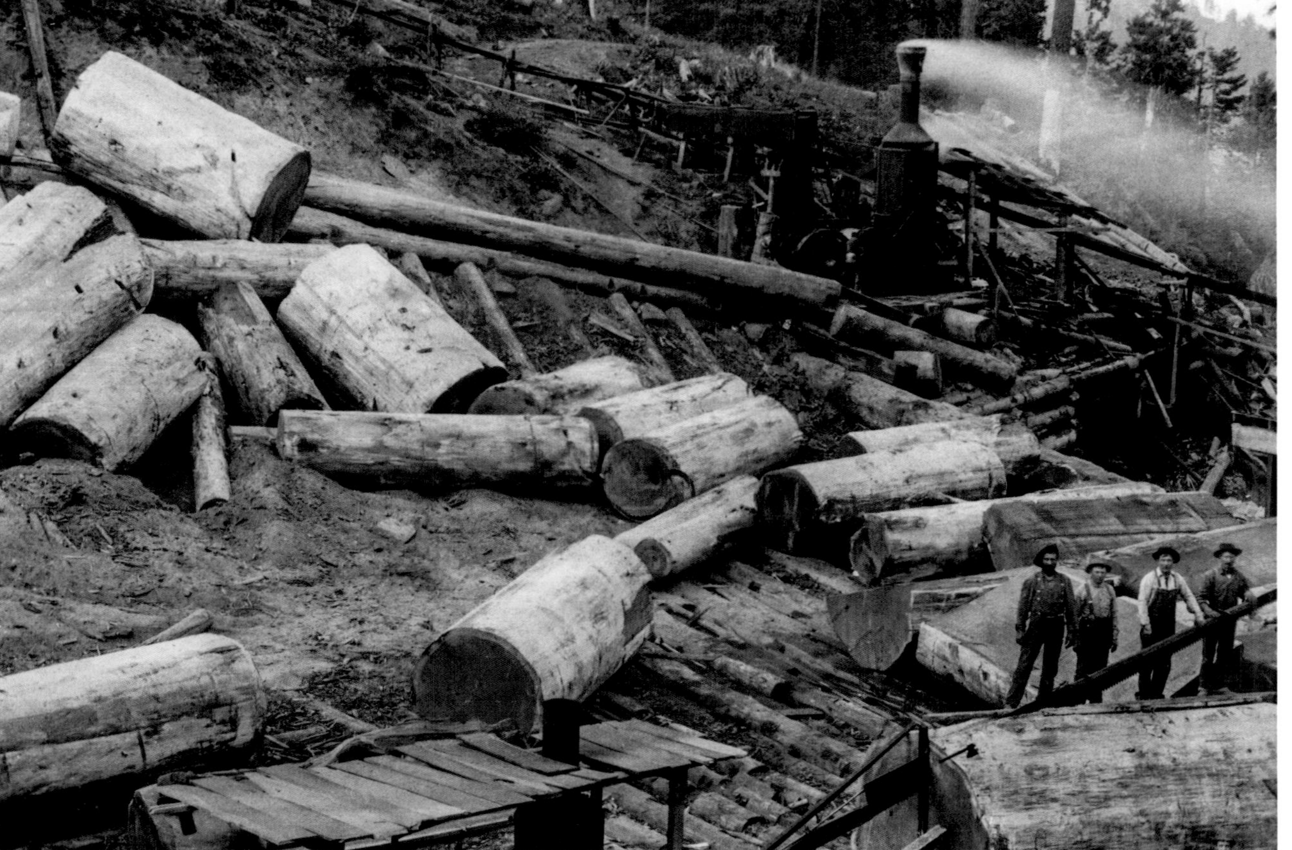

Beginning in the mid-1800s, the Santa Cruz Mountains were steadily stripped bare of trees, expedited by steam-powered sawmills, as shown in this photo from the 1890s. The demand for timber was triggered first by the Gold Rush and later by the need to rebuild San Francisco after the disastrous earthquake and fire of 1906.

LOGGING REDWOODS, APTOS
Photo by A. R. Moore / Covello & Covello Historical Collection

RESTORING THE BAY

A grove of primeval redwoods along the San Lorenzo River was acquired by the Cowell family in 1865. Nearly a century later, Samuel Cowell donated the land for a state park, which opened in 1954 and still preserves monumental giants like this one.

ANCIENT REDWOOD, HENRY COWELL REDWOODS STATE PARK

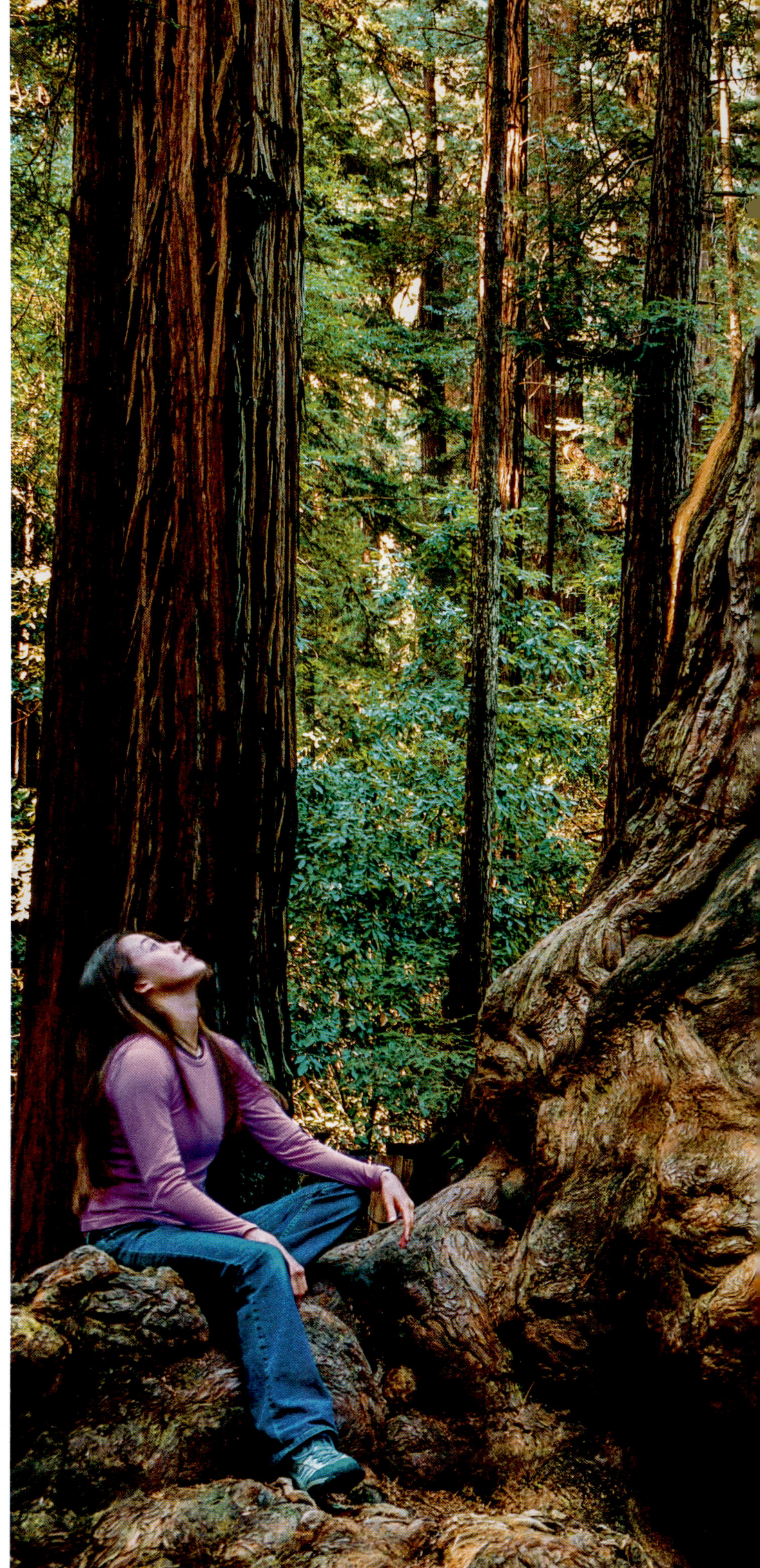

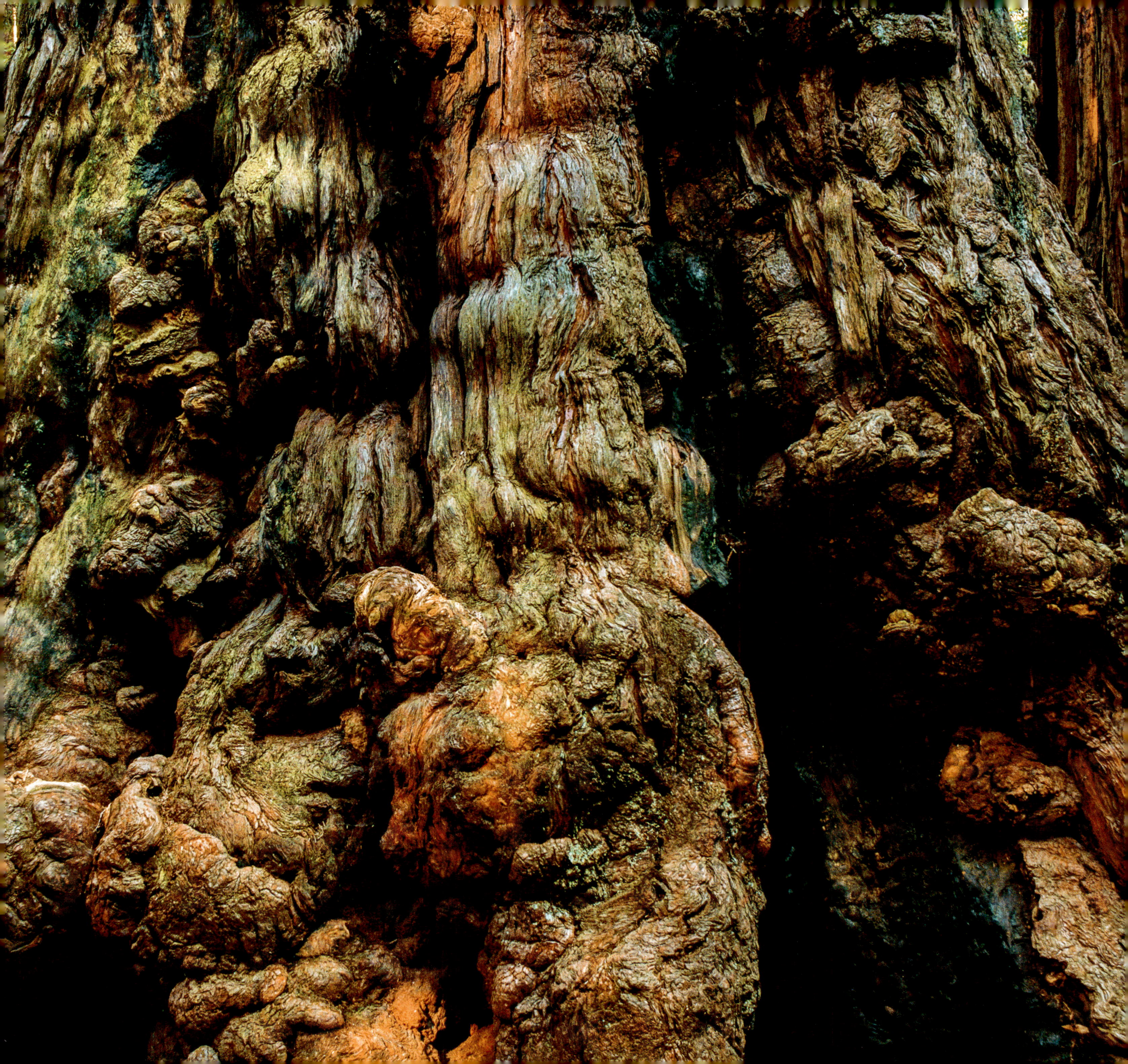

California's State Parks system relies on volunteers like David Neidel, who uproots non-native ice plant invading coastal grasslands at Soberanes Point. This fast-growing succulent from South Africa smothers slower-growing native species in habitats bordering the bay.

Invasive Plant Eradication, Garrapata State Park

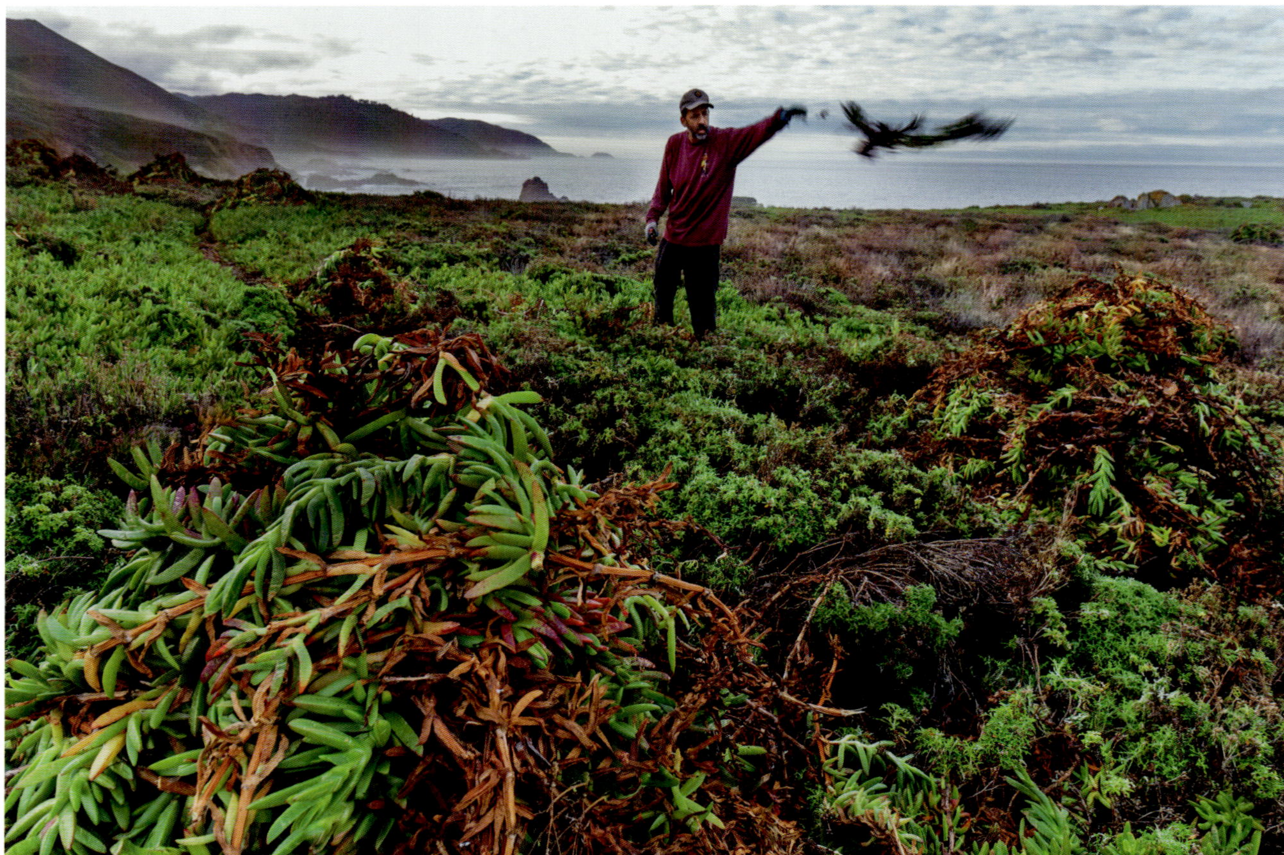

Steelhead trout and coho salmon have had a hard time surviving in coastal streams because of habitat loss due to logging, water diversions, and dams. And now climate change is warming their spawning streams. The fish need help, and Dave Straub did just that at the Monterey Bay Salmon and Trout Project hatchery, the only facility of its kind in the bay.

Steelhead Support, Scott Creek

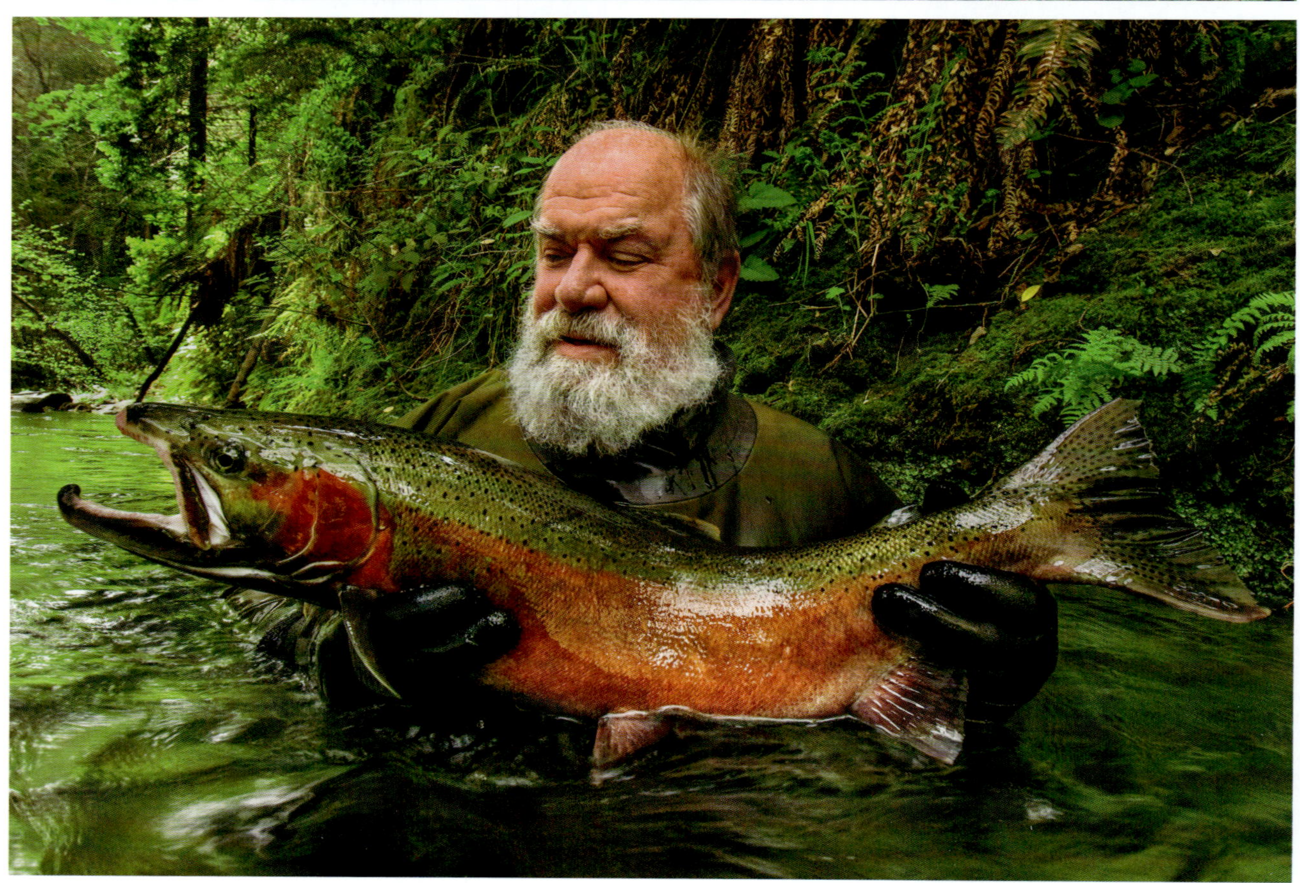

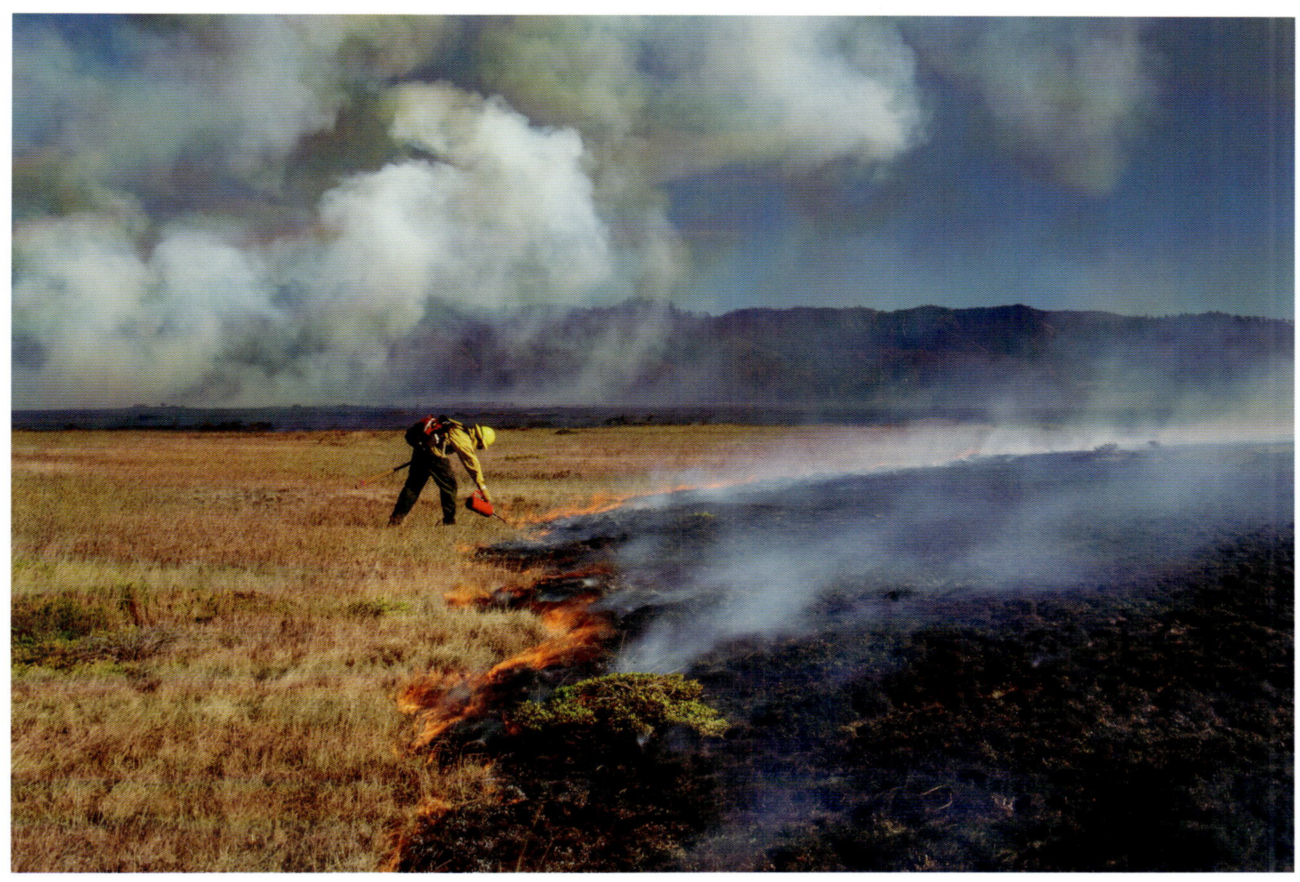

Fire is an important habitat-management tool to maintain the quality of coastal grasslands, which benefit from periodic burning. Trained teams from State Parks ignite grasses at Cascade Field, as they have done every other year for two decades. What was once an overgrown field of invasive species is now one of the best expressions of native coastal prairie in the region.

**Burning Grassland,
Año Nuevo State Park**

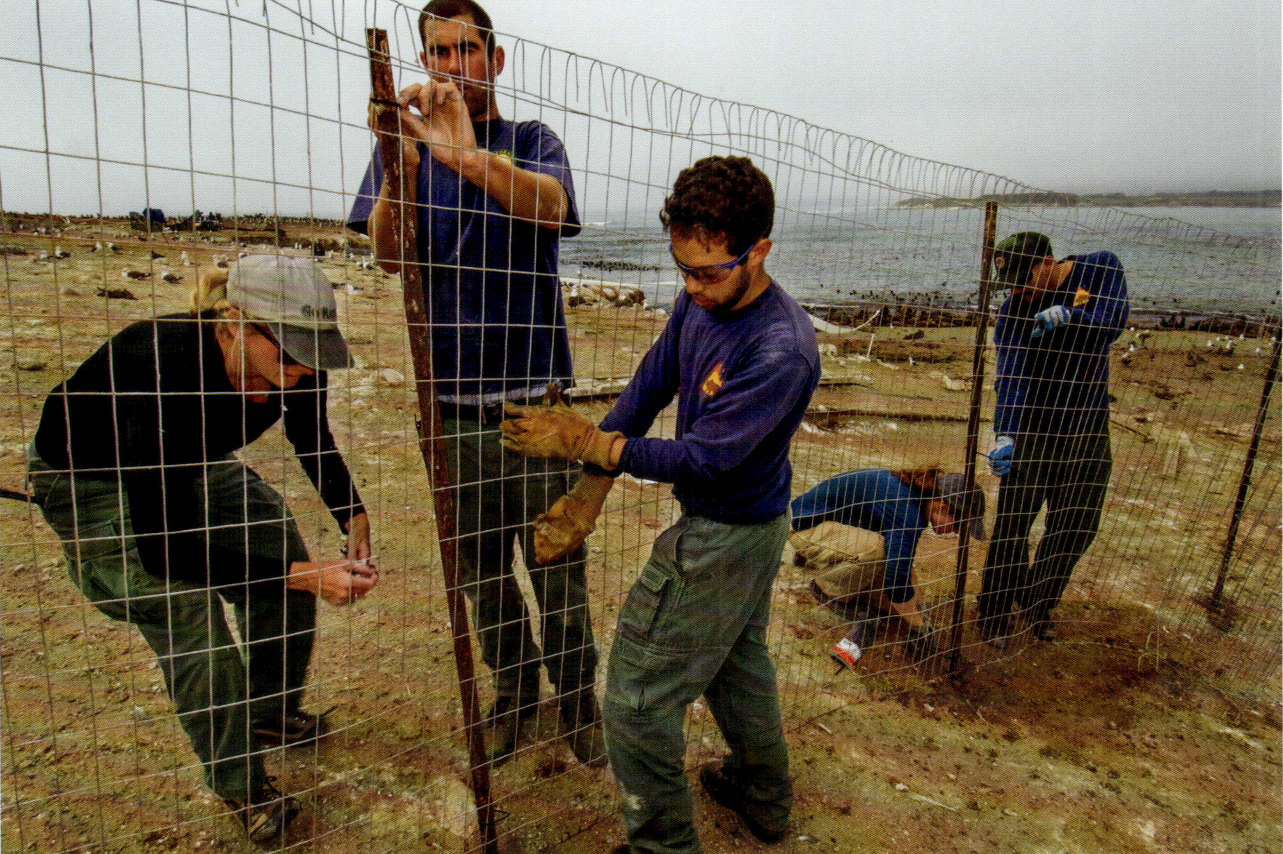

To protect sensitive seabird nesting areas on Año Nuevo Island, volunteers build a temporary fence—later replaced by a sustainable log fence integrated into the landscape. Populations of rare rhinoceros auklets, Cassin's auklets, and other birds have increased since the barrier was erected by Oikonos, a non-profit that protects and restores threatened ecosystems.

**Seabird Restoration,
Año Nuevo Island Reserve**

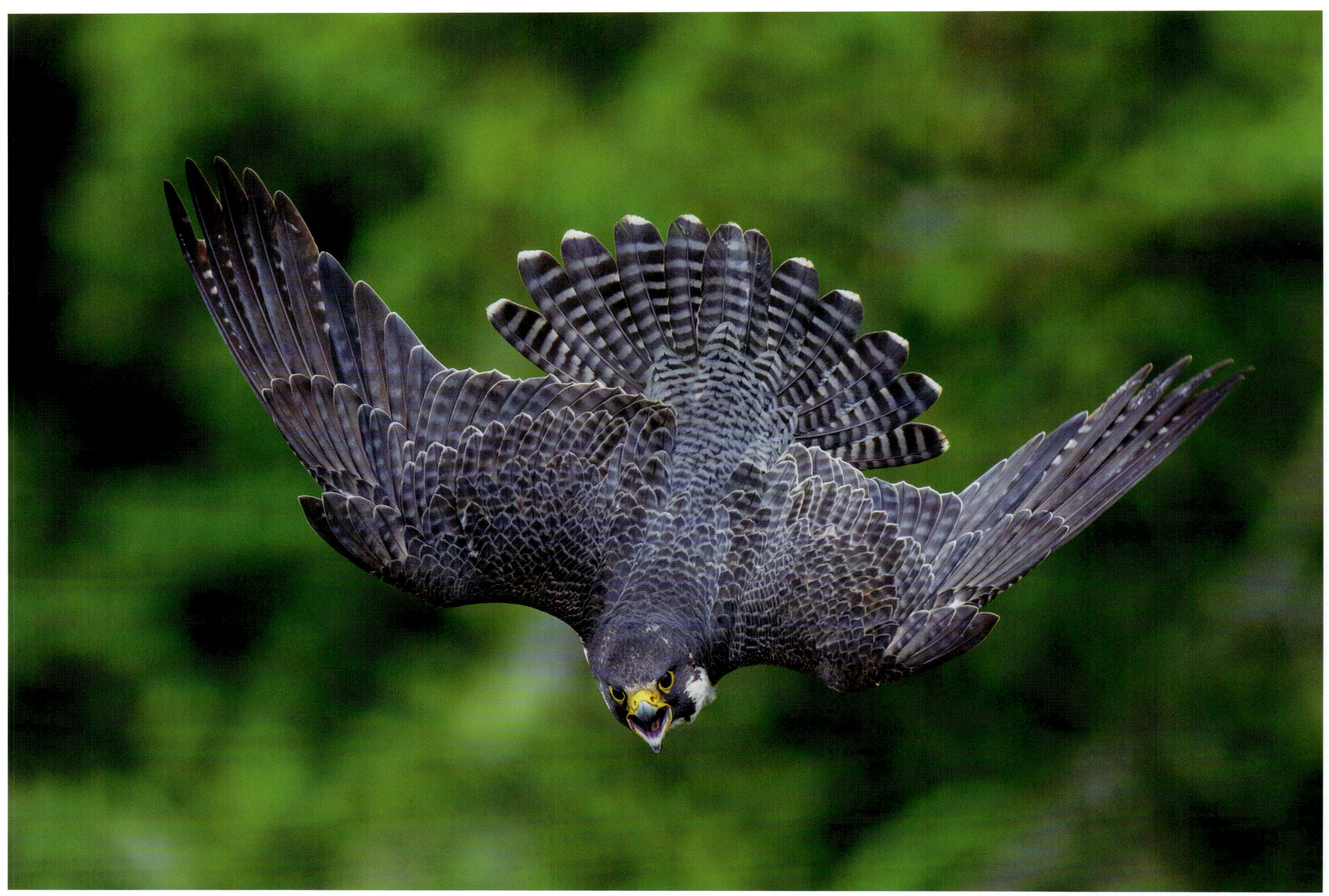

Peregrine falcons are the fastest birds on Earth, but they could not escape the poisonous effects of DDT, which thinned their eggshells, often fatally. Their population plummeted, but now they are back, thanks to protection provided by the 1973 Endangered Species Act and the hard work of UCSC's Predatory Bird Research Group, which led in the rewilding effort. Today these magnificent birds can be seen again around Monterey Bay.

Peregrine Falcon, Wilder Ranch State Park

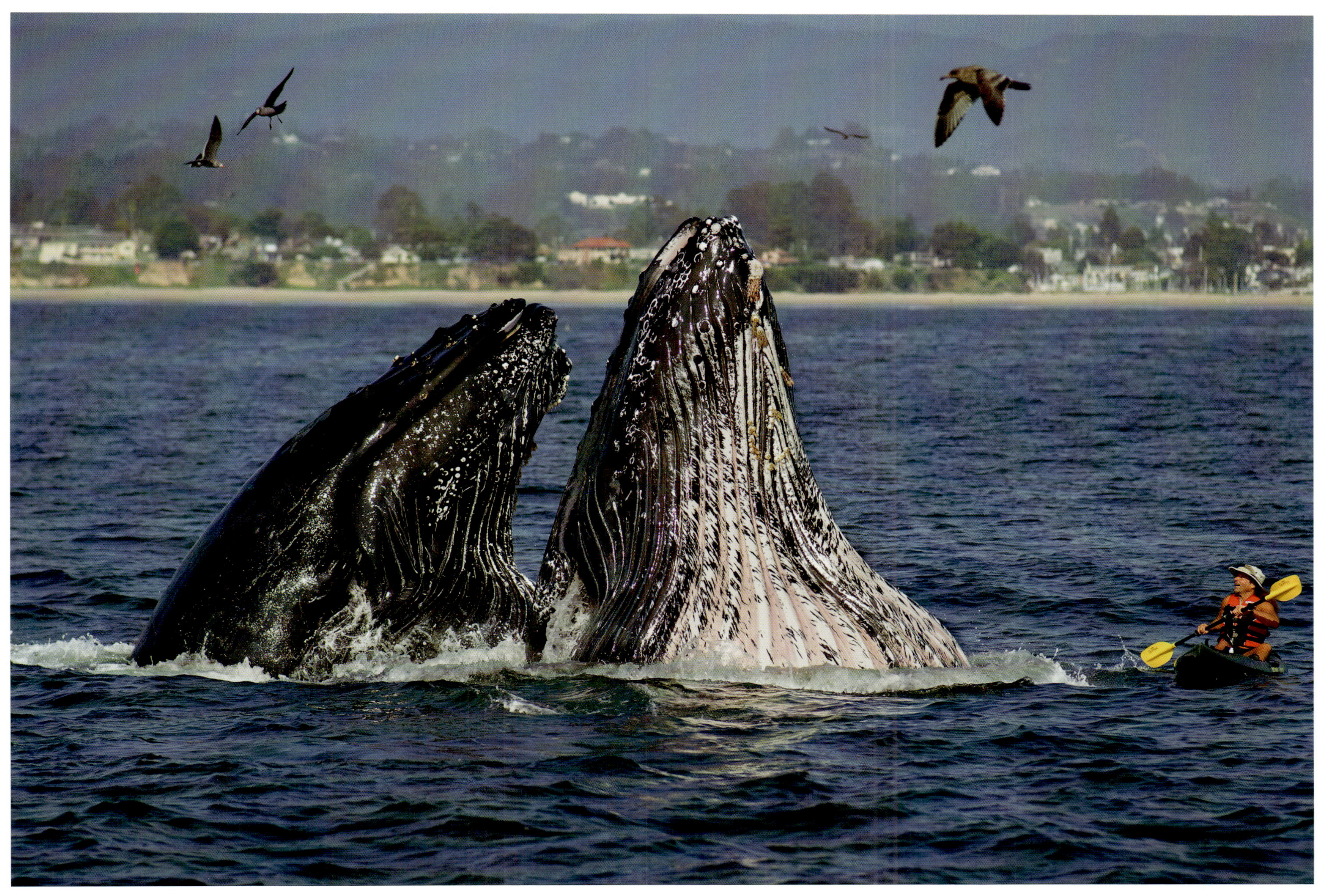

Lunge-feeding humpbacks surprise a kayaker off the Santa Cruz Wharf. The comeback of whales in Monterey Bay was boosted by the 1972 Marine Mammal Protection Act and the establishment, 20 years later, of the Monterey Bay National Marine Sanctuary.

HUMPBACK WHALES AND KAYAKER, SANTA CRUZ | *Photo by Paul Schraub*

SUSTAINING THE BAY

Rocks Ranch provides a critical link for mountain lions to
travel between the Santa Cruz Mountains and Gabilan Range.
It was purchased by the Land Trust of Santa Cruz County for
its strategic connectivity and to protect its open landscapes
from residential development, as seen in the distance.

ROCKS RANCH, AROMAS

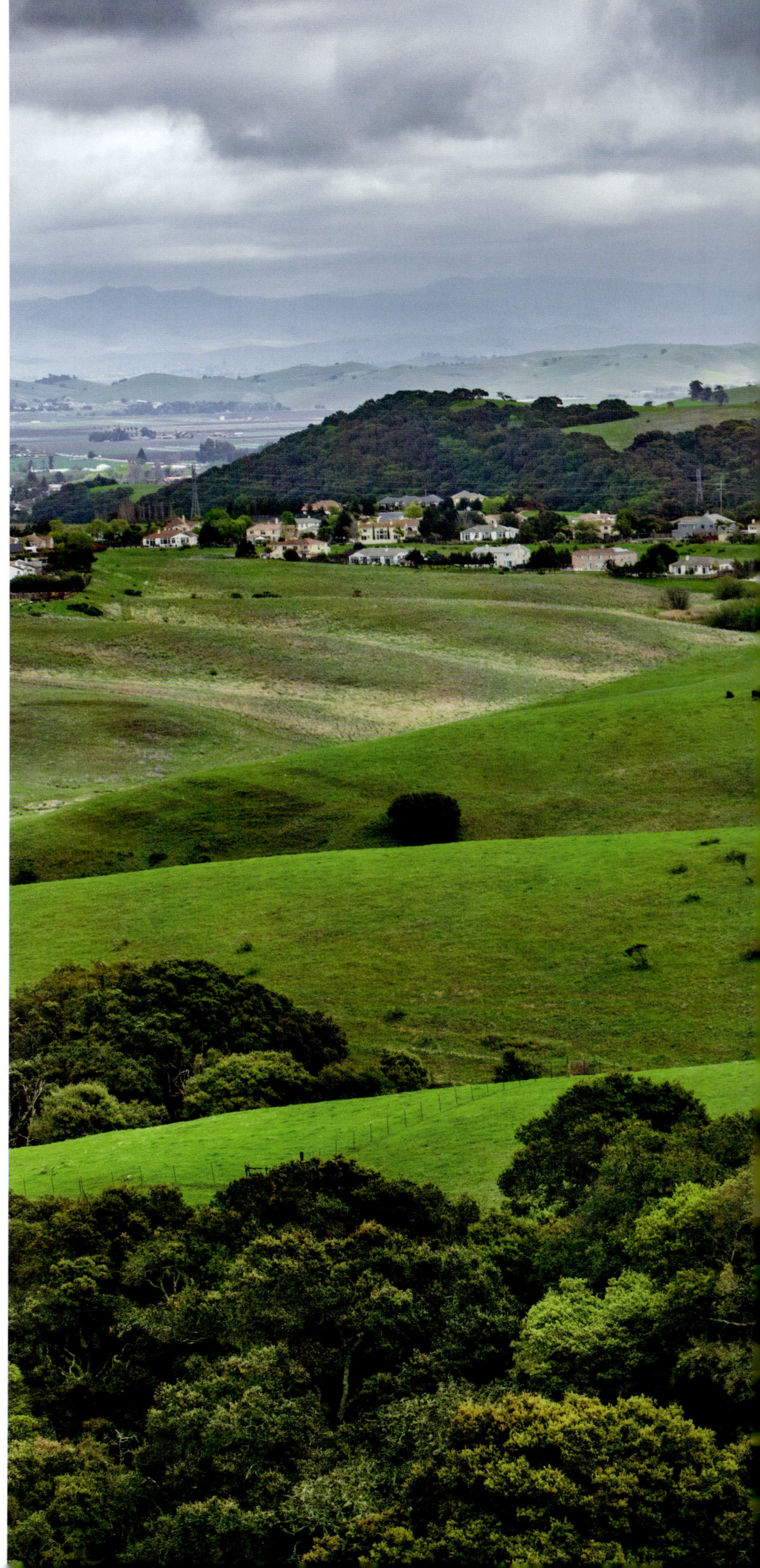

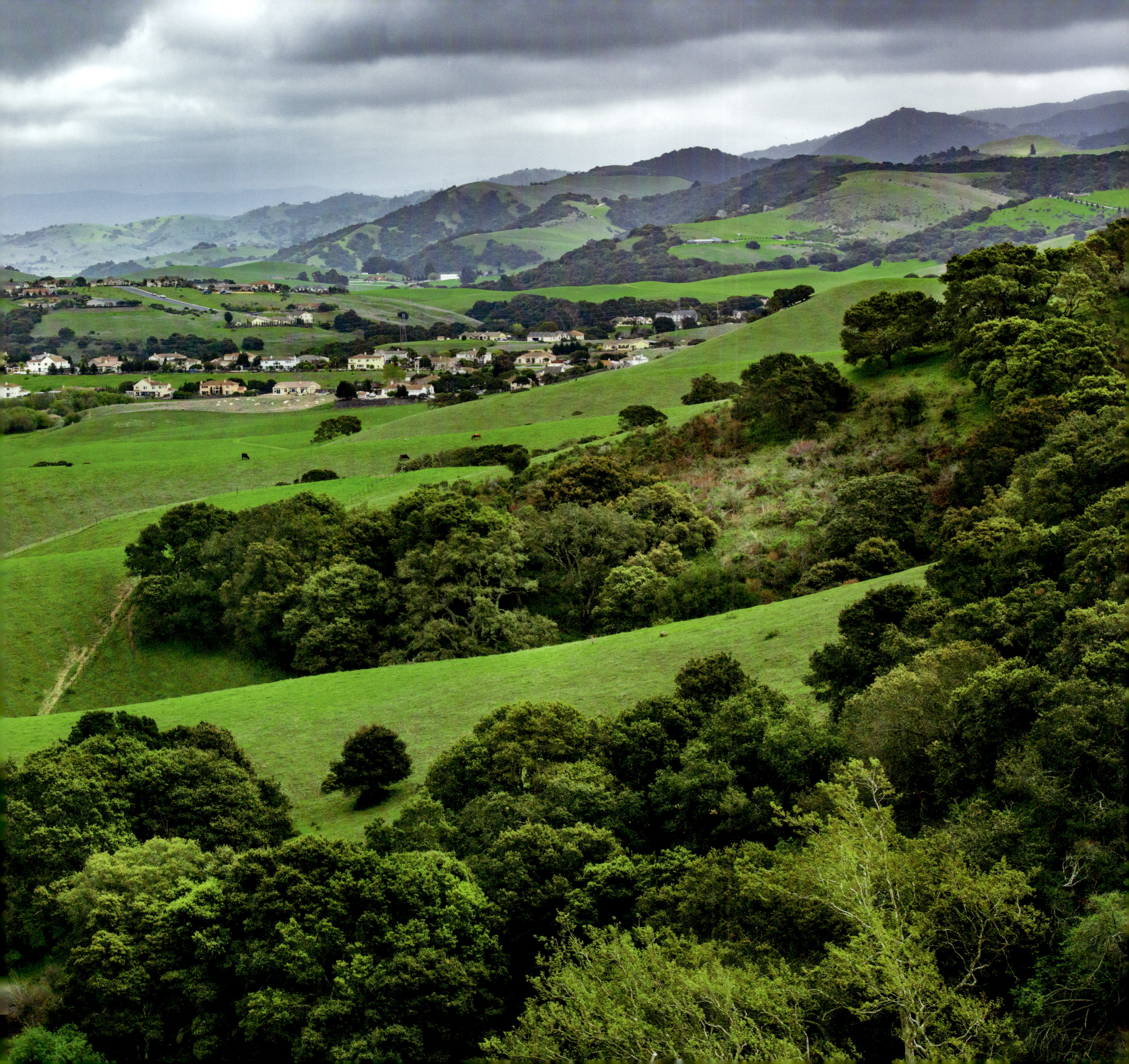

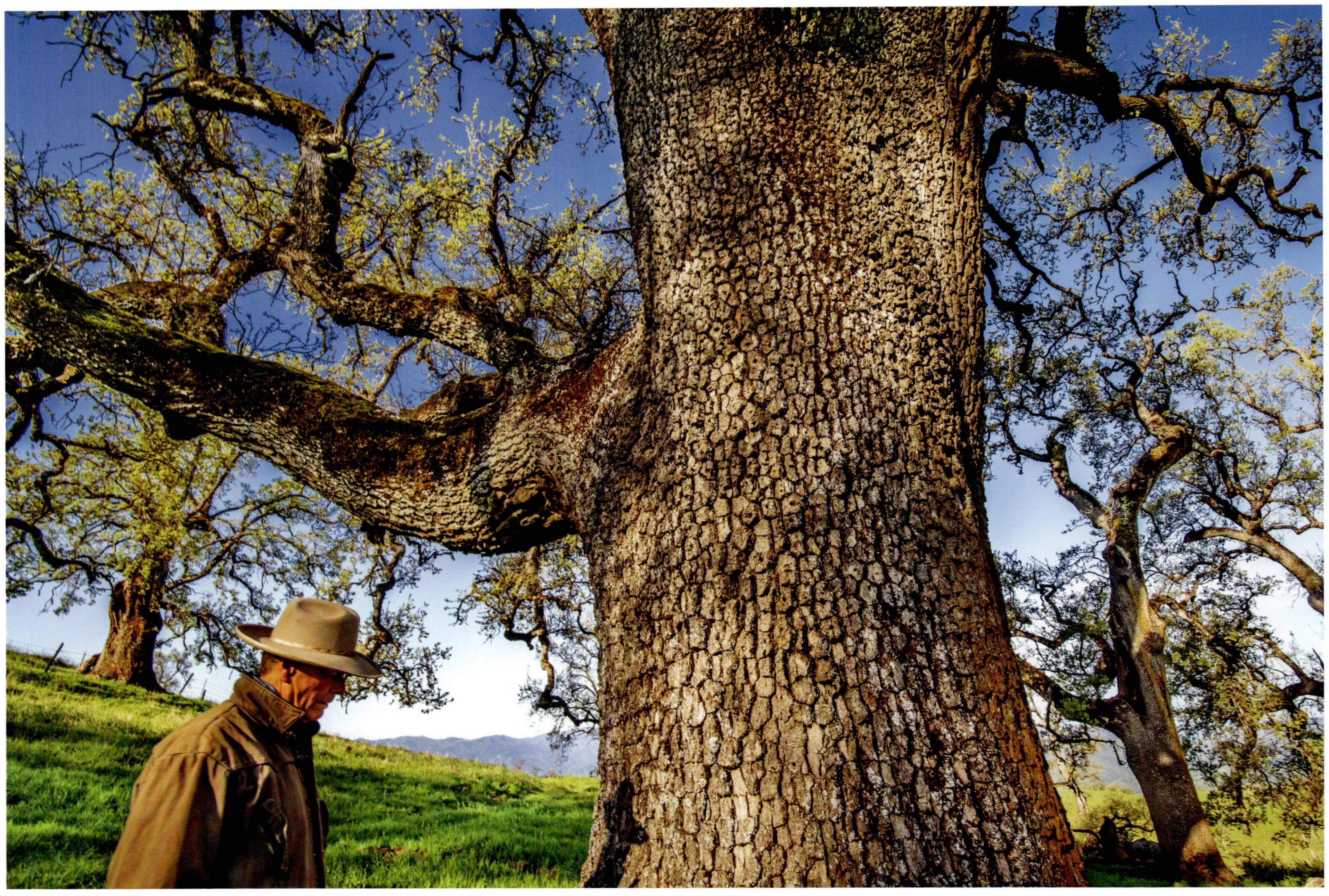

Steve Dorrance cares as much about the oak trees on his land as he does about the cattle he raises and the way of life his family has practiced for generations along the slopes of Mount Toro. He signed a conservation easement with The Nature Conservancy that protects him from pressures to sell the land for development and preserves the striking view of a prominent natural landmark visible around the bay.

Rancher and Oak Tree, Dorrance Ranch, Salinas

opposite: Lud and Bud McCrary helped set new standards of sustainable forestry practices during their lifetime of harvesting redwood trees in the Santa Cruz Mountains. The practical knowledge of foresters, ranchers, farmers, and fishers about earning a living from nature should be an important part of achieving a better balance between working lands and protected areas.

Foresters Lud and Bud McCrary, Swanton

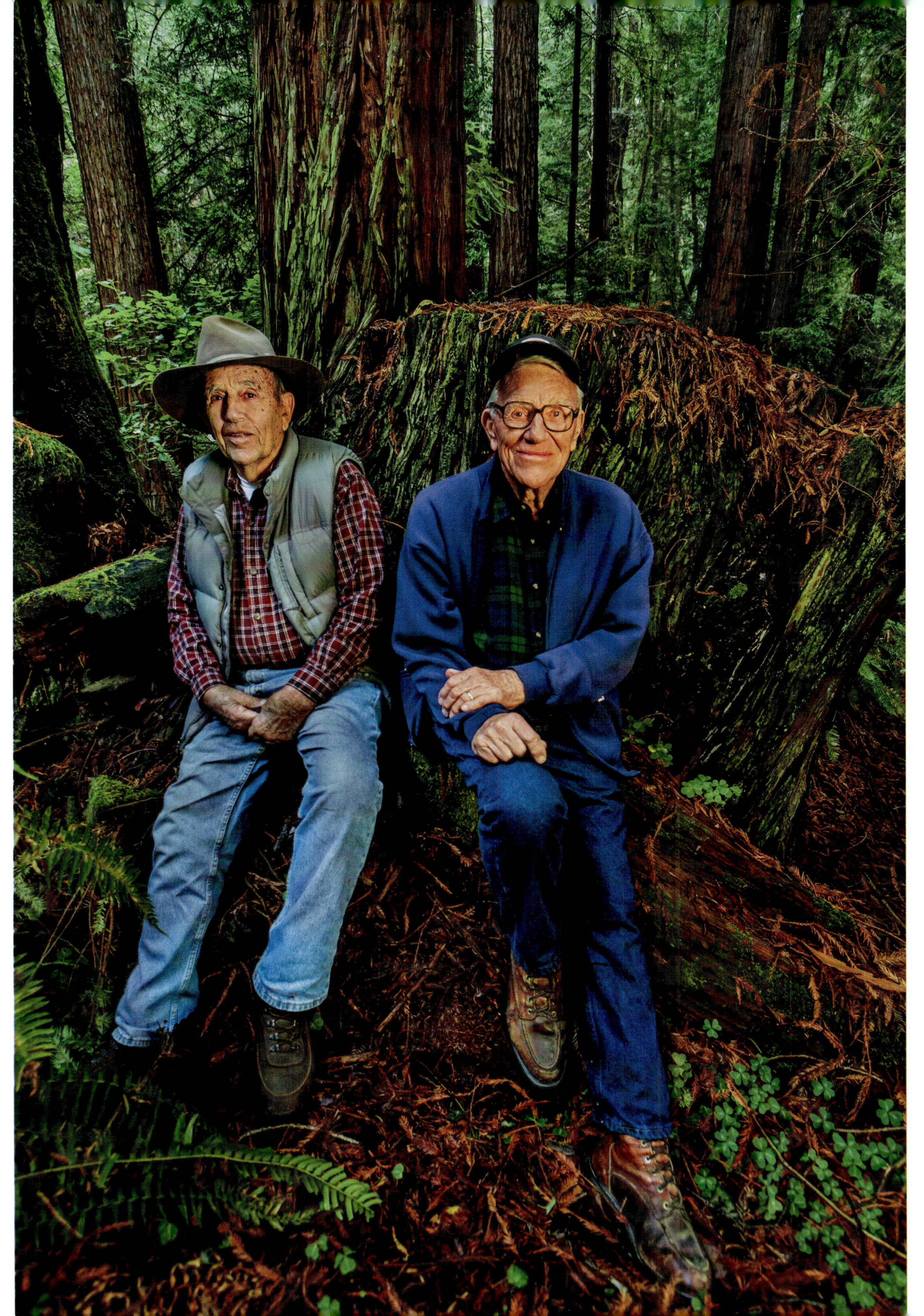

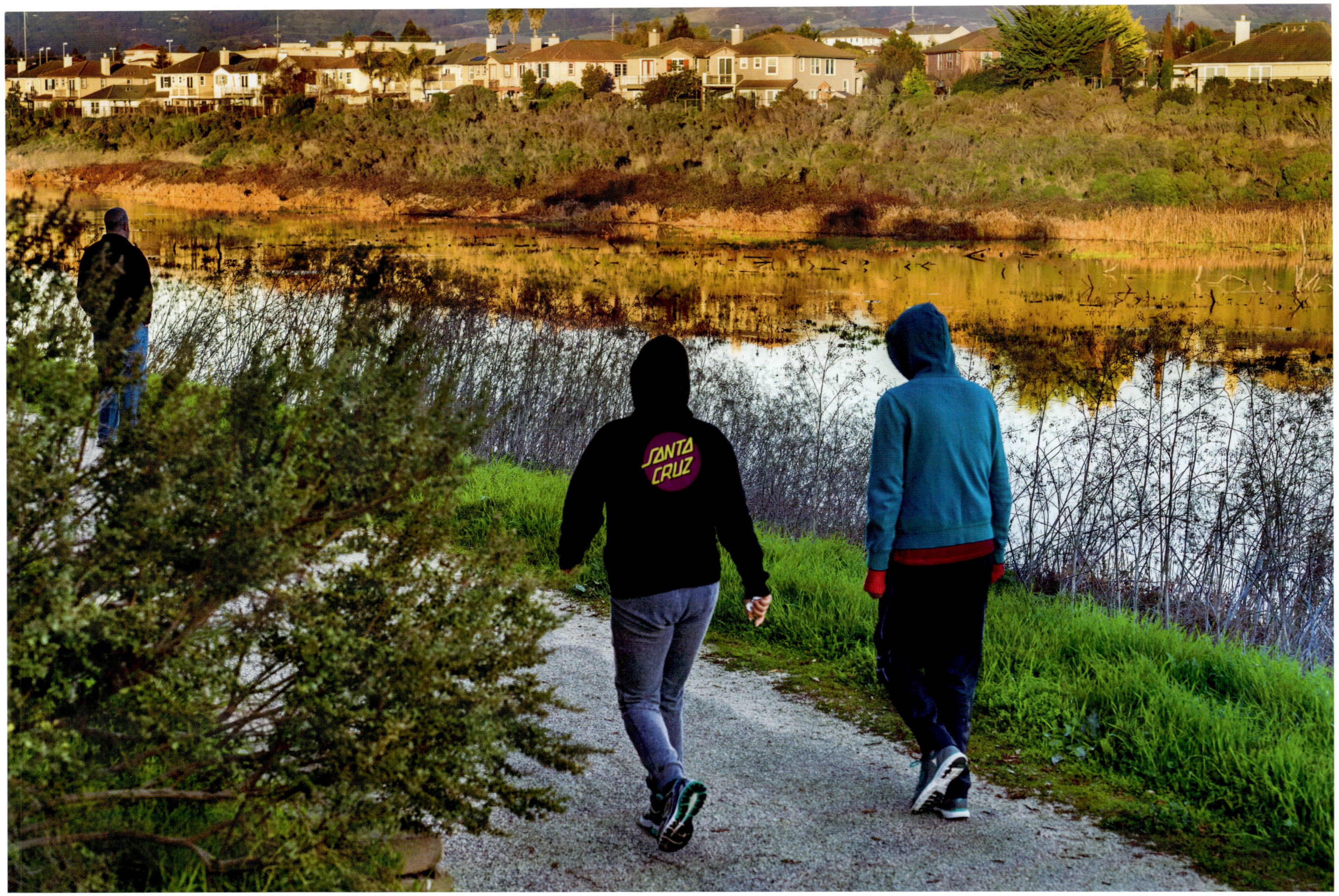

The sloughs around Watsonville are among the most significant freshwater wetlands along the California coast, and they attract a variety of wildlife. They are also an important place for people to connect with nature. Watsonville Wetlands Watch has played a key role in protecting the sloughs and promoting their value to the community.

HIKERS, STRUVE SLOUGH, WATSONVILLE

OPPOSITE: An aerial view of the Salinas River shows private farmlands bordering it on both sides. Only a handful of public access points exist between Camp Roberts and the Monterey Bay. People from inland rural communities and densely populated urban areas lack access to open spaces for recreation. In the city of Salinas, the Big Sur Land Trust has purchased part of Carr Lake to transform it into an urban park.

SALINAS RIVER AND FARMLAND, SALINAS VALLEY

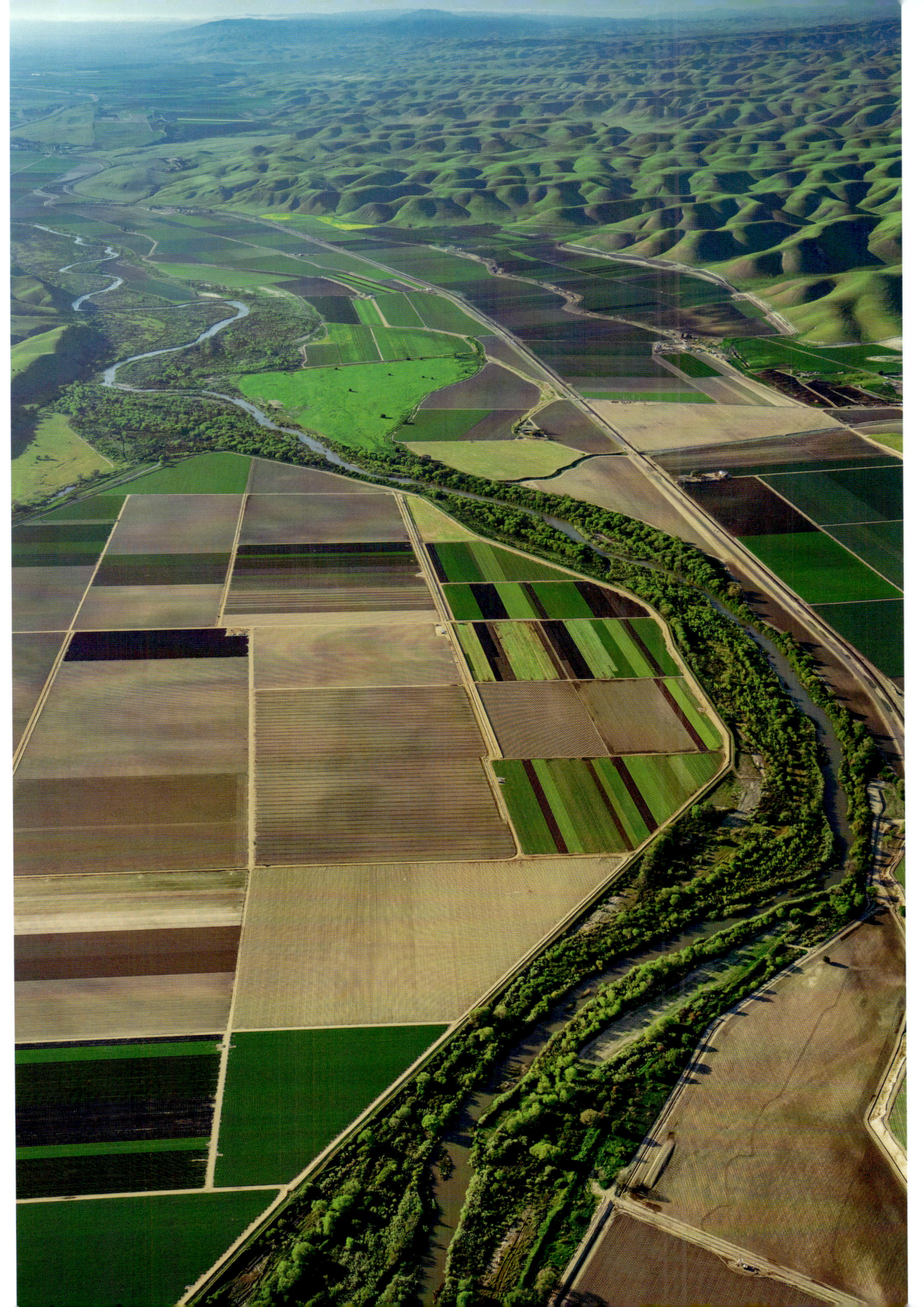

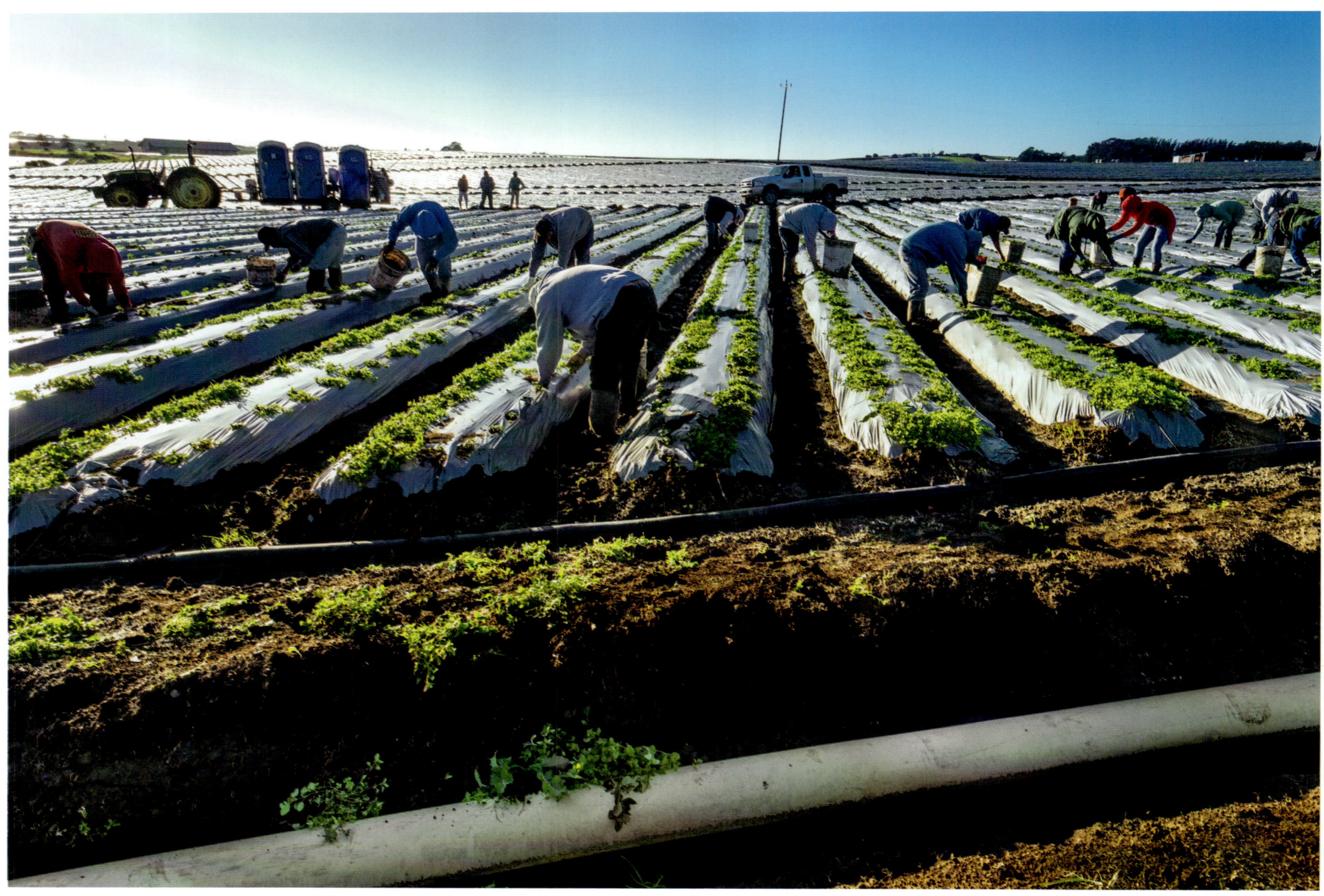

Generations of farmworkers have contributed to the prosperity of the agricultural industry in the Monterey Bay. Here, they tend to an organic strawberry crop on a farm owned by the Land Trust of Santa Cruz County near the Watsonville Slough. Purchased to safeguard wetlands, the property demonstrates how farming can coexist profitably with nature.

FARMWORKERS, WATSONVILLE SLOUGH FARM

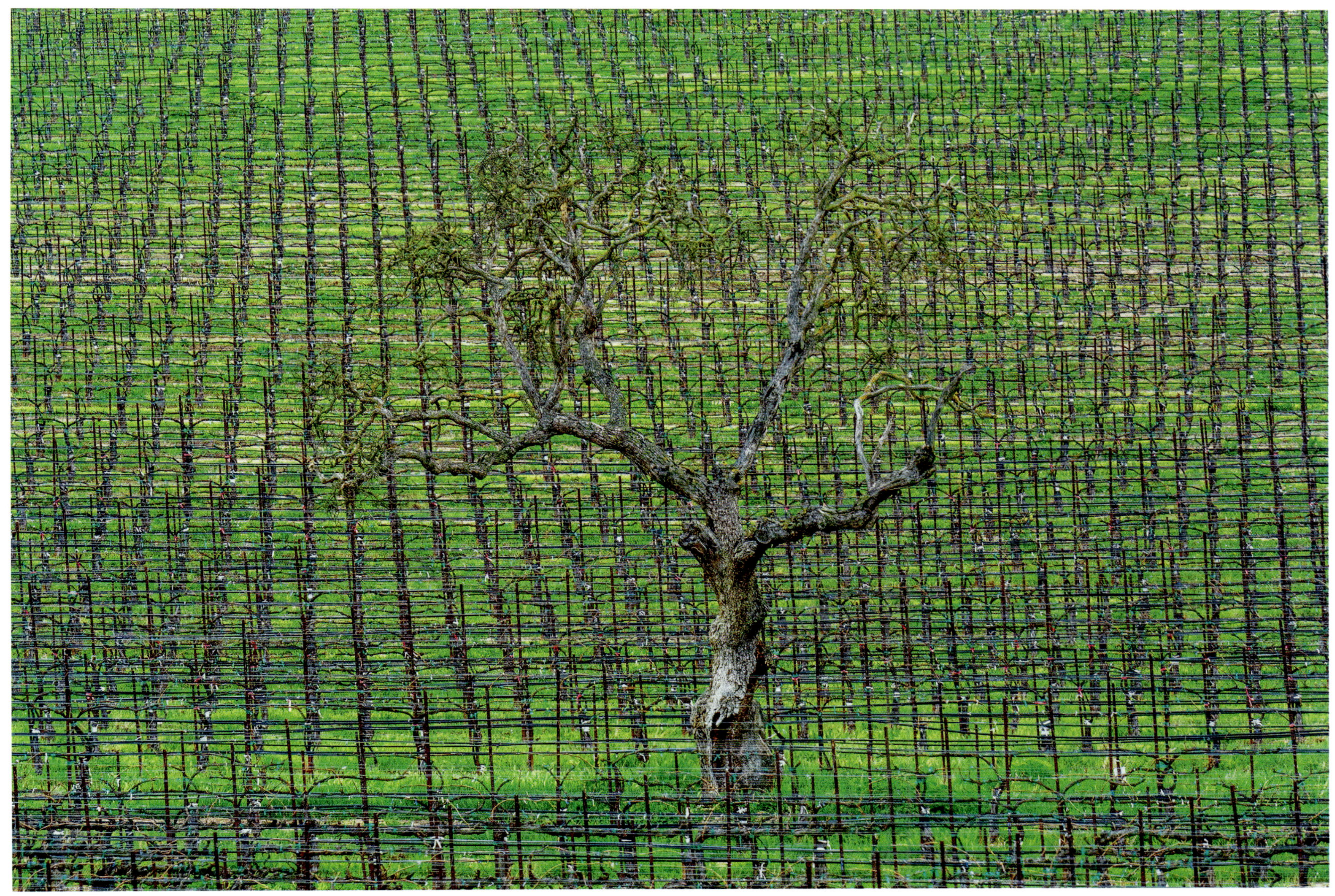

A withering oak tree surrounded by grape vines symbolizes the challenges faced by Monterey Bay's wine industry. Climate change is forcing growers to consider how to adapt their sensitive crop to a new reality that includes hotter weather and less water.

Oak Tree in Vineyard, Carmel Valley

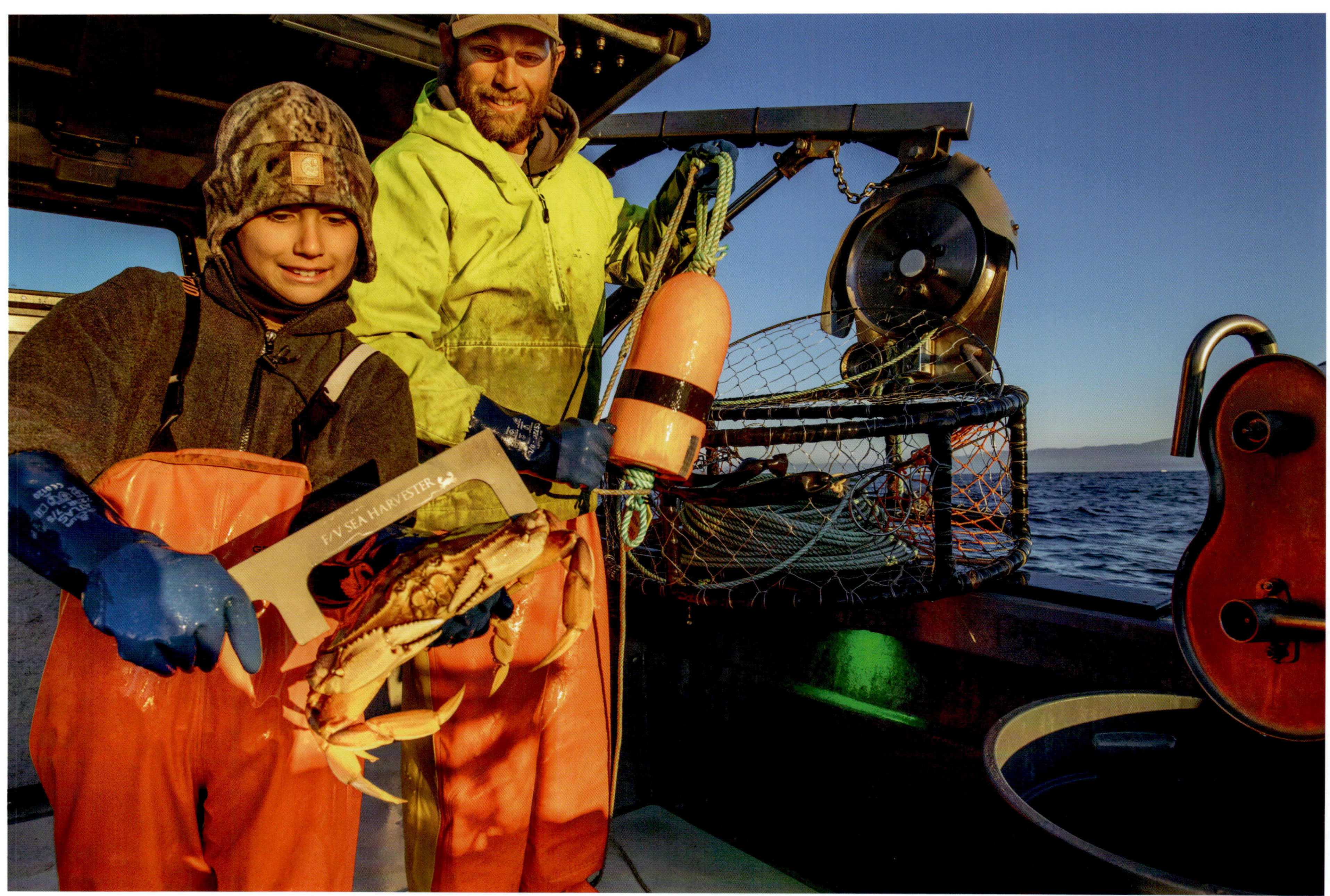

Miles Deyerle measures a crab to determine whether it is legal to keep while his father, Calder, looks on. All of their crabs and much of the fish they catch in the bay—from salmon to cod to halibut—ends up on local dinner plates. After a period of boom and bust, Monterey Bay's fisheries are more tightly regulated to meet sustainability goals. Crab season now ends when humpback whales show up, to minimize entanglement with crab pot lines.

CRAB FISHERMEN, MONTEREY BAY NATIONAL MARINE SANCTUARY

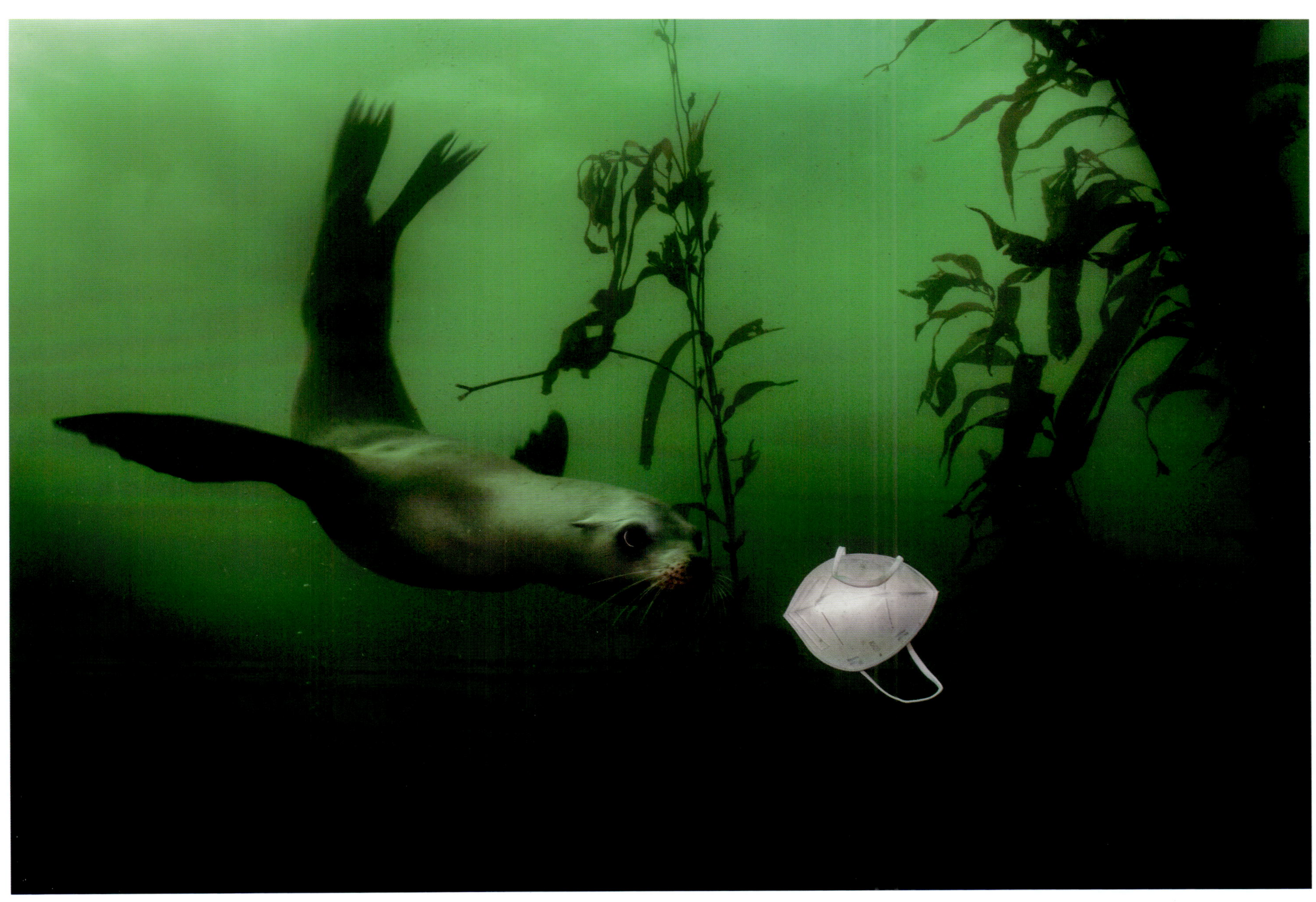

A curious sea lion approaches a face mask drifting underwater, but the encounter is a reminder of marine pollution. The health of the bay depends on how people along its shores manage the impacts of their lifestyles and livelihoods.

SEA LION AND FACE MASK, MONTEREY BAY NATIONAL MARINE SANCTUARY | *Photo by Ralph Pace*

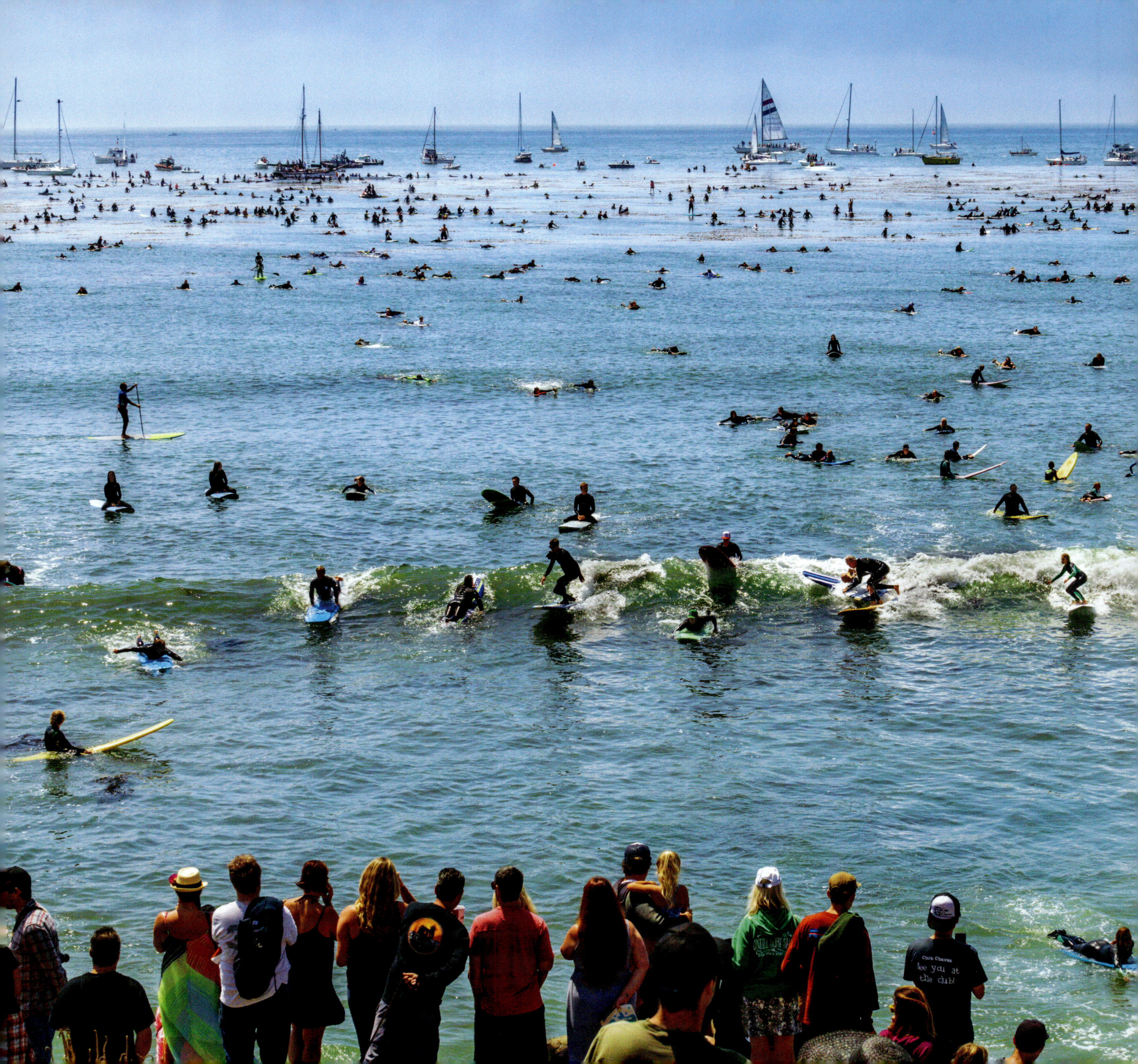

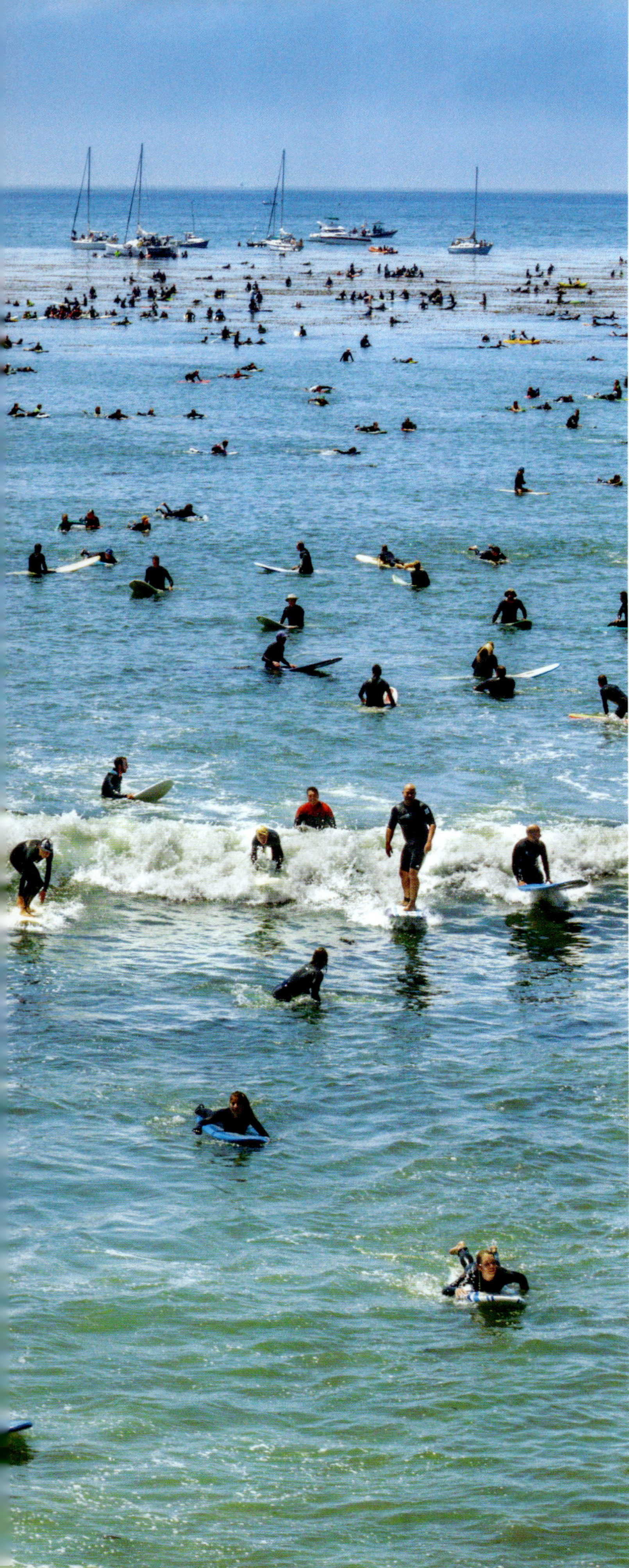

Thousands of surfers paddled out to honor surfing legend and ocean champion Jack O'Neill, and many more watched from the cliffs. It was a moving tribute to the man who helped pioneer the wetsuit, which enabled millions of people to plunge in and experience our blue planet firsthand. Along with groups like Save Our Shores, Save the Waves, and O'Neill Sea Odyssey, Monterey Bay surfers have long been passionate advocates for the protection of the bay and the ocean beyond.

JACK O'NEILL MEMORIAL PADDLE OUT, SANTA CRUZ

MAPS

The Monterey Bay National Marine Sanctuary borders nearly 300 miles of coastline and receives runoff from watersheds that cover 7,000 square miles and support a variety of land uses. The health of the sanctuary depends on the water quality from those drainages. This map shows the boundaries of coastal creeks and rivers that begin as far inland as Gilroy and Paso Robles, but they all feed into the bay.

Monterey Bay National Marine Sanctuary Watersheds

Map by the National Oceanic and Atmospheric Administration

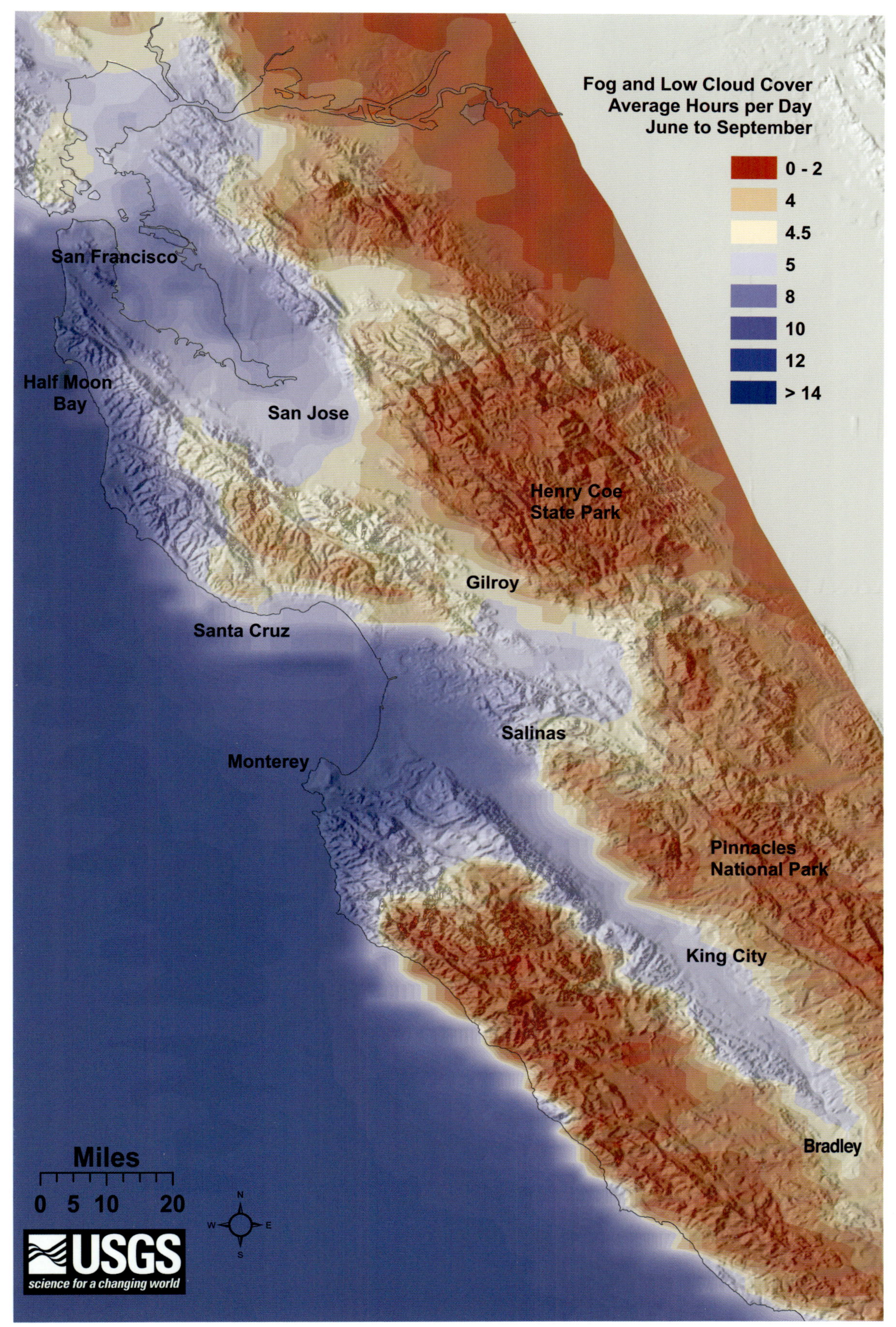

Coastal fog is an important feature of Monterey Bay, and its extent is one measure for defining the bay as an ecoregion. This map is based on the first detailed study of coastal fog, which measured its distribution over nine summer seasons between 1999 and 2009. Fog is more prevalent where land juts into the prevailing northwest winds, and it spreads into ocean-facing valleys as far south as Bradley.

Monterey Bay Region Coastal Fog

Map by the United States Geological Survey

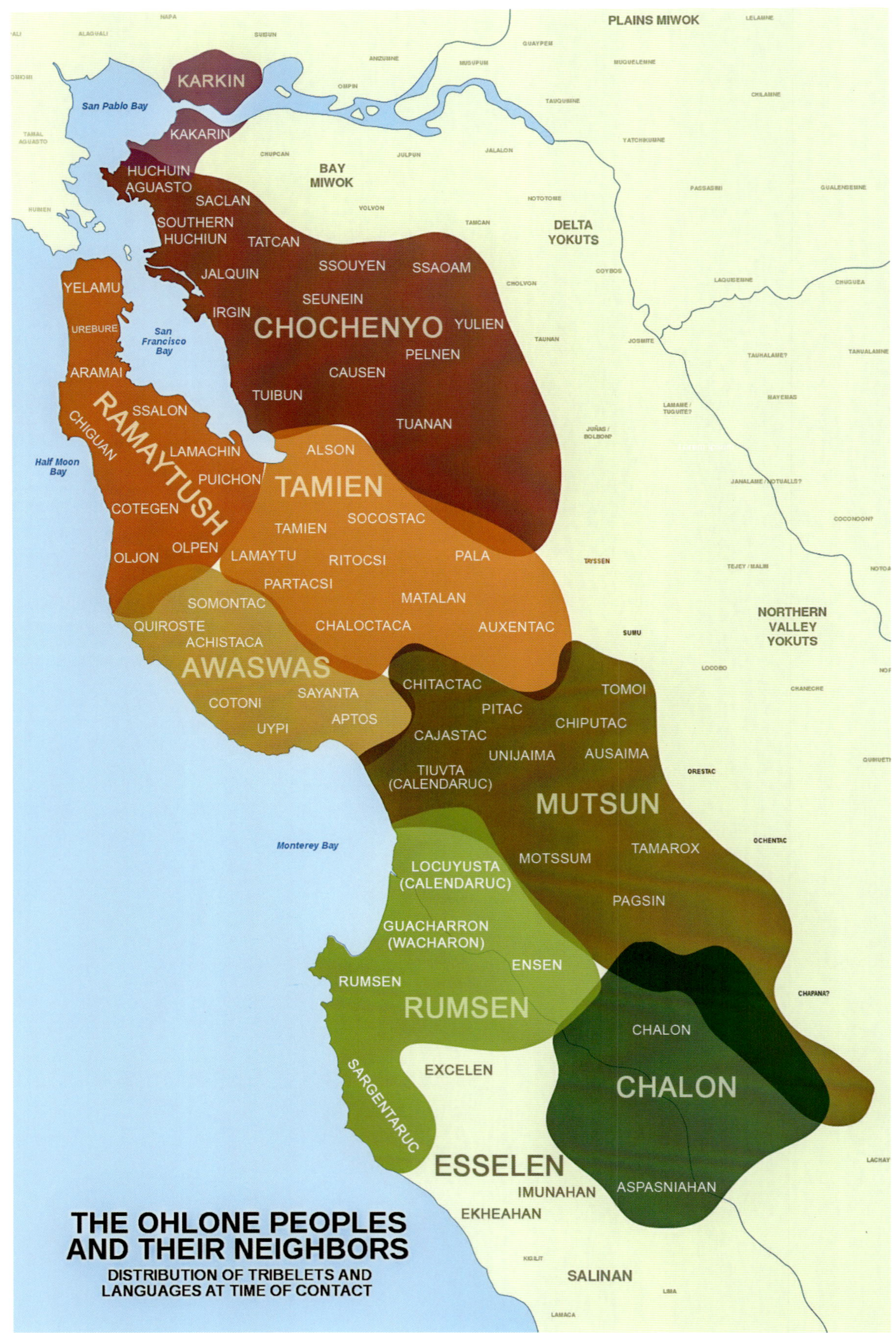

Prior to the arrival of Spanish colonizers in 1770, Northern California was one of the most densely populated regions north of Mexico. The indigenous people now referred to collectively as Ohlone did not view themselves as a single, unified group. They lived in more than 50 distinct communities. This map, based on the work of anthropologist Randall Milliken, shows the diversity of languages spoken in the greater Monterey Bay region. Approximate language boundaries, shown in different colors, overlay tribal designations.

THE OHLONE PEOPLE AND THEIR NEIGHBORS

Map by Randall Milliken

OPPOSITE: A dense mosaic of protected areas shelter Monterey Bay's unique ecological diversity and provide access for people to experience nature. Not shown are many private conservation easements in the region. This is impressive, but improvements need to be made to achieve better connectivity and to reach California's statewide goal to protect 30 percent of its land and marine areas by 2030—part of a global campaign known as "30 x 30."

MONTEREY BAY REGION PROTECTED AREAS

Map by GreenInfo Network

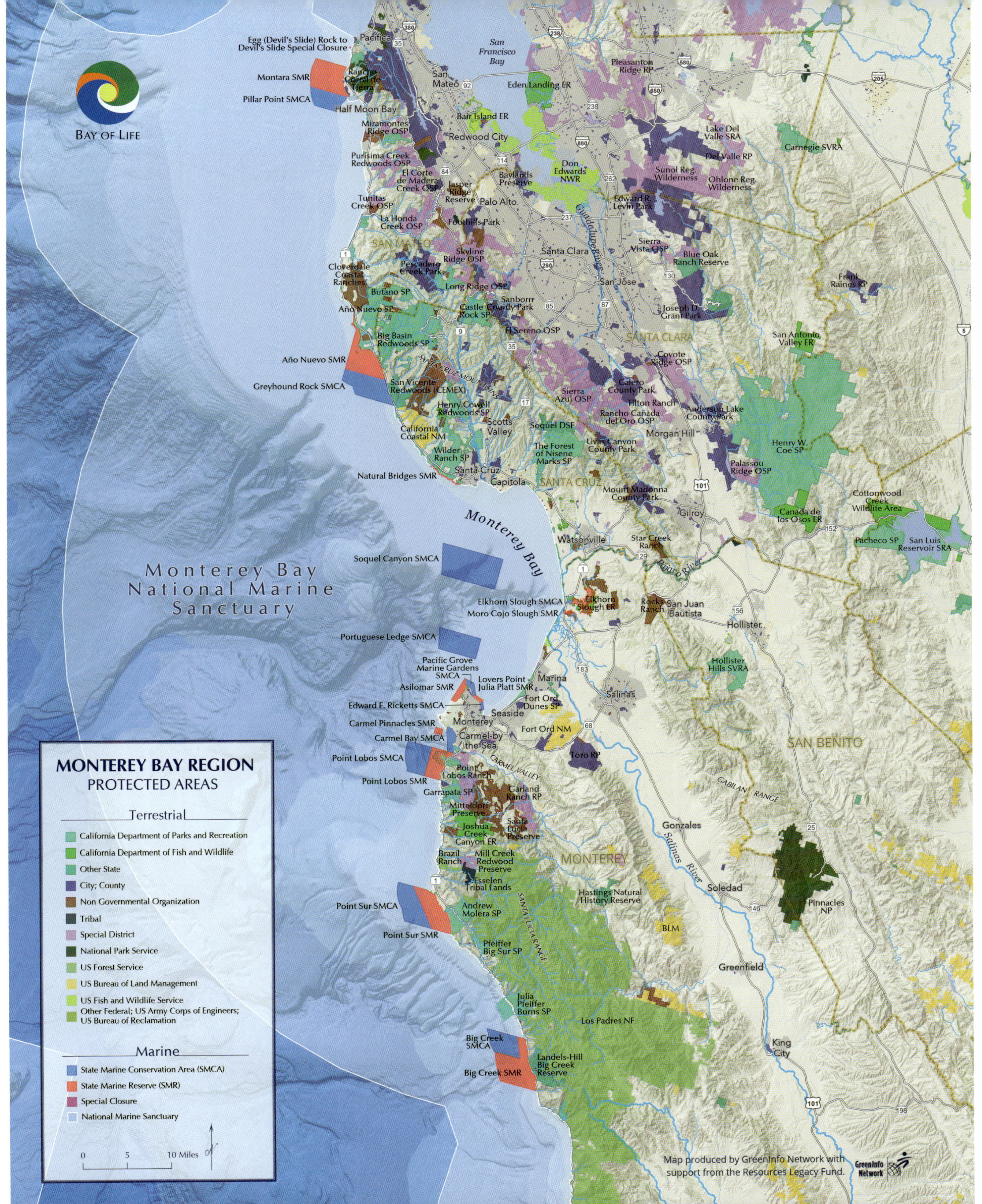

Bay of Life

Egg (Devil's Slide) Rock to Devil's Slide Special Closure
Montara SMR
Pillar Point SMCA

San Francisco Bay
Pacifica
San Mateo
Eden Landing ER
Pleasanton Ridge RP
Half Moon Bay
Bair Island ER
Redwood City
Miramontes Ridge OSP
Lake Del Valle SRA
Del Valle RP
Carnegie SVRA
Purisima Creek Redwoods OSP
Baylands Preserve
Don Edwards NWR
Sunol Reg. Wilderness
El Corte de Madera Creek OSP
Jasper Ridge Reserve
Palo Alto
Edward R. Levin Park
Ohlone Reg. Wilderness
Tunitas Creek OSP
Foothills Park
La Honda Creek OSP
Skyline Ridge OSP
Santa Clara
Sierra Vista OSP
Blue Oak Ranch Reserve
Frank Raines RP
SAN MATEO
Cloverdale Coastal Ranches
Pescadero Creek Park
Long Ridge OSP
San José
Butano SP
Sanborn County Park
Joseph D. Grant Park
Año Nuevo SP
Castle Rock SP
El Sereno OSP
SANTA CLARA
San Antonio Valley ER
Big Basin Redwoods SP
Coyote Ridge OSP
Año Nuevo SMR
San Vicente Redwoods (CEMEX)
Sierra Azul OSP
Calero County Park
Greyhound Rock SMCA
Henry Cowell Redwoods SP
Hilton Ranch
Rancho Cañada del Oro OSP
Anderson Lake County Park
California Coastal NM
Scotts Valley
Soquel DSF
Rancho Cañada del Oro OSP
Morgan Hill
Henry W. Coe SP
Wilder Ranch SP
The Forest of Nisene Marks SP
Uvas Canyon County Park
Palassou Ridge OSP
Natural Bridges SMR
Santa Cruz
Capitola
SANTA CRUZ
Mount Madonna County Park
Gilroy
Cañada de los Osos ER
Cottonwood Creek Wildlife Area
Monterey Bay
Watsonville
Star Creek Ranch
San Luis Reservoir SRA
Pacheco SP
Soquel Canyon SMCA
Monterey Bay National Marine Sanctuary
Rocks San Juan Bautista
Elkhorn Slough SMCA
Elkhorn Slough ER
Hollister
Moro Cojo Slough SMR
Portuguese Ledge SMCA
Hollister Hills SVRA
Pacific Grove Marine Gardens SMCA
Lovers Point Julia Platt SMR
Marina
Asilomar SMR
Fort Ord Dunes SP
Salinas
Edward F. Ricketts SMCA
Seaside
Carmel Pinnacles SMR
Monterey
Fort Ord NM
SAN BENITO
Carmel Bay SMCA
Carmel-by-the-Sea
Point Lobos SMCA
Point Lobos Ranch
Toro RP
Point Lobos SMR
CARMEL VALLEY
Garrapata SP
Garland Ranch RP
Mitteldorf Preserve
Joshua Creek Canyon ER
Santa Lucia Preserve
Gonzales
Brazil Ranch
Mill Creek Redwood Preserve
MONTEREY
Esselen Tribal Lands
Hastings Natural History Reserve
Soledad
Point Sur SMCA
Andrew Molera SP
SANTA LUCIA RANGE
BLM
Pinnacles NP
Point Sur SMR
Pfeiffer Big Sur SP
Greenfield
GABILAN RANGE
Julia Pfeiffer Burns SP
Los Padres NF
King City
Big Creek SMCA
Landels-Hill Big Creek Reserve
Big Creek SMR
Salinas River

MONTEREY BAY REGION
PROTECTED AREAS

Terrestrial
California Department of Parks and Recreation
California Department of Fish and Wildlife
Other State
City; County
Non Governmental Organization
Tribal
Special District
National Park Service
US Forest Service
US Bureau of Land Management
US Fish and Wildlife Service
Other Federal; US Army Corps of Engineers; US Bureau of Reclamation

Marine
State Marine Conservation Area (SMCA)
State Marine Reserve (SMR)
Special Closure
National Marine Sanctuary

0   5   10 Miles

Map produced by GreenInfo Network with support from the Resources Legacy Fund.
GreenInfo Network

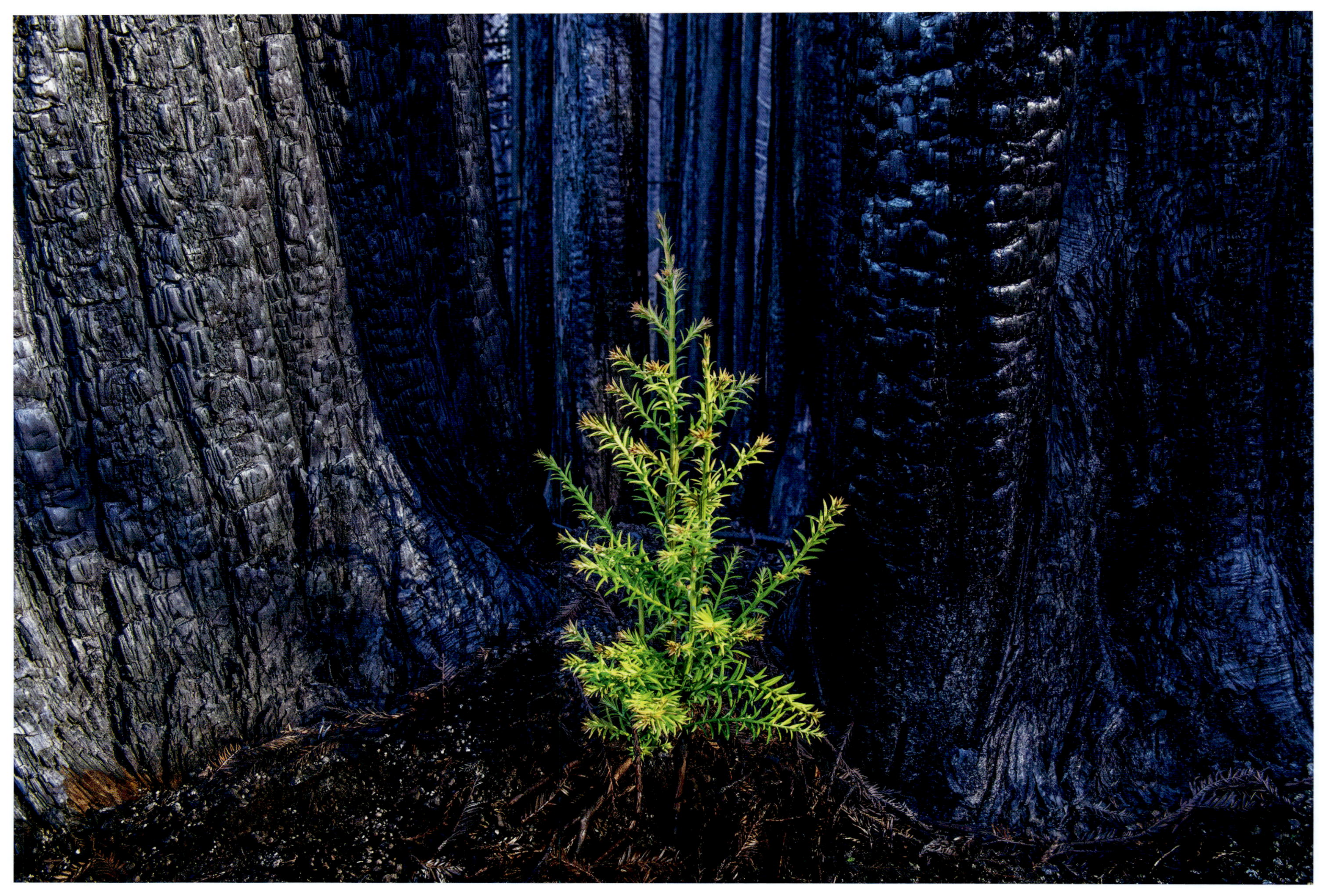

A new tree sprouting in a grove of fire-blackened redwoods
symbolizes the resilience of nature.

Young Redwood after Fire, K&S Ranch

PARTNERS

Many organizations have helped us to realize the Bay of Life Project. We offer our sincere appreciation to these partners in conservation and education for the important work they are doing in the Monterey Bay region. We hope you will support them too. Visit BayofLife.net for more information.

The **AMAH MUTSUN LAND TRUST** connects the Amah Mutsun Tribal Band to the lands, knowledge, and practices of their ancestors.

The **BIG SUR LAND TRUST** inspires conservation of Monterey County's unique landscapes and access to outdoor experiences for all.

CALIFORNIA STATE PARKS protects and preserves the best of California's natural and cultural history.

The **ELEPHANT SEAL RESEARCH GROUP** at UCSC studies the movements, foraging ecologies, and energetics of pinnipeds, cetaceans, and seabirds.

The **ELKHORN SLOUGH FOUNDATION** conserves and restores the Elkhorn Slough and its watershed.

The **LAND TRUST OF SANTA CRUZ COUNTY** protects, cares for, and connects people to the extraordinary lands that make this area special.

The **MONTEREY BAY AQUARIUM** is a window to marine life that inspires conservation of the ocean.

The **MONTEREY BAY AQUARIUM RESEARCH INSTITUTE** maintains a world center for advanced research and education in ocean science and technology.

The **MONTEREY BAY FISHERIES TRUST** advances the social, economic, and environmental sustainability of Monterey Bay fisheries.

The **MONTEREY BAY NATIONAL MARINE SANCTUARY FOUNDATION** inspires the public to protect the sanctuary through programs, projects, and partnerships.

The **MONTEREY BAY SALMON AND TROUT PROJECT** is dedicated to the recovery of native salmon and steelhead in the Monterey Bay region.

The **NATIONAL OCEANIC AND ATMOSPHERIC ADMINISTRATION** works to understand and predict changes in climate, weather, ocean, and coasts, and to conserve and manage marine resources.

OIKONOS studies and protects imperiled ecosystems through innovative scientific and artistic collaborations.

The **PENINSULA OPEN SPACE TRUST (POST)** protects open space on the San Francisco Peninsula and in the South Bay for the benefit of all.

The **PREDATORY BIRD RESEARCH GROUP** uses peregrine falcon recovery to inspire students and citizen scientists to monitor California's birds of prey.

The **RESOURCES LEGACY FUND** aims to secure a just and resilient world for people and nature by building alliances that advance bold solutions.

The **SANTA CRUZ MUSEUM OF ART AND HISTORY (THE MAH)** uses art, history, and culture to build a stronger, more connected community.

The **SANTA CRUZ MUSEUM OF NATURAL HISTORY** connects people with nature and science to inspire stewardship of the natural world.

The **SANTA CRUZ PUMA PROJECT** at UCSC monitors mountain lions to understand habitat requirements and movement corridors within and between the mountains of the Central Coast.

SAVE OUR SHORES protects and conserves the marine ecosystems of California's Central Coast.

SAVE THE WAVES is dedicated to preserving the world's surf spots and their surrounding environments and educating the public about their value.

The **SEMPERVIRENS FUND** preserves coast redwood forests and other important and scenic features of the Santa Cruz Mountains.

The **SEYMOUR MARINE DISCOVERY CENTER** brings the adventures and explorations of ocean science to life at its hands-on visitor and learning center.

THE TRUST FOR PUBLIC LAND creates parks and protects lands for people to ensure healthy, livable communities for generations to come.

The **UC SANTA CRUZ ARBORETUM & BOTANIC GARDEN** connects people with plants at its living museum of rare and unique Mediterranean-climate species.

The **VENTANA WILDLIFE SOCIETY** has dedicated the last 25 years to restoring California condors to the wild.

WATSONVILLE WETLANDS WATCH works to protect, restore, and foster appreciation of the wetlands of the Pajaro Valley.

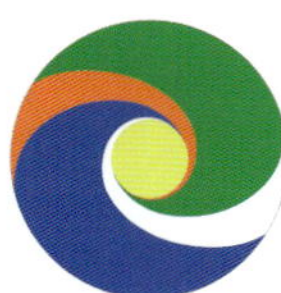

BAY OF LIFE PROJECT

The Bay of Life Project connects land and sea and people with nature to present a unified view of the Monterey Bay region through publications, exhibitions, events, and partnerships. The project aims to stimulate engagement and support that contribute to a sustainable future for the Bay of Life.

EXHIBITS:

The Santa Cruz Museum of Art and History hosts a traveling exhibition in 2023. It presents images and stories from the book along with videos and other content from the project.

EVENTS:

In collaboration with partners, a series of public presentations and private events are planned to highlight the project and promote the activities of organizations working to restore, protect, and promote appreciation of the Bay of Life.

WORKSHOPS:

We invite you to join Frans Lanting for one of his immersive Monterey Bay photo workshops, where he shares his skills and vision to help participants unleash their creativity while they focus their cameras on Monterey Bay's diverse landscapes, seascapes, wildlife, and floral wonders. Locations shown in this book are part of the itineraries. https://bayoflife.net/events/workshops/

WEBSITE:

BayofLife.net is a portal to images, stories, videos, and other content from the project along with a calendar of events. It includes links to partners' websites that showcase their work.

FINE PRINTS:

Frans Lanting's iconic images have been featured in exhibitions at museums and art galleries around the world. His archivally produced prints are included in many corporate, institutional, and private collections. Select images from *Bay of Life* are available as Limited Edition fine prints. Each print is signed and numbered by the artist. http://bayoflife.net/shop/

Frans Lanting Studio
Santa Cruz, California
office@lanting.com
www.lanting.com

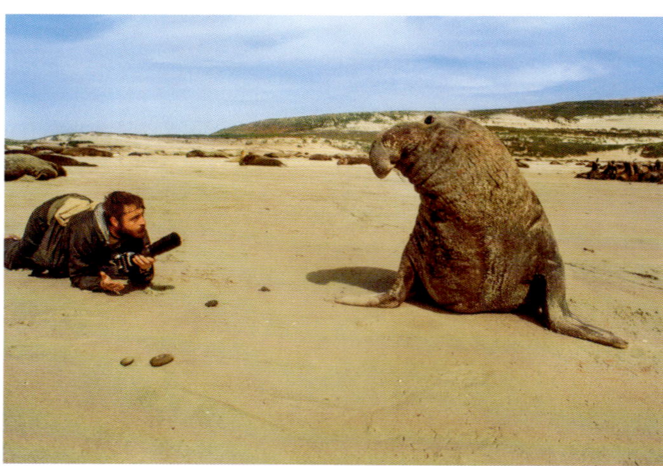

Frans Lanting makes himself small in front of a male elephant seal in the Channel Islands.

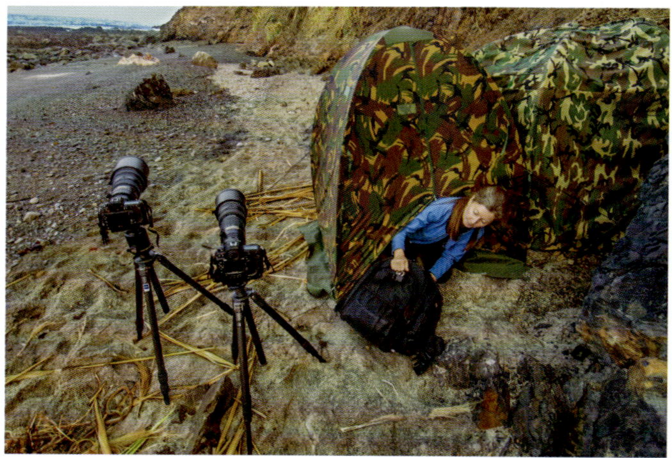

Chris Eckstrom disappears into a camera blind on a Big Sur beach where shy California condors forage on a dead whale.

ABOUT THE AUTHORS

Frans Lanting and Chris Eckstrom promote knowledge and understanding about the Earth through images and stories that convey a sense of wonder and concern about our living planet. Through their work and alliances, they create leverage for conservation efforts ranging from local initiatives to global campaigns.

Monterey Bay has been a home base and a source of inspiration to them for many years. Frans came to UCSC from the Netherlands to do research in environmental planning. He had a master's degree in environmental economics, but he changed careers and became a photographer, initially documenting the natural world of Monterey Bay, and eventually, exotic ecosystems around the world on assignment for National Geographic. There he met Chris, a staff writer at National Geographic, whose assignments had taken her from Namibia to Indonesia, with a focus on natural history. She joined Frans in Santa Cruz, and for the past 30 years they have worked together on projects ranging from bonobos in the Congo to macaws in Peru.

Frans and Chris live in Bonny Doon, on a secluded meadow with oak woodland and coastal prairie, which they have nurtured as habitat for animals from bluebirds to bobcats and mountain lions. They call their home "Rancho Refugio," for the 19th century land grant that once included their property. It is a fitting name for a place they consider a refuge, for themselves and the wild inhabitants with whom they share the land. During the CZU fire of 2020 and its aftermath, they worked with neighbors battling the fire close to their homes. They went into Big Basin right after it burned, and have chronicled its regeneration since then. A year after the fire, they captured rare video coverage of an endangered marbled murrelet fledging from a fire-scarred tree in Big Basin. In Big Sur, they huddled in blinds to watch shy condors come to forage on a whale carcass. Close to home, they discovered that endangered red-legged frogs had moved into a pond right by their kitchen window. Their appreciation for Monterey Bay has been enhanced by the ancestral knowledge of Native Americans, and by people who shared their stories about how they make a living on the land.

FRANS LANTING has been hailed as one of the great photographers of our time. His influential work appears in books, magazines, and exhibitions around the world. Lanting's books include *Into Africa*, *LIFE, Jungles, Eye to Eye*, and *Okavango*. Lanting is an ambassador for the World Wildlife Fund and has received numerous awards for his work, including the prestigious Wildlife Photographer of the Year's first Lifetime Achievement Award. HRH Prince Bernhard inducted him as a Knight in the Royal Order of the Golden Ark, the Netherlands' highest conservation honor.

CHRIS ECKSTROM is a writer and videographer. She is the author of *Forgotten Edens*, and as a staff writer she contributed to many books published by the National Geographic Society. She earned a Lowell Thomas Travel Journalism Award for Best Magazine Article on Foreign Travel for her *National Geographic Traveler* story "The Last Real Africa." The editor of Lanting's books, she has also produced stories for the National Geographic Channel.

ACKNOWLEDGMENTS

Many people have enriched our understanding of the Monterey Bay with their insights and made our work possible with their support. We express our heartfelt thanks and gratitude to all.

SPECIAL THANKS
Leon Panetta, Julie Packard; Steve Blank and Alison Elliott, Raoul Goff, Claire Perry, Jeff and Marieke Rothschild.

Lonnie Autry and Gigi Brisson, Alex and Sybilla Balkanski, Ted Benhari and Karla Hutton, Peter Beren, Bob Booth, George and Betsy Cameron, Val Cole, Freny Cooper, Mary Culley and Scott Smith, Caroline Getty, Grey Hayes, Mark Hylkema, Jay and Marlene Leite, Michael Mantell, Baldo and Kristen Marinovic, Vance Martin, Andreas Merkl and Donna Perrot, Stephanie Mills, Randy Repass and Sally-Christine Rogers, Kate and Buz Roberts, Kathleen Rose, Mat and Anne Rowley, Rob and Sally Smith, Fred Watson.

IN THE FIELD
Wilem Banks, Laura Beach, Greg Deaton, Calder and Miles Deyerle, Steve Dorrance, Amy Groesbeck, Becky Gustafson, Nadia Hamey, Lynn Huntzinger, Natalie McNear, Peter Mel, Monique Messié, Slater Moore, David Neidel, Dylan Neubauer and Tim Forsell, Alex Rinkert, Alan Rockefeller, Phil Sammet, Steven Singer, Gary and Terry Strachan, Shmuel Thaler, Brian Thom, Greg Turcott, Jim West, Zach Wormhoudt, Linda Yamane.

BIG CREEK LUMBER COMPANY: Lud and Bud McCrary, Janet McCrary Webb; CALIFORNIA NATIVE PLANT SOCIETY: Amy Patten; FUNGUS FEDERATION OF SANTA CRUZ: Phil Carpenter, Dan Tischler; KELLY-THOMPSON RANCH: Tamia Marg; LAKESIDE ORGANIC GARDENS: Dick Peixoto; MONTEREY BAY KAYAKS: Cass Schrock; MONTEREY BAY SALMON AND TROUT PROJECT: Ben Harris, Dave Straub; MORRIS GRASSFED: Joe Morris, Isaac Moreno; Buck Highberger; THE PLASTIC PICK-UP/THE GOLF BALL PROJECT: Alex Weber; Ethan Estess; VENTANA WILDLIFE SOCIETY: Joe Burnett.

CALIFORNIA STATE PARKS: Armando Quintero, Chris Spohrer; Ryan Diller, Susan Ferry, Portia Halbert, Elizabeth Hammack, Tim Hyland, Joanne Kerbavaz, Stanley Kopacz, Scott Sipes, Alex Tabone, James Weber.

UNIVERSITY OF CALIFORNIA, SANTA CRUZ: Don Croll, Jim Estes, Gary Griggs, Roger Luckenbach, Ken Norris, Vicki and John Pearse, Pete Raimondi, May Roberts; ARBORETUM & BOTANIC GARDEN: Martin Quigley; Brett Hall, Stephen McCabe; ELEPHANT SEAL RESEARCH: Roxanne Beltran, Dan Costa, Burney Le Boeuf, Pat Morris, Guy Oliver, Patrick Robinson; NORRIS CENTER: Christian Schwarz; PREDATORY BIRD RESEARCH GROUP: Zeka Glucs; John Schmitt, Glen Stewart, Brian Walton; SANTA CRUZ PUMA PROJECT: Chris Wilmers; SEYMOUR MARINE DISCOVERY CENTER: Jo Lynne and Fred Jones; Jonathan Hicken; Lauren Donnelly-Crocker, Julie Barrett Heffington; UC NATURAL RESERVE SYSTEM: Gage Dayton, Mark Readdie.

RESEARCH AND ENGAGEMENT
M. Kat Anderson, Kimberly Baker, Gary Breschini and Trudy Haversat, Ralph Buchsbaum, Jim Cochran, Don and Diane Cooley, Brandy Davis, Michael DeLapa and Rebecca Shaw, Burton Gordon, Sandy Lydon, Steve Reed, Nobby Riedy and Hilary Morgan, Celia and Peter Scott, Mark Shelley, Rachael Spencer, Robert Stephens, Eric Thiermann, Steve Webster, Jonathan Wittwer.

DIGITAL NEST: Jacob Martinez; ELKHORN SLOUGH FOUNDATION: Mark Silberstein; GREENINFO NETWORK: Maegan Leslie Torres; HOPKINS MARINE STATION: Chuck Baxter, Barbara Block, Steve Palumbi; MOSS LANDING MARINE LABORATORIES: Jim Harvey; PELAGIC SHARK RESEARCH FOUNDATION: Sean Van Sommeran; RESOURCES LEGACY FUND: Kaitilin Gaffney, Julie Turrini; SANTA CRUZ MUSEUM OF

NATURAL HISTORY: Felicia Van Stolk; Marisa Gomez; UNITED STATES GEOLOGICAL SURVEY: Josh Adams, Alicia Torregrosa; UNIVERSITY OF CALIFORNIA BERKELEY: Rob Cuthrell; UNIVERSITY OF CALIFORNIA SANTA BARBARA: Joshua Smith; VENTANA WILDERNESS ALLIANCE: Mike Splain; WATSONVILLE WETLANDS WATCH: Jonathan Pilch.

MONTEREY BAY AQUARIUM RESEARCH INSTITUTE (MBARI): Chris Scholin; Heidi Cullen, George Matsumoto, Raúl Nava, Bruce Robison.

MONTEREY BAY AQUARIUM: Kevin Connor, Aimee David, Ken Peterson, Margaret Spring.

NATIONAL OCEANIC AND ATMOSPHERIC ADMINISTRATION: Bill Douros, Lisa Wooninck; Sophie de Beukelaer, Warren Blier, Paul Michel, Becky Smyth, Lisa Uttal, Andre de Vogelaere.

MONTEREY BAY NATIONAL MARINE SANCTUARY FOUNDATION: Kris Sarri; Ginaia Kelly; Hilary Bryant, Dan Haifley.

LAND TRUSTS AND NON-PROFITS

AMAH MUTSUN LAND TRUST: Valentin Lopez; Adam French, Sara French, Kent Lightfoot, Arthur "Chico" Lopez, Esak Ordoñez, Gabriel Pineida, Steven Pratt, Alexii Sigona; BIG SUR LAND TRUST: Rachel Saunders; COMMUNITY FOUNDATION SANTA CRUZ COUNTY: Susan True; LAND TRUST OF SANTA CRUZ COUNTY: Sarah Newkirk; Terry Corwin, Bryan Largay; MONTEREY BAY FISHERIES TRUST: Sherry Flumerfelt; OIKONOS: Michelle Hester; Sara Acosta, Rozy Bathrick, Jessie Beck, Dave Calleri, Julie Thayer; PENINSULA OPEN SPACE TRUST: Walter Moore, Audrey Rust; SEMPERVIRENS FUND: Sara Barth; THE NATURE CONSERVANCY: Dick Cameron, Robin Cox, Mary Gleason.

ELECTED REPRESENTATIVES

Anna Eshoo, Sam Farr, Fred Keeley, John Laird, Robert Levy, Bruce McPherson, Henry Mello, Jimmy Panetta, Gary Patton, Mark Stone, Mardi Wormhoudt.

EXHIBIT PARTNERS

MUSEUM OF ART AND HISTORY (THE MAH): Robb Woulfe; Marla Novo, Everett Ó Cillín.

BAY PHOTO: Larry Abitbol; Steve Kurtz, Anya Thrash.

PHOTOGRAPHERS

Jon Anderson, Douglas Croft, Chase Dekker, Jodi Frediani, Justin Hofman, George Krieger, Steve Mandel, Karen Osborn, Kevin Osborn, Ralph Pace, Amy Patten, Joe Platko, Paul Schraub, Ann Thiermann (muralist), Kate Vylet, Patrick Webster.

Deep-sea images courtesy of the Monterey Bay Aquarium Research Institute (MBARI), and NOAA and the Ocean Exploration Trust.

Historic images: C.K. Tuttle and Donn I. Clickard, Pat Hathaway Photo Collection, with photo restoration by Michael Kenneth Hemp, The History Company; A. R. Moore, Covello & Covello Collection; Etching by Felix Darley courtesy of the Robert B. Honeyman Jr., Collection of Early Californian and Western American Pictorial Material, BANC PIC 1963.002:1435 (variant)—B, The Bancroft Library, University of California, Berkeley.

FRANS LANTING STUDIO

Talia Lipskind; Ross Daguio, Aliyah Nance, Doug Niven.

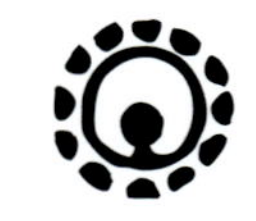

EARTH AWARE

An imprint of MandalaEarth
PO Box 3088
San Rafael, CA 94912
www.MandalaEarth.com

BAY OF LIFE

A production of the Frans Lanting Studio
108 High Road
Santa Cruz, CA 95060
www.BayofLife.net

Find us on Facebook: www.facebook.com/MandalaEarth
Follow us on Twitter: @mandalaearth

Produced by Earth Aware Editions in association with the Frans Lanting Studio.
www.lanting.com

Follow us on Instagram: www.instagram.com/franslanting and www.instagram.com/christineeckstrom
Find us on Facebook: www.facebook.com/FransLantingStudio and www.facebook.com/chris.eckstrom.3

Images from this book are available for licensing through the Frans Lanting Studio: photo@lanting.com.

CEO: Raoul Goff
Publisher: Roger Shaw
Editorial Director: Katie Killebrew
VP Creative: Chrissy Kwasnik
Project Editor: Claire Yee
Editorial Assistant: Amanda Nelson
Designer: Megan Sinead Harris
VP Manufacturing: Alix Nicholaeff
Production Manager: Joshua Smith
Sr Production Manager, Subsidiary Rights: Lina s Palma-Temena

Earth Aware would also like to thank Bob Booth for his copyediting.

Library of Congress Cataloging-in-Publication Data available.
ISBN: 978-1-64722-143-0

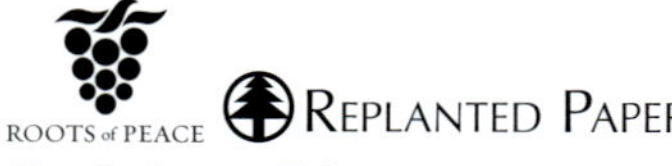

ROOTS of PEACE   REPLANTED PAPER

Earth Aware Editions, in association with Roots of Peace, will plant two trees for each tree used in the manufacturing of this book. Roots of Peace is an internationally renowned humanitarian organization dedicated to eradicating land mines worldwide and converting war-torn lands into productive farms and wildlife habitats. Roots of Peace will plant two million fruit and nut trees in Afghanistan and provide farmers there with the skills and support necessary for sustainable land use.

Manufactured in China by Insight Editions
10 9 8 7 6 5 4 3 2 1